Lecture Notes in Computer Science 5694

Commenced Publication in 1973
Founding and Former Series Editors:
Gerhard Goos, Juris Hartmanis, and J.

Álvaro Herrero   Emilio Corchado (Eds.)

Computational Intelligence in Security for Information Systems

4th International Conference, CISIS 2011
Held at IWANN 2011
Torremolinos-Málaga, Spain, June 8-10, 2011
Proceedings

 Springer

Volume Editors

Álvaro Herrero
Universidad de Burgos, Departamento de Ingeniería Civil
Francisco de Vitoria s/n, 09006 Burgos, Spain
E-mail: ahcosio@ubu.es

Emilio Corchado
Universidad de Salamanca, Departamento de Informática y Automática
Plaza de la Merced s/n, 37008 Salamanca, Spain
E-mail: escorchado@usal.es

ISSN 0302-9743   e-ISSN 1611-3349
ISBN 978-3-642-21322-9   e-ISBN 978-3-642-21323-6
DOI 10.1007/978-3-642-21323-6
Springer Heidelberg Dordrecht London New York

Library of Congress Control Number: 2011927852

CR Subject Classification (1998): K.6.5, D.4.6, C.2, E.3, H.4, H.3, J.1

LNCS Sublibrary: SL 4 – Security and Cryptology

Typesetting: Camera-ready by author, data conversion by Scientific Publishing Services, Chennai, India

Printed on acid-free paper

Springer is part of Springer Science+Business Media (www.springer.com)

Preface

The 4th International Conference on Computational Intelligence in Security for Information Systems (CISIS 2011) provided a broad and interdisciplinary forum to present the most recent developments in several very active scientific areas such as machine learning and intelligent methods, network security, cryptography, securying software and industrial perspective among others. The global purpose of the CISIS series of conferences has been to form a broad and interdisciplinary meeting ground offering researcher the opportunity to interact with the leading research team and industries actively involved in the critical area of security, and to get a picture of the current solutions adopted in practical domains.

This volume of *Lecture Notes in Computer Science* contains the accepted papers presented at CISIS 2011, which was held in one of the most famous resorts along the Costa del Sol, Torremolinos, Spain, during June 8–10, 2011. CISIS 2011 received about 70 technical submissions. After a thorough peer-review process, the International Program Committee selected 38 papers, which are published in these conference proceedings. This allowed the Scientific Committee to verify the vital and crucial nature of the topics involved in the event, and resulted in an acceptance rate close to 54%.

The selection of papers was extremely rigorous in order to maintain the high quality of the conference and we would like to thank the members of the Program Committee for their hard work in the reviewing process. This is a crucial process to the creation of a conference high standard and the CISIS conference would not exist without their help.

Our warmest and special thanks go to the IWANN 2011 Conference Chairs (Joan Cabestany, Gonzalo Joya and Ignacio Rojas) and Satellite Workshops Chair (Juan M. Corchado).

We also thank all the authors and participants for their great contributions that made this conference possible and all the hard work worthwhile.

June 2011

Álvaro Herrero
Emilio Corchado

Organization

Honorary Chairs

Antonio Silván Rodríguez   Consejero de Fomento - Regional Goverment of Castilla y León (Spain)

Carolina Blasco   Director of Telecommunication - Regional Goverment of Castilla y León (Spain)

General Chair

Emilio Corchado   University of Salamanca (Spain)

International Advisory Comittee

Antonio Bahamonde   President of the Spanish Association for Artificial Intelligence (AEPIA)

Michael Gabbay   Kings College London (UK)

Ajith Abraham   MIR Labs, Europe

Program Committee

Chairs

Álvaro Herrero   University of Burgos (Spain)

Emilio Corchado   University of Salamanca (Spain)

Members

Alain Lamadrid Vallina	Department of High Education (Cuba)
Alberto Peinado Domínguez	University of Malaga (Spain)
Alessandro Zanassi	Bocconi University (Italy)
Álvaro Herrero	University of Burgos (Spain)
Amparo Fúster Sabater	CSIC (Spain)
Ana Isabel González-Tablas-Ferreres	Carlos III of Madrid University (Spain)
Andre CPLF de Carvalho	University of São Paulo (Brazil)
Ángel Arroyo	University of Burgos (Spain)
Angel Grediaga Olivo	University of Alicante (Spain)
Angel Martín del Rey	University of Salamanca (Spain)
Angela I. Barbero Díez	University of Valladolid (Spain)
Antoni Bosch Pujol	Autonomous University of Barcelona (Spain)
Antonino Santos de Riego	University of La Coruña (Spain)
Antonio J. Tomeu Hardasmal	University of Cadiz (Spain)

Antonio Maña Gómez	University of Malaga (Spain)
Antonio Zamora Gómez	University of Alicante (Spain)
Araceli Queiruga Dios	University of Salamanca (Spain)
Arturo Ribagorda Garnacho	Carlos III of Madrid University (Spain)
Belén Vaquerizo	University of Burgos (Spain)
Benjamín Ramos Alvarez	Carlos III of Madrid University (Spain)
Bernardete Ribeiro	University of Coimbra (Portugal)
Borja Sanz Urquijo	University of Deusto (Spain)
Bruno Baruque	University of Burgos (Spain)
Candelaria Hernández Goya	University of La Laguna (Spain)
Carlos Laorden	University of Deusto (Spain)
Carlos Marcelo Martínez Cagnazzo	University of La República (Uruguay)
Carlos Munuera Gómez	University of Valladolid (Spain)
Carlos Pereira	Universidade de Coimbra (Portugal)
César Hervás-Martínez	University of Córdoba (Spain)
Chelo Malagón Poyato	CSIC (Spain)
Constantino Malagón Luque	University Antonio de Nebrija (Spain)
Cristina Alcaraz Tello	University of Malaga (Spain)
Daniel Sadornil Renedo	University of Cantabria (Spain)
Danilo Pastor Ramírez	Higher Polytechnic School of Chimborazo (Ecuador)
Danilo Pástor Ramírez	Polytechnic High School of Chimborazo (Ecuador)
Dario Forte	University of Milano Crema (Italy)
David García Rosado	University of Castilla la Mancha (Spain)
Davide Anguita	University of Genoa (Italy)
Davide Leoncini	University of Genoa (Italy)
Debasis Giri	Haldia Institute of Technology (India)
Diego Andina	Polytechnic University of Madrid (Spain)
Diego Avila Pesantez	Higher Polytechnic School of Chimborazo (Ecuador)
Domingo Gómez Pérez	University of Cantabria (Spain)
Edgar Martínez Moro	University of Valladolid (Spain)
Eduardo Carozo Blumsztein	University of Montevideo (Uruguay)
Eduardo Fernández-Medina Patón	University of Castilla la Mancha (Spain)
Emilio Corchado	University of Salamanca (Spain)
Enrico Appiani	Elsag Datamat (Italy)
Enrique Daltabuit	National Autonomous University of México (México)
Enrique De la Hoz de la Hoz	University of Alcalá (Spain)
Enrique González Jiménez	Autonomous University of Madrid (Spain)
Fabián Velásquez Clavijo	University of los Llanos (Colombia)
Fausto Montoya Vitini	Institute of Applied Physics (CSIC) (Spain)
Federico García Crespí	Miguel Hernández University (Spain)

Fernando Piera Gómez	Computer Technicians Association (ATI) (Spain)
Fernando Tricas García	University of Zaragoza (Spain)
Francisco Fernández-Navarro	University of Córdoba (Spain)
Francisco Herrera	University of Granada (Spain)
Francisco José Navarro Ríos	University of Granada (Spain)
Francisco Plaza	University of Salamanca (Spain)
Francisco Rodríguez Henríquez	CINVESTAV IPN (México)
Francisco Valera Pintor	Carlos III of Madrid University (Spain)
Gabriel Díaz Orueta	UNED (Spain)
Gabriel López Millán	University of Murcia (Spain)
Gerald Schaefer	Loughborough University (UK)
Gonzalo Alvarez Marañón	CSIC (Spain)
Gonzalo Martínez Ginesta	Alfonso X University (Spain)
Guillermo Morales-Luna	CINVESTAV (Mexico)
Gustavo Adolfo Isaza Echeverry	University of Caldas (Colombia)
Hector Alaiz	University of León (Spain)
Hugo Pagola	University of Buenos Aires (Argentina)
Hujun Yin	University of Manchester (UK)
Ignacio Arenaza	University of Mondragon (Spain)
Ignacio Luengo Velasco	University of Madrid Complutense (Spain)
Igor Santos Grueiro	University of Deusto (Spain)
Isaac Agudo Ruiz	University of Malaga (Spain)
Janusz Kacprzyk	Systems Research Institute, Polish Academy of Sciences (Poland)
Javier Areitio Bertolín	University of Deusto (Spain)
Javier Carbó Rubiera	Carlos III of Madrid University (Spain)
Javier Fernando Castaño Forero	University of los Llanos (Colombia)
Javier Sánchez-Monedero	University of Córdoba (Spain)
Jesús Esteban Díaz Verdejo	University of Granada (Spain)
Jesús María Minguet Melián	UNED (Spain)
Joan Borrel Viader	Autonomous University of Barcelona (Spain)
Joan-Josep Climent	University of Alicante (Spain)
Joaquín García-Alfaro	Carleton University (Canada)
Jordi Herrera Joancomartí	Autonomous University of Barcelona (Spain)
Jorge Diéz Pelaéz	University of Oviedo (Spain)
Jorge Eduardo Sznek	Nacional del Comahue University (Argentina)
Jorge López Hernández-Ardieta	Carlos III of Madrid University (Spain)
Jorge Ramió Aguirre	Universidad Politécnica de Madrid (Spain)
José Ángel Domínguez Pérez	University of Salamanca (Spain)
José Antonio Montenegro Montes	University of Málaga (Spain)
José Antonio. Onieva	University of Málaga (Spain)
José Daniel Britos	National University of Córboda (Argentina)

Rodrigo Adolfo Cofré Loyola	Católica del Maule University (Chile)
Rosanna Costaguta	National University of Santiago del Estero (Argentina)
Rosaura Palma Orozco	CINVESTAV IPN (México)
Rubén Vázquez Medina	National Polytechnic Institute (Mexico)
Salvador Alcaraz Carrasco	Miguel Hernández University (Spain)
Santiago Martín Acurio Del Pino	Católica del Ecuador Pontificial University (Ecuador)
Seema Verma	Banasthali University (India)
Sergi Robles Martínez	Autonomous University of Barcelona (Spain)
Sergio Bravo Silva	University of Bío Bío (Chile)
Sergio Decherchi	University of Genoa (Italy)
Sergio Pozo Hidalgo	University of Seville (Spain)
Sorin Stratulat	University Paul Verlaine - Metz (France)
Tomás Jímenez García	University of Murcia (Spain)
Tzai-Der Wang	Cheng Shiu University (Taiwan)
Urko Zurutuza Ortega	University of Mondragon (Spain)
Valentina Casola	University of Naples Federico II (Italy)
Valentina Casola	University of Naples Federico II (Italy)
Vincenzo Mendillo	Central University of Venezuela (Venezuela)
Wei Wang	University of Luxembourg (Luxembourg)
Wenjian Luo	University of Science and Technology of China (China)
Wilfred Torres Moya	Andrés Bello Catholic University (Venezuela)
Wiltord Pedrycz	University of Alberta (Canada)
Xiangliang Zhang	King Abdullah University of Science and Technology (Saudi Arabia)
Xiuzhen Chen	ParisTech (France)

Organizing Committee

Álvaro Alonso	University of Burgos (Spain)
Ángel Arroyo	University of Burgos (Spain)
Bruno Baruque	University of Burgos (Spain)
Leticia Curiel	University of Burgos (Spain)
Emilio Corchado	University of Salamanca (Spain)
Álvaro Herrero	University of Burgos (Spain)
Santiago Porras	University of Burgos (Spain)
Javier Sedano	University of Burgos (Spain)

Table of Contents

Chapter 1: Machine Learning and Intelligence

Chapter 2: Network Security

Chapter 3: Cryptography

Chapter 4: Securing Software

Chapter 5: Applications of Intelligent Methods for Security

Collective Classification for Spam Filtering

Carlos Laorden, Borja Sanz, Igor Santos, Patxi Galán-García,
and Pablo G. Bringas

DeustoTech Computing - S³Lab, University of Deusto
Avenida de las Universidades 24, 48007 Bilbao, Spain
{claorden,borja.sanz,isantos,patxigg,pablo.garcia.bringas}@deusto.es

Abstract. Spam has become a major issue in computer security because it is a channel for threats such as computer viruses, worms and
phishing. Many solutions feature machine-learning algorithms trained
using statistical representations of the terms that usually appear in the
e-mails. Still, these methods require a training step with labelled data.
Dealing with the situation where the availability of labelled training instances is limited slows down the progress of filtering systems and offers
advantages to spammers. Currently, many approaches direct their efforts
into Semi-Supervised Learning (SSL). SSL is a halfway method between
supervised and unsupervised learning, which, in addition to unlabelled
data, receives some supervision information such as the association of
the targets with some of the examples. Collective Classification for Text
Classification poses as an interesting method for optimising the classification of partially-labelled data. In this way, we propose here, for the first
time, Collective Classification algorithms for spam filtering to overcome
the amount of unclassified e-mails that are sent every day.

Keywords: Spam filtering, collective classification, semi-supervised
learning.

1 Introduction

Flooding inboxes with annoying and time-consuming messages, more than 85%
of received e-mails are spam[1].

Several approaches have been proposed by the academic community to solve
the spam problem [1,2,3,4]. Among them, the termed as *statistical approaches*
[5] use machine-learning techniques to classify e-mails. These approaches have
proved their efficiency detecting spam and are the most extended technique to
fight it. In particular, the use of the Bayes' theorem is widely used by the anti-
spam filters (e.g., SpamAssasin [6], Bogofilter [7], and Spamprobe [8]).

These statistical approaches are usually supervised, i.e., they need a training set of previously labelled samples. These techniques perform better as more
training instances are available. It means that a significant amount of previous
labelling work is needed to increase the accuracy of the models. This work includes a gathering phase in which as many e-mails as possible are collected. Then,

---

[1] http://www.junk-o-meter.com/stats/index.php

Á. Herrero and E. Corchado (Eds.): CISIS 2011, LNCS 6694, pp. 1–8, 2011.

each e-mail has to be classified as spam or legitimate. Finally, machine-learning models are generated based upon the labelled data.

This task is usually performed for text categorisation. Since text classification mostly uses the content of the documents and external sources to build accurate document classifiers, there is a great effort in the scientific community [9,10,11] directed towards the link structure among documents, to improve the performance of document classification.

The connections that can be found within documents vary from the most common citation graph, such as papers citing other papers or websites linking other websites, to links constructed from relationships including: co-author, co-citation, appearance at a conference venue, and others. The combination of these connections leads to the creation of an interlinked collection of text documents.

In some cases, it is interesting to determine the topic of not just a single document, but to infer it for a collection of unlabelled documents. Collective classification tries to collectively optimise the problem taking into account the connections present among the documents. This is a semi-supervised technique, i.e., uses both labelled and unlabelled data – typically a small amount of labelled data and a large amount of unlabelled data – that reduces the labelling work.

Given this background, we propose the first spam filtering system that uses collective classification to optimise the classification performance. Through this approach, we minimise the necessity of labelled e-mails without a significant penalisation of the accuracy of detection.

Summarising, our main findings are the following: (i) we describe how to adopt collective classification for spam filtering, (ii) we try to determine which is the optimal size of the labelled dataset for collective-classification-based spam filtering, and (iii) we show that this approach can reduce the efforts of labelling e-mails while maintaining a high accuracy rate.

The reminder of this paper is organised as follows. Section 2 describes the process of using collective classification applied to the spam filtering problem. Section 3 details the experiments performed and presents the results. Finally, Section 4 concludes and outlines avenues for future work.

2   Collective Classification for Spam Filtering

Collective classification is a combinatorial optimization problem, in which we are given a set of documents, or nodes, $\mathcal{D} = \{d_1, ..., d_n\}$ and a neighbourhood function N, where $N_i \subseteq \mathcal{D} \setminus \{\mathcal{D}_i\}$, which describes the underlying network structure [12]. Being $\mathcal{D}$ a random collection of documents, it is divided into two sets $\mathcal{X}$ and $\mathcal{Y}$ where $\mathcal{X}$ corresponds to the documents for which we know the correct values and $\mathcal{Y}$ are the documents whose values need to be determined. Therefore, the task is to label the nodes $\mathcal{Y}_i \in \mathcal{Y}$ with one of a small number of labels, $\mathcal{L} = \{l_1, ..., l_q\}$.

Since the spam problem can be tackled as a text classification problem, we use the *Waikato Environment for Knowledge Analysis* (WEKA) [13] and its

Semi-Supervised Learning and Collective Classification plugin[2]. In the remainder of this section we review the collective algorithms used in the empirical evaluation.

2.1   CollectiveIBk

It uses internally WEKA's classic IBk algorithm, implementation of the *K-Nearest Neighbour* (KNN), to determine the best k on the training set and builds then, for all instances from the test set, a neighbourhood consisting of k instances from the pool of train and test set (either a naïve search over the complete set of instances or a k-dimensional tree is used to determine neighbours). All neighbours in such a neighbourhood are sorted according to their distance to the test instance they belong to. The neighbourhoods are sorted according to their 'rank', where 'rank' means the different occurrences of the two classes in the neighbourhood.

For every unlabelled test instance with the highest rank, the class label is determined by majority vote or, in case of a tie, by the first class. This is performed until no further unlabelled test instances remain. The classification terminates by returning the class label of the instance that is about to be classified.

2.2   CollectiveForest

It uses WEKA's implementation of RandomTree as base classifier to divide the test set into folds containing the same number of elements. The first iteration trains using the original training set and generates the distribution for all the instances in the test set. The best instances are then added to the original training set (being the number of instances chosen the same as in a fold).

The next iterations train with the new training set and generate then the distributions for the remaining instances in the test set.

2.3   CollectiveWoods and CollectiveTree

CollectiveWoods works like CollectiveForest using CollectiveTree instead of RandomTree.

Collective tree is similar to WEKA's original RandomTree classifier, it splits the attribute at that position that divides the current subset of instances (training and test instances) into two halves. The process finishes if one of the following conditions is met:

- Only training instances would be covered (the labels for these instances are already known).
- Only test instances in the leaf, case in which distribution from the parent node is taken.
- Only training instances of one class, case in which all test instances are considered to have this class.

---

[2] http://www.scms.waikato.ac.nz/~fracpete/projects/collectiveclassification

To calculate the class distribution of a complete set or a subset, the weights are summed up according to the weights in the training set, and then normalised. The nominal attribute distribution corresponds to the normalised sum of weights for each distinct value and, for the numeric attribute, distribution of the binary split based on median is calculated and then the weights are summed up for the two bins and finally normalised.

2.4   RandomWoods

It works like WEKA's classic RandomForest but using CollectiveBagging (classic Bagging, a machine learning ensemble meta-algorithm to improve stability and classification accuracy, extended to make it available to collective classifiers) in combination with CollectiveTree in contrast to RandomForest, which uses Bagging and RandomTree.

3   Empirical Evaluation

To evaluate the collective algorithms we used the *Ling Spam*[3] and *SpamAssassin*[4] datasets. Ling Spam consists of a mixture of both spam and legitimate messages retrieved from the *Linguistic list*, an e-mail distribution list about *linguistics*. It comprises 2,893 different e-mails, of which 2,412 are legitimate e-mails obtained by downloading digests from the list and 481 are spam e-mails retrieved from one of the authors of the corpus (for a more detailed description of the corpus please refer to [14,15]). From the 4 different datasets provided in this corpus, each of one with different pre-process steps, we choose the *Bare* dataset, which has no pre-processing.

The SpamAssassin public mail corpus is a selection of 1,897 spam messages and 4,150 legitimate e-mails. Unfortunately, due to computational restrictions we were obliged to reduce the dataset to a 50%, so the final used dataset comprises 3,023 e-mails, of which 964 are spam e-mails and 2,059 are legitimate messages.

In addition, we performed for both datasets a *Stop Word Removal* [16] based on an external stop-word list[5] and removed any non alpha-numeric character.

We then used the *Vector Space Model* (VSM) [17], an algebraic approach for *Information Filtering* (IF), *Information Retrieval* (IR), indexing and ranking, to create the model. This model represents natural language documents in a mathematical manner through vectors in a multidimensional space.

We extracted the top 1,000 attributes using *Information Gain* [18], an algorithm that evaluates the relevance of an attribute by measuring the information gain with respect to the class: $IG(j) = \sum_{v_j \in R} \sum_{C_i} P(v_j, C_i) \cdot (P(v_j, C_i)/(P(v_j) \cdot P(C_i)))$ where C_i is the i-th class, v_j is the value of the j-th interpretation, $P(v_j, C_i)$ is the probability that the j-th attribute has the value v_j in the class

---

[3] http://nlp.cs.aueb.gr/software_and_datasets/lingspam_public.tar.gz
[4] http://spamassassin.apache.org/publiccorpus/
[5] http://www.webconfs.com/stop-words.php

C_i, $P(v_j)$ is the probability that the j-th interpretation has the value v_j in the training data, and $P(C_i)$ is the probability of the training dataset belonging to the class C_i.

We constructed an *ARFF* file [19] (i.e., Attribute Relation File Format) with the resultant vector representations of the e-mails to build the aforementioned WEKA's classifiers.

To evaluate the results, we measured the most frequently used for spam: precision, recall and Area Under the ROC Curve (AUC). We measured the precision of the spam identification as the number of correctly classified spam e-mails divided by the number of correctly classified spam e-mails and the number of legitimate e-mails misclassified as spam, $S_P = N_{s \to s}/(N_{s \to s} + N_{l \to s})$, where $N_{s \to s}$ is the number of correctly classified spam and $N_{l \to s}$ is the number of legitimate e-mails misclassified as spam.

Additionally, we measured the recall of the spam e-mail messages, which is the number of correctly classified spam e-mails divided by the number of correctly classified spam e-mails and the number of spam e-mails misclassified as legitimate, $S_R = N_{s \to s}/(N_{s \to s} + N_{s \to l})$.

Finally, we measured the *Area Under the ROC Curve* (AUC), which establishes the relation between false negatives and false positives [20]. The ROC curve is represented by plotting the rate of true positives (TPR) against the rate of false positives (FPR). Where the TPR is the number of spam messages correctly detected divided by the total number of junk e-mails, $TPR = TP/(TP + FN)$, and the FPR is the number of legitimate messages misclassified as spam divided by the total number of legitimate e-mails, $FPR = FP/(FP + TN)$.

For our experiments we tested the different configurations of the collective algorithms with sizes for the $\mathcal{X}$ set of known instances, varying from a 10% to a 90% of the instances used for training (i.e., instances known during the test).

Fig. 1 shows the precision of the different algorithms. Collective KNN shows significant improvements with Ling Spam when the number of known instances

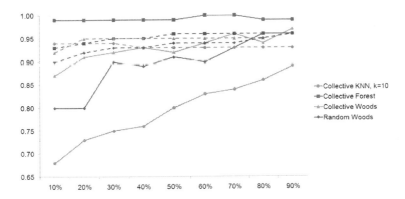

Fig. 1. Precision of the evaluation of collective algorithms for spam filtering with different sizes for the $\mathcal{X}$ set of known instances. Solid lines correspond to Ling Spam and dashed lines correspond to SpamAssassin.

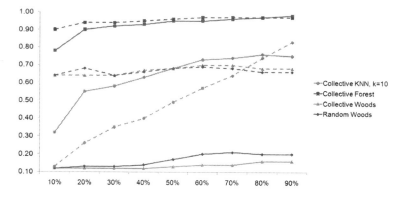

Fig. 2. Recall of the evaluation of collective algorithms for spam filtering with different sizes for the $\mathcal{X}$ set of known instances. Solid lines correspond to Ling Spam and dashed lines correspond to SpamAssassin.

increases (from 0.68 with 10% to 0.89 with 90%), but remains constant with SpamAssassin (between 0.93 and 0.94). Collective Forest was the best collective algorithm when evaluating the precision achieving between 0.99 and 1.00 for Ling Spam and no less than 0.93 for SpamAssassin. Finally, Collective Woods and Random Woods experience some improvements when increasing the number of known instances when testing with both datasets.

Fig. 2 shows the recall of the different algorithms. Again, Collective KNN shows better results, although not good enough, when the number of known instances increases: from a 0.32 with 10% to 0.75 with 90% for Ling Spam and from 0.13 with 10% to 0.83 with 90%. Collective Forest presents a poor 0.78 for 10% with Ling Spam but behaves better with the rest of configurations in both datasets: a minimum of 90% and a maximum of 0.97. Finally, Collective Woods

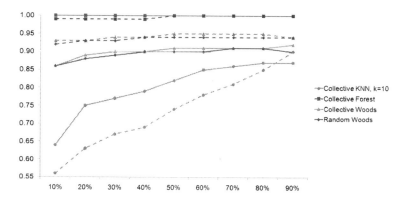

Fig. 3. Area under de ROC curve (AUC) evaluation of collective algorithms for spam filtering with different sizes for the $\mathcal{X}$ set of known instances. Solid lines correspond to Ling Spam and dashed lines correspond to SpamAssassin.

and Random Woods behave similar, with very poor recall, achieving maximums with 90% of 0.16 and 0.20 respectively for Ling Spam and 0.68 and 0.66 for SpamAssassin.

Finally, Fig. 3 shows the Area under de ROC curve (AUC) of the different algorithms. Once more, the performance of Collective KNN increases with more known instances: from 0.64 with 10% to 0.87 with 90% for Ling Spam and from 0.56 to 0.90 for SpamAssassin. Collective Forest offers a perfect 1.00 for every configuration with Ling Spam and a minimum of 0.99 with SpamAssassin posing as a suitable choice for collective classification. Finally, Collective Woods and Random Woods offer similar results, increasing from 0.86 both to 0.92 and 0.90 respectively with Ling Spam and from 0.93 and 0.92 to 0.94 both with SpamAssassin.

4   Discussion and Concluding Remarks

Collective Classification algorithms for spam filtering pose as a suitable approach for optimising the classification of partially-labelled data and, therefore, overcome the amount of unclassified spam e-mails that are created every day.

In particular, Collective Forest shows great results for every configuration of known instances (i.e., different sizes for the $\mathcal{X}$ set of known instances), with values above 0.93 of precision, above 0.90 of recall (only offering a poor recall of 0.78 with a 10% of $\mathcal{X}$) and almost 1.00 for all configurations of AUC.

Since precision and AUC are slightly affected with the variation of known instances, values of $\mathcal{X}$, to determine the optimal size of labelled data, and assuming that Collective Forest is the chosen algorithm, the recall should be the factor to take into account. For a value of $\mathcal{X} = 60\%$, CollectiveForest achieves its maximums, only experiencing a loss of 0.03 of recall for Ling Spam.

As the number of unsolicited bulk messages increases, the classification and labelling steps, that commonly supervised methods make use of, become more unattainable. To revert this situation, we propose the first spam filtering system that uses collective classification to optimise classification performance. Through the algorithms introduced, the necessity of labelled e-mails is minimised, by a 40%, without a significant penalisation in the detection capabilities.

Future work will be focused on three main directions. First, we plan to extend our study of collective classification by applying more algorithms to the spam problem. Second, we will select different features as data to train the models. Finally, we will perform a more complete analysis on the effects of the labelled degree of the data.

References

1. Robinson, G.: A statistical approach to the spam problem. Linux J. 3 (March 2003)
2. Chirita, P., Diederich, J., Nejdl, W.: MailRank: using ranking for spam detection. In: Proceedings of the 14th ACM International Conference on Information and Knowledge Management, pp. 373–380. ACM, New York (2005)

3. Schryen, G.: A formal approach towards assessing the effectiveness of anti-spam procedures. In: Proceedings of the 39th Annual Hawaii International Conference on HICSS 2006, vol. 6, pp. 129–138. IEEE, Los Alamitos (2006)
4. Chiu, Y., Chen, C., Jeng, B., Lin, H.: An Alliance-Based Anti-spam Approach. In: Third International Conference on ICNC 2007, vol. 4, pp. 203–207. IEEE, Los Alamitos (2007)
5. Zhang, L., Zhu, J., Yao, T.: An evaluation of statistical spam filtering techniques. ACM Transactions on Asian Language Information Processing (TALIP) 3(4), 243–269 (2004)
6. Mason, J.: Filtering spam with spamassassin. In: HEANet Annual Conference (2002)
7. Raymond, E.: Bogofilter: A fast open source bayesian spam filters (2005)
8. Burton, B.: Spamprobe-bayesian spam filtering tweaks. In: Proceedings of the Spam Conference (2003)
9. Dengel, A., Dubiel, F.: Clustering and classification of document structure-a machine learning approach. In: International Conference on Document Analysis and Recognition, vol. 2, p. 587 (1995)
10. Fujisawa, H., Nakano, Y., Kurino, K.: Segmentation methods for character recognition: from segmentation to document structure analysis. Proceedings of the IEEE 80(7), 1079–1092 (2002)
11. Denoyer, L., Gallinari, P.: Bayesian network model for semi-structured document classification. Information Processing & Management 40(5), 807–827 (2004)
12. Namata, G., Sen, P., Bilgic, M., Getoor, L.: Collective classification for text classification. Text Mining, 51–69 (2009)
13. Garner, S.: Weka: The Waikato environment for knowledge analysis. In: Proceedings of the New Zealand Computer Science Research Students Conference, pp. 57–64 (1995)
14. Androutsopoulos, I., Koutsias, J., Chandrinos, K., Paliouras, G., Spyropoulos, C.: An evaluation of naive bayesian anti-spam filtering. In: Proceedings of the Workshop on Machine Learning in the New Information Age, pp. 9–17 (2000)
15. Sakkis, G., Androutsopoulos, I., Paliouras, G., Karkaletsis, V., Spyropoulos, C., Stamatopoulos, P.: A memory-based approach to anti-spam filtering for mailing lists. Information Retrieval 6(1), 49–73 (2003)
16. Wilbur, W., Sirotkin, K.: The automatic identification of stop words. Journal of Information Science 18(1), 45–55 (1992)
17. Salton, G., Wong, A., Yang, C.S.: A vector space model for automatic indexing. Communications of the ACM 18(11), 613–620 (1975)
18. Kent, J.: Information gain and a general measure of correlation. Biometrika 70(1), 163–173 (1983)
19. Holmes, G., Donkin, A., Witten, I.H.: Weka: a machine learning workbench, 357–361 (August 1994)
20. Singh, Y., Kaur, A., Malhotra, R.: Comparative analysis of regression and machine learning methods for predicting fault proneness models. International Journal of Computer Applications in Technology 35(2), 183–193 (2009)

Detecting Bad-Mouthing Attacks on Reputation Systems Using Self-Organizing Maps

Z. Banković, J.C. Vallejo, D. Fraga, and J.M. Moya

Dep. Ingeniería Electrónica, Universidad Politécnica de Madrid, Av. Complutense 30,
28040 Madrid, Spain
{zorana,jcvallejo,dfraga,josem}@die.upm.es

Abstract. It has been demonstrated that rating trust and reputation of individual nodes is an effective approach in distributed environments in order to improve security, support decision-making and promote node collaboration. Nevertheless, these systems are vulnerable to deliberate false or unfair testimonies. In one scenario the attackers collude to give negative feedback on the victim in order to lower or destroy its reputation. This attack is known as bad mouthing attack, and it can significantly deteriorate the performances of the network. The existing solutions for coping with bad mouthing are mainly concentrated on prevention techniques. In this work we propose a solution that detects and isolates the abovementioned attackers, impeding them in this way to further spread their malicious activity. The approach is based on detecting outliers using clustering, in this case self-organizing maps. An important advantage of this approach is that we have no restrictions on training data, and thus there is no need for any data pre-processing. Testing results demonstrates the capability of the approach in detecting bad mouthing attack in various scenarios.

Keywords: reputation systems, bad mouthing detection, self-organizing maps.

1 Introduction

Trust and reputation have recently been suggested as an effective security mechanism for open and distributed environments (Ad Hoc networks [2], WSNs [1, 2], P2P networks [3], etc.). In essence, the nodes that do not behave properly (according to the established policy of "proper" behavior) will have low reputation, so the rest of the nodes will avoid any collaboration with them, which is equivalent to its isolation from the network. Extensive research has been done on modeling and managing trust and reputation, and it has been demonstrated that rating trust and reputation of individual nodes is an effective approach in distributed environments in order to improve security, support decision-making and promote node collaboration.

There are many different definitions of trust and reputation, but in essence trust is a belief about future behavior that one node holds in others and it is based on its own experience, thus its main characteristic is subjectivity. On the other hand, reputation is considered to be the global perception of the behavior of a node based on the trust that others hold in it, thus considered to be objective [2]. The common way of defining a trust value is by using policies or credentials, so a node that behaves according to the established policy system will have high reputation and vice versa.

Á. Herrero and E. Corchado (Eds.): CISIS 2011, LNCS 6694, pp. 9–16, 2011.
© Springer-Verlag Berlin Heidelberg 2011

Alternatives to reputation systems can be incentive systems [4], where it is advantageous for the nodes to act in a way that the resulting global welfare is optimal. In these systems the nodes receive some sort of payment if they behave properly. Rational peers have no reason (in other words, incentive) to deviate from the equilibrium behavior. Different variations of reputation systems have been developed for various purposes. The distinguishing characteristics of all of them are the following: representation of information and classification, use of second-hand information, definition of trust and redemption and secondary response.

Among the principal threats on reputation systems we can include colluding attacks. Here we distinguish two opposite scenarios: *ballot stuffing,* where a number of entities agree to give positive feedback on an entity (often with adversarial intentions), resulting in it quickly gaining high reputation, and the opposite case, known as *bad mouthing,* where the attackers collude to give negative feedback on the victim, resulting in its lowered or destroyed reputation. In this work we concentrate on detecting bad mouthing attack, although the similar principle could be applied to detect ballot stuffing as well.

Available solutions for coping with bad mouthing attack mostly rely on prevention techniques, such as cryptography. However, these methods only increase the effort the attacker has to make in order to make his attack successful. For this reason, we present a machine learning based solution for detecting the sources of the attack. In this work we are mainly concerned about the reputation systems used in distributed systems such as wireless sensor or mesh networks, where these are mainly used for isolating anomalous behavior. However, the approach can easily be adapted for the situations where the entities in the network are humans. The main idea consists in detecting great inconsistencies in appraising an entity by other entities that have been in contact with it. The inconsistencies are treated as data outliers and are being detected using self-organizing maps.

The rest of the work is organized as follows. Previous work is surveyed in Section 2. Section 3 details the principles of the proposed solution, while Section 4 provides its evaluation. Finally, conclusions are drawn in Section 5.

2   Previous Work

As already mentioned, the majority of the existing solutions for coping with bad mouthing attack rely on prevention techniques. A typical solution is the one given in [5] that relies on cryptography. However, with the existence of side channel attacks [6], the attacker can easily guess the secret keys and compromise the cryptography-based protocols. Another solution proposes to use "controlled anonymity" [7], where the identities of the communicating entities are not known to each other. In this way, each entity has to provide ratings based on the quality of service provided, and as they can no longer identify their "victims", bad-mouthing and negative discrimination can be avoided. However, this is not always possible, for example in the case of online hotel ratings. All these solutions in essence increase the effort the attacker needs to introduce in order to compromise the system, but it will not protect the system from all the attacks. Thus, a second line of defense that would detect the attacks and stop their further spreading is necessary.

For this reason, in the recent past solutions for detecting collusion attacks on reputation systems started to appear. Machine learning has always been an attractive solution, given that it copes well the uncertainties that exist in security. A representative solution using hierarchical clustering is given in [8]. This solution, as many others, after the training assign the clusters that contain the majority of the data as "good" clusters. However, this imposes restrictions on training data, as if the algorithm does not process the "unclean" data during the training, it will not be able to detect attacks. A solution based on graph theory is given in [9]. This solution, instead of using the count-based scheme that considers the number of accusations, uses the community-based scheme that achieves the detection of up to 90% of the attackers, which permits the correct operation of the system.

Thus, our aim is to design a detection based solution that would overcome the abovementioned issues. Namely, we want to provide a solution that would not have any restrictions regarding training data, and that would be capable of detecting up to 100% of malicious entities.

3 Proposed Solution

3.1 Feature Extraction and Formation of Model

For each entity, the feature vector is formed of the recommendation the others give on it. The main idea is to find inconsistencies in recommendations. In the case the reputation system considers separately different services each entity has to offer, each service is characterized and examined independently. The characterization is based on the idea of k-grams and it is performed in equidistant moments of time using the recommendations between the consecutive moments. The features are different sets of recommendations (k-grams) and their occurrence or their frequency during the characterization period. Let the recommendations issued for the node n from five different nodes during 10 sample periods be those given in Table 1.

Table 1. Example of recommendations

	n1	n2	n3	n4	n5
1	100	99	100	95	99
2	100	99	100	95	99
3	100	99	100	95	99
4	98	99	98	98	99
5	98	99	98	98	99
6	98	99	98	98	99
7	98	99	98	98	99
8	95	95	97	97	08
9	95	95	97	97	08
10	95	95	97	97	08

In this case, the extracted k-grams, i.e. features, and their corresponding feature values are given in Table 2. From this example it is obvious that the extracted number of different k-grams does not have to be the same in all characterization period. Thus, we cannot use any of the standard distance measurements. The distance between the instances of the presented model is taken from [10]. It is designed to calculate the distance between two sequences. We have elected this one (among all given in [10]) since it is proven to be the most efficient in the terms of the absolute execution time. The deployed distance function is actually is equivalent to Manhattan distance after making the following assumption: the feature that does not exist in the first vector while exists in the second (and vice versa) actually exists with the value equal to 0, since we can say that it occurs with 0 frequency. In this way, we get two vectors of the same size and the distance between the centre and an input is between 0 (the vectors have the same features with the same feature values) and 2 (the vectors have different features with the values greater than 0). In the same way, if the set of the features of one is the subset of the feature set of the other, the distance will be between 0 and 1.

In many situations this can result in having huge number of combinations. In this case, it is necessary to apply one of the following possibilities for reducing this number. One possibility is to divide the range [0,100] into few equidistant ranges (usually three to five), and assign a unique value or meaning to all the values that belong to one range. This significantly reduces the number of possible k-grams. Another possibility is to take an average of the values that belong to a certain range.

Table 2. The characterization of the previous example

Features	Occurrence	Frequency
100 99 100 95 99	3	0.3
98 99 98 98 99	4	0.4
95 95 97 97 98	3	0.3

3.2 Detection and Isolation of Bad Mouthing Attack

As previously mentioned we treat attacks as data outliers and deploy clustering techniques. In this work we will use the self-organizing maps (SOM) algorithm, as they are relatively fast and inexpensive when the dimensionality of the data is huge, which can happen in our case.

There are two possible approaches for detecting outliers using clustering techniques [11] depending on the following two possibilities: detecting outlying clusters or detecting outlying data that belong to non-outlying clusters. For the first case, we calculate the average distance of each node to the rest of the nodes (or its closest neighborhood) (*MD*). In the latter case, we calculate quantization error (*QE*) of each input as the distance from its group center. If we train the SOM algorithm with clean data, it is obvious that we will have the second scenario. On the other hand, if the traces of attacks existed during the training, both situations are possible. Thus, we can detect attacks in the situation we do or do not have the traces of attacks during the training, which means that we do not have any restrictions on the training data. This further means that we avoid time consuming and error prone process of pre-processing the training data.

In the first step we examine the recommendations for each node in order to find the inconsistencies. Having in mind that the attacks will often result in creating new k-grams, it is reasonable to assume that the extracted vector in the presence of attackers will not be a subset of any vector extracted in normal situation, thus the distance will never be lower than 1. Thus, the suspicious values of both QE and MD are greater than 1. Upon detecting suspicious values, we pass to the second step.

In the second step the aim is to find the origin(s) of the suspicion. First, the deviations from either the mode, median or mean values of all the recommendations assigned to the node are calculated. The rationale behind this is that the majority of the nodes will assign correct recommendations, which will result in higher deviations from each of the above values in the cases of the wrong recommendations. This information can further be used in various ways, yet we choose to couple it with the reputation system, in the way the origins of the bad mouthing will result in lowered reputation, and their recommendations will not be considered. Thus, the calculated deviations are normalized to the range [0, 1], in the way the entity that is the origin of the maximal deviation has the lowest reputation, i.e. 0, while the origin of the minimal one has the highest reputation, i.e. 1. The reputations of the rest of the nodes are linearly interpolated between 0 and 1.

3.3 Self-Organizing Maps Algorithm

The self-organizing maps (SOM) algorithm [12] follows the standard steps of SOM execution, as given in [12]. The only problem-specific point is the centre, i.e. node representation and updating. Each centre is implemented as a collection whose size can be changed on the fly and whose elements are the k-grams defined in the previous text with assigned occurrence or frequency. The adjustment of nodes (that belong to the map area to be adjusted) is performed in the following way:

- If an n-gram of the input instance $v(t)$ exists in the node, its value) is modified according to the centre update given in [12];
- If an n-gram of the instance $v(t)$ does not exist in the cluster centre, the n-gram is added to the centre with occurrence equal to 1.

4 Experimental Evaluation

The proposed algorithm has been tested on the reputation systems simulator developed by our research group and designed using the C++ programming language. The network consists of a number of distributed entities, and it can simulate a number of distributed systems, such as wireless sensor networks, wireless mesh networks, etc. The reputation can be calculated in various ways, which are the implementation of the class *ReputationServer*. In the testing scenario, the entities assign recommendations to their neighbors. The bad mouthing attack is initiated at a certain moment and is composed of a number of malicious nodes that falsely assign low reputation to some of their neighbors in a random fashion. The time in the simulator is measured in time ticks, where the ticks are the moments of time the recommendations are being published to the rest of the world.

In the following experiments we will present the performance of the approach in various scenarios, varying the attack strength and the starting point of the attack. There will be two typical situations: in the first case the attack will start after the end of training, so the training will be performed with "clean" data, while in the second case we will have the situations where the training data contains the traces of attacks as well. The aim of these experiments is to show that no constraints on training data exist and that the approach is capable of detecting 100% of the malicious entities even in the cases they make a significant part of the network.

The scenario is based on 50 entities that can take one of the possible 300 positions. In the experiments we fix the number of the entities that take part in the bad mouthing attack, where each entity gives false accusations about 10% of the entities in its closest neighborhood.

In the first experiment the attack starts after the end of training, so the training is performed with so-called clean data. In Fig. 1.a. we present the reputation evolution of the situation of the most aggressive attack that can be detected with 100% detection rate with 0% false positive rate, which is the case when the bad nodes make 28.6% of all the nodes. In Fig.1.b. the dependence of both detection rate (DR) and false positive rate (FPR) on the number of bad nodes is presented. As expected, as the number of bad nodes increases, detection rate decreases, while false positive rate increases. The simulation stops at the moment the total number of bad entities makes 61.5% of total, when the undetected bad entities make the majority of non-isolated entities. In this case the reputation system becomes compromised and stops providing correct reputation values.

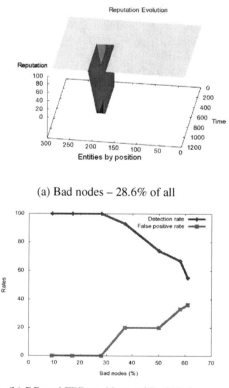

(a) Bad nodes – 28.6% of all

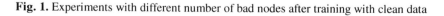

(b) DR and FPR vs. Num. of Bad Nodes

Fig. 1. Experiments with different number of bad nodes after training with clean data

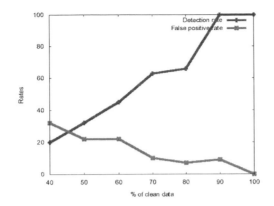

Fig. 2. DR and FPR vs. amount of clean data during the training

Now we will present the results of the experiments where the SOM algorithm is being trained with the data that contains the traces of attacks. Bad nodes make 28.6% of all the nodes. The results are presented in Fig.2. We can observe that the detection rate decreases, as the amount of the clean data during the training also decreases, while the false positive rate increases. This could be expected, as the "unclean" data makes bigger part of the training data, it is harder to distinguish it.

5   Conclusions

In this work we have presented an approach for detecting bad mouthing attack on reputation systems. The approach is based on outlier detection using SOM algorithm. We have proven that it is capable of achieving 100% detection rate with 0% false positive rate if trained with clean data and up to 28.6% of the nodes are malicious. For the last case, when 28.6% of the nodes are malicious, the detection of the attack is possible if at least 40% of the data are clean.

In the future we plan to test the approach on another colluding attack, ballot stuffing, where a number of entities agree to give positive feedback on an entity (often with adversarial intentions), resulting in it quickly gaining high reputation. In addition, we will test the performances of other clustering techniques instead of SOM, such as Growing Neural Gas [13].

Acknowledgments. This work was funded by the Spanish Ministry of Industry, Tourism and Trade, under Research Grant TSI-020301-2009-18 (eCID), the Spanish Ministry of Science and Innovation, under Research Grant TEC2009-14595-C02-01, and the CENIT Project Segur@.

References

1. Moya, J.M., Araujo, A., Bankovic, Z., de Goyeneche, J.M., Vallejo, J.C., Malagon, P., Villanueva, D., Fraga, D., Romero, E., Blesa, J.: Improving security for SCADA sensor networks with reputation systems and Self-Organizing maps. Sensors 9, 9380–9397 (2009)
2. Boukerch, A., Xu, L., EL-Khatib, K.: Trust-based Security for Wireless Ad Hoc and Sensor Networks. Comput. Commun. 30, 2413–2427 (2007)

3. Papaioannou, T.G., Stamoulis, G.D.: Effective use of reputation of peer-to-peer environments. In: Proceedings of IEEE/ACM CCGRID 2004, GP2PC Workshop, April 19-22, pp. 259–268. IEEE Comp. Soc., Chicago (2004)
4. Antoniadis, P., Courcoubetis, C., Efstathiou, E., Polyzos, G., Strulo, B.: Peer-to-Peer wireless LAN consortia: Economic modeling and architecture. In: 3rd IEEE International Conference on Peer-to-Peer Computing, pp. 198–199. IEEE Comp. Soc., Los Alamitos (2003)
5. Lou, J.-K., Chen, K.-T., Lei, C.-L.: A collusion-resistant automation scheme for social moderation systems. In: 6th IEEE Conference on Consumer Communications and Networking Conference, pp. 571–575. IEEE Press, Piscataway (2009)
6. Bar El, H.: Introduction to Side Channel Attacks. White Paper. Discretix Technologies Ltd. (2003)
7. Dellarocas, C.: Immunizing online reputation reporting systems against unfair ratings and discriminatory behavior. In: 2nd ACM Conference on Electronic Commerce, pp. 150–157. ACM, New York (2000)
8. Liu, S., Miao, C., Theng, Y.-L., Kot, A.C.: A clustering approach to filtering unfair testimonies for reputation systems (Extended Abstract). In: van der Hoek, Kaminka, L., Luck., Sen (eds.) Int. Conf. on Autonomous Agents and Multiagent Systems, pp. 1577–1578 (2010)
9. Lou, J.-K., Chen, K.-T., Lei, C.-L.: A collusion-resistant automation scheme for social moderation systems. In: 6th IEEE Conference on Consumer Communications and Networking Conference, pp. 571–575. IEEE Press, Piscataway (2009)
10. Rieck, K., Laskov, P.: Linear Time Computation of Similarity for Sequential Data. J. Mach. Learn. Res. 9, 23–48
11. Lopez, J., Roman, R., Agudo, I., Fernandez-Gago, C.: Trust management systems for wireless sensor networks: Best practices. Comput. Commun. (2010)
12. Haykin, S.: Neural networks - A comprehensive foundation, 2nd edn. Prentice-Hall, Englewood Cliffs (1999)
13. Fritzke, B.: A Growing Neural Gas Network Learns Topologies. In: Tesauro, G., Touretzky, D.S., Leen, T.K. (eds.) Advances in Neural Information Processing Systems, vol. 7, pp. 625–632. MIT Press, Cambridge (1995)

Approach Based Ensemble Methods for Better and Faster Intrusion Detection

Emna Bahri, Nouria Harbi and Hoa Nguyen Huu

ERIC Laboratory, University of Lyon, 5, Avenue Pierre-Mendes France 69500, France
{emna.bahri,nouria.harbi,Hoa.nguyenHuu}@univ-lyon2.fr

Abstract. This study introduces a new method based on Greedy-Boost, a multiple classifier system, for better and faster intrusion detection. Detection of the anomalies in the data-processing networks is regarded as a problem of data classification allowing to use data mining and machine learning techniques to perform intrusion detection. With such automatic processing procedures, human expertise only focuses on a small set of potential anomalies which may result in important time savings and efficiency. In order to be scalable and efficient, these kinds of approaches must respect important requirements. The first is to obtain a high level of precision, that is to be able to detect a maximum of anomalies with a minimum of false alarms. The second is to detect potential anomalies as fast as possible. We propose Greedy-Boost, a new approach of boosting which is based on an adaptive combination of multiple classifiers to perform the precision of the detection. This approach uses an aspect of smooth that ensures stability of the classifier system and offers speed of detection. The experimental results, conducted on the KDD99 dataset, prove that our proposed approach outperforms several state-of-the-art methods, particularly in detecting rare attack types.

Keywords: Ensemble methods, boosting, data mining, intrusion detection systems, Greedy-Boost.

1 Introduction

During the past decades, the noticeable proliferation of sophisticated attack tools has not only posed a big challenge to computer security community but also been a great anxiety of organizations in defending their assets from illicitly intrusive activities. The increase of attacks proves that security mechanisms such as firewalls and anti-virus are not strong enough to protect network systems. Within such a context, many intrusion detection approaches have been proposed to handle computer and network security problems. We find two common analysis techniques for intrusion detection : misuse and anomaly detection. In fact, misuse detection uses a collection of known attacks to construct a misuse model that is usually in forms of set of rules (or signatures). However, anomaly detection builds a model by employing information (dataset) about normal behavior. The detection mechanism here is based on the deviation between an instance

Á. Herrero and E. Corchado (Eds.): CISIS 2011, LNCS 6694, pp. 17–24, 2011.

needed for detection and the model such as in [13] and[14]. Taking advantages from these two techniques, hybrid methods are proposed. These methods can more efficiently handle both misuse and anomaly detection problems. It is worth noting that recently proposed methods are prone to hybridized mechanisms, e.g., ensemble or aggregation systems. This type of approach presents the subject of this paper.

We introduce a new approach of intrusion detection that inherits at the same time the attributes bases of the anomaly detection approach and misuse detection approach. This hybrid approach is based on a new ensemble method, Greedy-Boost, adapted to the data networks to improve the reliability of the intrusion detection systems and to reduce the time of intrusion detection. The use of aggregation reduces the number of false alarms (false-positives) and especially the number of undetected attacks (false-negative).

This paper is organized as follows. In section 2, we present the state of the art of principals hybrid intrusion detection methods, i.e., ensemble methods, systematically summarize and compares several related works to find out new applicable research directions. In section 3, we present our hybrid approach based on an ensemble method we called Greedy-Boost and detail the principle of the new algorithm. We also prove theoretically the stability (convergence) of the approach. This is the essential feature of our algorithm because it shows why Greedy-Boost leads to more efficient and scalable results than classical ensemble methods. The dataset used in the experiments, as well as the results are presented in section 4. Finally, in section 5, we conclude and give several future works issues.

2   Hybrid Methods for IDS Using Ensemble Methods

The main idea of ensemble method is to build several classifiers and then aggregate the outputs of all classifiers to make decision for the final outcome. The core purpose of an ensemble is to increase classification accuracy and decrease error rate. Because each type of classifier can produce different results, ensemble method takes advantages of the strong points of each individual classifier to induce a better final outcome. There are many types of ensemble proposed in the machine learning literature. With respect to architecture, individual classifiers can in general be structured in forms of parallel (e.g., bagging), sequential (e.g., boosting), or hybrid. For making decision, the composer of classifiers can apply various mechanisms such as majority voting, Bayesian combination, distribution summation, entropy weighting, and so on. Many studies have applied the diversity of ensemble methods to the intrusion detection problem. It is worth noting that most of the studies report that ensemble method considerably enhances the efficiency of 'rare-class' detection and anomaly detection. Giacinto et al. introduce an ensemble system including three groups of classifiers that correspond to three subsets of features (i.e., intrinsic features, traffic features, and content features) [2]. Each group of classifiers is trained from one out of the three above feature subsets. Then, three simple fusion functions (i.e., majority vote, average, and belief) are employed for aggregation. A subsequent work of the same authors describes an ensemble architecture including multiple one-class k-means classifiers [6]. Each classifier is trained from a training subset containing a specific attack type belonging to a specific attack class (e.g., Neptune is one of twenty one attack types and belongs to DoS attack class in the KDD99 dataset). The process of ensemble is based on the Decision Template method. The proposed architecture aims at labeling a given instance to belong to a normal or known attack class, and thus is called misuse detection. More adaptively, Abadeh et al. employ Fuzzy Logic Theory to develop an ensemble method [7]. This study introduces a parallel genetic local search algorithm to generate fuzzy rule sets for each class label in the training set. Each of these rule sets is utilized to build a fuzzy classifier. Then, a decision fusion procedure is in charge of determining a class label for a given instance. Comparably, Zainal et al. describe an ensemble model that utilizes three different learning algorithms (classifiers), i.e., linear genetic programming, neural fuzzy inference system, and random forest [3]. Each classifier is trained by the same training set and assigned to a weight calculated given the strength of the classifier. For decision making, a composer of classifiers determines a class label for a given instance according to the weights of classifiers.

Xiang et al. build a multi-level hybrid model by combining two techniques, i.e., supervised decision tree and unsupervised Bayesian classification [1]. The classifier model is hierarchically structured in forms of class labels in training set. By experimenting on the KDD99 dataset, the authors motivated that the model is especially efficient in improving false negative rate compared to other methods. Apart from other methods that build classifiers from network header data, Perdisci et al. introduce a multiple classifier system for anomaly detection given network payload data [4]. This ensemble system comprises several one-class SVM classifiers. In this study, different compact representations of payload in different feature spaces are obtained by applying a dimensionality reduction algorithm. Then, each one-class SVM classifier is trained by using these different representations of payload. Given the outputs of classifiers, a final decision is made by applying some fusion functions (e.g., average, product, majority vote). The experiment is conducted on three datasets, i.e., Attack-Free Darpa Dataset, Attack-Free Gatech (a dataset of Georgia Institute of Technology) and HTTP-Attack Dataset. Based on ROC Curve Graph, detection rate of the proposed method fluctuates from 80% to 99%. Zhang et al. apply a Random Forest Algorithm, an ensemble method, to intrusion detection [9]. Random Forest produces a forest of classification trees in which each tree is built from a different bootstrap sample. Instead of using the class label attribute of training dataset for classification analysis, the proposed method only uses the attribute service type (e.g., HTTP, FTP) as the purpose of classification. In misuse detection, a given instance is passed through the trees and then a 'majority vote' mechanism is applied to label this instance. For outlier detection, the general idea is that if an instance is classified as the one that is different from its own service type, then this instance is regarded as an outlier. For example, if an HTTP connection record is classified as FTP service type, this connection record is determined as an outlier. More diversely, Makkamala et al. build an ensemble model using five classifiers, i.e., resilient back propagation NN, scaled conjugate gradient NN, one-step-secant NN, SVM, and multivariate adaptive regression spline [8]. All these five classifiers are operated independently and concurrently. In this model, a final classification decision is made by majority voting.

Finally, authors in [15] use boosting strategy to improve the accuracy of intrusion detection system by developing a Multi-Class SLIPPER (MC-SLIPPER) from a boosting-based learning algorithm. The system is built from multiple available binary SLIPPER modules. Multiple prediction-confidence based strategies are proposed and applied to arbitrate the final prediction among predictions from all binary SLIPPER modules. The experimental results show that the system achieves the best performance using the BP neural network.

3   New Approach for Better and Faster Detection

An effective intrusion detection system is an essential step for the computer security. To solve the problem of the detection system performance, we choose the classifiers aggregation method specially the adaptive strategies such as boosting [11] that is presented by its algorithm AdaBoost. In fact, the idea of boosting is the construction of many models which are then incorporated by a weighted average of estimates or a vote. It differs clearly on the way of to build the family of models: each model is an adaptive version of the precedent by giving more weight to badly predicted observations. Intuitively, this algorithm thus concentrates its efforts on the observations most difficult to correctly predict while the models aggregation avoid the over-fitting. Good results are given by this approach thanks to the adaptive way used to detect non evident observations. Based on the performance of boosting, we propose a new approach adapted to the context on intrusion detection. Compared to [15], this new approach must be robust against huge and noisy data, one of problem of network data and must classify the connection type as speed as possible such we work in real time. A response to the exigences of network data, we propose Greedy-Boost.

3.1   New Method to Perform Detection Intrusion: Greedy-Boost

To make boosting and specially Adaboost resistant to the noise and to avoid these chaotic cyclic behaviors preventing convergence, it appears necessary to modify its update of the weights (distributions). Our idea consists in taking into account with an iteration T, not only the last assumption generated to put the up to date weights, but all the assumptions or models previously generated. We propose Greedy-Boost which based on the greedy process.

3.2   Explication of Greedy-Boost

Greedy-Boost is a pure generator of models which seeks in each iteration the model that predicts at best the examples badly predicted by the linear combination of the models previously generated. Two differences distinguish Greedy-Boost from AdaBoost. First, the current classifier is not one simple model but a linear combination of models. Then, the algorithm calculates the update of

Algorithm 1. Greedy-Boost algorithm

$S = (x_1, y_1), ..., (x_n, y_n)$ is a set of labeled instances (connections)
for $i = 1$ **to** n **do**
    Initialize $p_0(x_i) = 1/n$
end for
for $t = 1$ **to** T **do**
    Choose S_t from S using bootstrap sampling.
    Construct model h_t for S_t using weal learner A
    Calculate ϵ_t the error rate of h_t
    Calculate score of classifier $\alpha_t = 1/2ln((1 - \epsilon_t)/\epsilon_t)$.
    for $j = 1$ **to** m **do**
        $P_{t+1}(x_j) \leftarrow (p_0(x_j)/Z_t)e^{-\alpha_t}$
        If $argmax(\sum_{i=1}^{t} \alpha_i h_i(x_j)) = y_j$ (the connection is well classified)
        $P_{t+1}(x_j) \leftarrow (p_0(x_j)/Z_t)e^{+\alpha_t}$
        If $argmax(\sum_{i=1}^{t} \alpha_i h_i(x_j)) \neq y_j$ (The connection is badly classified)
        Use Z_t to normalize with $\sum_{j-1}^{n} p_t(x_j) = 1$)
    end for
end for
return $H(x) = argmax \ \ y \in Y \sum_{t=1}^{T} \alpha_t$

the distribution based on the initial distribution instead of the previous one (all examples with the same weight). In other words, we evaluate the examples badly classified by the standard model. This produces a new sample which will be used to generate a new model. The interest of such a process is the fact that it necessarily converges towards a stable solution under the hypotheses that on each iteration, we are able to find a weak learner, i.e, with an error $\epsilon_t < 1/2$ on the weighted sample.

Theorem. *Based on the hypotheses that for each iteration, the learner construct by Greedy-Boost is at least a weak learner, i.e, $\forall t$, $\epsilon_t < 1/2$, Greedy-boost converges necessarily towards a stable solution when $T \to \infty$.*

Proof : The proof is based on a theorem of [12] which ensures that in iteration $t+1$, the error on the learning sample of the combined classifier H_{t+1} of AdaBoost is lower than the one of H_t, the combined classifier of iteration t [12]:

$$err(H_{t+1}) < err(H_t) \times \sqrt{1 - 4(1 - \epsilon_t)^2} \qquad (1)$$

err(.) is the empirical error. With $\epsilon_t < 1/2$, we have $\sqrt{1 - 4(1 - \epsilon_t)^2} < 1$ so $err(H_{t+1}) < err(H_t)$. We consider that the solution of Greedy-Boost is equivalent to the solution of AdaBoost in the two fist iterations $H_1^{GLO}(x) = H_1^{ADA}(x)$. After, for each iteration, we change the distribution P_t with the same way of AdaBoost, based on the linear combination of models previously generated. This process is equivalent to applying AdaBoost on the current classifier H_t^{GRE}. So based on (1), we have $H_{t+1}^{GRE} < H_t^{GRE} \times \sqrt{1 - 4(1 - \epsilon_t)^2}$. Consequently, in iteration T, we have :

$$H_T^{GRE} \leq \prod_{t=1}^{T} \sqrt{1 - 4(1 - \epsilon_t)^2}. \tag{2}$$

Based on [12], we have also :

$$\prod_{t=1}^{T} \sqrt{1 - 4(1 - \epsilon_t)^2} \leq \exp\left(-2\sum_{t=1}^{T}(1 - \epsilon_t)^2\right) \tag{3}$$

Finally, for $\epsilon_t < 1/2$, we have:

$$\exp\left(-2\sum_{t=1}^{T}(1 - \epsilon_t)^2\right)_{T\to\infty} \to 0 \tag{4}$$

(4) ensures that the distribution P_t will not be modified once reaching a sufficient number of iterations, and so the convergence of the process. (4) shows that, similarly as for AdaBoost, Greedy-Boost decreases the learning error exponentially fast. Greedy-Boost stops when its error is equal to 0. Practically, Greedy-Boost reduces the error with a speedy way (only after few iterations). Consequently, Greedy-Boost performs the classification quickly in real time.

4   Experiments and Results

The used data are a sampling from KDD99 benchmark intrusion detection dataset. It's a standards data which were prepared and controlled by the MIT Lincoln laboratories for the DARPA 1998 program. These data are also used for the intrusion detection challenge of KDD 99 [10]. In this section, we compare the precision and the recall of AdaBoost, C4.5 and Greedy-Boost applying 10 cross-validation to evaluate the model. We use 10 iterations for AdaBoost and Greedy-Boost experiments.

Results in table1 show the superiority of Greedy-Boost concerning the precision of the minority classes (Probe, U2R and R2L). Indeed, the precision of the prediction of these classes varies between 88% and 100% for Greedy-Boost. However, for Boosting and C4.5, the prediction precision of these classes cannot even be calculated since these methods are unable to label a connection of these classes. Moreover, the precision ensured by Greedy-Boost (Normal and DOS) are close to 100%. These results are higher than those assured by C4.5 and Boosting.

We calculated the recalls of the various classes ensured by each of the 3 algorithms. Table 2 shows the superiority of greedy-Boost compared with C4.5 and Boosting, concerning the recall of minority classes. Whereas this recall is null for C4.5 and Boosting, Greedy-Boost obtains between 44% and 97,1% of recall for each one of these classes, which constitutes a clear improvement. In the case of the two most classes, the rates of recall of greedy-Boost are close to 90%, whereas that of Boosting goes down to 82.0% for the Normal class and that of C4.5 falls to 89.2% for the DoS class!

Based on the costs matrix table used on KDD99 challenge, the results obtained on 3 shows that Greedy-Boost presents the lowest average costs compared to

Table 1. Precision of Boosting, C4.5 and Greedy-Boost

Class	Precision		
	Boosting	C4.5	Greedy-Boost
0 : Normal	82.6	66.7	**99.1**
1 : Probe			**99.0**
2 : DoS	95.0	99.9	**100.0**
3 : U2R			**88.5**
4 : R2L			**93.2**

Table 2. Recall of Boosting, C4.5 and Greedy-Boost on KD99

Class	**Recall**		
	Boosting	C4.5	Greedy-Boost
0 : Normal	82.0	99.8	**100.0**
1 : Probe			**97.1**
2 : DoS	96.7	89.2	**100.0**
3 : U2R			**44.2**
4 : R2L			**71.9**

Table 3. Results of the cost

	Boosting	**C4.5**	**Greedy-Boost**
Cost average	0,1467	0,1949	0,0060
Standard deviation	0,5307	0,6067	0,1358

C4.5 and Boosting. Greedy-Boost has more the average low costs (0.0060), this thanks to its effectiveness on the minority classes, because the minority classes are the classes whose cost of bad classification is most important.

5   Conclusion and Perspectives

This study provides an efficient design method to generate a robust ensemble system for the intrusion detection problem. The main motivation behind this method is that the use of aggregation decision for classification ensures the strengthens of the ensemble system in term of both quantitative and qualitative sides of members, but also achieves a high diversity degree between members. The keystone of our proposed solution approach is systematically addressed through a modification of boosting, specifically, the techniques to update the weight of examples badly classified. Our theatrical study proves that our approach greedy-Boost converges quickly. It is experimentally proven that, as a whole, our algorithm clearly outperform several other algorithms, when evaluated on the KDD99 dataset. We believe that our attempt in this paper is a useful contribution to the development of ensemble-based intrusion detection systems.

References

1. Xiang, C., Yong, P.C., Meng, L.S.: Design of multiple-level hybrid classifier for intrusion detection system using Bayesian clustering and decision trees. Pattern Recognition Letters 29 (2008)
2. Giacinto, G., Roli, F.: Intrusion detection in computer networks by multiple classifier systems. In: 16th International Conference on Pattern Recognition, Quebec City, Canada (2003)
3. Zainal, A., Maarof, M.A., Shamsuddin, S.M., Abraham, A.: Ensemble of one-class classifiers for network intrusion detection system. In: Information Assurance and Security (2008)
4. Perdisci, R., Ariu, D., Fogla, P., Giacinto, G., Lee, W.: McPAD: A multiple classifier system for accurate payload based anomaly detection. Computer Networks 53(6), 864–881 (2009)
5. Giacinto, G., Perdisci, R., Rio, M.D., Roli, F.: Intrusion detection in computer networks by a modular ensemble of one-class classifiers. Information Fusion 9, 69–82 (2008)
6. Giacinto, G., Perdisci, R., Roli, F.: Network Intrusion Detection by Combining One-class Classifiers. In: International Conference on Image Analysis and Processing (2005); Special Session on Intrusion Detection, ICIAP
7. Abadeh, M.S., Habibi, J., Barzegar, Z., Sergi, M.: A parallel genetic local search algorithm for intrusion detection in computer networks. In: Engineering Applications of Artificial Intelligence, vol. 20, pp. 1058–1069 (2007)
8. Mukkamala, S., Sung, A.H., Abraham, A.: Intrusion detection using an ensemble of intelligent paradigms. Network and Computer Applications 28, 167–182 (2005)
9. Zhang, J., Zulkernine, M.: Anomaly Based Network Intrusion Detection with Unsupervised Outlier Detection. In: IEEE International Conference on Communications, ICC 2006, pp. 2388–2393 (2006)
10. DARPA dataset,
    http://www.ll.mit.edu/mission/communications/ist/corpora/ideval/data/
11. Shapire, R.: The strength of weak learnability. Machine Learning 5, 197–227 (1990)
12. Freund, Y., Schapire, R.E.: A decision-theoretic generalization of on-line learning and an application to *Boosting*. J. Comput. Syst. Sci. 55(1), 119–139 (1997)
13. Shafi, K., Abbass, H.A.: An adaptive genetic-based signature learning system for intrusion detection. Expert Systems with Applications 36(10), 12036–12043 (2009)
14. Jiang, S.Y., Song, X., Wang, H., Han, J.J., Li, Q.H.: A clustering-based method for unsupervised intrusion detections. Pattern Recognition Letters 27, 802–810 (2006)
15. Yu, Z., Tsai, J.J.P.: An efficient intrusion detection system using a boosting-based learning algorithm. International Journal of Computer Applications in Technology Achive 27(4) (2006)

Application of the Generic Feature Selection Measure in Detection of Web Attacks

Hai Thanh Nguyen[1], Carmen Torrano-Gimenez[2], Gonzalo Alvarez[2],
Slobodan Petrović[1], and Katrin Franke[1]

[1] Norwegian Information Security Laboratory,
Gjøvik University College, Norway
{hai.nguyen,katrin.franke,slobodan.petrovic,}@hig.no
[2] Instituto de Física Aplicada,
Consejo Superior de Investigaciones Científicas, Madrid, Spain
{carmen.torrano,gonzalo}@iec.csic.es

Abstract. Feature selection for filtering HTTP-traffic in Web application firewalls (WAFs) is an important task. We focus on the Generic-Feature-Selection (GeFS) measure [4], which was successfully tested on low-level package filters, i.e., the KDD CUP'99 dataset. However, the performance of the GeFS measure in analyzing high-level HTTP-traffic is still unknown. In this paper we study the GeFS measure for WAFs. We conduct experiments on the publicly available ECML/PKDD-2007 dataset. Since this dataset does not target any real Web application, we additionally generate our new CSIC-2010 dataset. We analyze the statistical properties of both two datasets to provide more insides of their nature and quality. Subsequently, we determine appropriate instances of the GeFS measure for feature selection. We use different classifiers to test the detection accuracies. The experiments show that we can remove 63% of irrelevant and redundant features from the original dataset, while reducing only 0.12% the detection accuracy of WAFs.

Keywords: Web attack detection, Web application firewall, intrusion detection systems, feature selection, machine learning algorithms.

1 Introduction

Web attacks pose many serious threats to modern Internet. The number of Web attacks is steadily increasing, consequently Web application firewalls (WAFs) [8] need to be more and more effective. One of the approaches for improving the effectiveness of WAFs is to apply the feature selection methods. Achieving reduction of the number of relevant traffic features without negative effect on detection accuracy is a goal that greatly increases the available processing time of WAFs and reduces the required system resources. As there exist many feature selection algorithms (see, for example [2,3]), the question that arises is which ones could be applied in intrusion detection in general and in Web attack detection in particular. The most of the feature selection work in intrusion practice is still done manually and the quality of selected features depends strongly on expert knowledge. For automatic feature selection, the wrapper

Á. Herrero and E. Corchado (Eds.): CISIS 2011, LNCS 6694, pp. 25–32, 2011.
© Springer-Verlag Berlin Heidelberg 2011

and the filter models from machine learning are frequently applied [2,3]. The wrapper model assesses the selected features by learning algorithm's performance. Therefore, the wrapper method requires a lot of time and computational resources to find the best feature subsets. The filter model considers statistical characteristics of dataset directly without involving any learning algorithms. Due to the computational efficiency, the filter method is usually used to select features from high-dimensional datasets, such as intrusion detection systems. Moreover, this method allows to estimate feature subsets not only by their relevance, but also by the relationships between features that make certain features redundant. A major challenge in the IDS feature selection process is to choose appropriate measures that can precisely determine the relevance and the relationship between features of given dataset.

Since the relevance and the relationship are usually characterized in terms of correlation or mutual information [2,3], we focus on the recently proposed generic feature selection (GeFS) measure for intrusion detection [4]. This measure consists of two instances that belong to the filter model from machine learning: the correlation feature selection (CFS) measure and the minimal-redundancy-maximal-relevance (mRMR) measure. In given dataset, if there are many features that are linearly correlated to each other, then the CFS measure is recommended for selecting features. Otherwise, the mRMR measure is alternatively chosen as it considers non-linear relations through the analysis of mutual information between the features. The GeFS measure was successfully tested on the KDD CUP 1999 benchmarking dataset for IDS [9]. However, this dataset is out of date and it was heavily criticized by the IDS community (see, for example [7]). Moreover, the KDD CUP 1999 dataset does not contain enough HTTP traffic for training and testing WAFs and the Web attacks of this dataset are not representative for currently existing Web attacks. Therefore, the question about the performance of the GeFS measure perform in Web attack detection is still open.

In this paper, we propose to use the GeFS measure for selecting features in Web attack detection. We conducted experiments on the ECML/PKDD 2007 dataset, which was generated for the ECML/PKDD 2007 Discovery Challenge [6]. However, the attack requests of this dataset were constructed blindly [6] and did not target any real Web application. Therefore, we additionally generated our new CSIC 2010 dataset, which contains the traffic directed to an e-commerce Web application. From our expert knowledge about Web attacks, we listed 30 features that we considered relevant for the detection process. Then, we extracted the values of these 30 relevant features from the datasets. By applying the GeFS measure, we wanted to know within the particular datasets which features among the 30 extracted features are the most important for the Web attack detection process. In order to do that, we analyzed the statistical properties of the datasets to see whether they had linear correlation or non-linear relations between features. To do that, the data points of the datasets were visualized in the two-dimensional space and the correlation coefficients were computed. We then chose the CFS measure for feature selection from the CSIC 2010 dataset and the mRMR measure for the ECML/PKDD 2007 dataset. The detection accuracies obtained after the feature selection by means of four different classifiers were tested. The experiments show that by using appropriate instances of the GeFS measure, we could remove 63% of irrelevant and redundant features from the original dataset, while reducing only 0.12% the detection accuracy of WAFs.

The paper is organized as follows. Section 2 describes the generic feature selection (GeFS) measure for intrusion detection and its instances in more detail. Section 3 shows our experiments on the CSIC 2010 dataset and the ECML/PKDD 2007 dataset. The last section summarizes the findings.

2   Generic Feature Selection for Intrusion Detection

In this subsection, we give an overview of the generic feature selection (GeFS) measure together with two instances applied in intrusion detection: the correlation-feature-selection (CFS) measure and the minimal-redundancy-maximal-relevance (mRMR) measure [4].

Definition: The feature selection problem by means of the generic feature selection (GeFS) measure is to find $x \in \{0,1\}^n$ that maximizes the function GeFS(x):

$$\max_{x \in \{0,1\}^n} GeFS(x) = \frac{a_0 + \sum_{i=1}^{n} A_i(x)x_i}{b_0 + \sum_{i=1}^{n} B_i(x)x_i} \tag{1}$$

In this definition, binary values of the variable x_i indicate the appearance ($x_i = 1$) or the absence ($x_i = 0$) of the feature f_i; a_0, b_0 are constants; $A_i(x)$, $B_i(x)$ are linear functions of variables $x_1, ..., x_n$.

The Correlation Feature Selection (CFS) Measure: This measure characterizes the relevance of features and their relationships in terms of the linear correlation. For a given dataset, if there are many features that are linearly correlated to each other, the CFS measure is recommended for selecting features. In [4], it was shown that the CFS measure is an instance of the GeFS measure.

The minimal-Redundancy-Maximal-Relevance (mRMR) Measure: The mRMR measure considers non-linear relations through the analysis of mutual information between the features. Therefore, it was recommended for selecting features from datasets that have many non-linearly correlated features. It was also shown that the mRMR measure belongs to the generic feature selection (GeFS) measure [4].

The feature selection problem (1) can be solved by means of the optimization approach proposed in [4]. The main idea is that the problem (1) is transformed into mixed 0-linear programming problem, which can be solved by using the branch and bound algorithm.

The search strategy for obtaining subsets of relevant features by means of the GeFS measure is:

-*Step 1*: Analyze the statistical properties of the given dataset in order to choose the appropriate feature selection instance (CFS or mRMR) from the generic feature selection measure GeFS. We choose the CFS measure if the dataset has many features that are linearly correlated to the class label and to each other. Otherwise, the mRMR measure is chosen.

-*Step 2*: According to the choice from Step 1, construct the optimization problem (1) for the CFS measure or for the mRMR measure. In this step, we can use expert knowledge by assigning the value to the variable if the feature is relevant and the value 0 otherwise.

-*Step 3*: Transform the optimization problem of the GeFS measure to a mixed 0-linear programming (M01LP) problem, which is to be solved by means of the branch-and-bound algorithm. A non-zero integer value of x_i from the optimal solution x indicates the relevance of the feature f_i regarding the GeFS measure.

3 Experiment

In this section, we show the application of the generic feature selection (GeFS) measure in Web attack detection. We first describe two datasets, on which the experiments were conducted: the ECML/PKDD 2007 dataset [6] and our new CSIC 2010 dataset. We then discuss the 30 features that we consider relevant for Web attack detection. We analyze the statistical properties of these datasets containing the 30 extracted features to choose appropriate instances from the GeFS measure. Since there is no standard Web application firewall (WAF), we apply four different machine learning algorithms to evaluate the detection accuracy on datasets containing the selected features.

3.1 Data Sets

We conducted experiments on the ECML/PKDD 2007 dataset, which was generated for the ECML/PKDD 2007 Discovery Challenge [6]. In fact, we used the training set, which is composed of 50,000 samples including 20% of attacks (i.e. 10,000 attacks and 40,000 normal requests). The requests are labeled with specifications of attack classes or normal traffic. The classes of attacks in this dataset are: Cross-Site Scripting, SQL Injection, LDAP Injection, XPATH Injection, Path traversal, Command Execution and SSI attacks. However, the attack requests of this dataset were constructed blindly and did not target any real Web application. Therefore, we additionally generated our new CSIC 2010 dataset for experiments.

The CSIC 2010 dataset contains the generated traffic targeted to an ecommerce Web application developed at our department. In this web application, users can buy items using shopping cart and register by providing some personal information. The dataset was generated automatically and contains 36,000 normal requests and more than 25,000 anomalous requests. In this data set the requests are labeled as normal or anomalous. We included attacks such as SQL injection, buffer overflow, information gathering, files disclosure, CRLF injection, XSS, server side include, parameter tampering and so on. In order to generate the traffic, we collected thousands of normal and anomalous values for the parameters of the web application. Then, we generated requests for every web-page and the values of the parameters, if any, were filled with the values collected (the normal values for the normal traffic and the anomalous ones for the anomalous traffic). Further details can be found in [5].

Table 1. Names of 30 features that are considered relevant for the detection of Web attacks. $\star$ refers to features selected by the CFS from the CSIC-2010 dataset; † refers to features selected by the mRMR from the CSIC 2010 dataset; refers to features • selected by the CFS from the ECML/PKDD 2007 dataset; and ◊ refers to features selected by the mRMR from the ECML/PKDD 2007 dataset.

Feature Name	Feature Name
Length of the request $\star$ ◊	Length of the path $\star$
Length of the arguments $\star$ ◊	Length of the header "Accept" †
Length of the header "Accept-Encoding" †	Length of the header "Accept-Charset" †
Length of the header "Accept-Language" †	Length of the header "Cookie" †
Length of the header "Content-Length" †	Length of the header "Content-Type"
Length of the Host †	Length of the header "Referer" †
Length of the header "User-Agent" †	Method identifier
Number of arguments $\star$	Number of letters in the arguments $\star$
Number of digits in the arguments $\star$	Number of 'special' char in the arguments $\star$ † • ◊
Number of other char in the arguments • ◊	Number of letters char in the path $\star$
Number of digits in the path $\star$ †	Number of 'special' char in the path $\star$
Number of other char in path †	Number of cookies †
Minimum byte value in the request ◊	Maximum byte value in the request $\star$ †
Number of distinct bytes	Entropy ◊
Number of keywords in the path	Number of keywords in the arguments

3.2 Experimental Settings

From our expert knowledge about Web attacks, we listed 30 features that we considered relevant for the detection process (see Table 1). Some features refer to the length of the request, the length of the path or the headers, as length is important for detecting buffer-overflow attacks. From our expert knowledge, we observed that the non-alphanumeric characters were present in many injection attacks. Therefore, we considered four types of characters: letters, digits, non-alphanumeric characters which have a special meaning in a set of programming languages (in Table 1 we refer to them as 'special' char) and other characters.

We analyzed their appearances in the path and in the argument's values. We also studied the entropy of the bytes in the request. Additionally, we collected the keywords of several programming languages that were often used in the injection attacks and counted the number of their appearances in different parts of the request as a feature.

Then, we extracted the values of these 30 relevant features from the CSIC 2010 and from the ECML/PKDD 2007 datasets and analyzed their statistical properties to see whether they had linear or non-linear relations between features. From this analysis, the appropriate feature selection instance from the GeFS measure was chosen for each dataset according to the Step 1 of the search method described above. In order to do that, we first visualized the whole datasets in the two-dimensional space to get a plot matrix, in which each element was the distribution of data points depending on the values of feature and the class label or the values of two features. For instance, Fig.1 and Fig. 2 show the sample distributions of data points of the CSIC 2010 dataset and the ECML/PKDD 2007 dataset, respectively. We then calculated the correlation coefficients between the features. From these, we observed that the CSIC 2010 dataset had many features that were linearly correlated to each other, whereas in the ECML/PKDD 2007 dataset the non-linear relations between features were more representative. In fact, in the CSIC 2010 dataset, more than 63 % of the correlation coefficients were greater than 0.5, whereas in the ECML/PKDD 2007 dataset more than 83% of the correlation coefficients were less than 0.09. Therefore, we chose the CFS measure for selecting features from the CSIC 2010 dataset, and the mRMR measure for selecting features from the ECML/PKDD 2007 dataset. Moreover, the CFS and the mRMR measures were also applied to the ECML/PKDD 2007 and to the CSIC 2010 datasets, respectively, to see how the wrong choice of feature selection methods would negatively affect the detection performance.

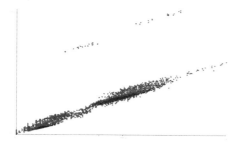 

Fig. 1. Sample distribution of data points of the CSIC 2010 dataset

Fig. 2. Sample distribution of data points of the ECML/PKDD 2007 dataset

We applied the optimization algorithm proposed in [4] to find globally optimal feature subsets by means of the CFS and the mRMR measures. Four classifiers with 10-fold cross validation were used to evaluate detection performances before and after feature selection: C4.5, CART, RandomTree and RandomForest [1]. All the obtained results are given in the Tables 2, 3 and 4.

3.3 Experimental Results

Table 2 shows the number of full-set features before feature selection and the number of features selected by the CFS measure and the mRMR measure (Table 1 shows which features were selected). Table 3 and Table 4 summarize the detection rate as well as the false positive rate of four different classifiers performed on the CSIC 2010 dataset and the ECML/PKDD 2007 dataset, respectively.

Table 2. Full-set features and the number of selected features

Data Set	Full-set	CFS	mRMR
CSIC 2010	30	11	14
ECML/PKDD 2007	30	2	6

Table 3. Experimental results on the CSIC 2010 dataset

Classifiers	Detection rate			False Positive Rate		
	Full-set	CFS	mRMR	Full-set	CFS	mRMR
C4.5	94.49	94.06	79.80	5.9	6.8	25.7
CART	94.12	93.71	79.85	6.2	6.8	25.3
Random Tree	92.30	92.70	71.36	8.3	7.8	30.6
Random Forest	93.71	93.68	71.70	7.2	7.2	30.5
Average	**93.65**	**93.53**	**75.67**	**6.9**	**7.1**	**28**

Table 4. Experimental results on the ECML/PKDD 2007 dataset

Classifiers	Detection rate			False Positive Rate		
	Full-set	CFS	mRMR	Full-set	CFS	mRMR
C4.5	96.37	86.45	91.62	3.7	17.6	9.9
CART	96.11	86.45	91.54	4.3	17.6	10
Random Tree	96.89	86.39	93.41	2.6	17.7	6.4
Random Forest	98.80	86.39	95.18	1.2	17.7	5.0
Average	**97.04**	**86.42**	**92.93**	**2.95**	**17.6**	**7.8**

It can be observed from Table 2 and Table 3 that the CFS measure performed well on the CSIC 2010 dataset and gave better results than the mRMR measure. In fact, the CFS measure removed the number of irrelevant and redundant features from the dataset by more than 63%, while reducing very slightly (only 0.12%) the detection accuracy. In this case, the mRMR measure gave much worse results in comparison with the full-set features.

From Table 2 and Table 4, it can be seen that the mRMR measure removed 80% of irrelevant and redundant features from the ECML/PKDD 2007 dataset, whereas the detection accuracies were a bit lower than the ones obtained with the full-set feature. The CFS measure did not work well in this case.

Therefore, based on all these experiments we can say that the effectiveness of WAFs would be improved by choosing and using appropriate feature selection methods of the GeFS measure.

4 Conclusions

We have proposed to use the generic feature selection (GeFS) measure for Web attack detection. We analyzed statistical properties of the new generated CSIC 2010 dataset and the ECML/PKDD 2007 dataset. Based on this analysis, the CFS measure and the mRMR measure were chosen for selecting features from the CSIC 2010 dataset and the ECML/PKDD 2007 dataset, respectively. The detection accuracies obtained after the feature selection by means of four different classifiers were tested. The experiments show that by choosing appropriate instances of the GeFS measure, we could remove 63% of irrelevant and redundant features from the original dataset, while reducing only 0.12% the detection accuracy of WAFs.

Acknowledgements. We would like to thank Gjøvik University College, Norwegian Information Security Laboratory, project CUCO (MTM2008-02194) from the Ministerio de Ciencia e Innovación, program JAE/I3P from the Consejo Superior de Investigaciones Científicas.

References

1. Duda, R.O., Hart, P.E., Stork, D.G.: Pattern Classification. John Wiley & Sons, USA (2001)
2. Guyon, I., Gunn, S., Nikravesh, M., Zadeh, L.A.: Feature Extraction: Foundations and Applications. Series Studies in Fuzziness and Soft Computing. Springer, Heidelberg (2005)
3. Liu, H., Motoda, H.: Computational Methods of Feature Selection. Chapman & Hall/CRC, Boca Raton (2008)
4. Nguyen, H., Franke, K., Petrović, S.: Towards a Generic Feature-Selection Measure for Intrusion Detection. In: 20th International Conference on Pattern Recognition, Istanbul, Turkey, pp. 1529–1532 (August 2010)
5. Torrano-Gimenez, C., Perez-Villegas, A., Alvarez, G.: A Self-Learning Anomaly-Based Web Application Firewall. In: Proceedings of Computational Intelligence In Security For Information Systems (CISIS 2009), pp. 85–92 (2009)
6. Rassi, C., Brissaud, J., Dray, G., Poncelet, P., Roche, M., Teisseire, M.: Web Analyzing Traffic Challenge: Description and Results. In: Proceedings of the Discovery Challenge ECML/PKDD 2007, pp. 47–52 (2007)
7. McHugh, J.: Testing Intrusion Detection Systems: Critique of the 1998 and 1999 DARPA Intrusion Detection System Evaluations as Performed by Lincoln Laboratory. Proc. ACM Transactions on Information and System Security (TISSEC) 3(4), 262–294 (2000)
8. Becher, M.: Web Application Firewalls. VDM Verlag Dr. Mueller e.K. (February 1, 2007); ISBN-10: 383640446X, ISBN-13: 978-3836404464
9. Lee, W.: A data mining framework for building intrusion detection models. In: IEEE Symposium on Security and Privacy, Berkeley, California, pp. 120–132 (1999)

Data Aggregation Based on Fuzzy Logic for VANETs*

P. Caballero-Gil, J. Molina-Gil, and C. Caballero-Gil

Department of Statistics, OR and Computing, University of La Laguna, Spain
{pcaballe,jmmolina,ccabgil}@ull.es

Abstract. Data aggregation is mainly used to combine similar or equal information sent by different nodes of a network before forwarding it with the aim of reducing the number of messages. This is particularly important in Vehicular Ad-hoc NETworks (VANETs) where vehicles broadcast information about the road traffic situation, what can lead to overload the network. In this paper we propose a system for data aggregation based on the primary computational intelligence approach of fuzzy logic. The scheme is automatically launched in case of incident, without any fixed structure on the road, but through the spontaneous formation of aggregation groups. Fuzzy logic is mainly applied in decision-making regarding aggregation and diffusion of aggregated information, while data aggregation is based on digital signature combination. The proposed protocol also uses probabilistic verification of aggregated data in order to reduce computation overhead and delay.

Keywords: Data aggregation; fuzzy logic; vehicular ad-hoc network.

1 Introduction

Vehicular Ad-hoc Networks (VANETs) are self-organized networks formed by vehicles and used to provide drivers with advance notification of traffic congestion or hazard events using wireless communication. In this type of networks, warning messages affect decisions taken by drivers so that any wrong message could lead to higher transportation times, fuel consumption, environmental contamination and impact of road constructions, and, in the worst-case scenario, more traffic accidents. In the near future, this type of networks will allow the reduction of the number of deaths due to car accidents, and the provision of real-time information on traffic and on roads. For example, drivers will be able to exchange information with their neighbors and with the road so that they can receive warnings about potentially dangerous events such as accidents, obstacles on the road, etc. Other practical applications of VANETs are, for instance, to provide the ability to find free parking spaces or to disseminate traffic information.

* This work was supported by the Ministerio de Ciencia e Innovación and the European FEDER Fund under Project TIN2008-02236/TSI and FPI scholarship BES-2009-016774, and by the Agencia Canaria de Investigación, Innovación y Sociedad de la Información under PI2007/005 Project and FPI scholarship BOC Number 60.

Á. Herrero and E. Corchado (Eds.): CISIS 2011, LNCS 6694, pp. 33–40, 2011.

VANETs are composed of two different types of nodes: On-Board Units (OBUs), which are wireless devices on vehicles, and Road-Side Units (RSUs), which form the network infrastructure on the road. While in other resource-constrained wireless networks such as sensor networks, data aggregation is used mainly to save energy, in VANETs it may be used both to ensure that the transmitted information is reliable and to reduce the number of repeated warnings.

This paper is organized as follows. Related works are summarized in Section 2. Basic concepts about the fuzzy logic approach that is followed in the scheme are described in Section 3. The probabilistic verification included in the scheme is presented in Section 4. Finally, conclusions are presented in Section 5.

2   Related Works

In the literature we can find many trust models applied to VANETs domain. Many of them are cited in the recent survey on trust management for VANETs [13]. With respect to practical cryptographic solutions, there are several papers proposing the use of Public-Key Infrastructures (PKI) in VANETs so that thanks to the use of digital signatures, the source and integrity of messages can be verified [6]. However, none of those proposals protect against malicious attacks such as false content generation where an adversary could try to inject false information that does not correspond to what it is really detecting.

Data aggregation for VANETs has been analyzed in several papers. [8] presents a protocol for relaying information in VANETs under the assumption that vehicles form clusters, and details about speed and traffic information are exchanged within nodes in the same cluster. Such a mechanism reduces the amount of data transmitted in a cluster, but the paper does not include any specific scheme to combine aggregated data. VESPA [3] proposes that not only fresh data are considered for warning, but also aggregated data histories are maintained for disseminating knowledge among vehicles. Another proposal can be found in [5], where the aggregation of multiple messages describing the same event and the use of revocation messages allowing vehicles to report false information are proposed. However, such a mechanism has an important weakness because real messages can be revoked through it. In [11] the proposed solution is based on the use of a tamper-proof device and consists in asking an aggregator vehicle about a random aggregated record. The main disadvantage of this method is the dependency on a tamper-proof device since an attacker could easily skip this service in order to compose malicious aggregated data. Finally, [4] proposes another mechanism to provide security through aggregation in a scheme where streets are divided into fixed size segments corresponding to Wi-Fi signal coverage. However, this aggregation criterion uses a fixed segmentation of the road, what has been shown that does not work properly with a high number of vehicles in large areas, like for example in big traffic jams covering kilometers.

In order to overcome all the aforementioned problems, the use of fuzzy logic combined with a probabilistic verification scheme is here proposed for the definition of a data aggregation protocol. The idea of using fuzzy aggregation in trust models has been modeled and proposed by several authors [1] [2]. A close and recent paper [9] proposed an algorithm for hierarchical aggregation in VANETs based on a probabilistic approximation to data. However, in our proposal the probabilistic approach is applied on the verification of fuzzily aggregated data.

Various proposals have been made to promote cooperation and enhance security in VANETs through the use of authentication, key management and pseudonyms [10]. However, to the best of our knowledge no tools that allow ensuring that the generated information is true have been proposed till now. A quite logical initial approach to address this problem is by providing nodes of a mechanism to verify the packet content accuracy. In this paper nodes will be called agents from now on, according to the Artificial Intelligence literature.

When data aggregation is possible because the vehicle has received several packets informing about the same event, various known schemes based on clusters may be used [7] [12]. In those proposals, the so-called cluster-heads are responsible for adding the information submitted by their cluster members, and also for forwarding it. Consequently, those schemes can be seen as proposals based on a hierarchy, which increases the amount of necessary communications for cluster management, especially in highly dynamic networks such as VANETs. In this paper we propose a new scheme that replaces such a static hierarchical point of view by a fuzzy-logic based dynamic approach.

3   Fuzzy Logic Approach

Aggregation schemes are usually based on three sequential phases. The first phase is decision-making, when the system must allow deciding whether two pieces of information are similar enough to add them or not. The second phase is data aggregation. Once the system has concluded that the received packets must be added, it has to apply an aggregation method for combining them. The third and last step is the aggregated data delivery. After the two previous steps, the system must allow the dissemination of the aggregated data.

In the literature we can find several proposals for the two last stages. However, schemes for making decision are normally based on predefined clusters, trees or fixed structures, which are not suitable for their use in VANETs. Thus, a new aggregation scheme is here proposed where decisions regarding whether two received pieces of information are similar enough to be added are based on the content of such packets. Such decisions take into account possible inaccuracies or approximations regarding space and time data to define an event. Therefore, our proposal for the application of fuzzy logic is focused especially on the description of the decision criteria of the first phase of the aggregation scheme.

In the proposed scheme information is aggregated based mainly on two dimensions: space and time. On the one hand, the approximate location of an event in a road or a map is a fundamental parameter. On the other hand, a time interval in which the persistence of an announced event must be taken into account. When applying a fuzzy approach on such parameters the best decision on aggregation is made because it allows a flexible reasoning that takes into account all possible values in packets announcing the same event. This enables a dynamic approach

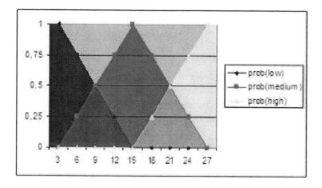

Fig. 1. Fuzzification Function of SD and TD

when considering clusters for aggregation. Before the implementation of the system, and depending on the particular application, it is possible to identify other possible parameters apart from spatial and temporal location, with possible influence on the decision of aggregation, such as distance between agents or speeds. The input values corresponding to all influential parameters are real numbers, which the system has to assign to adjectives. The next step is to formulate rules that express the combination of the chosen influential parameters. In particular, according to such rules, the degrees of the influential parameters adjectives are combined using fuzzy Boolean operators such as AND, OR and NOT, defined as the minimum, maximum, and complement, respectively. The output of the application of every rule is defined as two possible values: YES and NO. This fuzzy decision making process allows combining all possible influential parameters in order to conclude whether two received warnings refer to the same event because the complexity of the original real values of such parameters are hidden behind the mapping to adjectives.

As an example of fuzzy decision making based on rules we propose to choose and combine the influential parameters of spatial and temporal location denoted Space-Distance (SD) and Time-Distance (TD). Fig. 1 exemplifies this process for both variables representing the influence of both parameters considering as x-coordinate respectively SD in meters or TD in minutes, and the y-coordinate is the probability corresponding to the adjectives LOW, MEDIUM and HIGH. Each of these adjectives is described by a membership function that maps the real valued input value of the corresponding influence factor to a membership degree corresponding to the adjective described by the function. In the depicted example, according to the fact that a typical error in normal GPS is about 23 meters of ambiguity, an input SD of less than 3 meters is fuzzified as being LOW with a degree of 1. For example, the output of the function for a SD of about 9 meters is classified at the same time as LOW and as MEDIUM with a degree of 0.5. From 27 meters on, SD is considered HIGH with probability 1. The same is considered for TD in minutes.

The next step after fuzzification is to formulate particular rules that express the combination of the influences. As an example, a possible simple basic structure of such fuzzy logic rules is as follows:

Algorithm 1. Fuzzy Rules
01: **if** (SD **is** LOW) **OR** ((SD **is** MEDIUM) **AND** (TD **is NOT** HIGH))
02: **then**
03:   Aggregation-Decision **is YES**;
04: **else**
05:   Aggregation-Decision **is NO**;
06: **endif**

The above rules can be also represented according to Table 1.

There can be more than one rule assigning values to the aggregation decision. In this case, the assignments to the aggregation decision are combined by an implicit AND, so that the corresponding probability of the Aggregation-Decision is given by the minimum between both input probabilities for SD and LD. After all rules have been evaluated, the decision will be either YES or NO depending on which of the two has got the higher assigned probability by the rules.

For example, if the SD is 10 m and so it is fuzzified to LOW with a degree of 0.32 and to MEDIUM with a degree of 0.68, and for the same pair of packets the TD is 20 min and so the TD is fuzzified to MEDIUM with a degree of 0.58 and to HIGH with a degree of 0.42, the Aggregation-Decision would be YES with a degree 0.58 and NO with a degree 0.42, so the final decision is YES and we aggregate both packets because we concluded they refer to the same event.

Data received by an agent must be stored in a local database with the objective not only of aggregation but also because the channel could get overload, restricting the amount of data that can be sent, and in this case, the agent is allowed to send only a subset of its database. In order to solve the problem of selection, we might use an approach also based on fuzzy logic to take into account relevant parameters for spreading the more adequate and accurate information that is currently available in the database. Then, each agent should carry out a qualification process of the data in its database in order to conclude which are the most relevant data stored that must be sent according to the restrictions of the channel. Several factors, such as severity or antiquity of an event, can play an important role in this selection. As of the aggregation decision, rating relevance of different parameters of a piece of information often depends on the specific application. Relevance ranking provides an order on the parameters to be considered and on data stored so that according to this order, the agent always knows which packages should be sent without collapsing the channel.

Table 1. Fuzzy Rules

HIGH	NO	NO	NO
MEDIUM	YES	YES	NO
LOW	YES	YES	YES
SD/TD	LOW	MEDIUM	HIGH

4   Probabilistic Verification

Message verification only applies to vehicles that are unable to check directly the received information. That is to say, when a vehicle receives a warning message about an incident that is not under the coverage of its antenna, and wants to confirm the authenticity of the received message, it has two options depending on its location with respect to the source of the warning. First we consider the case when the receiver cannot confirm the information directly, but it is so close to the supposed event that it has to make a decision quickly because in a short period of time it will be too near to avoid it. In this case, if a vehicle receives an aggregated packet signed by several vehicles, it should use a verification mechanism fast enough to verify the signatures of the packet. As we already mentioned, on the one hand it is inefficient to verify all the signatures contained in a packet, but on the other hand it is necessary to verify the information before accepting it as valid. In order to fix this problem, only a few signatures are proposed to be verified according to a probabilistic scheme. Secondly, we consider the case when agents are far enough from the hazard so they behave according to the store-and-carry paradigm, collecting evidences about the hazard in the form of aggregated packets. In this case, the vehicle has enough time to collect and check several aggregated messages before it has to make a decision. In particular, it has to check some signatures for each received aggregated packet as in the previous case. However, in this case the vehicle may perform more complete verifications that will provide a higher level of certainty.

As aforementioned, probabilistic verification will be only used by vehicles that are unable to verify directly the information that reaches them. The proposed verification algorithm uses threads, which are lightweight processes that allow a concurrent execution for a faster execution of the whole protocol. In the algorithm shown below, $H[i]$ denotes a thread for the variable i that takes an integer value between 1 and n, where n denotes the number of aggregated signatures. When an agent receives a message and decides to verify its signatures, the main process launches as many threads as signatures the message contains. Before the main process launches the threads, it checks whether the message contains enough signatures to determine whether the message has been signed by a significant number of agents. This minimal number of signatures to validate a message shows the degree of closeness between data packets referring to the message, and is usually called intimacy level in trust literature. In our probabilistic verification scheme, such an intimacy level will be given by a combination of two factors: the average number of authenticated vehicles and the space-distance between the locations of the receiving agent and the event announced in the aggregated packet. Thus, in order to calculate the threshold for the minimal number of required signatures, for example the agent could compute the average number of authenticated users per minute in the current session and the SD between both aforementioned locations. Then, the intimacy level might be given by the average of users when the distance is below 30 m. For distances between 30 m and 1000 m the level can decrease linearly with the distance, until reaching the minimal value of 2, which might be the intimacy level for any distance greater than 1000 m.

Each thread $H[i]$ determines whether to verify the signature with a verification probability p. If $H[i]$ defines a verification, and the signature is proved to be valid, $H[i]$ returns a *true* value informing that it is a valid signature. Otherwise, it returns a *false* value. The result of all those threads are stored in a structure P. If all fields in the structure P are proved to be valid, it is interpreted as evidence that all the verified signatures are correct so the message is accepted as valid. On the other hand, if P contains some thread results that is invalid, this could be interpreted as false message. If most threads indicate that the message is false, it is taken as invalid message, otherwise it is valid. If there is a tie or a questionable amount of false signatures, the reputation information stored by the receiving agent about the different agents that have signed the message is checked. In this case, only those agents that have a good reputation due to their active and correct participation in the network are trusted and accepted.

Algorithm 2. Probabilistic Verification of Signatures

```
01: function Main(...)
02:    bool P[c];
03:    Thread H[c];
05:    for (i=0;i¡c;i++) do
06:       if (ProbH[i]=1) then
07:          P[j]=H[i](VerifySignature(S,M));
08:          j++;
09:       end if
10:    end for
11:    if (IsTrueAll(P)) then
12:       return ReliableMessage;
13:    else
14:       if (NotIsTrueAll(P)) then
15:          return NotReliableMessage;
16:       else
17:          return VerifyNodeReputation;
18:       end if
19:    end if
20: end Main

21: bool function VerifySignature(Signature S,text M)
22:    if (IsValid(S)) then
23:       return true;
24:    else
25:       return false;
26:    endif
27: end function
```

5   Conclusions

This paper proposes a new scheme for data aggregation with the aim of reducing the number of sent messages in VANETs. Different ideas have been combined in a new data aggregation method so that those agents who agree with the generated information sign the packet. The proposed aggregation system is based on fuzzy logic mainly during the phase of decision-making regarding aggregation. When an aggregated packet reaches a vehicle, this may verify the information by checking the attached signatures. In order to avoid the delay produced by signature verification, a probabilistic scheme is proposed according to which only a number of signatures given by the intimacy level are chosen to be checked. The implementation of the proposal is part of a work in progress.

References

1. Lee, K.M., Hwang, K.-S., Lee, J.-H., Kim, H.-J.: A Fuzzy Trust Model Using Multiple Evaluation Criteria. In: Wang, L., Jiao, L., Shi, G., Li, X., Liu, J. (eds.) FSKD 2006. LNCS (LNAI), vol. 4223, pp. 961–969. Springer, Heidelberg (2006)
2. Castelfranchi, C., Falcone, R.: Trust is Much More Than Subjective Probability: Mental Components and Sources of Trust. In: Proc. Hawaii International Conference on System Sciences (2000)
3. Delot, T., Cenerario, N., Ilarri, S.: Vehicular Event Sharing with a Mobile Peer-to-Peer Architecture. Transportation Research Part C: Emerging Technologies 18(4), 584–598 (2010); ISSN: 0968-090X
4. Dietzel, S., Schoch, B., Konings, E., Weber, M., Kargl, F.: Resilient secure aggregation for vehicular networks. IEEE Network (2010)
5. Eichler, S., Merkle, C., Strassberger, M.: Data aggregation system for distributing inter-vehicle warning messages. In: Proc. IEEE Conf. on Local Computer Networks, pp. 543–544. IEEE Computer Society, Los Alamitos (2006)
6. Gollan, L., Meinel, C.: Digital signatures for automobiles. In: Proc. Systemics, Cybernetics and Informatics, pp. 225–230 (2002)
7. Heinzelman, W.R., Chandrakasan, A., Balakrishnan, H.: Energy-Efficient Communication Protocol for Wireless Microsensor Networks. In: Proc. Hawaii International Conference on System Sciences, vol. 8, p. 8020. IEEE, Los Alamitos (2000)
8. Ibrahim, K., Weigle, M.C.: Accurate data aggregation for VANETs. In: Proc. ACM International Workshop on Vehicular Ad Hoc Networks (2007)
9. Locherta, C., Scheuermann, B., Mauvea, M.: A probabilistic method for cooperative hierarchical aggregation of data in VANETs. Ad Hoc Networks 8(5), 518–530 (2010)
10. Molina-Gil, J., Caballero-Gil, P., Caballero-Gil, C.: Enhancing Collaboration in Vehicular Networks. In: Luo, Y. (ed.) CDVE 2010. LNCS, vol. 6240, pp. 77–80. Springer, Heidelberg (2010)
11. Picconi, F., Ravi, N., Gruteser, M., Iftode, L.: Probabilistic Validation of Aggregated Data in Vehicular Ad-Hoc Networks. In: Proc. International Workshop Vehicular Ad Hoc Networks, pp. 76–85. ACM Press, New York (2006)
12. Yao, Y., Gehrke, J.: The cougar approach to in-network query processing in sensor networks. SIGMOD Rec. 31(3), 9–18 (2002)
13. Zhang, J.: A Survey on Trust Management for VANETs. In: Proc. International Conference on Advanced Information Networking and Applications, AINA (2011)

Digging into IP Flow Records with a Visual Kernel Method

Cynthia Wagner, Gerard Wagener, Radu State, and Thomas Engel

University of Luxembourg - SnT,
Campus Kircherg, L-1359 Luxembourg, Luxembourg
{cynthia.wagner,jerome.francois,
radu.state,thomas.engel}@uni.lu
http://www.securityandtrust.lu

Abstract. This paper presents a network monitoring framework with an intuitive visualization engine. The framework leverages a kernel method with spatial and temporal aggregated IP flows for the off/online processing of Netflow records and full packet captures from ISP and honeypot input data and is operating on aggregated Netflow records and is supporting network management activities related to the anomaly and attack detection.

Keywords: Netflow records, Visualization, Kernel Function, Honeypot.

1 Introduction

The business of network monitoring has been studied a lot and still, there are a lot of problems to be solved. Problems, as full automation of monitoring processes respectively the evaluation are still challenging. Network incidents may have most different natures, i.e. attacks, component failures or unusual user activities. In most cases, incident evaluation requires strong and fast interpretation skills of network operators, because countermeasures have to be taken quickly. Another challenge is the quantity of available data. Information on network borders are mostly Netflow[1] records, which can also be exported by most commercially available routers today, but evaluating these large quantities of Netflow records in real time remains an open issue. A convenient solution is to use condensed forms of packets or to refer to a more novel approach by spatially aggregating flow records over time. In this paper, a new network monitoring framework for on/off-line processing of temporal-spatial aggregated IP flows is described, which aims to detect network incidents/attacks and to visualize them in an intuitive way. For the network monitoring task, a modified version of the Aguri tool [2] is used, which monitors IP flow records and summarizes them into traffic profiles. These traffic profiles are applied to a specific kernel method for evaluation purpose. The kernel function captures topological and traffic changes without having a manual profile comparison. The kernel results are then mapped

---

[1] Netflow records: RFC3954, http://tools.ietf.org/html/rfc3954

Á. Herrero and E. Corchado (Eds.): CISIS 2011, LNCS 6694, pp. 41–49, 2011.

onto an intuitive image with adaptive colour gradients. To proof the validity of this method, two different data sets were applied to PeekKernelFlows. The first data set is originated from an ISP and the second from an High Interaction Honeypot [10] with a vulnerable ssh-server.

Section 2 describes the different modules of the framework PeekKernelFlows. A short description of IP flow aggregation is given, the kernel method described and the visualization method is explained. In Section 3, the evaluation of the monitoring framework is given. Section 4 presents relevant work in this area and section 5 describes future work and presents the conclusions.

2 The Monitoring Framework

The following section presents the theoretical components and implemented features of the monitoring framework PeekKernelFlows (see Fig. 1). The routers with Netflow record exporting functionality log Netflow records from the network and store them on the Collector. Then, Netflows are processed by PeekKernelFlows, which has four main components. The first module, modifed Aguri, is

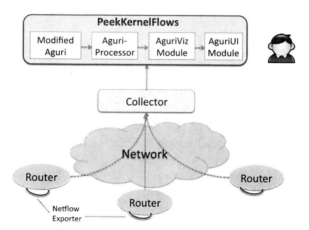

Fig. 1. The Monitoring Framework PeekKernelFlows

the monitoring feature, which accepts Netflow records and performs the spatial-temporal aggregation task. The AguriProcessor-module included the kernel calculus model. The AguriViz-module maps the outcomes of the kernel calculus onto an image by referring to an adaptive colour gradient. The AguriUI-module is the interface towards the end-user of the system.

2.1 Aggregated Netflow Records in Space Over Time η

Aguri [2] is a near real-time flow-monitoring tool that spatially aggregates IP flows over time. The advantage is that instead of considering single flow records, an overview on subnet layer can be given due to aggregation. This module has been modified by implementing a custom import interface, such that the input format are Netflow records, called `modified Aguri`. The spatial-aggregation task is performed by assembling small records into larger ones in prefix based trees. This means, for a time period of η seconds, Aguri generates a traffic profile by spatially summarizing subnets, hosts and traffic volumes. The tool can generate 4 distinct profiles: source address profile, destination address profile, source protocol profile and destination protocol profile. An example for a source address profile is shown in Fig. 3, reflecting the local network activity for 32 seconds in a tree-like structure. By inspecting the Aguri tool, it has been detected that monitored time intervals are not constantly η seconds, but sometimes $\eta + \tau$ seconds. A source code analysis showed that the monitoring time period (start and end time) are deduced from packet captures and not based on a simple timing mechanism. A consequence of this is that moments of silence, where no packets are transmitted, are not taken into consideration, such that a time interval becomes $\eta + \tau$ seconds.

2.2   Digging into Netflow Records with a Kernel Function

Kernel functions are an interesting tool for the evaluation of high dimensional data. Referring to [11], a kernel function is defined as a simple mapping $K : X \times X \rightarrow [0, \infty[$ from input space X to a similarity score $K(x, y) = \sum_i \phi_i(x)\phi_i(y) = \phi(x) \cdot \phi(y)$, where $\phi_i(x)$ is a feature vector over x. In the module `Aguri-Processor`, a new kernel function based on topology and traffic volume has been defined to compare Aguri profiles.

$$K(T_n, T_m) = \sum_{i \in N_{T_n}, j \in N_{T_m}} s(a_i, b_j) \times v(a_i, b_j) \tag{1}$$

The kernel function is defined by two kernel function parts. The first part $s(a_i, b_j)$ assesses topological changes in the network by considering suffix lengths of nodes (see Eq. 2). The second part $v(a_i, b_j)$ is a Gaussian kernel treating traffic volume changes in tree nodes (see Eq. 3).

$$s(a_i, b_j) = \begin{cases} \frac{2^{suffixlength_j}}{2^{suffixlength_i}} & \text{if } prefix_i \text{ prefix of } prefix_j \\ \frac{2^{suffixlength_i}}{2^{suffixlength_j}} & \text{if } prefix_j \text{ prefix of } prefix_i \\ 0 & \text{otherwise} \end{cases} \tag{2}$$

$$v(a_i, b_j) = exp\left(-\frac{|\, vol\_percentage_i - vol\_percentage_j\,|^2}{\sigma^2}\right) \tag{3}$$

A more comprehensive version of the kernel function is presented in [12]. The kernel function takes as input successive Aguri profiles, i.e. (T_1, T_2) and determines the similarity between $K(T_1)$ and $K(T_2)$. The higher the K-value, the more similar are the successive trees.

2.3 Visualizing Processed Netflow Records

The visualization task has two modules, the `AguriViz`-module is the mapping of kernel values into an image and the `AguriUI`-module is the user interface. The main task is the mapping of a kernel function value K_i onto an RGB scheme image. A vector v describing the traffic evolution is created and mapped into a colored rectangle. The colour of the rectangle is a function over a kernel score K_i, where the colour intensity describes the evolution of the network topology and traffic load. An RGB [3]-mapping function is used for the generation of the image. The simplified RGB 3-byte scheme is used, where each byte stands for a different colour. By this, a kernel value K_i is mapped onto the RGB-scheme where the lower bits represent the colour 'blue', the next bits are colour 'green' and the higher bits are the colour 'red'. The RGB mapping function k'_i is defined as

$$k'_i = \frac{k_i \cdot B}{\sum(k_i \cdot B)} \cdot 2^{24} + I \tag{4}$$

where B is a brightness factor providing a higher decimal precision of a kernel value K_i. I is an intensity factor to linearly shift the kernel values in the RGB-space for better visibility. The rectangles are sequentially mapped onto the image that is defined as a 2-dimensional space having a (x, y) coordinate system. The rectangle has a size of rxr pixels. The first rectangle is located in the top left corner of the image having coordinates (x_0, y_0). The i-th rectangle is placed on coordinates $(x_i + r, y_i)$. When inserting a line break, coordinates for x are reset to 0 and for y are incremented by the rectangle height r. To have an actual view of the network traffic, a freshness parameter Γ has been introduce for the image,

$$\Gamma = \eta \cdot width \cdot height \tag{5}$$

where η is the time window for exporting Aguri trees and $height, width$ the image size. This freshness parameter has been introduced, because the data window size impacts the image freshness, so a small window means fresher images, whereas for large data windows an image reflects an network evolution overview.

The main interests are first, the detection if a host performs scanning on other systems or, if there are dominant (i.e. like ssh-brute force attack) respectively long-lasting TCP sessions on the network and secondly, to get insights into the traffic to a host.

The `AguriUI`-module represents the outcomes of the `AguriViz`-module on a visual user interface. It shows the outcomes for the Aguri source profiles as well as the outcomes for the destination profiles. Different configuration parameters can be realized on this interface by a network operator. The graphical representation looks similar to a Self-Organizing-Map, but is only a simple graphical representation. A representation of the `AguriUI`-module is shown in Fig. 2. The different parameters can be adjusted by the network operator, like the monitoring time for Aguri profiles (η), Brightness (B) or Intensity (I). Additionally, statistical information in text-form has been added.

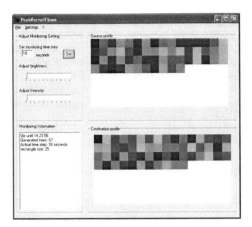

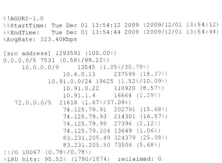

```
!AGURI-1.0
%%StartTime: Tue Dec 01 13:54:12 2009 (2009/12/01 13:54:12)
%%EndTime:   Tue Dec 01 13:54:44 2009 (2009/12/01 13:54:44)
%AvgRate: 323.40Kbps

[src address] 1293591 (100.00%)
0.0.0.0/5 7531 (0.58%/99.22%)
       10.0.0.0/9     13545 (1.05%/30.79%)
              10.4.0.13      237599 (18.37%)
              10.91.0.0/24 19625 (1.52%/10.09%)
              10.91.0.22     110920 (8.57%)
              10.91.1.4      16664 (1.29%)
       72.0.0.0/5  21618 (1.67%/37.09%)
              74.125.79.91  202791 (15.68%)
              74.125.79.93  214301 (16.57%)
              74.125.79.99   27396 (2.12%)
              74.125.79.104 13649 (1.06%)
              83.231.205.49 324379 (25.08%)
              83.231.205.50 73506 (5.68%)
::/0 10067 (0.78%/0.78%)
%LRU hits: 95.52% (1790/1874)  reclaimed: 0
```

Fig. 2. PeekKernelFlows GUI

Fig. 3. Aguri Profile Tree

3   Experimental Results

For the experimental part, two different data sets have been used to evaluate the framework PeekKernelFlows. The first data set, uses Netflow records from an ISP and the second data set is from an honeypot [10], both are given in Table 1. In the experiments, Aguri parameters have been set as such: Aguri-profile generation η set to $\eta=$ 5 seconds and the aggregation threshold $t =$ 1%, to give a fine-grained view of the network. In the first part, only source profiles generated by Aguri have been used. Different tests for the accuracy evaluation and performance for the kernel function have been done. In Fig. 4, the influence of the kernel function by adding hosts to the network can be seen. It can be distinguished between normal traffic on the network and an injection attack, where hosts are added to the network, represented by the peek value. By studying different cases of incidents on networks, it can be illustrate that a kernel function per se can be helpful in the identification of network incidents. To validate the kernel function performance, a clustering algorithm called K.-T.R.A.C.E [1] has been used. The aim is to classify kernel function values obtained from the network traffic into attacks or benign traffic. The K.-T.R.A.C.E algorithm is a an iterative $k - means$ algorithm variant, supporting

Table 1. ISP Network Monitoring Data Set Description

ISP data set		Honeypot data set	
Average number of nodes	42	Number of addresses	47 523
Number of flows	3733680	Exchanged TCP packets	1 183 419
Total bytes	19.36G	Operation time	24 hrs
Global capture duration	300 s	Used Bandwidth	64 Kbits/s
Average bandwidth	528Mbit/s	Colour (bit)	24

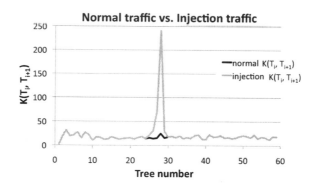

Fig. 4. Normal Traffic vs. Traffic with Injected Nodes

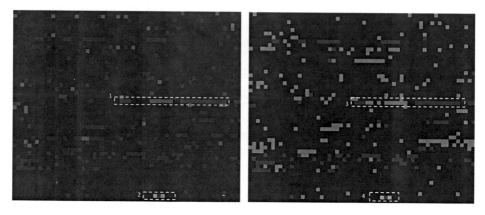

Fig. 5. PeekKernelFlows Results for Source (left) and Destination (right) Profile

a revised method of T.R.A.C.E. (Total Recognition by Adaptive Classification Experiments). It is a supervised learning algorithm that estimates k barycenters for each class and data is assigned to a class such that the Euclidean distance to a barycenter is minimal. The K.-T.R.A.C.E input are similarity scores estimated by the kernel function $K(T_n, T_m) = s(a_i, b_j) \times v(a_i, b_j)$. By adjusting the different parameters in the kernel function, classification results between 77 to 98% were obtained.

In the second data set, a high interaction honeypot exposing a vulnerable ssh-server for 1-day on a public IP-address has been operated and logged. Fig. 5 summarizes the graphical evaluation of the honeypot data set for source (left picture) and destination (right picture) profiles. The picture resolutions are 1 200×1 000 pixels, Aguri kernel values have a 20 × 20 pixels size each and the monitoring time is $\eta = 5$ seconds. A figure holds 4 000 Aguri trees, the equivalent of 4 hours monitoring. To validate the visual results, a manual investigation of the data set has been additionally realized. A problem of manual investigations is that a honeypot is under most different attacks, which can generate a lot of noise in the data set. In the visual traffic representation a lot of 'noise' can be observed by looking at the black rectangles in the images. From a kernel function perspective this means that Aguri trees are thoroughly different, whereas a 'white' colour in the image means similar Aguri profiles.

Common attacks on honeypots are brute-force attacks against the honeypot or attacks compromising the honeypot in order to control the system or to scan/launch new attacks against other targets. In the graphical representation, four relevant patterns can be seen in Fig. 5 for the source profile (left). By help of a manual exploration of the Netflow record data set, the three successive 'green' lines, annotated by 1 represent `ssh brute-force` attacks. In the bottom of the source profile representation a 'coloured' line, annotated by 2 can interpreted as scanning activities of the operated honeypot against other hosts. For the scanning activities it has been observed that attackers nearly used the full available bandwidth for scanning entire sub-networks. These activities can be observed because the scanning activities last over a longer time period inducing that more Aguri profiles have similar structures.

The destination profile image (Fig. 5 right) gives a more fine-grained overview about the targets of the attacker. The same pattern as for the source profile on the left figure, annotated by 3 and 4 can be observed, which represent the communication intensity of both parties. Different patterns as the coloured segments (4) represent the durations of the attackers stay at a dedicated target and the amount of exchanged traffic. Another observation is that dominant TCP sessions, like ssh brute-force attacks, are represented in intense colours, whereas scanning activities are represented by dark colours. This can be explained by the used kernel function, which has a dominant topological kernel part in the volume/traffic part. It is shown that PeekKernelFlows can first detect anomalies by the evaluation of the kernel function and then easily represent them on the visual interface for the network operators.

4   Related Work

Netflow records are commonly used in network monitoring activities. A feature is that they can be generated for most different traffic types. Since most commercially available routers support netflow exports today, costs have been cut a lot. The main drawback of Netflow records is the storage or the mechanisms for online analysis. While introducing Netflow sampling [7], the problem is partially solved, but finding good sampling rates remains difficult. In recent past, a lot of significant progress has been made in the evaluation of Netflow data, pure statistics have been replaced by complex machine learning techniques as Flow Mining [9] or kernel methods. The analysis of Netflow records is time-consuming, complex and error prone. To facilitate network operators duty, it is often referred to visualization for the analysis of large scale data. Goodall et al. [5] present a visualization tool for port usage, called FlowViz. Their tool refers to a rectangle coloration technique, such that the idea of rectangles is similar to our, but we refer to a mapping of a kernel value onto the RGB-color space. Mansmann et al. [6] use TreeMaps for their intrusion detection system evaluation.

Glanfield et al. [4] have presented a tool called OverFlow, where flow relationships are represented by concentric circles following flow hierarchies. PeekKernelFlows respects flow hierarchies by using Aguri, but we focus more on the differences between flows over time. A first version of the theoretical analysis of PeekKernelFlows is presented in [12], where a game-theory driven model has been used to assess the performance of the framework. Furthermore, in [12] different attack strategies and defense measures are described, as for example the manipulation of traffic load or hidden attacks. Nevertheless, a detailed and complete overview of this framework has not been described yet.

5   Conclusion

In this paper, a framework called PeekKernelFlows, for the evaluation of spatial and temporarily aggregated Netflow records has been presented. PeekKernelFlows uses a kernel function that maps Aguri trees onto a similarity score that is further mapped onto the RGB color-space in on/off-line mode. Furthermore the visualization technique has a an easily understandable outcome representation. A limitation of PeekKernelFlows is that by generating too much noise, an attacker can not be detected anymore. To improve PeekKernelFlows, in future work a new method for the spatial aggregation of Netflow records is planned and the Human-Machine interaction increased by implementing additional features like zoom or decisional features.

Acknowledgments

This project is supported by the FNR Luxembourg and we address special thanks to RESTENA Luxembourg for their support.

References

1. Cifarelli, C., Nieddu, L., Seref, O., Pardalos, P.M.: K.-T.R.A.C.E.: A kernel k-means procedure for classification. Computers and Operations Research 34(10), 3154–3161 (2007)
2. Cho, K., Kaizaki, R., Kato, A.: Aguri: An aggregation-based traffic profiler. In: Smirnov, M., Crowcroft, J., Roberts, J., Boavida, F. (eds.) QofIS 2001. LNCS, vol. 2156, pp. 222–242. Springer, Heidelberg (2001)
3. Cowlishaw, M.F.: Fundamental Requirements for Picture Presentation. Proceedings of the Society for Picture Presentation 26(2), 101–107 (1985)
4. Glanfield, J., Brooks, S., Taylor, T., Paterson, D., Smith, C., Gates, C., McHugh, J.: OverFlow: An Overview Visualization for Network Analysis. In: 6th International Workshop on Visualization for Cyber Security, Atlantic City, NJ (2009)
5. Goodall, J.R., Tesone, D.R.: Visual Analytics for Network Flow Analysis. In: Conference for Homeland Security, Cybersecurity Applications & Technology, pp. 199–204. IEEE, Los Alamitos (2009)

6. Mansmann, F., Fischer, F., Keim, D.A., North, S.C.: Visual Support for Analyzing Network Traffic and Intrusion Detection Events using TreeMap and Graph Representations. In: Proceeding of ACM CHiMitiT 2009, Balitmore, Maryland, pp. 19–28 (2009)
7. Paredes-Oliva, I.: Portscan Detection with Sampled NetFlow. In: Papadopouli, M., Owezarski, P., Pras, A. (eds.) TMA 2009. LNCS, vol. 5537, pp. 26–33. Springer, Heidelberg (2009)
8. Patole, V.A., Pachghare, V.K., Kulkarni, P.: Self Organizing Maps to build Intrusion Detection Systems. Journal of Computer Applications 1(8) (2010)
9. Rieck, K.: Machine Learning for Application-layer Intrusion Detection. In: Fraunhofer Institute FIRST and Berlin Institute of Technology, Berlin, Germany (2009)
10. Spitzner, L.: Honeypots: Tracking Hackers. Addison-Wesley Professional, Reading (2002)
11. Vapnik, V.: Statistical Learning Theory. Wiley, Chichester (1998)
12. Wagner, C., Wagener, G., State, R., Dulaunoy, A., Engel, T.: Game Theory Driven Monitoring of Spatial-Aggregated IP-Flow Records. In: 6th International Conference on Network and Services Management, Niagara Falls, Canada (2010)

Opcode-Sequence-Based Semi-supervised Unknown Malware Detection

Igor Santos, Borja Sanz, Carlos Laorden, Felix Brezo, and Pablo G. Bringas

S^{3}Lab, DeustoTech - Computing, Deusto Institute of Technology
University of Deusto,
Avenida de las Universidades 24, 48007
Bilbao, Spain
{isantos,borja.sanz,claorden,felix.brezo,pablo.garcia.bringas}@deusto.es

Abstract. Malware is any computer software potentially harmful to both computers and networks. The amount of malware is growing every year and poses a serious global security threat. Signature-based detection is the most extended method in commercial antivirus software, however, it consistently fails to detect new malware. Supervised machine learning has been adopted to solve this issue, but the usefulness of supervised learning is far to be complete because it requires a high amount of malicious executables and benign software to be identified and labelled previously. In this paper, we propose a new method of malware detection that adopts a well-known semi-supervised learning approach to detect unknown malware. This method is based on examining the frequencies of the appearance of opcode sequences to build a semi-supervised machine-learning classifier using a set of labelled (either malware or legitimate software) and unlabelled instances. We performed an empirical validation demonstrating that the labelling efforts are lower than when supervised learning is used while the system maintains high accuracy rate.

Keywords: malware detection learning, machine learning, semi-supervised learning.

1 Introduction

Malware is defined as any computer software explicitly designed to damage computers or networks. While in the past malware writers seek 'fame and glory', currently their motivation has evolved to malicious economic considerations [1].

The commercial anti-malware software is highly dependant on a signature database [2]. A signature is a unique sequence of bytes that is always present within malicious executables and in the files already infected. The main issue of this approach is that malware analysts must wait until new malware has harmed several computers to generate a signature file and provide a solution. Analysed suspect files are compared with this list of signatures. When the signatures match, the file being tested is classified as malware. Although this approach has been proven as effective when threats are known in beforehand, these signature methods are surpassed with large amounts of new malware.

Á. Herrero and E. Corchado (Eds.): CISIS 2011, LNCS 6694, pp. 50–57, 2011.
© Springer-Verlag Berlin Heidelberg 2011

Machine-learning-based approaches train classification algorithms that detect new malware, by means of datasets composed of several characteristic features of both malicious and benign software. Schultz et al. [3] were the first to introduce the concept of applying machine-learning models to the detection of malware based on their respective binary codes. Specifically, they applied several classifiers to three different feature sets: (i) program headers, (ii) strings and (iii) byte sequences.

Later, Kolter et al. [4] improved Schulz's results by applying n-grams (i.e., overlapping byte sequences) instead of non-overlapping sequences. This approach employed several algorithms, achieving the best results with a boosted decision tree. Likewise, substantial research has focused on n-gram distributions of byte sequences and data-mining [5,6].

Additionally, opcode sequences have recently been introduced as an alternative to byte n-grams [7]. This approach appears to be theoretically better than byte n-grams because it relies on source code rather than the bytes of a binary file that can be easier changed than code [8].

However, these supervised machine-learning classifiers require a high number of labelled executables for each of the classes. Sometimes, we can omit one class for labelling, such as in anomaly detection for intrusion detection [9]. It is quite difficult to obtain this amount of labelled data for a real-world problem such as malicious code analysis. To gather these data, a time-consuming process of analysis is mandatory, and in the process, some malicious executables are able to surpass detection.

Semi-supervised learning is a type of machine-learning technique specially useful when a fixed amount of labelled data exists for each file class. These techniques generate a supervised classifier based on labelled data and predict the label for every unlabelled instance. The instances whose classes have been predicted surpassing a certain threshold of confidence are added to the labelled dataset. The process is repeated until certain conditions are satisfied (a commonly used criterion is the maximum likelihood found by the expectation-maximisation technique). These approaches enhance the accuracy of fully unsupervised methods (i.e., no labels within the dataset) [10].

Given this background, we propose here an approach that employs a semi-supervised learning technique for the detection of unknown malware. In particular, we utilise the method *Learning with Local and Global Consistency* (LLGC) [11] able to learn from both labelled and unlabelled data and capable of providing a *smooth* solution with respect to the intrinsic structure displayed by both labelled and unlabelled instances. For the representation of executables, we propose the adoption of LLGC for the detection of unknown malware based on opcode sequences [7]. However, the presented semi-supervised methodology is scalable to any representation susceptible to be represented as a feature vector.

Summarising, our main findings in this paper are: (i) we describe how to adopt LLGC for opcode-sequence-based unknown malware detection, (ii) we empirically determine the optimal number of labelled instances and we evaluated how this parameter affects the final accuracy of the models and (iii) we demonstrate that labelling efforts can be reduced in the malware detection industry, while still maintaining a high rate of accuracy in the task.

2   Opcode-Sequence Features for Malware Detection

To represent executables using opcodes, we extract the *opcode-sequences* and their frequency of appearance. Specifically, we define a program ρ as a set of ordered opcodes o, $\rho = (o_1, o_2, o_3, o_4, ..., o_{\ell-1}, o_\ell)$, where ℓ is the number of instructions I of the program ρ. An opcode sequence os is defined as a subset of opcodes within the executable file where $os \subseteq \rho$; it is made up of opcodes o, $os = (o1, o2, o3, ..., o_{m1}, o_m)$ where m is the length of the sequence of opcodes os. Consider an example code formed by the opcodes mov, add, push and add; the following sequences of length 2 can be generated: $s_1 = (\text{mov}, \text{add})$, $s_2 = (\text{add}, \text{push})$ and $s_3 = (\text{push}, \text{add})$.

Afterwards, we compute the frequency of occurrence of each opcode sequence within the file by using *term frequency* (tf) [12] that is a weight widely used in information retrieval: $tf_{i,j} = \frac{n_{i,j}}{\sum_k n_{k,j}}$ where $n_{i,j}$ is the number of times the sequence $s_{i,j}$ (in our case opcode sequence) appears in an executable e, and $\sum_k n_{k,j}$ is the total number of terms in the executable e (in our case the total number of possible opcode sequences).

We define the *Weighted Term Frequency* (WTF) as the result of weighting the relevance of each opcode when calculating the term frequency. To calculate the relevance of each individual opcode, we collected malware from the Vx-Heavens website[1] to assemble a malware dataset of 13,189 malware executables and we collected 13,000 executables from our computers. Using this dataset, we disassemble each executable and compute the mutual information gain for each opcode and the class: $I(X;Y) = \sum_{y \in Y} \sum_{x \in X} p(x,y) \log \left(\frac{p(x,y)}{p(x) \cdot p(y)} \right)$ where X is the opcode frequency and Y is the class of the file (i.e., malware or benign software), $p(x,y)$ is the joint probability distribution function of X and Y, and $p(x)$ and $p(y)$ are the marginal probability distribution functions of X and Y. In our particular case, we defined the two variables as the single opcode and whether or not the instance was malware. Note that this weight only measures the relevance of a single opcode and not the relevance of an opcode sequence.

Using these weights, we computed the WTF as the product of sequence frequencies and the previously calculated weight of every opcode in the sequence: $wtf_{i,j} = tf_{i,j} \cdot \prod_{o_z \in S} \frac{weight(o_z)}{100}$ where $weight(o_z)$ is the calculated weight, by means of mutual information gain, for the opcode o_z and $tf_{i,j}$ is the *sequence frequency measure* for the given opcode sequence. We obtain a vector v composed of weighted opcode-sequence frequencies, $v = ((os_1, wtf_1), ..., (os_n, wtf_n))$, where os_i is the opcode sequence and wtf_i is the weighted term frequency for that particular opcode sequence.

---

[1] http://vx.netlux.org/

3   Overview of LLGC

Learning with Local and Global Consistency (LLGC) [11] is a semi-supervised algorithm that provides *smooth* classification with respect to the intrinsic structure revealed by known labelled and unlabelled points. The method is a simple iteration algorithm that constructs a smooth function coherent to the next assumptions: (i) nearby points are likely to have the same label and (ii) points on the same structure are likely to have the same label [11].

Formally, the algorithm is stated as follows. Let $\mathcal{X} = \{x_1, x_2, ..., x_{\ell-1}, x_\ell\} \subset \mathbb{R}^m$ be the set composed of the data instances and $\mathcal{L} = \{1, ..., c\}$ the set of labels (in our case, this set comprises two classes: malware and legitimate software) and $x_u(\ell + 1 \le u \le n)$ the unlabelled instances. The goal of LLGC (and every semi-supervised algorithm) is to predict the class of the unlabelled instances. $\mathcal{F}$ is the set of $n \times c$ matrices with non-negative entries, composed of matrices $F = [F_1^T, ..., F_n^T]^T$ that match to the classification on the dataset $\mathcal{X}$ of each instance x_i. with the label assigned by $y_i = \text{argmax}_{j \le c} F_{i,j}$. F can be defined as a vectorial function such as $F : \mathcal{X} \to \mathbb{R}^c$ to assign a vector F_i to the instances x_i. Y is an $n \times c$ matrix such as $Y \in F$ with $Y_{i,j} = 1$ when x_i is labelled as $y_i = j$ and $Y_{i,j} = 0$ otherwise. Considering this, the LLGC algorithm performs as follows:

if $i \ne j$ and $W_{i,i} = 0$ then

    Form the affinity matrix W defined by $W_{i,j} = \exp\left(\frac{-||x_i - x_j||^2}{2 \cdot \sigma^2}\right)$;

Generate the matrix $S = D^{-1/2} \cdot W \cdot D^{-1/2}$ where D is the diagonal matrix with its (i, i) element equal to the sum of the i-th row of W;

while $\neg$ *Convergence* do

    $F(t + 1) = \alpha \cdot S \cdot F(t) + (1 - \alpha) \cdot Y$ where α is in the range $(0, 1)$;

F^* is the limit of the sequence $\{F(t)\}$;

Label each point x_i as $\text{argmax}_{j \le c} F_{i,j}^*$;

Fig. 1. LLGC algorithm

The algorithm first defines a pairwise relationship W on the dataset $\mathcal{X}$ setting the diagonal elements to zero. Suppose that a graph $G = (V, E)$ is defined within $\mathcal{X}$, where the vertex set V is equal to $\mathcal{X}$ and the edge set $\mathcal{E}$ is weighted by the values in W. Next, the algorithm normalises symmetrically the matrix W of G. This step is mandatory to assure the convergence of the iteration. During each iteration each instance receives the information from its nearby instances while it keeps its initial information. The parameter α denotes the relative amount of the information from the nearest instances and the initial class information of each instance. The information is spread symmetrically because S is a symmetric matrix. Finally, the algorithm sets the class of each unlabelled specimen to the class of which it has received most information during the iteration process.

4   Empirical Validation

The research question we seek to answer through this empirical validation is the following one: *What is the minimum number of labelled instances required to assure a suitable performance using LLGC?*

To this end, we collected a dataset comprising 1,000 malicious executables and 1,000 benign ones. For the malware, we gathered random samples from the website VxHeavens, which has assembled a malware collection of more than 17,000 malicious programs, including 585 malware families that represent different types of current malware such as Trojan horses, viruses and worms. Although they had already been labelled according to their family and variant names, we analysed them using Eset Antivirus[2] to confirm this labelling. For the benign dataset, we collected legitimate executables from our own computers. We also performed an analysis of the benign files using Eset Antivirus to confirm their legitimacy. Although we have already computed the IG values for the complete VxHeavens database, due to computational limitations in order to calculate the unique byte n-grams we have selected only 1,000 executables randomly to perform the final validation.

Hereafter, we extracted the opcodes-sequence representation for each file in the dataset for a sequence length of 2. Because the total number of features we obtained was high, we applied a feature selection step employing mutual information gain, selecting the 1,000 top ranked sequences.

Next, we split the dataset into different percentages of training and test instances the dataset. In other words, we changed the number of labelled instances from 10% to 90% to measure the effect of the number of previously labelled instances on the final performance of LLGC in detecting unknown malware.

We used the LLGC implementation provided by the *Semi-Supervised Learning and Collective Classification* package[3] for the well-known machine-learning tool WEKA [13]. Specifically, we configured it with a transductive stochastic matrix W [11] and we employed the Euclidean distance with 5 nearest neighbours.

In particular, we measured the *True Positive Ratio* (TPR), i.e., the number of malware instances correctly detected divided by the total number of malware files: $TPR = TP/(TP + FN)$ where TP is the number of malware cases correctly classified (true positives) and FN is the number of malware cases misclassified as legitimate software (false negatives). We also measured the *False Positive Ratio* (FPR), i.e., the number of benign executables misclassified as malware divided by the total number of benign files: $FPR = FP/(FP + TN)$ where FP is the number of benign software cases incorrectly detected as malware and TN is the number of legitimate executables correctly classified. Furthermore, we measured *accuracy*, i.e., the total number of the hits of the classifiers divided by the number of instances in the whole dataset: $Accuracy(\%) = (TP + TN)/(TP + FP + TP + TN)$ Besides, we measured the *Area Under the ROC Curve* (AUC) that establishes the relation between false negatives and false positives [14]. The ROC curve is obtained by plotting the TPR against the FPR.

---

[2] http://www.eset.com/

[3] Available at: http://www.scms.waikato.ac.nz/~fracpete/projects/collective-classification/downloads.html

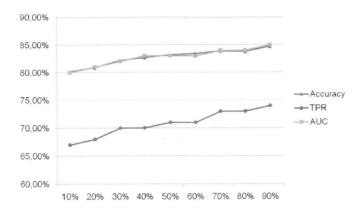

Fig. 2. Accuracy, TPR and AUC results. The X axis represent the percentage of labelled instances. The precision of the model increases along with the size of the labelled set.

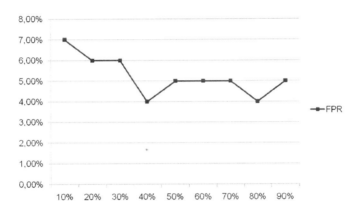

Fig. 3. FPR results. The X axis represent the percentage of labelled instances. The FPR decreases as the size of the labelled set increases. In particular, the best results were obtained with a size of the labelled dataset of 40%.

Fig. 2 and Fig. 3 show the obtained results. In particular, we found out that the greater the size of the labelled instances set the better the results. Specifically, the best overall results were obtained with a training set containing 90% of labelled instances. However, the results are above the 80% of accuracy and AUC when only the 10% of the instances are labelled. These results indicate that we can reduce the efforts of labelling software in a 90% while maintaining a accuracy higher than 80%. However ,the FPR are not as low as they should be, with a lowest value of 4% of false positives. Although for a commercial system this value can be too high, due to the nature of our method, which is devoted to detect new malware, this value is assumable.

We consider that these results are significant for the anti-malware industry. The reduction of the efforts required for unknown malware can help to deal with the increasing amount of new malware. In particular, a preliminary test with a Bayesian Network trained with Hill climber shows an accuracy of 86.73% which only a bit higher that the presented semi-supervised approach. However, because of the static nature of the features we used with LLGC, it cannot counter *packed* malware. Packed malware is produced by cyphering the payload of the executable and having it deciphered when finally loaded into memory. Indeed, broadly-used static detection methods can deal with packed malware only by using the signatures of the packers. Accordingly, dynamic analysis seems to be a more promising solution to this problem [15]. One solution for this obvious limitation of our malware detection method is the use of a generic dynamic unpacking schema such as PolyUnpack [16], Renovo [15], OmniUnpack [17] and Eureka [18].

5   Concluding Remarks

Unknown malware detection has become an important topic of research and concern owing to the growth of malicious code in recent years. Moreover, it is well known that the classic signature methods employed by antivirus vendors are no longer completely effective in facing the large volumes of new malware. Therefore, signature methods must be complemented with more complex approaches that provide the detection of unknown malware families. While machine-learning methods are a suitable approach for unknown malware, they require a high number of labelled executables for each classes (i.e., malware and benign datasets). Since it is difficult to obtain such amounts of labelled data in a real-word environment, a time-consuming process of analysis is mandatory.

In this paper, we propose the use of a semi-supervised learning approach for unknown malware detection. This learning technique does not need a large amount of labelled data; it only needs several instances to be labelled. Therefore, this methodology can reduce efforts in unknown malware detection. By labelling 50% of the software, we can achieve results with more than 83% accuracy.

Future work will be focused on three main directions. First, we plan to extend our study of semi-supervised learning approaches by applying more algorithms to this issue. Second, we will use different features for training these kinds of models. Finally, we will focus on facing packed executables with a hybrid dynamic-static approach.

References

1. Ollmann, G.: The evolution of commercial malware development kits and colour-by-numbers custom malware. Computer Fraud & Security 2008(9), 4–7 (2008)
2. Lanzi, A., Balzarotti, D., Kruegel, C., Christodorescu, M., Kirda, E.: AccessMiner: using system-centric models for malware protection. In: Proceedings of the 17th ACM Conference on Computer and Communications Security, pp. 399–412. ACM, New York (2010)

3. Schultz, M., Eskin, E., Zadok, F., Stolfo, S.: Data mining methods for detection of new malicious executables. In: Proceedings of the 22nd IEEE Symposium on Security and Privacy, pp. 38–49 (2001)
4. Kolter, J., Maloof, M.: Learning to detect malicious executables in the wild. In: Proceedings of the 10th ACM SIGKDD International Conference on Knowledge Discovery and Data Mining, pp. 470–478. ACM, New York (2004)
5. Zhou, Y., Inge, W.: Malware detection using adaptive data compression. In: Proceedings of the 1st ACM Workshop on Workshop on AISec, pp. 53–60. ACM, New York (2008)
6. Santos, I., Penya, Y., Devesa, J., Bringas, P.: N-Grams-based file signatures for malware detection. In: Proceedings of the 11th International Conference on Enterprise Information Systems (ICEIS), vol. AIDSS, pp. 317–320 (2009)
7. Santos, I., Brezo, F., Nieves, J., Penya, Y.K., Sanz, B., Laorden, C., Bringas, P.G.: Opcode-sequence-based malware detection. In: Massacci, F., Wallach, D., Zannone, N. (eds.) ESSoS 2010. LNCS, vol. 5965, pp. 35–43. Springer, Heidelberg (2010)
8. Christodorescu, M.: Behavior-based malware detection. PhD thesis (2007)
9. Perdisci, R., Gu, G., Lee, W.: Using an ensemble of one-class svm classifiers to harden payload-based anomaly detection systems. In: Proceedings of 6th International Conference on Data Mining (ICDM), pp. 488–498. IEEE, Los Alamitos (2007)
10. Chapelle, O., Schölkopf, B., Zien, A.: Semi-supervised learning. MIT Press, Cambridge (2006)
11. Zhou, D., Bousquet, O., Lal, T., Weston, J., Schölkopf, B.: Learning with local and global consistency. In: Proceedings of the 2003 Conference Advances in Neural Information Processing Systems, vol. 16, pp. 595–602 (2004)
12. McGill, M.J., Salton, G.: Introduction to modern information retrieval. McGraw-Hill, New York (1983)
13. Garner, S.: Weka: The Waikato environment for knowledge analysis. In: Proceedings of the New Zealand Computer Science Research Students Conference, pp. 57–64 (1995)
14. Singh, Y., Kaur, A., Malhotra, R.: Comparative analysis of regression and machine learning methods for predicting fault proneness models. International Journal of Computer Applications in Technology 35(2), 183–193 (2009)
15. Kang, M., Poosankam, P., Yin, H.: Renovo: A hidden code extractor for packed executables. In: Proceedings of the 2007 ACM Workshop on Recurring Malcode, pp. 46–53 (2007)
16. Royal, P., Halpin, M., Dagon, D., Edmonds, R., Lee, W.: Polyunpack: Automating the hidden-code extraction of unpack-executing malware. In: Proceedings of the 22nd Annual Computer Security Applications Conference (ACSAC), pp. 289–300 (2006)
17. Martignoni, L., Christodorescu, M., Jha, S.: Omniunpack: Fast, generic, and safe unpacking of malware. In: Proceedings of the 23rd Annual Computer Security Applications Conference (ACSAC), pp. 431–441 (2007)
18. Sharif, M., Yegneswaran, V., Saidi, H., Porras, P.A., Lee, W.: Eureka: A framework for enabling static malware analysis. In: Jajodia, S., Lopez, J. (eds.) ESORICS 2008. LNCS, vol. 5283, pp. 481–500. Springer, Heidelberg (2008)

A New Alert Correlation Algorithm Based on Attack Graph

Sebastian Roschke, Feng Cheng, and Christoph Meinel

Hasso Plattner Institute (HPI), University of Potsdam,
P.O.Box 900460, 14440, Potsdam, Germany
{sebastian.roschke,feng.cheng,meinel}@hpi.uni-potsdam.de

Abstract. Intrusion Detection Systems (IDS) are widely deployed in computer networks. As modern attacks are getting more sophisticated and the number of sensors and network nodes grows, the problem of false positives and alert analysis becomes more difficult to solve. Alert correlation was proposed to analyze alerts and to decrease false positives. Knowledge about the target system or environment is usually necessary for efficient alert correlation. For representing the environment information as well as potential exploits, the existing vulnerabilities and their Attack Graph (AG) is used. It is useful for networks to generate an AG and to organize certain vulnerabilities in a reasonable way. In this paper, we design a correlation algorithm based on AGs that is capable of detecting multiple attack scenarios for forensic analysis. It can be parameterized to adjust the robustness and accuracy. A formal model of the algorithm is presented and an implementation is tested to analyze the different parameters on a real set of alerts from a local network.

Keywords: Correlation, Attack Graph, IDS.

1 Introduction

Intrusion Detection Systems (IDS) have been proposed for years as an efficient security measure and is nowadays widely deployed for securing critical IT-Infrastructures. The problem of false positive alerts is a well known problem for many IDS implementations [1]. Suboptimal patterns or insufficient thresholds for pattern-based and anomaly-based IDS approaches are the main reasons for a huge number of false-positive alerts. By deploying the IDS sensors in a distributed environment, the number of false positive alerts increases as a single event may be detected and reported multiple times by different involved sensors. The popular solution to address this problem is correlation and clustering of relative or similar alerts[2]. Modern algorithms for alert correlation are using environment information, e.g., attack graphs (AG) [3,4], to improve their performance. The approach proposed in [5] correlates IDS alerts in a memory-efficient way by using an AG and a matching function. The algorithm works with implicit alert correlations, considering only the last alert of a certain type per node in the attack graph. While it is memory-efficient, the approach can not easily be used for forensic analysis. It takes many additional efforts to identify similar attack scenarios having the same anatomy, i.e., using the same exploits on the same hosts at different times. Furthermore, the approach does not consider different mapping functions and aggregation of alerts in detail.

Á. Herrero and E. Corchado (Eds.): CISIS 2011, LNCS 6694, pp. 58–67, 2011.

In this paper, we design an AG based correlation algorithm to overcome the above mentioned drawbacks of the algorithm proposed in [5]. By running the algorithm on hardware[6] with 2 TB of main memory on a single machine, we can make all the correlations between alerts explicit. Therefore, the algorithm is capable of identifying multiple attack scenarios of the same anatomy using an attack graph. The algorithm consists of a mapping of alerts to nodes in the attack graph, an alert aggregation, a building of an alert dependency graph, and a function for finding suspicious alert subsets. Apart from the formal model of the correlation algorithm, we analyze multiple possibilities for AG node matching and aggregation by parameterizing the algorithm. A proof-of-concept implementation is tested using a real data set with alerts from our university network.

The rest of the paper is organized as follows. Section 2 provides an overview on different approaches of alert correlation. In Section 3, the proposed correlation algorithm is described by a formal model. Its capabilities for detecting multiple attack scenarios is discussed. Section 4 presents some experiments and discusses the influence of selected parameters for the algorithm. Section 5 provides a short summary of the contributions and future works.

2   Alert Correlation

The alerts created by the distributed sensors are usually gathered by a central management system and processed by correlation algorithms. The quality of a correlation depends on accuracy and speed. The speed depicts how many correlations can be found in a certain amount of time. The accuracy depicts how many of the identified correlations represent real existing relations between these alerts. Due to more complex attacks and large scale networks, the amount of alerts increases significantly which yields the requirement for improved quality of the correlation. The correlation accuracy depends on the used correlation algorithm. It is obvious that using environmental information can help to improve the quality of alert correlation. Environmental information can be host addresses, running services, active users, network configurations, existing policies, known vulnerabilities in general, and existing vulnerabilities on hosts. To represent the listed information, AG are usually constructed for further processing and analysis. Attack Graphs have been proposed as a formal way to simplify the modeling of complex attacking scenarios. Based on the interconnection of single attack steps, they describe multi-step attacks. Attack Graphs not only describe one possible attack, but many potential ways for an attacker to reach a goal. In an attack graph, each node represents a single attack step in a sequence of steps. Each step may require a number of previous attack steps before it can be executed, denoted by incoming edges, and on the other hand may lead to several possible next steps, denoted by outgoing edges. With the help of attack graphs most of possible ways for an attacker to reach a goal can be computed. This takes the burden from security experts to evaluate hundreds and thousands of possible options. At the same time, representing attack graphs visually allows security personal a faster understanding of the problematic pieces of a network [7,4].

The alert correlation framework usually consists of several components [8]: *Normalization, Aggregation (Clustering), Correlation, False Alert Reduction, Attack Strategy Analysis*, and *Prioritization*. Over the last years, alert correlation research focused on new methods and technologies of these components. IDMEF [9] and CVE [10] are important efforts in the field of *Normalization*. Approaches of aggregation are mostly based on similarity of alerts [11] or generalization hierarchies [12]. The correlation algorithms [8] can be classified as: *Scenario-based correlation* [13,14], *Rule-based correlation* [15], *Statistical correlation* [16], and *Temporal correlation* [17,18]. The proposed approach can be classified as *Scenario-based correlation*: attack scenarios are specified by a formal language and alerts are correlated, if they can be combined to one of the known scenarios, i.e., alerts are matched in a specific path of the graph which can be considered as attack scenario (e.g., [5]). False alert reduction can be done by using such techniques as data mining [19] or fuzzy techniques [20]. Attack strategy analysis often depends on reasoning and prediction of attacks missed by the IDS [21]. In terms of Prioritization, the alerts are categorized based on their severity, e.g., using attack ranks [22]. To solve problems of alert correlation, a variety of disciplines are used, e.g., machine learning, data mining [19], or fuzzy techniques [20].

An Attack graph based correlation has been introduced in [5]. This approach maps alerts into the AG for correlation, and provides possibilities for hypothesizing and prediction of alerts. It uses a matching function which maps the alerts by comparing the alert type, the source, and the target address of each alert. Furthermore, this approach distinguishes between implicit and explicit correlation. It significantly reduces the number of explicit correlations by considering only the last alert in a set of similar alerts, i.e., the alert type, the source, as well as the target are identical. The explicitly correlated alerts are stored in a data structure called Queue Graph (QG) which tries to reduce the memory consumption.

3   Towards High-Quality Attack-Graph-Based Correlation

In this paper, a modified AG based correlation algorithm is proposed which only creates explicit correlations. Implicit correlations as described in [5] make it difficult to use the correlated alerts in the graph for forensic analysis of similar attack scenarios. Furthermore, the hardware environment used for the In-Memory databases provides machines with huge amounts of main memory which downgrades the priority of memory efficiency for this work. The algorithms consists of five steps, while each step can be parameterized to fine tune the results: 1) preparation, 2) alert mapping, 3) aggregation of alerts, 4) building of an alert dependency graph, and 5) searching for alert subsets that are related. In the preparation phase, all necessary information is loaded, i.e., the system and network information is gathered, the database with alert classifications is imported, and the AG for the network is loaded. We use the MulVAL [3] tool to generate an AG which describes the corresponding system and network information for the target network. The algorithm is based on a set of basic definitions.

3.1   Definitions

Let $\mathcal{T}$ be the set of all timestamps, $\mathcal{H}$ be the set of possible hosts, and $\mathcal{C}$ be the set of classifications. $\mathcal{A}$ can be defined as:

$$\mathcal{A} = \mathcal{T} \times \mathcal{H} \times \mathcal{H} \times \mathcal{C} \tag{1}$$

Let a single alert $a \in \mathcal{A}$ be a tuple $a = (t, s, d, c)$ while the following functions are defined:

- $ts(a) = t$ - returns $t \in T$, the timestamp of the alert
- $src(a) = s$ - returns $s \in H$, the source host of the alerts
- $dst(a) = d$ - returns $d \in H$, the destination host of the alert
- $class(a) = c$ - returns $c \in C$, the classification of the alert

Let $\mathcal{I}$ be the set of impacts described by MulVAL [3] and $\mathcal{VR}$ be the set of known vulnerabilities. Let V be a set of vertices defined as:

$$V = \mathcal{I} \times \mathcal{H} \times \mathcal{VR} \tag{2}$$

For each triple $v = (im, h, r), v \in V$, the following functions are defined:

- $imp(v) = im$ - returns $im \in \mathcal{I}$, the impact of the vertex
- $host(v) = h$ - returns $h \in \mathcal{H}$, the host if the vertex
- $ref(v) = r$ - returns $r \in \mathcal{VR}$, the vulnerability reference of the vertex

Let $AG = (V, E)$ be an AG with vertices V and edges E. An edge $e \in E \subseteq V^2$ is an ordered tuple of vertices (v, v') with $v \in V \wedge v' \in V$. PAG defines all the paths in the AG. The path $P \in PAG$ is defined as a set of edges $P = (v, v') \in E$. $ord(P)$ defines the number of edges in the path P. $in(v, P)$ depicts whether a vertex lies in the path:

$$in(v, P) := \exists (v, v') \in P \vee \exists (v', v) \in P \tag{3}$$

3.2 Mapping

The mapping function map_i maps matching alerts to specific nodes in the AG and is defined as:

$$map_i : a \mapsto \{v \in V \mid \Phi_i(a, v)\} \tag{4}$$

There are different kinds of $\Phi_i(a, v)$ defined in (5), (6), (7), (8), and (9) to parameterize the mapping function.

$$\Phi_1(a, v) := \exists v' \in V : (src(a) = host(v'))$$
$$\wedge (dst(a) = host(v)) \wedge (class(a) = ref(v)) \tag{5}$$

$$\Phi_2(a, v) := \exists v' \in V : (dst(a) = dst(v)) \wedge (class(a) = ref(v)) \tag{6}$$

$$\Phi_3(a, v) := \exists v' \in V : (class(a) = ref(v)) \tag{7}$$

$$\Phi_4(a, v) := \exists v' \in V : (src(a) = host(v')) \wedge (dst(a) = host(v)) \tag{8}$$

$$\Phi_5(a, v) := \exists v' \in V : (dst(a) = host(v)) \tag{9}$$

We will refer to match modes when using a specific $\Phi_i(a, v)$. The match modes are named as follows:

- $\Phi_1(a, v)$ - match mode *cvesrcdst*
- $\Phi_2(a, v)$ - match mode *cvedst*
- $\Phi_3(a, v)$ - match mode *cve*
- $\Phi_4(a, v)$ - match mode *srcdst*
- $\Phi_5(a, v)$ - match mode *dst*

3.3 Aggregation

Let $A \subset \mathcal{A}$ be the set of alert that is supposed to be aggregated. Let th be a threshold and $x \in A, y \in A$ two alerts, then the relation R_A is defined as:

$$R_A = \{(x, y) \in A^2 :$$
$$(\mid ts(x) - ts(y) \mid < th) \wedge (src(x) = src(y))$$
$$\wedge (dst(x) = dst(y)) \wedge (class(x) = class(y))\} \tag{10}$$

R_A^* defines an equivalence relation on the transitive closure of R_A. The alert aggregation combines alerts that are similar but where created together in a short time, i.e., the difference of the timestamps is below a certain threshold th. It defines a set of equivalence classes $A_{/R_A^*}$ over the equivalence relation R_A^*.

3.4 Alert Dependencies

Let $A_m \subset A$ be the set of alerts that have been matched to a node in an AG:

$$A_m = \{[a] \in A_{/R_A^*} \mid map_i(a) \neq \emptyset\} \tag{11}$$

The alert dependencies are represented by a graph $DG = (A_m, E_{m,k})$, with $E_{m,k}$ as defined in (12).

$$E_{m,k} = \{([x], [y]) \in (A_{/R_A^*})^2 \mid \Psi_k([x], [y])\} \tag{12}$$

The set $E_{m,k}$ can be parameterized by the functions Ψ_k as shown in (13), (14), and (15).

$$\Psi_1([x], [y]) := (ts([x]) < ts([y]))$$
$$\wedge (\exists (v, w) \in E : (v \in maps_i(x) \wedge w \in maps_i(y))) \tag{13}$$

$$\Psi_2([x], [y]) := (ts([x]) < ts([y]))$$
$$\wedge (\exists P \in PAG : (ord(P) = n) \wedge (\exists v, w :$$
$$(v \in maps_i(x) \wedge w \in maps_i(y)$$
$$\wedge in(v, P) \wedge in(w, P)))) \tag{14}$$

$$\Psi_3([x], [y]) := (ts([x]) < ts([y]))$$
$$\land(\exists P \in PAG : \exists v, w :$$
$$(v \in maps_i(x) \land w \in maps_i(y)$$
$$\land in(v, P) \land in(w, P))) \tag{15}$$

The dependency graph DG is defined by the matched and aggregated alerts A_m as vertices and the relations between these alerts as edges $E_{m,k}$. There are three possible ways to define these relations using Psi_k. Psi_1 defines two alerts as related, if they are mapped to neighboring vertices in AG. Psi_2 defines two alerts as related, if they are mapped to two vertices in AG that are connected by the path P with the length of n. Psi_3 defines two alerts as related, if they are mapped to two vertices in AG that are part of the same path P.

3.5   Searching

Each path in the alert dependency graph DG identifies a subset of alerts that might be part of an attack scenario. DG is used in the last step to determine the most interesting subsets of alerts, respectively the most interesting path in the alert dependency graph. The last step of searching alert subsets is done by performing a Floyd Warshall algorithm [24,25] to find all the shortest paths. Furthermore, the diameter dia (i.e. the value of the longest instance of the shortest paths) is determined and each path DP_i that has the length $ord(DP) = dia$ is converted in subsets of alerts. All the subsets S_x are defined as:

$$S_x = \{a \in A \mid in(a, DP_i)\} \tag{16}$$

With a simple optimization, the algorithm allows to identify multiple different attack scenarios of the same anatomy. By sorting the suspicious alert subsets according to the smallest difference between alert a_1 and a_n, the algorithm will identify the alerts that are near each other on the time-line as related to one attack scenario. Let $as_1 = \{a_1, ..., a_n\}$ and $as_2 = \{b_1, ..., b_n\}$ be two alert sets where the only difference between a_i and b_i is the times-tamp $ts(a_i) \neq ts(b_i)$. There are three different combinations how these alerts can be located on a time-line:

1. as_1 and as_2 are not overlapping at all, i.e., $ts(a_n) < ts(b_1)$
2. $as_1 = \{a_1, a_2, ..., a_k, ...a_n\}$ and $as_2 = \{b_1, ..., b_n\}$ are partially overlapping, i.e., $\exists k \in \mathbb{N} \forall a_{i \in \{1,k\}} \mid ts(a_k) > ts(b_1)$
3. as_2 is completely overlapped by as_2, i.e., $(ts(a_1) < ts(b_1)) \land (ts(a_n) > ts(b_n))$

The modified algorithm can identify both suspicious alert sets in case 1, which is impossible for the algorithm in [5]. Due to the memory limitation, this algorithm only considers the last matching alert for each node in the AG.

4 Experiment and Discussion

The algorithm is implemented on a modularized correlation platform which is designed based on in-memory techniques and a multi-core hardware [6]. For testing the correlation algorithm, we created a data set of IDMEF alerts by running a Snort[23] sensor in our university network. The sensor gathered 43485 alerts in 6 days of runtime. Meanwhile, we had a Snort sensor running in several vulnerable subnets of our university network which include several vulnerable hosts. The AG for this subnet is constructed accordingly. We performed a multi-step attack covering multiple hosts in the existing subnets. This provides us with a set of alerts we consider as attack trace in the following work. By injecting this attack trace into the clean data set of the whole university network, we can simulate alert sets without running the real attacks over the production network of our university. The attack is done by compromising 5 hosts in the vulnerable network spread over 4 subnets. We conducted multiple experiments using the data set and the attack trace.

For this set of experiments, we injected one attack trace into the clean data set to test if it can be found in a real set of alerts. Furthermore, we analyzed selected parameters of the algorithm and their influence on the actual result, such as the match mode, the aggregation threshold, the dependency build mode, and the searching algorithm for alert subsets. We fixed the parameters for defining dependencies between alerts and searching for suspicious subsets of alerts. A dependency between two alerts is defined by $E_{a,1}$ using Ψ_1, i.e., alerts that are mapped to adjacent nodes fulfilling the timing constraint are dependent. The dependency graph $DG = (D_a, E_{a,1})$ is used to find all the shortest paths by performing a Floyd-Warshall algorithm and defining the diameter. As shown in Table 1, the match modes using the CVE[10] as criteria work precisely and can identify attacks that follow the AG.

With the alert set from our experiment, this match mode filters about 99.98% of the alerts. The match modes that ignore CVE and are based on the source and destination address are less accurate in terms of the vulnerability used. In our experiments it still showed a filtering rate of 95.58%. The advantage of this match mode is that an attacker can use different vulnerabilities to compromise a host covered in the AG and can still be recognized by the correlation. In the CVE based matching, there is only one suspicious alert set found, basically the one which is supposed to be found. The matching without CVE identifies much more suspicious alert sets. By looking at these alert sets, we recognized that most of the alert sets are using similar alerts and that the high number of the alert sets is due to the fact that there are two hosts which seem to be frequently used and that the Snort sensor produces more false positives for them. To improve it, we can

Table 1. Experiment results - match modes with fixed aggregation threshold of 2s

	Matched alerts	% filtered	Suspicious alert sets
cvesrcdst	5	99.99	1
cvedst	5	99.99	1
cve	8	99.98	1
srcdst	1836	95.78	1010
dst	1923	95.58	1010

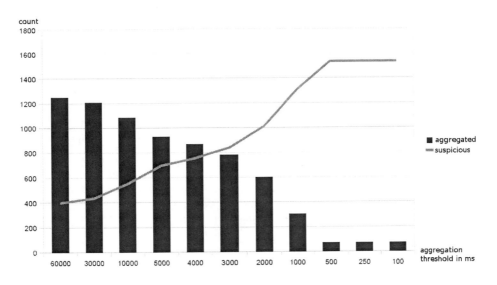

Fig. 1. Experiment results - aggregated alerts and suspicious alert sets for different aggregation thresholds with match mode *srcdst*

try to filter more alerts in the matching by using a matching mode that is based on alert categories, e.g., we do not need to match alerts that are related to an attacks categorized as Denial-of-Service (DoS).

As shown in Figure 1, the aggregation threshold influences the number of suspicious subsets, as a lot of matched alerts can be filtered. The diagram shows the amount of aggregated/filtered alerts as blocks and the amount of identified suspicious alert subsets as line. The overall positive effect of aggregation seen in the diagram is due to the high similarity of consecutive alerts in our data set. We realized multiple alerts in a row that are pretty similar and most likely belong to the same communication. These alert clusters can be aggregated without loosing accuracy of correlation result. An aggregation threshold of $60s$ or larger filters 1246 out of 1836 alerts, i.e., 67.86% of the matched alerts can be filtered in the best case. The algorithm determined 398 suspicious alert sets for this case, which is a significant improvement over the 1010 suspicious alert sets for the threshold of 2 seconds. Thresholds smaller than 2 seconds do not show reasonable effect.

5   Conclusion

In this paper, an AG based correlation algorithm is proposed that overcomes the drawbacks of the algorithm described in [5]. It creates only explicit correlations and enables the identification of multiple attack scenarios of the same anatomy. The algorithm consists of a mapping of alerts to AG nodes, the alert aggregation function, a function for building an alert dependency graph, and a function for finding suspicious subsets using the Floyd-Warshall algorithm and the diameter value. In addition to the formal model of the correlation algorithm, we analyzed multiple possibilities for the node matching and aggregation function in detail to parameterize the algorithm. Finally, we tested the capabilities and analyzed the influence of the parameters by using a real data set of alerts generated from our university network.

The algorithm is implemented and tested based on real data. As this data set is still small, we want to conduct more experiments using larger data sets. Running multiple attacks against the secured network that (partially) cover the AG is also useful to analyze the efficiency and performance of the algorithm. Although the *srcdst* based matching filters about 95% of the alerts, it might still be possible to improve this matching by using attack categories or ontologies. This can improve the filtering without getting inaccurate in the results. Furthermore, the algorithm needs some computing power to consume, especially the Floyd-Warschall algorithm. This can be improved by providing a multi-core-compliant version of the algorithm. Apart from IDMEF alerts, there are additional data sources (e.g., log files) that can be used for AG-based correlation. It should be supported by a more flexible mapping function.

References

1. Northcutt, S., Novak, J.: Network Intrusion Detection: An Analyst's Handbook. New Riders Publishing, Thousand Oaks (2002)
2. Kruegel, C., Valuer, F., Vigna, G.: Intrusion Detection and Correlation: Challenges and Solutions. AIS, vol. 14. Springer, Heidelberg (2005)
3. Ou, X., Govindavajhala, S., Appel, A.: MulVAL: A Logic-based Network Security Analyzer. In: Proceedings of 14th USENIX Security Symposium, p. 8. USENIX Association, Baltimore (2005)
4. Noel, S., Jajodia, S.: Managing attack graph complexity through visual hierarchical aggregation. In: Proceedings of Workshop on Visualization and Data Mining for Computer Security (VizSEC/DMSEC 2004), pp. 109–118. ACM, Washington DC (2004)
5. Wang, L., Liu, A., Jajodia, S.: Using attack graphs for correlation, hypothesizing, and predicting intrusion alerts. Journal of Computer Communications 29(15), 2917–2933 (2006)
6. Roschke, S., Cheng, F., Meinel, C.: A Flexible and Efficient Alert Correlation Platform for Distributed IDS. In: Proceedings of the 4th International Conference on Network and System Security (NSS 2010), pp. 24–31. IEEE Press, Melbourne (2010)
7. Sheyner, O., Haines, J., Jha, S., Lippmann, R., Wing, J.M.: Automated Generation and Analysis of Attack Graphs. In: Proceedings of the 2002 IEEE Symposium on Security and Privacy (S&P 2002), pp. 273–284. IEEE Press, Washington, DC (2002)
8. Sadoddin, R., Ghorbani, A.: Alert Correlation Survey: Framework and Techniques. In: Proceedings of the International Conference on Privacy, Security and Trust (PST 2006), pp. 1–10. ACM Press, Markham (2006)
9. Debar, H., Curry, D., Feinstein, B.: The Intrusion Detection Message Exchange Format, Internet Draft. Technical Report, IETF Intrusion Detection Exchange Format Working Group (July 2004)
10. Mitre Corporation: Common vulnerabilities and exposures CVE Website, http://cve.mitre.org/ (accessed March 2009)
11. Valdes, A., Skinner, K.: Probabilistic alert correlation. In: Lee, W., Mé, L., Wespi, A. (eds.) RAID 2001. LNCS, vol. 2212, pp. 54–68. Springer, Heidelberg (2001)
12. Julisch, K.: Clustering intrusion detection alarms to support root cause analysis. ACM Transactions on Information and System Security 6(4), 443–471 (2003)

13. Debar, H., Wespi, A.: Aggregation and correlation of intrusion-detection alerts. In: Lee, W., Mé, L., Wespi, A. (eds.) RAID 2001. LNCS, vol. 2212, pp. 85–103. Springer, Heidelberg (2001)

14. Al-Mamory, S.O., Zhang, H.: IDS alerts correlation using grammar-based approach. Journal of Computer Virology 5(4), 271–282 (2009)

15. Ning, P., Cui, Y., Reeves, D.: Constructing attack scenarios through correlation of intrusion alerts. In: Proceedings of the 9th ACM Conference on Computer and Communications Security (CCS 2002), pp. 245–254. ACM Press, Washington, DC (2002)

16. Qin, X.: A Probabilistic-Based Framework for INFOSEC Alert Correlation, PhD thesis, Georgia Institute of Technology (2005)

17. Qin, X.: Statistical causality analysis of INFOSEC alert data. In: Vigna, G., Krügel, C., Jonsson, E. (eds.) RAID 2003. LNCS, vol. 2820, pp. 73–93. Springer, Heidelberg (2003)

18. Oliner, A.J., Kulkarni, A.V., Aiken, A.: Community epidemic detection using time-correlated anomalies. In: Jha, S., Sommer, R., Kreibich, C. (eds.) RAID 2010. LNCS, vol. 6307, pp. 360–381. Springer, Heidelberg (2010)

19. Manganaris, S., Christensen, M., Zerkle, D., Hermiz, K.: A data mining analysis of rtid alarms. Computer Networks 34(4), 571–577 (2000)

20. Siraj, A., Vaughn, R.B.: A cognitive model for alert correlation in a distributed environment. In: Kantor, P., Muresan, G., Roberts, F., Zeng, D.D., Wang, F.-Y., Chen, H., Merkle, R.C. (eds.) ISI 2005. LNCS, vol. 3495, pp. 218–230. Springer, Heidelberg (2005)

21. Ning, P., Xu, D., Healey, C.G., Amant, R.S.: Building attack scenarios through integration of complementary alert correlation method. In: Proceedings of the Network and Distributed System Security Symposium (NDSS 2004). The Internet Society, San Diego (2004)

22. Porras, P.A., Fong, M.W., Valdes, A.: A mission-impact-based approach to INFOSEC alarm correlation. In: Wespi, A., Vigna, G., Deri, L. (eds.) RAID 2002. LNCS, vol. 2516, pp. 95–114. Springer, Heidelberg (2002)

23. Snort IDS: WEBSITE, http://www.snort.org/ (accessed November 2009)

24. Floyd, R.: Algorithm 97 (SHORTEST PATH). Communications of the ACM 5(6), 345 (1962)

25. Warshall, S.: A Theorem on Boolean Matrices. Journal of the ACM 9(1), 11–12 (1962)

A Qualitative Survey of Active TCP/IP Fingerprinting Tools and Techniques for Operating Systems Identification

João Paulo S. Medeiros[1], Agostinho de Medeiros Brito Júnior[2], and Paulo S. Motta Pires[2]

LabSIN – Security Information Laboratory
LabEPI – Elements of Information Processing Laboratory
[1]Department of Exact and Applied Sciences – DCEA
[2]Department of Computer Engineering and Automation – DCA
Federal University of Rio Grande do Norte – UFRN
Natal, 59.078-970, RN, Brazil
{joaomedeiros,ambj,pmotta}@dca.ufrn.br

Abstract. TCP/IP fingerprinting is the process of identifying the Operating System (OS) of a remote machine through a TCP/IP based computer network. This process has applications close related to network security and both intrusion and defense procedures may use this process to achieve their objectives. There are a large set of methods that performs this process in favorable scenarios. Nowadays there are many adversities that reduce the identification performance. This work compares the characteristics of four active fingerprint tools (Nmap, Xprobe2, SinFP and Zion) and how they deal with test environments under adverse conditions. The results show that Zion outperforms the other tools for all test environments and it is suitable even for use in sensible systems.

1 Introduction

The remote identification of operating systems, also known as OS fingerprinting (Operating System fingerprinting), is a process that aims at the discovery of the operating system of a remote machine. We consider remote a machine that is accessible through a computer network. This identification is accomplished by the use of data from the remote machine. More specifically, the process of OS fingerprinting is illustrated in Fig. 1.

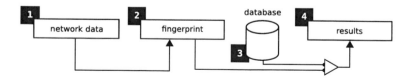

Fig. 1. Representation of the OS fingerprinting process [11]

Á. Herrero and E. Corchado (Eds.): CISIS 2011, LNCS 6694, pp. 68–75, 2011.
© Springer-Verlag Berlin Heidelberg 2011

The process at all has four components: (1) the acquired network data, (2) a fingerprint made by refinement of the data, (3) a fingerprint database where each fingerprint is labeled according to the OS in which it represents, and (4) the results produced by a matching algorithm applied to the database and the fingerprint made from the acquired data. These four components are distributed into two sub processes, called *fingerprinting* and *matching*.

The techniques used for this purpose differ according to the data they use and how these data are acquired. The OS fingerprinting process can be divided in two subsequent tasks: which we call characterization and classification. In the characterization task a *fingerprint* is created for an OS, while in the classification use some procedure is applied to a database of these pictures to classify (*match*) the OS. According to how data are created and captured the methods can be grouped in two classes:

- **Active:** the machine that performs the identification sends messages to the remote machine. The responses to these messages (or the lack of responses) are used in the identification process;
- **Passive:** the machine that performs the identification does not send messages through the network to perform identification. The remote machine data is captured when it communicates with a third machine. This implies that the identification machine must have access to the communication channel between the remote and the third machine.

The way these two categories of tools performs fingerprinting is very important because it closely related to the tool efficiency. Choosing the appropriate tool for OS fingerprinting is an important question to consider, once it will be (usually) applied on security tests. We will show some of the most important characteristics of the most well known tools and how these characteristics are important for an security expert.

This paper is followed by more 4 sections. The criteria used and to select tools, OSes and the test bed used to assessment are presented in Section 2. The results are presented in Section 3. Explanations about the results are done in Section 4, and Section 5 concludes the paper.

2   Scenario

When the OS fingerprinting process uses TCP/IP network data the process is called TCP/IP stack fingerprinting, which takes advantage of details that differ from implementation to implementation of the TCP/IP [8]. The selection of the tools used in this survey is conducted by four reasons: (i) greater acceptance by the security community [1]; (ii) widely used [9]; (iii) techniques used are at least mentioned in papers [4,12]; (iv) and use active OS fingerprinting. The last presented reason was adopted because unlike passive methods, the active ones can produce the data it needs not depending on third devices, and the techniques used to create fingerprints depends only on data. For such reason, other well known TCP/IP stack fingerprinting tools such as p0f, PRADS, Ettercap,

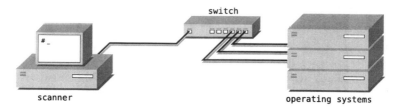

Fig. 2. First test environment

NetworkMiner, PacketFence and Satori) were not included in the tests. The chosen tools were: Nmap [9] (version 5.21), SinFP [4] (version 2.07), Xprobe2 [3] (version 0.3), and Zion [12] (version 0.1).

Each selected tool underwent a series of tests related to its ability to identify, and robustness against the presence of network security devices (e.g. firewalls). Initially, tests were conducted in a controlled environment without the presence of security devices. In this case, the tools are, theoretically, under ideal conditions. Therefore, the results related to these tests express the best possible results for each tool. This initial test environment is shown in Fig. 2. The operating systems used are installed on the machines in the right side, and in the *scanner* machine the fingerprinting tools were installed.

The OSes were chosen obeying three criteria: (i) they are widely used, so the fingerprinting database of each tool most probably have their signatures; (ii) just one of OSes that have the same, or almost the same, TCP/IP stack implementation (e.g. QNX or NetBSD, MacOS or FreeBSD) [13,14]; (iii) and not to be a newest system that probably can not be in the fingerprint databases of some old tools like Xprobe2 (for example, there are no fingerprints of Windows 7 and Vista on Xprobe2 database). The selected OSes are shown in Table 1.

Now we introduce some security devices to create a more realistic shot of a machine on the Internet. Assuming an environment in which the firewall is intended to protect a given set of services (e.g. HTTP and SSH) all traffic not associated with these services could (or should) be blocked. This blockage may imply that all UDP and ICMP traffic could be discarded. As result, the tools whose use data from these protocols will not produce reasonable results.

Regarding the traffic normalization, almost all the peculiarities exploited by TCP/IP stack fingerprinting methods, present in specially crafted packets, sent

Table 1. Used operating systems

Operating system	Detailed version
Debian	Linux debian 2.6.26-1-686
FreeBSD	6.4-RELEASE i386
NetBSD	4.0.1 GENERIC i386
OpenBSD	4.4 GENERIC#1021 i386
OpenSolaris	SunOS 5.11 snv_101b i86pc
Windows 2000	5.00.2195 Service Pack 4
Windows XP	Version 2002 Service Pack 2

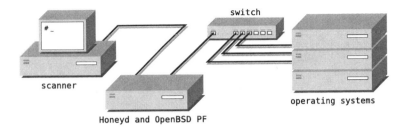

Fig. 3. Second test environment, using Honeyd and OpenBSD Packet Filter

to the remote machine, are removed or may cause the drop of the packet [10]. If traffic normalization is performed on all protocols (IP, TCP, UDP and ICMP) practically all fingerprinting tools will be affected.

Another problem that affects fingerprint tools is created by the use of SYN proxies. SYN proxies are one of the widely used techniques to prevent servers against DoS (Denial of Service) attacks [6]. The SYN+ACK synchronization message of sent in response to TCP SYN requests are not originated from the target machine, but instead, from the firewall itself. As result, the use of SYN proxies also directly affects an identification tool that uses TCP.

Other problem is related to the use of PAT (Port Address Translation) [7,20]. PAT is a technology in which a mapping between the device's port internal network and the device port exposed to the Internet is made explicitly. The use of PAT complicates the identification process because the operating system to be identified depends on which port the tool collects the information. If the identification tool uses more than one open TCP port to create your fingerprint this signature will not properly represent the TCP/IP stack of either machine (remote or the one who perform PAT).

Beyond the use of firewalls there are tools that aim to fool OS fingerprinting [19]. The Honeyd is a tool that aims to simulate machinery, services and operating systems on the network [17,18]. Therefore, this tool simulates different implementations of the TCP/IP stack. In this sense, considering the use of OpenBSD Packet Filter [2] and the presence of Honeyd, the architecture of Fig. 2 was modified and used as a second test environment, presented in Fig. 3.

This last test environment can reproduce all the security mechanisms introduced in this section. Next section will presents the results for each tool in the following conditions: (i) in a clean environment, without the use of any security mechanism; (ii) using PAT; (iii) using packet normalization; (iv) using a SYN proxy; (v) and using fake machines made with Honeyd.

3   Experiments

In Table 2 are summarized the results of the tests for each analyzed tool, where: full black circle means correct, half means imprecise and empty means wrong.

Table 2. Classification results

Network setup	Nmap	SinFP	Xprobe2	Zion
Clean environment	●	●(a)	●(a)	●
Using Port Address Translation	◐(b)	●	○(c)	●
Using Packet Normalization	◐(d)	●	○	●
Using SYN proxy	○	○	○	●(f)
Using Honeyd	○	○(e)	○	●(g)

The notes in each part of Table 2 are associated to these facts and events:

(a) unable to distinguish between Windows 2000 and XP;
(b) the Debian GNU/Linux operating system was not precisely recognized: it was classified as Linux 2.6.X and OpenBSD 4.X with the same grade of certainty (85%);
(c) because Xprobe2 uses only network layer information it cannot distinguish the operating system using information associated to transport layer;
(d) the Debian GNU/Linux operating system was not precisely recognized: it was classified as Linux 2.6.X and OpenBSD 4.X with almost the same grade of certainty (approximated 86%);
(e) the Honeyd use was not recognized, but the Honeyd mimic was not good enough to produce the wrong result;
(f) the Zion tool was able to recognize the use of the SYN proxy;
(g) the Zion tool was able to recognize the use of Honeyd.

Until this point what we showed when each analyzed tool fails in the task on recognize operating systems remotely. Although only the active tools have been analyzed the methods used by passive tools are also fragile since the information used by these methods are also affected by the security mechanisms used here. In the next section will be verified what information can be used to perform OS fingerprinting even in the presence of PF and Honeyd.

4   Why Zion Outperforms?

The TCP ISN (Initial Sequence Number) is responsible for maintaining consistency in TCP communications (i.e. to avoid duplicated segments originated from the reuse of sequences of previous connections [16]). The way the generation of these numbers is implemented can lead to security problems. After the discovery of these problems a new recommendation was established in 1996 by RFC 1948 [5]. Michal Zalewski first showed that some operating systems have a distinct way of implement the generation of these numbers [21,22].

To use the TCP ISNs as data to create a signature to perform OS fingerprinting will consider the PRNG (Pseudo Random Number Generation) of the operating systems. The current recommendation for the generation of these numbers through a function $G_{isn}(t)$ is expressed as [5]:

$$G_{isn}(t) = M(t) + F(\cdot) \tag{1}$$

$$M(t) = M(t-1) + R(t) \tag{2}$$

$$F(\cdot) = f(connection\_id, secret\_key) \tag{3}$$

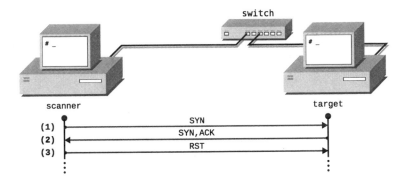

Fig. 4. Illustration of TCP ISN sample acquisition process

where $G_{isn}(t)$ is the function responsible for generating the initial number of sequence at time t, $M(t)$ is a composite function by its previous value adding the value of the function $R(t)$ and $F(\cdot)$, which consists in apply a function $f(\cdot)$ to the identifier of the connection, comprising the addresses and ports of origin and destination and a optional secret key. To estimate the function $R(t)$ using only samples of $G_{isn}(t)$ is important to note that $F(\cdot)$ can be assumed constant for a same link identifier (*connection_id*). Thus, one can obtain from Equations 1, 2 and 3 a estimative, $\hat{R}(t)$, of the function $R(t)$:

$$\hat{R}(t) = G_{isn}(t) - G_{isn}(t-1). \tag{4}$$

The process of sample acquisition is illustrated in Fig. 4.

One feature to consider is that intervals of sending packets SYN sufficiently short, can characterize a SYN flooding attack. Mainly because RST messages are not sent in response to SYN+ACK message from the target machine [6]. The process of acquisition of TCP ISN samples are performed according to Fig. 4, that is: (1) the scanner sends a synchronization message (SYN); (2) the target receives the message confirming the synchronization and acquisition of the TCP ISN (via SYN+ACK); (3) the scanner sends a RST message to cancel synchronization to prevent (and thus avoid detection of) SYN flooding.

In our experiments we find that the analyzed versions of the operating systems Debian, NetBSD, OpenSolaris, Windows 2000 and Windows XP adopt the recommendation proposed by RFC 1948. In cases where the recommendation proposed by RFC 1948 is not adopted, will used their own samples of the $G_{isn}(t)$ in place of the estimate $\hat{R}(t)$. In Fig. 5 presents sketches of the 100 first samples of the $\hat{R}(t)$ for each operating system and Honeyd. This graphical representation of each of these series shows how each one is different from others.

A SYN proxy tends to send the same TCP ISN for a quite long period of time (see FreeBSD sketch). Also, the TCP ISN generator of Honeyd produces a deterministic signal. These facts imply that both SYN proxies and Honeyd can be detectable easily. Zion uses intelligent methods to create a signature for each operating systems and classify them using $\hat{R}(t)$ samples. The theoretical foundation to accomplish this task is already presented in literature [11,12,15].

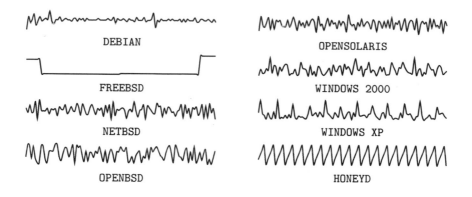

Fig. 5. Sketch of the time series compound of 100 samples of $\hat{R}(t)$

5 Conclusion

The paper presented the aspects related to efficiency and reliability of tools for remote identification of operating systems through active OS fingerprinting and confirms the benefits of using feature extraction and pattern matching on the analysis of TCP ISNs. The results demonstrate the feasibility of the computational intelligent methods developed by the Zion for OS fingerprinting. Since Zion use only well-formed packets on the identification process, it can be used against sensible machine, such as SCADA devices. We showed also the reason for each wrong identification of analyzed tools when a set of network security countermeasures are incorporated in test bed. We exploited the TCP ISN of several OSes to bring about why Zion is not influenced by the use of packet normalization or PAT and can detect SYN proxies and Honeyd.

Acknowledgment. The authors would like to express their gratitude to the Department of Exact and Applied Sciences, Department of Computer Engineering and Automation, Federal University of Rio Grande do Norte, Brazil, and REDIC (Instrumentation and Control Research Network) for supporting this work.

References

1. Nmap Hackers Mailing List: Top 2 OS Detection Tools (2008)
2. The OpenBSD Packet Filter (2010), http://www.openbsd.org/faq/pf/ (OpenBSD version 4.7)
3. Arkin, O., Yarochkin, F.: XProbe2 A 'Fuzzy' Approach to Remote Active Operating System Fingerprinting. Tech. rep., Sys-security (August 2002)
4. Auffret, P.: SinFP, unification de la prise d'empreinte active et passive des systmes d'exploitation. In: Proc. Symposium sur La Securit des Technologies de L'Information et des Communications (2008)
5. Bellovin, S.: Defending Against Sequence Number Attacks. RFC 1948 (Informational) (May 1996)

6. Eddy, W.: TCP SYN Flooding Attacks and Common Mitigations. RFC 4987 (Informational) (August 2007)
7. Egevang, K., Francis, P.: The IP Network Address Translator (NAT). RFC 1631 (Informational) (May 1994)
8. Fyodor.: Remote OS Detection via TCP/IP Fingerprinting. Phrack Magazine 8 (1998)
9. Fyodor.: Nmap Network Scanning. Insecure.Com LLC (2009)
10. Handley, M., Paxson, V., Kreibich, C.: Network Intrusion Detection: Evasion, Traffic Normalization, and End-to-End Protocol Semantics. In: Proceedings of the 10th USENIX Security Symposium (2001)
11. Medeiros, J.P.S., Brito, A.M., Pires, P.S.M.: A New Method for Recognizing Operating Systems of Automation Devices. In: Proc. IEEE Conference on Emerging Technologies & Factory Automation (ETFA 2009), pp. 772–775 (2009)
12. Medeiros, J.P.S., Brito, A.M., Pires, P.S.M.: An Effective TCP/IP Fingerprinting Technique Based on Strange Attractors Classification. In: Garcia-Alfaro, J., Navarro-Arribas, G., Cuppens-Boulahia, N., Roudier, Y. (eds.) DPM 2009. LNCS, vol. 5939, pp. 208–221. Springer, Heidelberg (2010)
13. Medeiros, J.P.S., Brito, A.M., Pires, P.S.M.: Using Intelligent Techniques to Extend the Applicability of Operating System Fingerprint Databases. Journal of Information Assurance and Security 5(1), 554–560 (2010)
14. Medeiros, J.P.S., Cunha, A.C., Brito Jr., A.M., Motta Pires, P.S.: Application of Kohonen Maps to Improve Security Tests on Automation Devices. In: Lopez, J., Hämmerli, B.M. (eds.) CRITIS 2007. LNCS, vol. 5141, pp. 235–245. Springer, Heidelberg (2008)
15. Medeiros, J.P.S., dos Santos, S.R., Brito, A.M., Pires, P.S.M.: Advances in Network Topology Security Visualisation. International Journal of System of Systems Engineering 1(4), 387–400 (2009)
16. Postel, J.: Transmission Control Protocol. RFC 793 (Standard) (September 1981)
17. Provos, N.: Honeyd (May 2007), http://www.honeyd.org/ (version 1.5c)
18. Provos, N., Holz, T.: Virtual Honeypots: From Botnet Tracking to Intrusion Detection. Addison-Wesley, Reading (2008)
19. Smart, M., Malan, G., Jahanian, F.: Defeating TCP/IP stack fingerprinting. In: Proceedings of the 9th USENIX Security Symposium (2000)
20. Srisuresh, P., Egevang, K.: Traditional IP Network Address Translator (Traditional NAT). RFC 3022 (Informational) (January 2001)
21. Zalewski, M.: Strange Attractors and TCP/IP Sequence Number Analysis. Tech. rep., Coredump (2001)
22. Zalewski, M.: Strange Attractors and TCP/IP Sequence Number Analysis – One Year Later. Tech. rep., Coredump (2002)

Security Alert Correlation Using Growing Neural Gas

Francisco José Mora-Gimeno, Francisco Maciá-Pérez, Iren Lorenzo-Fonseca,
Juan Antonio Gil-Martínez-Abarca, Diego Marcos-Jorquera,
and Virgilio Gilart-Iglesias

Department of Computer Technology,
University of Alicante, AP.99-03080, Alicante, Spain
{fjmora,pmacia,ilorenzo,gil,dmarcos,vgilart}@dtic.ua.es

Abstract. The use of alert correlation methods in Distributed Intrusion Detection Systems (DIDS) has become an important process to address some of the current problems in this area. However, the efficiency obtained is far from optimal results. This paper presents a novel approach based on the integration of multiple correlation methods by using the neural network Growing Neural Gas (GNG). Moreover, since correlation systems have different detection capabilities, we have modified the learning algorithm to positively weight the best performing systems. The results show the validity of the proposal, both the multiple integration approach using GNG neural network and the weighting based on efficiency.

Keywords: Alert correlation, Neural networks, Intrusion detection, Growing neural gas.

1 Introduction

When an intrusion detection system (IDS) detects an attack – or any other malicious activity – an alert is reported to the system administrator. However, an attack will rarely occurs in isolation, but belongs to a higher scenario composed of a series of attacks [1]. The logical connection between several alerts belonging to the same scenario, the large number of alerts that makes it impossible to manual processing and the tendency to include in the analysis alerts from other security systems different than the IDS, are three of the reasons for the use of alert correlation mechanisms [2].

The correlation methods are generally classified mainly into three types: *specification of scenarios*, which defines the whole scenarios using an attack description language and modeling the correlation process as a pattern recognition problem [3]; another approach defines the *prerequisites and consequences* of each individual attack and, in the correlation process, the approach relates consequences of a previous attack with prerequisites of a subsequent [4]; and finally, the *clustering* approach is based on finding similarities or relationships between attributes of the alerts, so that the alerts with similar values on their attributes belong to the same class, and therefore, to the same scenario [2].

Each of the above approaches has different features. For example, the first approach can efficiently detect known scenarios, but is unable to correlate new scenarios. By contrast, clustering methods can detect unknown attacks, but produce a high

Á. Herrero and E. Corchado (Eds.): CISIS 2011, LNCS 6694, pp. 76–83, 2011.

volume of false positives. For this reason, the literature proposes the integration of pairs of methods in other to achieve better performance [3], [4].

This work proposes an approach that integrates or combines the results of multiple correlation methods, not just a pair. This multiple integration was performed using an artificial neural network (ANN), in particular, the network Growing Neural Gas (GNG) [5]. We use the GNG network due to its clustering capabilities. Moreover, we have taken into account the performance or efficiency of the methods, with the aim that the integration process is conditioned by the best methods.

Having reviewed the state of the art (ch. 2) in related subjects, our proposal is showed, which covers the metric to evaluate the correlation systems and the integration method (ch. 3); subsequently, (ch. 4) a test scenario is built using several correlation systems and the GNG, and the proposal evaluation is showed; finally, (ch. 5) the main conclusions deriving from research, as well as appropriate lines for future investigation are presented.

2 Related Works

ANN is one of the most widely used techniques in the IDS, because the neural networks have shown themselves to be powerful classifiers with tremendous generalization and learning ability. On the other hand, the use of ANN for IDS are based on their flexibility and adaptation to natural changes which may occur in the environment, and particularly to the ability to detect patterns of unknown attacks [6].

Unsupervised learning techniques like *Self-organizing map* (SOM) algorithm have been used to cluster the content of the network packets. Others like *multilayer perceptron* (MLP) with *backpropagation* learning algorithm has been used to recognize host attacks, and its analysis is based on both logs and system calls [7].

The research carried out by [8] presents a neural network-based intrusion detection method for the internet-based attacks on a computer network. In particular, *feedforward* neural networks with the back propagation training algorithm were employed in this study. The experimental results on real-data showed promising results on detection and prediction of intrusions.

In [9] an integrated IDS using multiple ANN is developed. The approach used in this work include the combination of two component neural networks, growing neural gas and self-organizing map. An important feature of this system is that it can be adapted to both anomaly and misuse detections for intrusive outsiders.

In the work carried out by [6] nine IDS based on ANN were implemented and tested with several experiments and topologies. An important result of this research is that, in average, the neural networks provided very good results, in some cases, detection rates of 99,60% are achieved.

The *specification of scenarios* correlation methods define the whole scenarios using an attack description language and model the correlation process as a pattern recognition problem [10], [11]. These systems have very favorable results in terms of detection capabilities, they have a high probability of recognizing the scenarios stored in the database and rarely produce false positives. However, they have limitations such as time needed to encode the scenarios and, above all, their inability to detect new scenarios not specified in the database [3].

In the approach of *prerequisites and consequences* of each individual attack relates consequences of a previous attack with prerequisites of a subsequent attack [1], [4], [12]. Such systems have the advantages of requiring less time to define the preconditions and consequences, and have some ability to detect small variations of well-defined scenarios. On the contrary, has the disadvantage of not detecting new scenarios or large variations and, also, this approach presents the problem of false positives.

The *clustering* approach looks for similarities or relationships between attributes of the alerts, so that those having similar or related values on their attributes belong to the same class and, therefore, at the same scenario [2], [13]. Clustering methods have the advantage of detecting new and unknown scenarios. However, they have the problem of obtaining a very high rate of false positives.

Using the approach of integration of two methods, [3] develops a system that complements a prerequisites and consequences correlation engine with other system based on statistical analysis (clustering). The main conclusion of this work is that it improves the performance respect to another paper by the same authors, which they only use clustering [2].

Finally, [14] also uses an integrative approach of prerequisites and consequences with clustering techniques, in particular, the work employs a Bayesian network and a probabilistic causality test. As in the previous case, the results are better than those obtained in previous work [4], which only used the probabilistic method.

3   Correlating IDS Alerts Using GNG

Our objective in this paper is to propose a new approach that joins together an extended view of two of the ideas revised in the previous section. On the one hand, we use the approach of integration, but to combine the results of multiple different correlation methods, not just a pair as in previous works. In addition, our novelty lies in the fact that the integration method is general, not ad-hoc as in previous papers. On the other hand, we use a neural network (GNG neural network) for grouping and correlating alerts, but we take into account the quality of these alerts to balance the learning process with the aim that the final result is conditioned by the best methods.

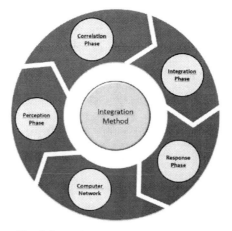

Fig. 1. Intrusion detection general model

In this paper, we will focus on the method used to perform alert correlation by DIDS. However, this correlation component is part of a generic intrusion detection model shown in Figure 1. The perception phase monitors the computer network and performs intrusion detection at low level through local IDS, for example, Snort sensor. The correlation component is divided into two phases, the first is the correlation itself through multiple correlation methods (not just one or a pair) and the second to integrate the results obtained by different methods above. Finally, the response phase which aims to act on the network when any attack occurs, reconfiguring a firewall, closing ports or any other method of active response.

3.1 Performance Measurement

Since we will modify the learning algorithm of the GNG neural network based on the quality of correlation methods, first, it is necessary to establish a quality measure. The weighting of each correlation method in the integration process is based on the evaluation of their performance, which is essential in the field of intrusion detection. This evaluation will focus on measuring the effectiveness of different systems in terms of its ability to classify or correlate properly. Therefore, we must have a metric to evaluate and compare the quality of each correlation methods objectively [15]. Of course, the quality measure of each method may vary over time depending on its successes and failures.

Generally, the most frequently used indices are the true positives rate (TP-True Positive) and the false positives rate (FP-False Positive). TP and FP rates are often used combined using ROC curves (Receiver Operating Characteristic). In our case, we use a measure defined in [15] called *intrusion detection capability* (C_{ID}), because its calculation is based on previous rates and this metric is an objective measure that returns a real value directly comparable.

3.2 Correlation Process

The correlation process has been divided into two phases identified in the general model of Figure 1: correlation phase and integration phase. The correlation phase in which low-level alerts generated by local IDS are related by multiple local correlation methods. We can use any number of different correlation techniques, not just a pair as in traditional approaches. The output of any correlation method will be an alert in the standard format for the exchange of information between detection systems called IDMEF (Intrusion Detection Message Exchange Format) [16].

The second stage is the integration phase which receives as input IDMEF alerts generated by the correlation methods in the previous phase. The integration will combine these alerts, and scenarios in the highest abstraction level will be obtained. To perform the integration, we have been used a clustering method, the same idea that the correlation clustering approach but operating in a higher abstract level.

We have used GNG neural network as integration algorithm due to its clustering capabilities and its ability to learn new scenarios without retraining the network with all the above. Input features to the network will be the fields of IDMEF alerts, examples of these fields are the source IP address of the attack, destination IP address, source port, destination port and time. It is important to consider that our integration method is general (GNG neural network algorithm), not ad-hoc as in previous works.

However, we propose a minor modification of the GNG learning algorithm [5], using the C_{ID} measure (to prioritize, in the integration process, the more reliable and efficient methods). These methods will have more weight in the final result. Specifically, we modify the adaptation criteria of the reference vectors of winner neuron and its neighbors with respect to the input patterns, using the C_{ID} measure of each correlation method. So, the increase of reference vectors of the winning neuron and its neighbors will be as great as the performance measure of the correlation method associated to the input pattern.

$$\Delta w_{s_1} = C_{ID_i} \varepsilon_1 (\mu - w_{s_1})$$

$$\Delta w_i = C_{ID_i} \varepsilon_2 (\mu - w_i), \forall i \in \mathcal{N}_{s_1}$$

Thus, the neurons of network will be closer to the greater quality input patterns. Finally, the final map will have learned mainly patterns of correlation methods with great ability to detect but unable to correlate new scenarios. But the map also will have learned patterns that can detect unknown attacks, as well as the inherent capacity of neural networks to generalize and recognize new patterns from other previously observed. Therefore, the neural network can detect known and new scenarios

4   Tests and Results

We built our test scenario in order to evaluate the outcome of our approach and compare it with other proposals. The Figure 2 shows the test scenario developed.

We have used Snort sensor as local IDS, possibly the world's most widely used IDS. In the correlation stage, because the approach allows multiple systems, we have deployed three systems: alertSTAT, a tool developed by the University of California, this tool belongs to the specification of scenarios type; PreCons module, that implements the prerequisites and consequences approach defined in [4], EMERALD [17], one of the well-known intrusion detection monitors, which perform the correlation process by clustering. GNG neural network has been used in the integration phase and a response module that basically generates reports.

For the tests are uniform, we have used as input characteristics to the GNG neural network the same attributes used in [17], addresses and ports of source and destination, attack class and time. Moreover, the learning parameters of the network have been $\lambda = 2000$, $\varepsilon_1 = 0.1$, $\varepsilon_2 = 0.01$, $\alpha = 0.5$, $\beta = 0.005$.

In order to validate the modification of the GNG algorithm, we must consider that the tests have been conducted both with the original algorithm and the modified algorithm. In addition, in order to obtain results that can be compared with other proposals, we need to use a standardized test data. To date, DARPA intrusion detection evaluation data is the most comprehensive set known to be generated for the purpose of evaluating the performance of any given IDS [18].

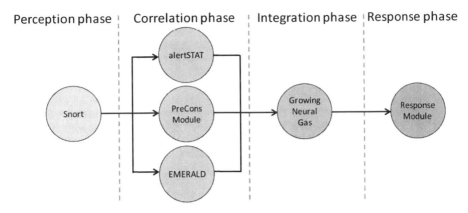

Fig. 2. Test scenario

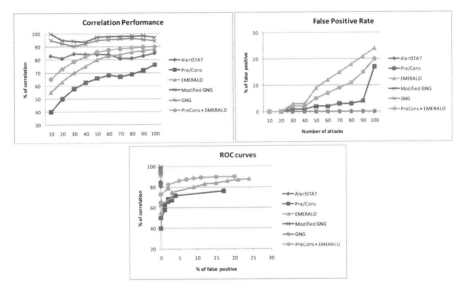

Fig. 3. Results of the test

As we can see in Figure 3, on average, PreCons shows the worst results, about 60% of correlation rate, while the probabilistic method (EMERALD) behaves better, correlation rate between 60% and 80%. The integration approach of pairs of methods (PreCons + EMERALD) improves the results of the previous two, but its performance is worse than our multiple integration approach. AlertSTAT showed a performance above 80% in all cases, very acceptable and predictable result. Finally, the integration approach of the three previous correlation methods achieves the best results, the performance is better in the modified GNG algorithm. The integration show rates over 90%, even close to 100% by modified GNG.

Table 1. C_{ID} value of the evaluated methods

Method	C_{ID} Value
Modified GNG	0.8787
GNG	0.8158
AlertSTAT	0.6311
EMERALD	0.2818
Pre-Cons	0.2100

Moreover, the false positive rate shows that AlertSTAT, GNG and modified GNG have not errors (there are three overlapping bottom lines). PreCons approach has a low false positive rate and EMERALD and the integration of pairs of methods have an excessive number of false positives.

When ROC curves intersect or overlap is difficult to determinate the best method, in order to compare through a real value the results obtained by different methods, we have used a measure of quality named C_{ID} [15] which is defined as follows:

$$C_{ID} = I(X;Y)/H(X)$$

The ratio between the mutual information of input and output ($I(X;Y)$) and the input entropy ($H(X)$). Mutual information measures the reduction of uncertainty of the IDS input by knowing de IDS output, this measure is normalized using the entropy (the original uncertainty) of the input. Table 1 shows the value of C_{ID} obtained by each of the tested approaches. The modified GNG neural network gets the best value.

5 Conclusion

This work present a method for the correlation of intrusion detection alerts based on the use of multiple correlation methods and the integration of its results. For this end, the ANN GNG has been used. The learning algorithm of the GNG network has been modified so that the best correlation methods weight the final result.

The results show that, the integration of multiple methods improves the performance obtained by each of the correlation methods alone. Moreover, the integration using the modified GNG algorithm has improved the performance of the classic version. Although the two versions obtain rates over 90%, in the case of the modified GNG are close to 100%.

We are currently working in the improvement of the proposed method to achieve the ability to be proactive, so that the system detects early stages of the attack scenarios with some probability. Moreover, we are evaluating new versions of self-organizing neural networks that open new ways to improve the performance. Finally, due to lack of real scenarios in the DARPA data set, we are working to validate the approach in real scenarios randomly generated.

References

1. Ren, H., Stakhanova, N., Ghorbani, A.: An Online Adaptive Approach to Alert Correlation. In: Kreibich, C., Jahnke, M. (eds.) DIMVA 2010. LNCS, vol. 6201, pp. 153–172. Springer, Heidelberg (2010)

2. Qin, X., Lee, W.: Statistical Causality Analysis of INFOSEC Alert Data. In: Vigna, G., Krügel, C., Jonsson, E. (eds.) RAID 2003. LNCS, vol. 2820, pp. 73–93. Springer, Heidelberg (2003)

3. Qin, X., Lee, W.: Discovering Novel Attack Strategies from INFOSEC Alerts. In: Samarati, P., Ryan, P.Y.A., Gollmann, D., Molva, R. (eds.) ESORICS 2004. LNCS, vol. 3193, pp. 439–456. Springer, Heidelberg (2004)

4. Ning, P., Cui, Y., Reeves, D.S.: Constructing Attacks Scenarios Through Correlation of Intrusion Alerts. In: Proceedings of the 9th ACM Conference on Computer and Communications Security. ACM Press, New York (2002)

5. Fritzke, B.: A growing neural gas network learns topologies. In: Advances in Neural Information Processing Systems, vol. 7. MIT Press, Cambridge (1995)

6. Abdel-Azim, M., Abdel-Fatah, A., Awad, M.: Performance Analys of Artificial Neural Network Intrusion Detection Systems. In: Proceedings of International Conference on Electrical and Electronics Engineering, Bursa, Turkey, pp. 385–389 (2009)

7. Lorenzo-Fonseca, I., Maciá-Pérez, F., Mora-Gimeno, F.J., Lau-Fernández, R., Gil-Martínez-Abarca, J.A., Marcos-Jorquera, D.: Intrusion Detection Method Using Neural Networks Based on the Reduction of Characteristics. In: Cabestany, J., Sandoval, F., Prieto, A., Corchado, J.M. (eds.) IWANN 2009. LNCS, vol. 5517, pp. 1296–1303. Springer, Heidelberg (2009)

8. Shun, J., Malki, H.A.: Network Intrusion Detection System Using Neural Networks. In: Proceedings of International Conference on Natural Computation, Jinan, China, pp. 242–249 (2008)

9. Liu, G., Wang, X.: An Integrated Intrusion Detection System by Using Multiple Neural Networks. In: Proceedings of IEEE Conference on Cybernetics and Intelligent Systems, Chengdu, China, pp. 22–27 (2008)

10. Tenfl, P., Payer, U., Fellner, R.: Event Correlation on the Basis of Activation Patterns. In: Proceedings of International Conference on Parallel, Distributed, and Network-Based Processing, Pisa, Italy, pp. 631–640 (2010)

11. Morin, B., Me, L., Debar, H., Ducasse, M.: A Logic-Based Model to Support Alert Correlation in Intrusion Detection. Information Fusion 10(4), 285–299 (2009)

12. Zhou, J., Hechman, M., Reynolds, B., Carlson, A., Bishop, M.: Modeling Network Intrusion Detection Alerts for Correlation. ACM Transactions on Information and System Security 10(1), 1–31 (2007)

13. Gu, T., Xiao, D., Liu, X., Xia, X.: Multilevel Event Correlation Based on Collaboration and Temporal Causal Correlation. In: Proceedings of International Conference on Wireless Communications, Networking and Mobile Computint, Beijing, China, pp. 1–4 (2009)

14 Ning, P., Xu, D., Healey, C.G., Amant, R.: Building Attacks Scenarios Through Integration of Complementary Alert Correlation Method. In: Proceedings of Network and Distributed System Security Symposium, San Diego, USA, pp. 69–84 (2004)

15. Gu, G., Fogla, P., Dagon, D., Lee, W., Skoric, B.: Measuring Intrusion Detection Capability: An Information_Theoretic Approack. In: Proceedings of ACM Symposium on Information, Computer and Communications Security. ACM Press, New York (2006)

16. Debar, H., Curry, D., Feinstein, B.: The Intrusion Detection Message Exchange Format (IDMEF). RFC 4765. IETF Trust (2007)

17. Valdes, A., Skinner, K.: Probabilistic Alert Correlation. In: Lee, W., Mé, L., Wespi, A. (eds.) RAID 2001. LNCS, vol. 2212, pp. 54–68. Springer, Heidelberg (2001)

18. MIT Lincoln Laboratory: DARPA Intrusion Detection Evaluation,
   http://www.ll.mit.edu/IST/ideval/index.html

A Comparative Performance Evaluation of DNS Tunneling Tools

Alessio Merlo[1,2], Gianluca Papaleo[2], Stefano Veneziano[2], and Maurizio Aiello[2]

[1] Dipartimento di Informatica, Sistemistica e Telematica (DIST), University of Genova,
Via All'Opera Pia, 13, 16145 Genova, Italy
alessio.merlo@dist.unige.it
[2] Istituto di Elettronica ed Ingeneria dell'Informazione e delle Telecomunicazioni
(IEIIT-CNR), Via De Marini, 6, 16142, Genova, Italy
{papaleo,veneziano,aiello}@ieiit.cnr.it

Abstract. DNS Tunnels are built through proper tools that allow embedding data on DNS queries and response. Each tool has its own approach to the building tunnels in DNS that differently affects the network performance. In this paper, we propose a brief architectural analysis of the current state-of-the-art of DNS Tunneling tools. Then, wepropose the first comparative analysis of such tools in term of performance, as a first step towardsthe possibility to relateeach tool with a proper behavior of DNS traffic. To this aim, we define an assessment of the toolsin three different network configurationswith three different performance metrics. We finallysummarize the most interesting results and provide some considerations on the performance of each tool.

1 Introduction

In the last years, Internet has grown so much that any organization from single restaurant and hotels to big companies are connected to it. In the same years, the evolution from early Web to Web 2.0 has seamlessly increased the number of applications available on the network. Both these aspects have indirectly taken organizations to the adoption of mechanisms (e.g. firewalls, captive portals) aimed at controlling the access to Internet. The reasons can be very different, from censorship in some countries to the selling of Internet connectivity. In general, such mechanisms acts as filters for proper network protocols (e.g. HTTP, FTP) while they often allow the transit of service protocols (DNS, ICMP) and they can't appropriately filter ciphered ones (e.g. HTTPS, Skype). Thus, many attempts have been made aimed at exploiting these latter protocols in order to hide information and build a communication channel to another system on Internet, avoiding the restrictions of firewalls. To this regard, many research activities [1] [2] [3] have been focused on hiding data into various network protocols like IPv4, IPv6, TCP ICMP, HTTP and HTTPS, just to cite some.

At present, a particularly interesting covert channel is the DNS tunnel, since DNS protocol is less filtered by security mechanisms of organizations. For instance, when dealing with captive portals, if an unauthenticated user tries to connect to a given site, the captive portal solves the DNS query before requesting credentials to the user. Thus, this means that each user within the network can produce DNS traffic to reach a destination over the Internet, independently from the identity of the requestor.

Á. Herrero and E. Corchado (Eds.): CISIS 2011, LNCS 6694, pp. 84–91, 2011.
© Springer-Verlag Berlin Heidelberg 2011

Fig. 1. Entities involved in a DNS Tunnel

The potential use of DNS queries as covert channels had taken to the development of proper DNS Tunneling tools aimed at hiding information inside the DNS requests/responses, using a customized client on the user machine and a colluded DNS server outside the organization, in the destination domain. A DNS Tunneling tool embeds data in DNS queries and delivers DNS requests and responses between the tunneled client and a rogue server, exchanging information in proper fields of DNS packets. The rogue server can then forward the received data to another destination client.

Each DNS Tunneling tool adopts its own strategies for building tunnels between the client and the rogue server, resulting in covert channels that show different characteristics. However, DNS covert channels (and tools) can be divided into two classes: (1) *IP over DNS* where IP packets are embedded and delivered through the tunnel, and (2) *TCP over DNS* that embeds one or more TCP-like communication channels, allowing the establishment of an SSH connection (or any kind of TCP connection) in the tunnel. Currently, there exist only few working and reliable DNS Tunneling tools, in particular for the second category. Each tool shows a unique strategy that has different aftermaths and backlashes on the legal DNS servers and network traffic. Thus, the possibility to relate some specific performance patterns to a proper DNS tool would be useful for a detection system to recognize the presence of a DNS tunnel.

To the best of our knowledge, a comprehensive and deep performance evaluation of all the current state-of-the-art in DNS tunneling tools has not been made yet. Thus, the aim of this paper is to provide a first attempt to compare distinct DNS Tunneling tools by characterizing their performance and the impact they have on the network.

The paper is organized as follows: Section 2 points out the related works on convert channels and, in particular, on DNS tunnels; Section 3 provides an introduction to current DNS Tunneling Tools. Section 4 introduces the testing network architecture, the network scenarios (i.e. proper configurations of the general architecture) and the metrics we used in our tests. Section 5 provides an analysis of the results and a characterization of each tool in term of network performance. Finally, Section 6 concludes the paper.

2   Related Works

Due to the growing proliferation of covert channels, many research activities have been focused on recognize unexpected patterns [7] or hidden information in plain and ciphered network protocols. Plain protocols (e.g. http) can be exploited to build covert channels. In particular, SSH can use HTTP to force the restriction of a firewall. In [4], HTTP traffic is analyzed in order to recognize covert channels built by Skype protocols. The proposed solution is feasible for real-time Skype detection over HTTP, providing a very low percentage of false positive.

On ciphered networks, many activities are focused in categorizing communication patterns of ciphered traffic by evaluating only features and metrics that are not affected by encryption. For instance, in [8] a methodology for recognizing application level protocols embedded on ciphered TCP channels is presented. Similarly, in [5] two traffic analysis techniques based on classification algorithms are used for retrieving web sites identities in ciphered HTTPS traffic.

In general, the information leakage in ciphered protocols is a sensitive problem: in [6], authors investigate how the behavior of anonymity systems (e.g. Tor) could take to an unwanted reduction of the real level of anonymity, allowing an attacker to discover information on the network location of a client.

DNS protocol has been deeply investigated in order to monitor and detect attack to single DNS servers and to the network of servers. In [9] monitoring algorithms are proposed for detecting attacks to DNS servers (e.g. cache poisoning). In the same article, a methodology for detecting DNS Tunneling is provided. To this regard, in [10] a statistical approach based on the analysis of the frequencies of characters in DNS request is provided: the idea is that characters in DNS tunnels have an evenly distributed frequency while in normal language (and so, real DNS query), the frequency follows the Zipf's law.

However, previous studies do not consider variation of performance due to the existence of DNS Tunneling in comparison to DNS traffic without tunnels. However, some early studies have been made under this perspective. In [11] the impact of DNS Tunnels on network performance is investigated. However, the study is limited to DNS tunnels built with DNSCat and on a network scenario distributed over Internet.

3   DNS Tunneling Tools

Existing DNS Tunneling Tools can be divided into two classes, depending on the abstraction layer at which the information is encapsulated. Each tool requires a real DNS server to administer the tunneling domain.

3.1 IP over DNS Tunnels

The main part of DNS Tunneling tools are aimed at building IP over DNS tunnels, namely encapsulating IP packets inside DNS queries:

- **NSTX** [13] has been the first tool to realize IP over DNS. To encode data into queries, it uses a non-compliant Base64 encoding (adding the character ``_" to the 63 characters allowed by the DNS RFC). Tunnels are realized on the tun0 interface and replies are encoded into TXT records. NTSX requires a rogue server running the NSTX tool. It also requires the client and server to have special kernel configurations.
- **DNSCat** [14] consists of two small programs, a server and client, written in Java. It is afast, efficient and highly configurable cross platform. The tunnel is made through the interface ppp0 and data in replies are encapsulated in the CNAME record. In comparison to NTSX, it does not require special kernel configuration. Thus, DNSCat is more flexible than NTSX.

- **Iodine** [15] is a more recent project. It uses either Base32 or a non-compliant Base64 encoding to encode the data (the choice is configurable). Replies are sent using NULL records. NULL records are described in RFC 1035 [5] section 3.3.10 as a container for any data, up to 65535 bytes long. It is used as a placeholder in some experimental DNS extensions. Additionally, Iodine uses EDNS0, a DNS extension that allows using DNS packets longer than the 512-byte asoriginallyproposed in RFC 1035. Both NSTX and Iodine split IP packets into several DNS packets and send them separately. Thusthey reassemble the IP packets at the endpoint (in a way similar to IP fragmentation).
- **TUNS** [12] isa new-coming tool. It works exclusively onUNIX-like systems(clients and servers) and encapsulates data in CNAME field. In comparison to NSTX and Iodine it does not split IP packets in smaller DNS packets. TUNS client polls periodically the rogue server with short queries. TUNS avoids duplicated queries made by DNS servers by using a cache. TUNS has been demonstrated to work on a wide range of networks.

3.2 TCP over DNS Tunnels

In TCP over DNS tunnels, only packets that use TCP as transport protocol are encapsulated in the tunnel. There are two tools that allowbuilding TCP over DNS tunnels:

- **Dns2TCP** [16] is composed by a server-side and a client-side part. The server has a list of resources, each of whom is a local or remote service listening for TCP connection. The client listens on a predefined TCP port and relays each incoming connection to the final service using DNS. Information is encapsulated in the TXT field. Differently from the IP-over-DNS tools, there is not a periodic polling activity from the client side
- **OzyManDNS** [17] is based on four Perl scripts. Two of them allow users to upload and download files using DNS. The other two form a server client pair. The server imitates a DNS server and listens on port 53 for incoming DNS requests. The client converts input to DNS requests, which are then sent to a given domain. These two scripts can be used in conjunction with SSH to create a tunnel. Users will then have to manually map ports to pass traffic through the resulting tunnel. Their use is transparent for applications.

4   Testing Environment

The previous tools have been tested on three different scenarios on the same network architecture at IEIIT-CNR (National Research Council in Genoa, Italy).

The network architecture is represented in Fig. 2. It is made by 4 networks connected by a Juniper Router with firewall. Each subnet contains a single participant in the DNS Tunneling. This choice allowed us to better isolate and analyze the traffic flow during the testing phase. Network 1 contains the DNS Tunnel client, where DNS Tunnel client of each tool is executed. Network 2contains the local DNS server only, which is authoritative for the domain of the client. Network 3 is made by a DNS rogue server, namely running the server part of the DNS Tunneling tool. Finally, Network 4 contains a further machine, recipient for the tunneled data.

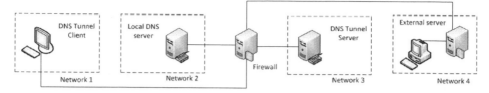

Fig. 2. IEIIT-CNR Testing architecture

We tested the tool suite using three different configurations. In each configuration, only some networks are involved:

- **Direct:** It involves the Network 1 and 3. The aim is to evaluate the performance of different tools, without taking into account the overheads of the network. To this aim, the DNS client is directly connected to the fake DNS server, without querying the local DNS. In the most part of real scenario this configuration is unfeasible, since DNS traffic is typically allowed only towards the local DNS or outer trusted DNS servers. However, this configuration allows each tool to build the tunnel independently from typical restriction of DNS server (e.g. filtering on DNS records like NULL, TXT, EDNS0 extension) in order to evaluate the behavior of tools in an ideal environment.
- **IEIIT:** It involves the first three networks. The DNS client connects to the local DNS server. The local server forwards the queries to the fake server. In this case, tools have to adapt their behavior depending on the restrictions settled by the local DNS server. A sensitive reduction of the performance of the tools is expected due to (1) server restriction and (2) traffic congestion. The comparison between *Direct* and *IEIIT* configurations allows characterizing the effects of local DNS on tunnels. IEIIT configuration is closed to a real use of DNS Tunneling. Indeed, in an organization all the DNS traffic must pass through the local DNS server in order to be forwarded to an outer DNS server. However, the fake DNS server is in general used as bridge for a remote machine that is waiting for data (i.e. it does not work as the destination of the tunneled data). This configuration does not take care of this final step to the remote machine.
- **NAT:** This configuration is similar to the previous one but the fake DNS decodes the request, extracts data and deliver them to a destination machine through a third external server (all networks are involved).

4.2 Performance Metrics

We defined three metrics in order to evaluate the performance of tools in the three configurations.

- **Throughput.** It assesses the bandwidth availability through the tunnel. This value measures the efficiency of the DNS tunneling tool implementation and allows understanding which kind of data (and, consequently, kinds of applications) can be embedded on a tunnel. For instance, low throughput tools can be used for short data transfers but are unsuitable for applications with time constraints (i.e. VOIP). We measured throughput in different time instants through the *Iperf*[18] tool. Real payloads have been used as tunneled data, in order to increase the realism of simulation and to avoid data compression.

- **Round Trip Time (RTT).** In our context, RTT measures the time elapsed between the sending of a packet to a destination and the receipt of the same packet from the source. The destination is forced to send back the received packet at once, in order to assess RTT. Latency has been measured through *hping3* [19] using different packet sizes from 16 to 1024 byte each. Also in this case, packets have been filled with real data.Since ping is not realizable in TCP over DNS tools, we built a proper tunneling interface for managing ICMP packets. In particular, we define a fake interface by customizing an SSH client and serverin order to avoid ciphering that would increase overhead.!
- **Overhead.** It measures the number of packets generated by tools that are not directly related to the transport of tunneled data. This includes, for instance, packets for polling the rouge DNS server. The overhead of each tool has been measured by calculating the number of packets in a tunnel in a ping session, and thus comparing it with the amount of packets in a ping session without tunneling. The amount of packets has been calculated through the *tshark* tool, synchronized with the ping session.

5 Testing and Analysis of Results

We tested all network configurations in terms of all metrics. Each test has been repeated several times.Due to the lack of space,we provide a summary with a global evaluation of the performance of each tool, without detailing the test results. The comparative analysis of performance has been made both analytically (making investigation at a granularity of single packets with Wireshark [20]) and graphically, by comparing the trend of single metrics among the different tools (e.g. Fig. 3).

The previous tests allow recognizing a unique set of characteristics for each tool in term of performance:

- **Dns2Tcp.** The TCP-over-Tunnel built with Dns2Tcp shows a higher throughput in comparison to the IP-over-DNS solutions and the RTT is low. However, a tunnel made through Dns2Tcp is easily recognizable by the high amount of packet overhead (around 1500%), which significantly lowers the global network performance.
- **NSTX.** It shows the lower RTT in all IP-over-DNS tools but it has globally a low throughput. Moreover, since NSTX is not configurable, it cannot be customized to different scenarios and, thus, the throughput cannot be raised. A high throughput has been measured only in the Direct configuration, that is, as remarked, an unrealistic case.
- **DnsCat.** It has an acceptable level of throughput and RTT, making it suitable for Internet surfing without sensitive delays. However, it is characterized by a non-regular trend and high overhead. Differently from NSTX, it is a highly configurable tool, so the overhead can potentially be reduced by properly customizing the tool if the network configuration is known.
- **Iodine.** Iodine is the only tool showing a linear behavior in all metrics and all configurations. Notwithstanding the average throughput, Iodine shows the lower overhead and a low RTT value. Since it is particularly configurable, it is suitable for almost all network scenarios.

- **TUNS.** It shows the lower performance in all configurations. Throughput and RTT are too low and too high, respectively, making hard its use for building channels exploitable by real applications. However, it shows a good overhead value and, differently from the other tools, its performance and design characteristics make it particularly reliable in choke networks.
- **OzyManDNS.** We were not able to assess the performance of OzyManDNS since it has revealed to be too buggy for an exhaustive evaluation. In particular, each test had crashed after few seconds. Thus, we argue that this tool is too unstable to be effectively used in real scenarios.

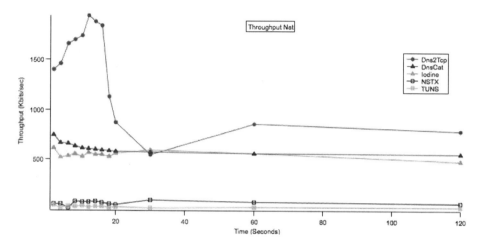

Fig. 3. A throughput test in the NAT configuration

6 Conclusions and Future Works

In this paper we have comparatively analyzed the characteristics of the current state-of-the-art in DNS Tunneling tools, providing both a testing environment and a brief and global analysis of the whole set of results. Such analysis allowed us to relate a relationship among values of the test metrics to a proper tool. Further work will regard the exhaustive and detailed analysis of the results and a behavioral analysis of the tools for intrusion detection and security purposes.

References

[1] Llamas, D., Allison, C., Miller, A.: Covert Channels in Internet Protocols:A Survey. In: 6th Annual Postgraduate Symposium about Convergence of Telecommunications, Networking and Broadcasting (2005)
[2] Rowland, C.H.: Covert channels in the TCP/IP Protocols Suite. First Monday 2(5) (1997)
[3] Zander, S., Armitage, G., Branch, P.: Covert channels and countermeasuresin computer network protocols. IEEE Communication Magazine 45(12) (2007)

[4] Freire, E.P., Ziviani, A., Salles, R.M.: Detecting Skype flowsin Web traffic. In: Network Operations and Management Symposium, NOMS 2008, April 7-11, pp. 89–96. IEEE, Los Alamitos (2008), doi:10.1109/NOMS.2008.4575121

[5] Liberatore, M., Levine, B.N.: Inferring the source of encrypted HTTP connections. In: Proceedings of the 13th ACM Conference on Computer and Communications Security (CCS 2006), pp. 255–263. ACM, New York (2006)

[6] Hopper, N., Vasserman, E.Y., Chan-Tin, E.: How much anonymitydoes network latency leak? In: Proc. of the 14th ACM Conf. on Computer and Communications Security, CCS 2007 (2007)

[7] Xu, K., Zhang, Z., Bhattacharyya, S.: Profiling internet backbone traffic: behavior models and applications. SIGCOMM Comput. Commun. Rev. 35(4), 169–180 (2005)

[8] Wright, C.V., Monrose, F., Masson, G.M.: On Inferring ApplicationProtocol Behaviors in Encrypted Network Traffic. J. Mach. Learn. Res. 7, 2745–2769 (2006)

[9] Karasaridis, A., Meier-Hellstern, K., Hoein, D.: Detection of DNS Anomalies using Flow Data Analysis. In: Global TelecommunicationsConference, GLOBECOM 2006, November 27 -December 1, pp. 1–6. IEEE, Los Alamitos (2006), doi:0.1109/GLOCOM.2006.280

[10] Born, K., Gustafson, D.: Detecting DNS Tunnels Using Character Frequency Analysis. In: Proceedings of the 9th Annual Security Conference, LasVegas, NV, April 7-8 (2010)

[11] van Leijenhorst, T., Lowe, D., Chin, K.-W.: On the Viability and Performance of DNS Tunneling. In: The 5th International Conference on InformationTechnology and Applications (ICITA 2008), Cairns, Australia, June 23-26 (2008)

[12] Nussbaum, L., Neyron, P., Richard, O.: On Robust Covert ChannelsInside DNS. Emerging Challenges for Security, Privacy and Trust. In: IFIPAdvances in Information and Communication Technology. Springer, Boston (2009)

[13] NSTX (October 2003), http://nstx.sourceforge.net/

[14] DNSCat (October 2004),
http://tadek.pietraszek.org/projects/DNScat/

[15] Iodine (February 2010), http://code.kryo.se/iodine/

[16] DNS2TCP,
http://www.hsc.fr/ressources/outils/dns2tcp/index.html.en

[17] Ozyman,
http://www.cship.info/mirror/dnstunnel/ozymandns_src0.1.tgz

[18] Iperf, http://sourceforge.net/projects/iperf/

[19] Hping, http://www.hping.org/

[20] tshark, http://www.wireshark.org/docs/man-pages/tshark.html

[21] WireShark, http://www.wireshark.org

Security Analysis and Complexity Comparison of Some Recent Lightweight RFID Protocols

Ehsan Vahedi, Rabab K. Ward, and Ian F. Blake

Department of Electrical and Computer Engineering,
The University of British Columbia, Vancouver, Canada
{vahedi,rababw,ifblake}@ece.ubc.ca

Abstract. Using RFID tags can simplify many applications and provide many benefits, but the privacy of the customers should be taken into account. A potential threat for the privacy of a user is that anonymous readers can obtain information about the tags in the system. In order to address the security issues of RFID systems, various schemes have been proposed. Among the various solutions, lightweight protocols have attracted much attention as they are more appropriate for the limited architecture of RFID tags. In this paper, we perform the security analysis of five lightweight protocols proposed in [1-4] and discuss their advantages and security issues. The computational complexity of these lightweight protocols are also compared in this work.

1 Introduction

Radio frequency identification (RFID) is a ubiquitous wireless technology which allows objects to be identified automatically. For pervasive deployment of RFID systems, one issue which causes public's concern is privacy. Many research activities have been devoted in the area of RFID security and privacy recently. Various attacks on the current algorithms, protocols and implementations showed that the privacy of RFID systems should be taken into account more seriously. Some customers are concerned about being tracked by other readers when they are carrying items (such as clothes, medicine or currency) embedded with RFID tags. In addition to tracking people, RFID tags may also be used to extract personal information such as the type of clothes somebody wears, the specific brand that an individual is interested in, or some medical information about the patient carrying an RFID-embedded container of medicine [5]. RFID tags may also be used by some malicious organizations or dealers that sell fake RFID embedded items and forge them as valuable items [5]. Denial of service (DoS) is another type of problem which can be caused by attackers whose aim is to disrupt an RFID system [6]. Moreover, some specific RFID applications demand specific considerations.

In order to cope with security issues of RFID systems, various schemes have been proposed. These solutions can be divided into two general groups. The first group uses blocking, jamming and physical solutions [7]. The other group uses cryptographic concepts and privacy preserving protocols. Cryptographic solutions for RFID security issues can be divided into two main groups, lightweight and complex cryptographic solutions. Some researchers believe that it is possible to

Á. Herrero and E. Corchado (Eds.): CISIS 2011, LNCS 6694, pp. 92–99, 2011.

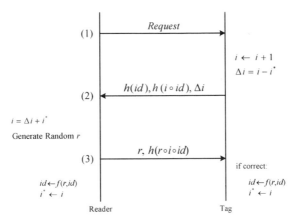

Fig. 1. The RFID protocol proposed by Henrici and Müller [1]

use complex cryptographic protocols in future RFID tags. Most RFID researchers, however, believe that the industry needs simple and low cost RFID tags (below 5 cents per item) with limited number of logical gates [5],[8]. For this case, many approaches that are based on the lightweight cryptographic solutions and protocols have been suggested [1-4]. Lightweight protocols have the advantage of keeping the computational demand and the price of RFID tags very low. In this work, we perform a security analysis of five lightweight protocols proposed in [1-4], and show that they are vulnerable to some simple security attacks.

2   Henrici-Müller RFID Protocol

In this Section, we explain the protocol proposed by Henrici and Müller [1]. In this protocol, each tag contains its current identifier id, the current session number i, and the last successful session number i^*. Similarly, the database contains a list of all identifiers, session numbers and the last successful session numbers for all the tags in the system. Both the reader and the tags are aware of the hash function h, and $\circ$ is a "simple XOR function" [1]. The communication process is performed as shown in Fig. 1. It should be noted that in this protocol, an entry is not deleted from the database after the third step, but a copy of the previous id and i^* is kept until the next successful session.

Although this protocol is simple, efficient and can solve many security issues of RFID systems, it is vulnerable to some simple attacks as explained below:

1. In this protocol, the tag increases the value of i by one, even if the session finally fails, while i^* is updated only if the session is successful and the reader is confirmed. Based on the above, an attacker can interrogate a tag several times to abnormally increase i and Δi. Therefore, an attacker is able to recognize its target by identifying and "tracking" the tag that sends abnormally large values of Δi.

2. After step (2) and before the legitimate reader sends r and $h(r \circ i \circ id)$ to the tag, the attacker can use a null element like $r' = \bar{0}$ and sends back the

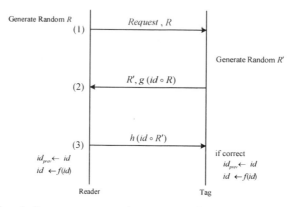

Fig. 2. The challenge-response trigger protocol proposed by Lim *et al.* [2]

r' and $h(r' \circ i \circ id)$ to the tag. As a result, the original r and $h(r \circ i \circ id)$ will not be accepted from the legitimate reader and it will be "desynchronized" from the tag.

3. As mentioned before, a copy of the previous id is kept in the database to make it possible for the reader to communicate with a tag whose id has not been updated for any reason. Using this fact, an attacker can simply save and then "replay" $\{h(id), h(i \circ id), \Delta i\}$ to the legitimate reader to "impersonate" itself as the real tag.

4. In Henrici-Müller protocol, when a legitimate reader interrogates a tag, an attacker can interrogate this tag before the reader carries out the third step. After receiving the request message from the attacker, the tag increases i by one. Thus, the hash value sent by the legitimate reader to the tag is conceived as an incorrect response and will not be accepted (desynchronization).

5. An attacker can repeatedly send the request message to the nearby tags and looks for the $h(id)$ in the received replies. As a result, the attacker can "track" a specific tag using its $h(id)$.

3   Lim *et al.* RFID Protocols

In this Section, we explain two RFID protocols proposed by Lim *et al.* [2]. The first protocol is named the "challenge-response trigger" and uses a challenge-response mechanism to provide the required security. In this scheme, each tag contains its current id, and a copy of all the tag ids is kept in the database. The communication process is shown in Fig. 2. Here, R and R' are random challenges, $\circ$ shows the XOR function, and g is a one-way hash function [2]. In the challenge-response trigger protocol, an entry is not deleted from the database after the third step. The challenge-response trigger protocol is vulnerable to some simple attacks as discussed below:

1. For most RFID applications, it is a reasonable assumption that a tag may be captured and analyzed by an attacker. The attacker can interrogate the captured tag for different values of R, and make a dictionary of some probable

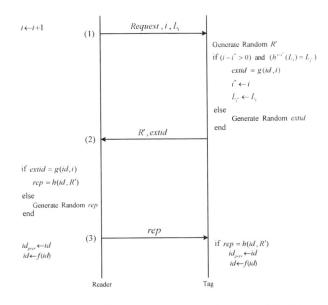

Fig. 3. The forward rolling trigger protocol proposed by Lim *et al.* [2]

challenges and related responses from the tag. The attacker can use this dictionary later to impersonate itself as the real tag to the legitimate reader.

2. As another attack, the above mentioned dictionary can be used to track a specific tag. The attacker would repeatedly send the request message and R to all tags and look for the $g(id, R)$ response known from the dictionary.

3. After the legitimate reader sends a request message to the tag in step (1) and before step (3), an attacker can repeat step (1) and send a request message to force the tag to reset the random challenge R'. Since the new random challenge is different from the previous one, the $h(id \circ R')$ message which the reader sends will not be accepted by the tag.

After the challenge-response trigger protocol, another scheme named the "forward rolling trigger" was proposed in [2]. This scheme takes advantage of Lamport's one-time password authentication scheme [9]. In the "forward rolling trigger" protocol, the tag only responds to a valid challenge from the reader or sends back some random values otherwise [2]. In this protocol, the reader stores a chain of hash functions like $h(w)$, $h^2(w) = h(h(w))$, ..., $h^{max}(w)$, where h is a secure one-way hash function, w is a secret random seed, and max is the length of the chain. The reader uses a hash value from this chain to authenticate itself to the tag over time. For each tag in the system, the last successful session (communication with the reader) is stored as i^* and the current session is shown by i. The reader uses $L_i = h^{max-i}(w)$ to authenticate itself to the tag. The communication process is shown in Fig. 3. As in the challenge-response trigger protocol, an entry is not deleted from the database after the third step, but a copy of the previous id is kept until the next successful session. The forward rolling trigger protocol has some security drawbacks, as stated below:

1. The total number of session requests which can be issued by the reader is limited to max for each tag, which makes the protocol vulnerable to DoS attacks.
2. The attacker may know the set of acceptable $\{i, L_i\}$ (or at least a large pair of this set) from another RFID system or by tampering. The attacker can send $i = max$ and L_{max} to a tag and waste its set of acceptable $\{i, L_i\}$.
3. The $(i - i^*) > 0$ condition makes the protocol vulnerable to DoS attack. Moreover, the reader needs to be aware of the tag which is going to be interrogated next, and this is not a plausible assumption for many applications. On the other hand, if we remove the $(i - i^*) > 0$ condition, the protocol becomes vulnerable to another attack. The attacker may listen to the communications between the tags and the reader in another RFID system, eavesdrop and save a valid (i, L_i) pair, and use it for an RFID system somewhere else to ruin the synchronization between the tag and the reader.
4. If we remove the $(i - i^*) > 0$ condition from the protocol, an attacker can eavesdrop on the previous communication between the tag and the reader and use one of the previously used valid (i, L_i) pairs to interrogate the tag again. The tag replies with $extid = g(id, i)$ and the attacker can track the tag by sending the request message repeatedly.
5. An attacker may find a valid (i, L_i) pair from another RFID system as explained above. Then, it can send the valid pair along with the request message to a captured tag and obtain the $\{R', extid = g(id, i)\}$ information in the second step. Using the $\{R', extid = g(id, i)\}$ information, the attacker is now able to impersonate itself as the actual tag to the legitimate reader.

4   Tan *et al.* RFID Protocol

In this Section, we explain the lightweight protocol proposed by Tan *et al.* [3]. This scheme uses a server-less authentication protocol that aims to provide the same level of security as the previous protocols, without needing a central database system. In this scheme, each reader has a unique identifier r_i where the index i is used to distinguish between different readers. Each tag has a unique identifier id and a unique secret t_j where the index j is used to distinguish between different tags. The secret t_j is only known by the tag itself and a central database. A one-way hash function h is known by both the tags and the readers and $f(a, b) = h(a||b)$ in which $||$ is the concatenation operation. It should be noted that the reader does not have access to the secret t_j of the tags, but it knows the value of $f(r_i, t_j)$ for each tag [3]. Details of the the server-less protocol is shown in Fig. 4. Here, $\oplus$ shows the XOR operation. This protocol can resist the DoS, cloning, replay and physical attacks [3]. However, it still has some security issues as explained below:

1. A malicious user can send a request message to the tag after step (3) and force it to generate a new challenge n'_j. At this point, the reader waits for $h(f(r_i, t_j))_m$ and $h(f(r_i, t_j)||n_i||n_j) \oplus id_j$ while the tag is expecting a new n'_i and r_i as the third step.

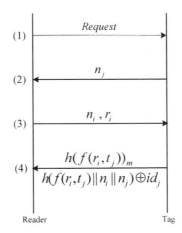

Fig. 4. The server-less protocol proposed by Tan *et al.* [3]

2. In step (4) of this scheme, $h(f(r_i, t_j))_m$ is sent by the tag. This is a static form of data which can be used by malicious users to track the tag.
3. It is possible that an attacker captures a tag, repeatedly sends the request message along with fixed values of r_i and n_i, and then stores the $\{h(f(r_i, t_j))_m, h(f(r_i, t_j)||n_i||n_j) \oplus id_j\}$ responses received for different values of n_j. This way, the attacker can make a table of responses and use this table in a fake tag to impersonate it as a real one.

5   Sun *et al.* Gen2$^+$ RFID Protocol

In order to solve the security issues of the EPCglobal Class-1 Generation-2 (*Gen2*) protocol, Sun *et al.* propose an improved version of *Gen2* called the *Gen2$^+$* protocol [4]. A typical *Gen2* tag contains a pseudorandom number generator (PRNG) and takes advantage of a cyclic redundancy code (CRC-16) to protect the message integrity [4]. The *Gen2$^+$* protocol uses the same PRNG and CRC-16 tools for privacy preserving. Sun *et al.* assume that each tag shares an *l*-word-long random string, called "keypool", with the back-end database. This string is randomly generated by the back-end database and is written into the tag before deployment [4]. A threshold *t* is also set in each tag to tolerate error bits in the received values and to boost the reading speed. Sun *et al.* assume that it is possible to design and add an extra Hamming distance calculator to each *Gen2* tag [4]. The *Gen2$^+$* protocol is depicted in Fig. 5. Although the *Gen2$^+$* protocol is easy to implement and inexpensive, it has some security problems as follow:

1. To obtain the *EPC data*, an attacker needs to be able to provide an acceptable ck' for each *RN*16 and *check* it receives in step (2). It was proven in [4] that if an attacker records approximately 16,384 failed sessions between a reader and a tag and analyzes them, it may be able to track the tag using the additional information provided by the *check* bits. Moreover, a passive

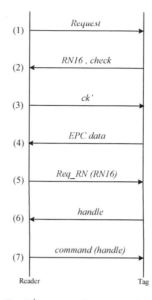

Fig. 5. The $Gen2^+$ protocol proposed by Sun *et al.* [4]

Table 1. Security comparison of the RFID protocols explained in Sections 2-5

Protocol\Attack	Tracking	Desynchronization	Replay	DoS	Impersonating a real tag
Henrici-Müller [1]	No	No	No	Yes	No
Challenge-Response Trigger [2]	No	No	Yes	Yes	No
Forward Rolling Trigger [2]	No	No	Yes	No	No
Server-less Method [3]	No	No	Yes	Yes	No
$Gen2^+$ [4]	No	No	No	Yes	No

Table 2. Complexity comparison of the RFID protocols explained in Sections 2-5

Protocol	Complexity
Henrici-Müller [1]	$4\alpha+3\gamma+2\lambda$
Challenge-Response Trigger [2]	$3\alpha+\beta+\gamma+2\lambda$
Forward Rolling Trigger [2]	$4\alpha+\beta+3\gamma$
Server-less Method [3]	$3\alpha+\beta+4\lambda$
$Gen2^+$ [4]	$2\beta+3\gamma+\lambda+\theta$

attacker can listen to the communication between the legitimate readers and the tags, and notice the presence of a specific tag, as the *EPC data* is sent in plaintext in the $Gen2^+$ protocol.

2. An attacker can eavesdrop on the communication between a legitimate reader and a tag, and extract its *EPC data*, *RN16* and *check*. The attacker can save this information on a fake tag. The fake tag then accepts any *ck'* it receives from the reader and sends its *EPC data* in step (4) to impersonate itself.

3. An attacker can wait until a tag is interrogated by a legitimate reader and sends its *RN16* and *check* in step (2). At this point and before the legitimate

reader calculates ck' and sends it to the tag, another request message can be sent to the tag by the attacker. As a result, the tag replies with another $RN16$ and does not accept the ck' which was sent by the legitimate reader.

6   Comparison and Conclusion

In this Section, we compare the five discussed protocols [1-4] from the security point of view. We also compare them from the complexity and computational costs aspect. Table 1 compares the robustness of discussed protocols against tracking, desynchronization, replay, DoS, and impersonation attacks. For each attack, the word "Yes" implies the considered protocol is robust against that attack while "No" means the protocol is vulnerable to that attack. Table 2 compares the computational costs (per successful session) imposed on the tags, for each of the discussed protocols. In this table, we only consider the complexity of implementing each protocol on RFID tags, and neglect the computational cost on the database side. In order to make a fair comparison of the complexity and computational costs, we denote the computational cost of each hash function by α, each random generation by β, each addition, subtraction or comparison by γ, each conjugation or concatenation function by λ, and each Hamming distance calculation by θ. Finally, interested readers are encouraged to refer to [10] for more details and the complete version of this paper.

References

1. Henrici, D., Müller, P.: Hash-based enhancement of location privacy for radio-frequency identification devices using varying identifiers. In: IEEE PERCOM, pp. 149–153 (2004)
2. Lim, T.L., Li, T., Gu, T.: Secure RFID identification and authentication with triggered hash chain variants. In: IEEE ICPADS, pp. 583–590 (2008)
3. Tan, C.C., Sheng, B., Li, Q.: Secure and server-less RFID authentication and search protocols. IEEE Trans. on Wireless Communications 7, 1400–1407 (2008)
4. Sun, H.M., Ting, W.C.: A Gen2-based RFID authentication protocol for security and privacy. IEEE Trans. on Mobile Computing 8, 1052–1062 (2009)
5. Juels, A.: RFID security and privacy: A research survey. IEEE J. on Selected Areas in Communication 24, 381–394 (2006)
6. Langheinrich, M.: A survey of RFID privacy approaches. J. of Personal and Ubiquitous Computing 13, 413–421 (2009)
7. Vahedi, E., Shah-Mansouri, V., Wong, V., Blake, I.F.: A probabilistic approach for detecting blocking attack in RFID systems. In: IEEE ICC, pp. 101–107 (2010)
8. Avoine, G., Oechslin, P.: RFID traceability: A multi-layer problem. Financial Cryptography and Data Security 3570, 125–140 (2005)
9. Lamport, L.: Password authentication with insecure communication. Communications of the ACM 24, 770–772 (1981)
10. www.ece.ubc.ca/~vahedi/CISIS-Full.pdf

A Secure and Efficient Searching Scheme for Trusted Nodes in a Peer-to-Peer Network

Jaydip Sen

TCS Innovation Labs, Tata Consultancy Services Ltd.,
Bengal Intelligent Park, Salt Lake Electronics Complex, Kolkata – 700091, India
Jaydip.Sen@tcs.com

Abstract. The existing search mechanisms for peer-to-peer (P2P) networks have several problems such as fake content distribution, free riding, white-washing and poor search scalability. Although, researchers have proposed several trust management and semantic community-based mechanisms for combating free riding and distribution of malicious contents, most of these schemes lack scalability due to their high computational, communication and storage overhead. This paper presents a trust management scheme for P2P networks that utilizes topology adaptation by constructing an overlay of trusted peers where the neighbors are selected based on their trust ratings and content similarities. It also increases the search efficiency by taking advantage of the implicit semantic community structures formed as a result of topology adaptation since most of the queries are resolved within the community of trustworthy peers. Simulation results demonstrate that the proposed scheme provides efficient searching to good peers while penalizing the malicious peers by increasing their search times.

Keywords: P2P network, topology adaptation, trust management, semantic community, malicious peer.

1 Introduction

The term *peer-to-peer* (P2P) system encompasses a broad set of distributed applications which allow sharing of computer resources by direct exchange between systems. The goal of a P2P system is to aggregate resources available at the edge of Internet and to share it cooperatively among users. Specially, the file sharing P2P systems have become popular as a new paradigm for information exchange among large number of users in Internet. They are more robust, scalable, fault tolerant and offer better availability of resources. Depending on the presence of a central server, P2P systems can be classified as centralized or decentralized [1]. In decentralized architecture, both resource discovery and download are distributed. Decentralized P2P application may be further classified as structured or unstructured network. In structured network, there is a restriction on the placement of content and network topology. In unstructured P2P network, however, placement of content is unrelated to topology. Unstructured P2P networks perform better than their structured counterpart in dynamic environment. However, they need efficient search mechanisms and suffer from

Á. Herrero and E. Corchado (Eds.): CISIS 2011, LNCS 6694, pp. 100–108, 2011.

fake content distribution, free riding (peers who do not share, but consume resources), whitewashing (peers who leave and rejoin the system in order to avoid penalties) and search scalability problems. Open and anonymous nature of P2P applications lead to complete lack of accountability of the content that a peer puts in the network. The malicious peers often use these networks to do content poisoning and to distribute harmful programs such as Trojan Horses and viruses [2].

To combat inauthentic downloads as well as to improve search scalability, this paper proposes an *adaptive trust-aware scalable* algorithm. The proposed scheme constructs an overlay of trusted peers where neighbors are selected based on their trust ratings and content similarities. It increases search efficiency by taking advantage of implicit semantic community structures formed as a result of topology adaptation. The novel contribution of the work is that it combines the functionalities of trust management and semantic community formation. While the trust management scheme segregates honest peers from malicious peers, the semantic communities adapt topology to form cluster of peers sharing similar contents.

The rest of the paper is organized as follows. Section 2 discusses some related work. Section 3 presents the proposed algorithm for trust management. Section 4 introduces various metrics to measure performance of the proposed algorithm, and presents the simulation results. Finally, Section 5 concludes the paper while highlighting some future scope of work.

2 Related Work

In [3], a searching mechanism is proposed that is based on discovery of trust paths among the peers in a peer-to-peer network. A global trust model based on distance-weighted recommendations has been proposed in [4] to quantify and evaluate the peers in a P2P network. In [5], a protocol named *adaptive peer-to-peer technologies* (APT) for the formation of adaptive topologies has been proposed to reduce spurious file download and free riding in a peer-to-peer network. The scheme follows a defensive strategy for punishment where a peer equally punishes both malicious peers as well as neighbors through which it receives response from malicious peers. This strategy is relaxed in the *reciprocal capacity-based adaptive topology protocol* (RC-ATP), where a peer connects to others which have higher *reciprocal capacity* [6]. Reciprocal capacity is defined based on the capacity of providing good files and of recommending source of download of the peers. While RC-ATP provides better network connectivity than APT, it has a large overhead of topology adaptation.

There are some significant differences between the proposed algorithm in this paper and APT and RC-ATP. First, in the proposed scheme, to avoid network partitioning, the links in the original overlays are never deleted. Second, the robustness of the proposed protocol in presence of malicious peers is higher than that of APT and RC-ATP protocols. Third, as APT and RC-ATP both use flooding to locate resources, they have poor search scalability. The proposed scheme, on the other hand, exploits the advantages of the formation of semantic communities to improve the quality of service (QoS) of search. Finally, unlike APT and RC-ATP, the proposed scheme punishes malicious peers by blocking queries initiated from them.

3 The Proposed Trust-Aware Algorithm

In this section, we describe the factors that are taken into account for designing the proposed scheme, and then present the details of the scheme.

(1) *Network topology and load*: Using the approach described in [5] and [6], the network has been modeled as a *power law graph*. In a power law network, degree distribution of nodes follows power law distribution, i.e. fraction of nodes having degree L is L^{-k} where k is a network dependent constant. Prior to each simulation cycle, a fixed fraction of peers chosen randomly is marked as malicious. As the algorithm proceeds, the peers adjust topology locally to connect those peers which have better chance to provide good files and drop malicious peers from their neighborhood. The network links are categorized into two types: *connectivity link* and *community link*. The connectivity links are the edges of the original power law network which provide seamless connectivity among the peers. To prevent the network from being fragmented they are never deleted. On the other hand, community links are added probabilistically between the peers who know each other. A community link may be deleted when perceived trustworthiness of a peer falls in the perception of its neighbors. A limit is put on the additional number of edges that a node can acquire to control bandwidth usage and query processing overhead in the network.

(2) *Content distribution*: The dynamics of a P2P network are highly dependent on the volume and variety of files each peer chooses to share. Hence a model reflecting real-world P2P networks is required. It has been observed that the peers are in general interested in a subset of the content on the P2P network [7]. Also, the peers are often interested only in files from a few content categories. Among these categories, some are more popular than others. It has been shown that Gnutella content distribution follows *zipf distribution* [8]. Keeping this in mind, both content categories and file popularity within each category is modeled with *zipf distribution* with $\alpha = 0.8$.

Content distribution model: The content distribution model in [8] is followed for simulation purpose. In this model, each distinct file $f_{c,r}$ is abstractly represented by the tuple (c, r), where c represents the content category to which the file belongs, and r represents its popularity rank within a content category c. Let content categories be $C = \{c_1, c_2, \ldots, c_{32}\}$. Each content category is characterized by its *popularity rank*. For example, if $c_1 = 1$, $c_2 = 2$ and $c_3 = 3$, then c_1 is more popular than c_2 and hence it is more replicated than c_2 and so on. Also there are more files in category c_1 than c_2.

Table 1. Hypothetical content distribution in peer nodes

Peers	Content categories
P_1	$\{C_1, C_2, C_3\}$
P_2	$\{C_2, C_4, C_6, C_7\}$
P_3	$\{C_2, C_4, C_7, C_8\}$
P_4	$\{C_1, C_2\}$
P_5	$\{C_1, C_5, C_6\}$

Each peer randomly chooses three to six content categories to share files and shares more files in more popular categories. Table 1 shows an illustrative content distribution among five peers. The category c_1 is more replicated as it is most popular. The

Peer $1(P_1)$ shares files in three categories: c_1, c_2, c_3 where it shares maximum number of files in category c_1, followed by category c_2 and so on. On the other hand, Peer 3 (P_3) shares maximum number of files in category c_2 as it's the most popular among the categories chosen by it, followed by c_4 and so on.

(3) *Query initiation model*: The peers usually query for files that exist on the network and are in the content category of their interest [8]. In each cycle of simulation, active peers issue queries. However number of queries a peer issues may vary from peer to peer, modeled by *Poisson* distribution as follows. If M is the total number of queries to be issued in each cycle of simulation and N is the number of peers present in the network, query rate $\lambda = M/N$ is the mean of the *Poisson* process. The expression $p(\#quries = K) = \dfrac{e^{-\lambda}\lambda^K}{K!}$ gives the probability that a peer issues K queries in a cycle. The probability that a peer issues query for the file $f_{c,r}$ depends on the peer's interest level in category c and rank r of the file within that category.

(4) *Trust management engine*: The trust management engine helps a peer to compute trust rating of other peer from past transaction history as well as recommendation from its neighbor. It allows a peer to join the network with default trust level and gradually build its reputation by providing good files to other peers. In the proposed scheme, each peer maintains a *least recently used* (LRU) data structure to keep track of recent transactions with almost 32 peers at a time. Each time peer i downloads a file from peer j, it rates the transaction as positive $(tr_{ij}=1)$ or negative $(tr_{ij}= -1)$ depending on whether downloaded file is authentic or fake. $S_{ij} = \dfrac{1}{TD}\sum tr_{ij}$ is the fraction of successful downloads peer i had made from peer j, where TD is the total number of downloads. Peer i considers peer j as trustworthy if $S_{ij} > 0.5$, and malicious if $S_{ij} < 0$. If $0 \le S_{ij} < 0.5$, peer i considers peer j as *average trustworthy*. Peer i seeks recommendations from other peers about peer j if the information is not locally available.

3.2 The Proposed Trust-Aware Algorithm

The proposed scheme uses three steps for its operation: (i) search, (ii) trust checking and (iii) topology adaptation. These steps are discussed in the rest of this section.

3.2.1 Search

The *time to live* (TTL) bound search is used which evolves along with topology. At each hop, query is forwarded to a fraction of neighbors, the number of neighbors is decided based on the local estimate of network connectivity, known as probability of community formation, $Prob_{com}$. For node x, $Prob_{com}$ is defined as in (1):

$$Prob_{com}(x) = \frac{degree(x) - initial\_degree(x)}{initial\_degree(x).(edge\_limit - 1)} \qquad (1)$$

When $Prob_{com}$ for a node is low, the peer has the capacity to accept new community edges. Higher the value of $Prob_{com}$, lesser the neighbors choose to disseminate queries. As simulation proceeds, connectivity of good nodes increases and reaches a maximum value. So, they focus on directing queries to appropriate community which may host the specific file rather than expanding communities. For example, if peer i can contact at most 10 neighbors and $Prob_{com}$ of j is 0.6, it forwards query to 10 x (1 – 0.6) = 4 neighbors only. The search strategy modifies itself from initial *TTL limited BFS* to *directed DFS* with the restructuring of the network. The search is carried out in two steps– *query initiation* and *query forward*. These are explained in the following.

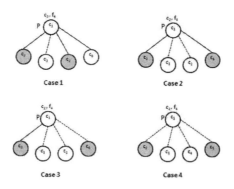

Fig. 1. Neighbor selection at P for query string (c2, f4). Community edges and connectivity edges are drawn with solid and dotted lines respectively. Nodes that dispatch query are shaded.

Query initiation: The initiating peer forms a query packet containing the name of the file (c, r) and forwards it to a certain fraction of neighbors along with the $Prob_{com}$ and the TTL values. The query is disseminated as follows. The neighbors are ranked based on both *trustworthiness* and the *similarity of interest*. Preference is given to the trusted neighbors who share similar contents. If there are insufficient community links, query is forwarded through connectivity links also. The various cases of *neighbor selection rule* are illustrated in Fig. 1. It is assumed that in each case only two neighbors are selected. When the query (c_2, f_4) reaches node P, following cases may occur. In first case, P has adequate community neighbors sharing file in category c_2, hence they are chosen. In *Case 2*, there are insufficient community neighbors sharing file in the requested category, the community neighbors sharing c_2 and c_6 preferred to the connectivity neighbor c_2 to forward query. In *Case 3*, only one community neighbor (c_2) shares the file. Hence it is chosen. From the remaining connectivity neighbors, most trusted c_6 is selected. In *Case 4*, only connectivity neighbor are present. Assuming all of them at the same trust level, the matching neighbor c_2 is chosen and from the rest c_5 is selected randomly. When a query reaches from peer j to i, the latter performs the *query forward* action, which is described in the following.

Query forward: (i) *Check trust level of peer j*: Peer i checks trust rating of peer j through *check trust rating* algorithm (explained later). Accordingly, the decision regarding further propagation of the query is taken. (ii) *Check the availability of file*: If the requested file is found, response is sent to peer j. If TTL value has not expired, the following steps are executed. (iii) *Calculate the number of messages to be sent*: It is calculated based on the value of $Prob_{com}$.(iv) *Choose neighbors*: Neighbors are chosen in using *neighbor selection rule*. The search process is shown in Fig. 2. It is assumed that the query is forwarded at each hop to two neighbors. The matching community

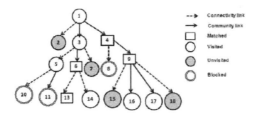

Fig. 2. The breadth first search (BFS) tree for the search procedure initiated by peer 1

links are preferred over connectivity links to dispatch query. Peer 1 initiates a query and forwards it to two community neighbors 3 and 4. The query reaches peer 8 via peer 4. However, peer 8 knows that peer 4 is malicious from previous transactions. Hence it blocks the query. The query forwarded by peer 5 is also blocked by peer 10 and 11 as both of them know that peer 5 is malicious. The query is matched at four peers: 4, 6, 9 and 13. The search process is shown in Fig. 2.

Topology Adaptation: Responses are sorted by the initiating peer i based on the reputation of resource providers, and the peer having highest reputation is selected as source of download. The requesting peer checks the authenticity of downloaded file. If the file is found to be fake, peer i attempts to download from other sources. It updates the trust rating and possibly adapts topology. The restructuring of network is controlled by a parameter known as *degree of rewiring* which is the probability with which a link is formed between two peers. Topology adaptation consists of the following operations: (i) *link deletion*: Peer i deletes the existing community link with peer j if it finds peer j as malicious. (ii) *link addition*: Peer i probabilistically forms community link with peer j if resource is found to be authentic.

In the example shown in Fig. 3, peer 1 downloads the file from peer 4 and finds that the file is spurious. It reduces the trust score of peer 4 and deletes the community link 1--4. It then downloads the file from peer 6 and gets an authentic file. Peer 1 now sends a request to peer 6, and the latter grants the request and adds the community edge 1--6. The malicious peer 4 loses one community link and peer 6 gains one community edge. However, the network still remains connected by connectivity edges.

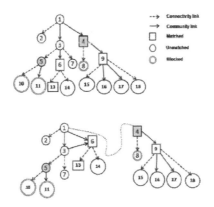

Fig. 3. Topology adaptation on the search in Figure 2. Malicious nodes are shaded in gray.

4 Performance Evaluation

To analyze the performance of the proposed scheme, three metrics are defined: attempt ratio, closeness centrality, and largest connected component. These metrics are discussed below and they are evaluated by simulation.

(1) *Attempt ratio* (AR): A peer keeps on downloading files from various sources based on their trust rating till it gets the authentic file. AR is the probability that the authentic file is downloaded in the first attempt. A high value of AR is desirable.

(2) *Closeness centrality* (CC): Since the topology adaptation brings the good peers closer to each other, the length of the shortest path between a pair of good peers decreases. The peers with higher CC values are topologically better positioned. If P_{ij} is the length of the shortest path between i and j through community edges and if V denotes the set of peers, then CC for peer i is given by: $CC_i = \dfrac{1}{\sum_{j \in V} P_{ij}}$.

(3) *Largest connected component* (LCC): The community edges form a trust-aware community overlay with the peers sharing similar contents. However, it will be highly probable that the trust-aware overly graph will be a disconnected graph. LCC is the largest connected component of this disconnected graph. LCC of the network can be taken as a measure of the goodness of the community structure.

A discrete time simulator written in C is used for simulation. In simulation, 6000 peer nodes, 18000 connectivity edges, 32 content categories are chosen. To make their detection difficult, the malicious peers occasionally provide authentic files with a probability known as the *degree of deception*. The value of this probability is taken as 0.1. The value of *degree of rewiring* is taken as 0.3. Due to formation of the semantic edges, the degrees of the peers are allowed to increase maximum to the extent of 30%. The TTL values for BFS and DFS are taken as 5s and 10 s respectively. Barabasi-Alabert generator is used to generate initial power law graphs with 6000 nodes and 18000 edges. The number of searches per generation and the number of generations per cycle are taken as 5000 and 100 respectively.

To check the robustness of the algorithm against attack from malicious peers, the percentage of malicious peers is gradually increased. Fig. 4 illustrates the cost incurred by each type of peers (honest and malicious) to download authentic files. It is evident that with the increase in the percentage of malicious peers, cost for malicious peers to download authentic files decreases. The reverse is the case for honest peers.

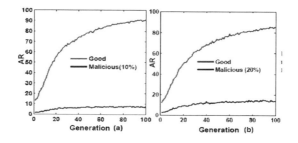

Fig. 4. AR vs. percentage of malicious nodes. In (a) 10%, in (b) 20% nodes are malicious.

Fig. 5 depicts the size of LCC for each of the 32 content categories. It may be observed that the average size of LCC for all content categories remains the same even if the percentage of malicious peers increases. This shows that the community formation among the honest peers is not affected by the presence of malicious nodes.

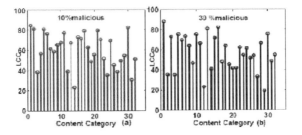

Fig. 5. Largest connected components for peers having different content categories

Fig. 6 presents how the *closeness centrality* (CC) of good and malicious peers varies in the community topology. It may be observed that the steady state value of CC for honest peers is around 0.12, irrespective of the percentage of malicious peers in the network. However, for the malicious peers, the CC value is found to lie between 0.03 to 0.07. This implies that the malicious peers are effectively driven to the fringe of the network while the good peers are rewarded.

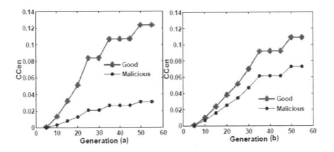

Fig. 6. Closeness centrality for (a) 20% and (b) 40% $Prob_{com}$ malicious nodes in the network

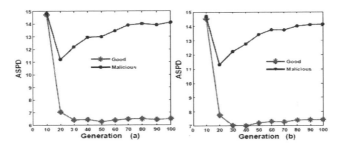

Fig. 7. Avg. shortest path length vs generations of search at the step of ten for various percentages of malicious peers. In (a) 30% and in (b) 40% nodes are malicious.

Higher values of CC also indicate that good peers have smaller average shortest path length between them. In the simulation, the diameter of the initial network is taken as 5. At the end of one simulation run, if there is no path between a pair of peers using community edges, then the length of the shortest path between that pair is assumed to be arbitrarily long, say 15 (used in Fig. 7). The *average shortest path distance* (ASPD) decreases for both honest and malicious nodes. However, the rate and the extent of decrease for honest peers are much higher due to the formation of semantic communities. For malicious peers, after an initial fall, the value of ASPD increases consistently and finally reaches the maximum value of 15. On the other hand, the average value of ASPD for honest peers is observed to be around 6. Since the honest nodes are connected with shorter paths, the query propagations will also faster for these nodes. This justifies the smaller value of TTL used in the simulation.

5 Conclusion

In this paper, a mechanism is proposed that solves multiple problems in peer-to-peer network e.g., inauthentic download, and poor search scalability and combating free riders. It is shown that by topology adaptation, it is possible to isolate the malicious peers while providing topologically advantageous positions to the good peers so that good peers get faster and authentic responses to their queries. Simulation results have demonstrated that the protocol is robust in presence of a large percentage of malicious peers. Analysis of message overhead of the protocol constitutes a future plan of work.

References

1. Risson, J., Moors, T.: Survey of Research Towards Robust Peer-to-Peer Networks. Computer Networks 50(7), 3485–3521 (2006)
2. Schafer, J., Malinks, K., Hanacek, P.: Peer-to-Peer Networks Security. In: Proc. of the 3rd Int. Conf. on Internet Monitoring and Protection (ICIMP), pp. 74–79 (2008)
3. de Mello, E.R., van Moorsel, A., da Silva Fraga, J.: Evaluation of P2P Search Algorithms for Discovering Trust Paths. In: Wolter, K. (ed.) EPEW 2007. LNCS, vol. 4748, pp. 112–124. Springer, Heidelberg (2007)
4. Li, X., Wang, J.: A Global Trust Model of P2P Network Based on Distance-Weighted Recommendation. In: Proc. of IEEE Int. Conf. of Networking, Architecture and Storage, pp. 281–284 (2009)
5. Condie, T., Kamvar, S.D., Garcia-Molina, H.: Adaptive Peer-to-Peer Topologies. In: Proc. of the 4th Int. Conf. on Peer-to-Peer Computing (P2P 2004), pp. 53–62 (2004)
6. Tain, H., Zou, S., Wang, W., Cheng, S.: Constructing Efficient Peer-to-Peer Overlay Topologies by Adaptive Connection Establishment. Computer Communication 29(17), 3567–3579 (2006)
7. Crespo, A., Garcia-Molina, H.: Semantic Overlay Networks for P2P Systems. Technical Report, Stanford University (2002)
8. Schlosser, M.T., Condie, T.E., Kamvar, S.D., Kamvar, A.D.: Simulating a P2P File-Sharing Network. In: Proc. of the 1st Workshop on Semantics in P2P and Grid Computing (2002)

Testing Ensembles for Intrusion Detection: On the Identification of Mutated Network Scans

Silvia González[1], Javier Sedano[1], Álvaro Herrero[2], Bruno Baruque[2], and Emilio Corchado[3]

[1] Instituto Tecnológico de Castilla y León
C/ López Bravo 70, Pol. Ind. Villalonquejar, 09001 Burgos, Spain
javier.sedano@itcl.es
[2] Department of Civil Engineering, University of Burgos, Spain
C/ Francisco de Vitoria s/n, 09006 Burgos, Spain
{ahcosio,bbaruque}@ubu.es
[3] Departamento de Informática y Automática, Universidad de Salamanca
Plaza de la Merced, s/n, 37008 Salamanca, Spain
escorchado@usal.es

Abstract. In last decades there have been many proposals from the machine learning community in the intrusion detection field. One of the main problems that Intrusion Detection Systems (IDSs) - mainly anomaly-based ones - have to face are those attacks not previously seen (zero-day attacks). This paper proposes a mutation technique to test and evaluate the performance of several classifier ensembles incorporated to network-based IDSs when tackling the task of recognizing such attacks. The technique applies mutant operators that randomly modifies the features of the captured packets to generate situations that otherwise could not be provided to learning IDSs. As an example application for the proposed testing model, it has been specially applied to the identification of network scans and related mutations.

Keywords: Network Intrusion Detection, Computational Intelligence, Machine Learning, IDS Performance, Classifiers.

1 Introduction

One of the most harmful issues of attacks and intrusions, which increases the difficulty of protecting computer systems, is the ever-changing nature of attack technologies and strategies.

For that reason, among others, IDSs [1], [2], [3] have become an essential asset in addition to the computer security infrastructure of most organizations. In the context of computer networks, an IDS can roughly be defined as a tool designed to detect suspicious patterns that may be related to a network or system attack. Intrusion Detection (ID) is therefore a field that focuses on the identification of attempted or ongoing attacks on a computer system (Host IDS - HIDS) or network (Network IDS - NIDS).

ID has been approached from several different points of view up to now; many different Computational Intelligence techniques - such as Genetic Programming [4],

Á. Herrero and E. Corchado (Eds.): CISIS 2011, LNCS 6694, pp. 109–117, 2011.

Data Mining [5], [6], [7], Expert Systems [8], Fuzzy Logic [9], or Neural Networks [10], [11], [12] among others - together with statistical [13] and signature verification [14] techniques have been applied mainly to perform a 2-class classification (normal/anomalous or intrusive/non-intrusive).

IDS evaluation is not a clear cut task [15]. Previous works have presented several techniques to test and evaluate misuse detection models for network-based IDSs. A testing technique to prove the effectiveness and capability of any visualization-based IDS, employing numerical data to confront unknown attacks has been previously proposed [16], [17]. In this case, the method is used to asses different classifiers in the detection of mutated network scans. The ability to detect such scans can help identifying wider and potentially more dangerous threats to a network. The main advantage of this testing model is that it provides the classifiers with brand new attacks - network scans in this case -.

A port scan may be defined as a series of messages sent to different port numbers to gain information on their activity status. These messages can be sent by an external agent attempting to access a host to find out more about the network services the host is providing. A port scan provides information on where to probe for weaknesses, for which reason scanning generally precedes any further intrusive activity. This work focuses on the identification of network scans, in which the same port is the target for a number of computers. A network scan is one of the most common techniques used to identify services that might then be accessed without permission [18].

The remaining sections of this study are structured as follows: section 2 introduces the proposed testing technique. While the applied classifiers are described in section 3, experimental results are presented in section 4. The conclusions of this study are discussed in section 5, as well as future work.

2   A Mutation Testing Technique for IDSs

Testing an ID tool is the only way to establish its effectiveness. This paper focuses on checking the performance of IDSs when confronting with unknown anomalous situations.

Misuse IDSs based on signatures rely on models of known attacks. The effectiveness of these IDSs depends on the "goodness" of their models. This is to say, if a model of an attack does not cover all the possible modifications, the performance of the IDS will be greatly impaired.

The proposed mutation testing model was previously applied to a visualization-based IDS [16], [17] and is based on mutating attack traffic. In general, a mutation can be defined as a random change. In keeping with this idea, the testing model modifies different features of the numerical information extracted from the packet headers.

The modifications created by this model may involve changes in aspects such as: attack length (amount of time that each attack lasts), packet density (number of packets per time unit), attack density (number of attacks per time unit) and time intervals between attacks. The mutations can also concern both source and destination ports, varying between the different three ranges of TCP/UDP port numbers: well known (from 0 to 1023), registered (from 1024 to 49151) and dynamic and/or private (from 49152 to 65535).

Time is another fascinating issue of great importance when considering intrusions since the chance of detecting an attack increases in relation to its duration. There are therefore two main strategies:

- Drastically reduce the time used to perform a scan.
- Spread the packets out over time, which is to say, reduce the number of packets sent per time unit that are likely to slip by unnoticed.

In this study, the mutations are applied to data related to network scans. It should be taken into account that any of the possible mutations may be meaningless such as a sweep of less than 5 hosts in the case of a network scan.

Changes can be made to attack packets taking the following issues into account:

- Number of scans in the attack (that is, number of addressed port numbers).
- Destination port numbers at which scans are aimed.
- Time intervals when scans are performed.
- Number of packets (density) forming the scans (number of scanned hosts).

3   Classifiers and Ensembles

As previously explained, one of the most interesting features of IDSs would be their capability to automatically detect whether a portion of the traffic circulating the network is an attack or normal traffic. Automated learning techniques are algorithms designed specifically for the purpose of deciding about new presented data.

Usually that kind of algorithms suffer from common problems, such as the over-fitting to the data used for training - and therefore, poor generalization capabilities -, the stuck on local minima in their learning function or a high computational complexity when dealing with complex data. One of the most widespread and useful techniques in order to avoid such problems is the ensemble learning scheme [19], [20]. The main idea behind this kind of meta-algorithms is to train several slightly different simpler classifiers and combine their results in order to improve the results obtained by a single, usually more complex, one [21].

In the present study several of these algorithms have been considered both for the base classifiers and for the ensemble training in order to have a significant wide array of possible algorithms to compare their performance results on mutated data sets.

Among the base classifiers, it should be mentioned clustering algorithms such as the k-Nearest Neighbours (IBK) [22], instance-based statistical classification algorithms such as the Simple Classification and Regression Decision Tree (CART) [23] and the REP-Tree [24] and artificial neural-network such as the Radial Basis Function Network [25].

Among the ensemble meta-algorithms that make use of the previous mentioned simple algorithms, the test performed has made use of basic algorithms such as the MultiClass Classifier [26], used to adapt binary classifiers to multi-class problems, Bagging [27], Adaptative Boosting (AdaBoost) [28], or Random Forest [29] and compared their results with more modern boosting algorithms such as the LogitBoost [30] or the StackingC [31]. As results prove, ensemble learning adds an important value to the analysis, as almost all variants consistently improve results obtained by the single classifier.

4 Experimental Results

This section describes the datasets used for evaluating the proposed testing method and how they were generated. Then, the obtained results are also detailed.

4.1 Datasets

Real-life datasets have been previously applied to perform ID [16], [17], it has been proved that this low-dimensional datasets allow the detection of some anomalous situations [11]. Packets travelling along the network are characterized by using a set of features, extracted from the packet headers contribute to build up the neural-network input vector, $x \in \Re^5$; these features can be listed as follows:

- Timestamp: the time the packet was sent.
- Source port: the port number of the device that sent the packet.
- Destination port: the port number of the target host, i.e. the host to which the packet is sent.
- Protocol ID: an integer number that identifies the protocol over TCP of the packet.
- Size: the packet size (in Bytes).

From these datasets, one of them was selected as the original one that was later mutated. It contained examples of two different attacks:

- Three different network scans aimed at port numbers 161, 162 and 3750. A time difference between the first and the last packet included in each sweep of 17 866 ms for port number 161, 22773 ms for port number 162 and 17755 ms for port number 3750.
- An MIB (Management Information Base) information transfer event. This anomalous situation and its potential risks are fully described in [17], [32].

On the basis of this original dataset, several mutations were generated according to the testing technique previously described.

Several testing data sets containing the following key features were obtained by mutating different characteristics of the original data:

- Case 1 (modifying both the amount of scans and the destination ports):
  - Data set 1.- only one scan: port 3750.
  - Data set 2.- two scans: ports 161 and 162.
  - Data set 3.- only one scan: port 1734.
  - Data set 4.- two scans: ports 4427 and 4439.
- Case 2 (modifying both time and the number of scans):
  - Data set 5.- three time-expanded scans: ports 161, 162 and 3750.
  - Data set 6.- three time-contracted scans: ports 161, 162 and 3750.
  - Data set 7.- one time-expanded scan: port 3750.
- Case 3 (modifying both the amount of packets and the destination ports):
  - Data set 8.- two 5-packet scans: ports 4427 and 4439.
  - Data set 9.- two 30-packet scans: ports 1434 and 65788.

The first issue to consider is the amount of scans. Data sets containing 1 scan (Data sets 1, 3 and 7), 2 sweeps (Data sets 2, 4, 8 and 9) or 3 sweeps (Data sets 5 and 6) have been used. Each scan is aimed at a different port number. The implications are crystal clear; hackers can check the vulnerability of as many services/protocols as they want.

A scan attempting to check port protocol/service can be aimed at any port number (from 0 to 65535). The data sets contain scans aimed at port numbers such as 161 and 162 (well known ports assigned to Simple Network Management Protocol), 1434 (registered port assigned to Microsoft-SQL-Monitor, the target of the W32.SQLExp.Worm), 3750 (registered port assigned to CBOS/IP ncapsalation), 4427 and 4439 (registered ports, as yet unassigned) and 65,788 (dynamic or private port).

In order to check the performance of the described ensembles in relation to the time-related strategies, data sets 5, 6 and 7 have been used. Data set 5 was obtained by spreading the packets contained in the three different scans (161, 162 and 3750) over the captured session. In this data set, there is a time difference of 247360 ms between the first (in the sweep aimed at port 161) and the last scan packet (in the scan aimed at port 3750). The duration of the captured session (all the packets contained in the data set) is 262198 ms, whereas in the original data set the scan lasts 164907 ms. In the case of data set 7, the same mutation has been performed but only for packets relating to the scan aimed at port 3750. On the other hand, the strategy of reducing the time was used to obtain data set 6. In this case, the time difference between the first and the last packet is about 109938 ms.

Finally, the number of packets contained in each scan was also considered. In the case of a network scan, each packet means a different host targeted by the scan. Data

Table 1. Results on data set 6 (two classes)

Ensembles	Classifier	Correctly Classified Instances
FilteredClassifier	MLP, REPTree, PART, id3, SMO, SMOreg, Winnow, SPegasos	Training (99.983%) Classification (100%)
Adaboost	JRip	Training (99.983%) Classification (100%)
MultiboostAB	JRip	Training (99.983%) Classification (100%)
MultiboostAB	REPTree	Training (99.9489%) Classification (100%)
RandomSubSpace	REPTree	Training (99.983%) Classification (100%)
RandomSubSpace	SImpleCart	Training (99.9659%) Classification (100%)
RotationForest	REPTree and PART	Training (99.983%) for both Classification (100%) for both
AttributeSelectedClassifier	SImpleCart	Training (99.8636 %) Classification (100%)
Bagging	REPTree	Training (99.9659%) Classification (100%)

sets 8 and 9 were designed in complying with this idea. Data set 8 contains low-density scans given that they have been reduced to only 5 packets. It was decided that a scan aimed at less than 5 hosts should not constitute a network scan. On the other hand, data set 9 contains medium-density scans. In this case, each one of them has been extended to 30 packets.

4.2 Results

For the sake of brevity, experiments were conducted only on two of the data sets described above: data set 6 and 9. All the classifiers were trained on the original data-set, comprising an MIB information transfer and scans aimed at port numbers 161, 162 and 3750.

To check the performance of the classifier ensembles when confronting different numbers of classes, the data sets were labeled in a different way. Two different labels were assigned to packets in dataset 6, differentiating attacks from normal traffic. On the other hand, four different classes were defined for data set 9, namely: normal, scan#1, scan#2, and MIB transfer.

Table 2. Results on data set 9 (four classes)

Ensembles	Classifier	Correctly Classified Instances
FilteredClassifier	MLP, REPTree, PART, id3, SMO	Training (99.9489%) for MLP Training (99.8977%) for Reptree Training (99.9489%) for PART Training (99.9148%) for id3 Training (99.9659%) for SMO Classification (81.25%) for all of then. 12 errors in the one of the classes.
Adaboost	JRip	Training (99.9148%) Classification (100%)
MultiboostAB	JRip	Training (99.9148%) Classification (100%)
MultiboostAB	REPTree	Training (99.983%) Classification (100%)
RandomSubSpace	REPTree	Training (99.9659%) Classification (100%)
RandomSubSpace	SImpleCart	Training (99.983%) Classification (100%)
RotationForest	REPTree and PART	Training (99.983%) for RepTree Classification (89.0625%) for RepTree. Training (99.983%) for PART Classification (53.125%) for PART.
AttributeSelectedClassifier	SImpleCart	Training (99.983%) Classification (100%)
Bagging	REPTree	Training (99.983%) Classification (100%)

WEKA software [33] was used to train and classify the data sets, with various ensembles and classifiers. In the experimentation, cross validation is used with a value of 10 K-fold. Tables 1 and 2 show the training and validation/classification performance of the applied models.

From Tables 1 and 2, it can be concluded that classification models are able to carry out the classification of the two data sets and get the right classification for more than 99.9% of the classes.

Table 3 shows the characteristics and options of the chosen ensembles, together with their tuned values.

Table 3. Selected options of the ensembles for experimental study

Ensembles	Options
FilteredClassifier	Name of the filter "Discretize"
Adaboost	Number of boost iterations (10), seed for resampling (1), use resampling instead of reweighting (false), percentage of weight mass (100).
MultiboostAB	Number of boost iterations (10), number of sub-committees (3), seed for resampling (1), use resampling instead of reweighting (false), percentage of weight mass (100).
RandomSubSpace	Number of iterations (10), Size of each subSpace (0.5), seed for resampling (1).
RotationForest	Maximum size of a group (3), Minimum size of a group (3), number of iterations to be performed (10), number of groups (false), filter used "Principal Components", percentage of instances to be removed (50), seed for resampling (1).
AttributeSelectedClassifier	Name of an attribute evaluator (CfsSubsetEval), name of a search method (BestFirst).
Bagging	Size of each bag (100), compute out of bag error (False), number of bagging iterations (10), seed for resampling (1).

5   Conclusions and Future Work

This paper has proposed a mutation testing model for classifiers ensembles performing ID on numerical traffic data sets. It is aimed at assessing the generalization capability of the applied classifiers when confronting with zero-day attacks.

Experimental results show that the applied classifier ensembles properly deal with the analyzed data, containing mutated network scans. It can then be concluded that the applied models are able to properly detect new attacks related with previously unseen scans.

Future work will be based on the mutation of some other attack situations and the broadening of considered classifiers and ensembles.

Acknowledgments

This research has been partially supported through the project of the Spanish Ministry of Science and Innovation TIN2010-21272-C02-01 (funded by the European

Regional Development Fund). The authors would also like to thank the vehicle interior manufacturer, Grupo Antolin Ingenieria S.A., within the framework of the MAGNO2008 - 1028.- CENIT Project also funded by the MICINN, the Spanish Ministry of Science and Innovation PID 560300-2009-11 and the Junta de Castilla y Len CCTT/10/BU/0002.

References

1. Computer Security Threat Monitoring and Surveillance. Technical Report. James P. Anderson Co. (1980)
2. Denning, D.E.: An Intrusion-Detection Model. IEEE Transactions on Software Engineering 13(2), 222–232 (1987)
3. Chih-Fong, T., Yu-Feng, H., Chia-Ying, L., Wei-Yang, L.: Intrusion Detection by Machine Learning: A Review. Expert Systems with Applications 36(10), 11994–12000 (2009)
4. Abraham, A., Grosan, C., Martin-Vide, C.: Evolutionary Design of Intrusion Detection Programs. International Journal of Network Security 4(3), 328–339 (2007)
5. Julisch, K.: Data Mining for Intrusion Detection: A Critical Review. In: Applications of Data Mining in Computer Security. AIS, pp. 33–62. Kluwer Academic Publishers, Dordrecht (2002)
6. Giacinto, G., Roli, F., Didaci, L.: Fusion of Multiple Classifiers for Intrusion Detection in Computer Networks. Pattern Recognition Letters 24(12), 1795–1803 (2003)
7. Chebrolu, S., Abraham, A., Thomas, J.P.: Feature Deduction and Ensemble Design of Intrusion Detection Systems. Computers & Security 24(4), 295–307 (2005)
8. Kim, H.K., Im, K.H., Park, S.C.: DSS for Computer Security Incident Response Applying CBR and Collaborative Response. Expert Systems with Applications 37(1), 852–870 (2010)
9. Tajbakhsh, A., Rahmati, M., Mirzaei, A.: Intrusion Detection using Fuzzy Association Rules. Applied Soft Computing 9(2), 462–469 (2009)
10. Sarasamma, S.T., Zhu, Q.M.A., Huff, J.: Hierarchical Kohonenen Net for Anomaly Detection in Network Security. IEEE Transactions on Systems Man and Cybernetics, Part B 35(2), 302–312 (2005)
11. Herrero, Á., Corchado, E., Gastaldo, P., Zunino, R.: Neural Projection Techniques for the Visual Inspection of Network Traffic. Neurocomputing 72(16-18), 3649–3658 (2009)
12. Zhang, C., Jiang, J., Kamel, M.: Intrusion Detection using Hierarchical Neural Networks. Pattern Recognition Letters 26(6), 779–791 (2005)
13. Marchette, D.J.: Computer Intrusion Detection and Network Monitoring: A Statistical Viewpoint. In: Information Science and Statistics. Springer, New York (2001)
14. Roesch, M.: Snort–Lightweight Intrusion Detection for Networks. In: 13th Systems Administration Conference (LISA 1999), pp. 229–238 (1999)
15. Ranum, M.J.: Experiences Benchmarking Intrusion Detection Systems. NFR Security Technical Publications (2001)
16. Corchado, E., Herrero, Á., Sáiz, J.M.: Testing CAB-IDS Through Mutations: On the Identification of Network Scans. In: Gabrys, B., Howlett, R.J., Jain, L.C. (eds.) KES 2006. LNCS (LNAI), vol. 4252, pp. 433–441. Springer, Heidelberg (2006)
17. Corchado, E., Herrero, Á.: Neural Visualization of Network Traffic Data for Intrusion Detection. Applied Soft Computing 11(2), 2042–2056 (2011)

18. Abdullah, K., Lee, C., Conti, G., Copeland, J.A.: Visualizing Network Data for Intrusion Detection. In: Sixth Annual IEEE Information Assurance Workshop - Systems, Man and Cybernetics, pp. 100–108 (2005)
19. Sharkey, A.J.C., Sharkey, N.E.: Combining Diverse Neural Nets. Knowledge Engineering Review 12(3), 231–247 (1997)
20. Polikar, R.: Ensemble Based Systems in Decision Making. IEEE Circuits and Systems Magazine 6(3), 21–45 (2006)
21. Ruta, D., Gabrys, B.: An Overview of Classifier Fusion Methods. Computing and Information Systems 7(1), 1–10 (2000)
22. Bailey, T., Jain, A.: A Note on Distance-Weighted k-Nearest Neighbor Rules. IEEE Transactions on Systems, Man and Cybernetics 8(4), 311–313 (1978)
23. Breiman, L., Friedman, J.H., Olshen, R.A., Stone, C.J.: Classification and Regression Trees, p. 358. Wadsworth Inc., Belmont (1984)
24. Zhao, Y., Zhang, Y.: Comparison of Decision Tree Methods for Finding Active Objects. Advances in Space Research 41(12), 1955–1959 (2008)
25. Moody, J., Darken, C.J.: Fast Learning in Networks of Locally-tuned Processing Units. Neural Computation 1(2), 281–294 (1989)
26. Allwein, E.L., Schapire, R.E., Singer, Y.: Reducing Multiclass to Binary: a Unifying Approach for Margin Classifiers. Journal of Machine Learning Research 1, 113–141 (2001)
27. Breiman, L.: Bagging Predictors. Machine Learning 24(2), 123–140 (1996)
28. Freund, Y., Schapire, R.E.: Experiments with a New Boosting Algorithm. In: International Conference on Machine Learning, pp. 148–156 (1996)
29. Breiman, L.: Random Forests. Machine Learning 45(1), 5–32 (2001)
30. Friedman, J., Hastie, T., Tibshirani, R.: Additive Logistic Regression: a Statistical View of Boosting. The Annals of Statistics 28(2), 337–407 (2000)
31. Seewald, A.K.: How to Make Stacking Better and Faster While Also Taking Care of an Unknown Weakness. In: Nineteenth International Conference on Machine Learning. Morgan Kaufmann Publishers Inc., San Francisco (2002)
32. Corchado, E., Herrero, Á., Sáiz, J.M.: Detecting Compounded Anomalous SNMP Situations Using Cooperative Unsupervised Pattern Recognition. In: Duch, W., Kacprzyk, J., Oja, E., Zadrożny, S. (eds.) ICANN 2005. LNCS, vol. 3697, pp. 905–910. Springer, Heidelberg (2005)
33. Hall, M., Frank, E., Holmes, G., Pfahringer, B., Reutemann, P., Witten, I.H.: The WEKA Data Mining Software: An Update. ACM SIGKDD Explorations Newsletter 11(1), 10–18 (2009)

An Intelligent Information Security Mechanism for the Network Layer of WSN: BIOSARP

Kashif Saleem, Norsheila Fisal, Sharifah Hafizah, and Rozeha A. Rashid

Telematic Research Group, Faculty of Electrical Engineering,
Universiti Teknologi Malaysia
81310 Skudai, Malaysia
{kashif_pg,sheila,sharifah,rozeha}@fke.utm.my

Abstract. In multihop wireless sensor network (WSN) users or nodes are constantly entering and leaving the network. Classical techniques for network management and control are not conceived to efficiently face such challenges. New mechanisms are required, to work in a self-organized manner. The techniques found in nature promises WSN, to self-adapt the environmental changes and also self-protect itself from the malicious stuff. This paper introduces a biological inspired secure autonomous routing protocol (BIOSARP). The self-optimized routing protocol is enhanced with artificial Immune System (AIS) based autonomous security mechanism. It enhances WSN in securing itself from the abnormalities and most common WSN routing attacks. NS2 based simulation analysis and results of BIOSARP are presented. The comparison of proposed intelligent protocol with SAID and SRTLD security mechanisms for WSN is further exhibited, in terms of processing time and energy consumption.

Keywords: Artificial Immune system, Human Immune Blood Brain Barrier System, Human Immune System, Intelligence, Self-Optimization, Self-Security, Wireless Sensor Network.

1 Introduction

Wireless communication plays an important role in telecommunication sector and has huge importance for future research. The communication is making the world's life easier with the development of sensing and monitoring systems. In these sensing and monitoring systems new gadgets and software advancement are frequently available to the end-user. In infrastructure less networks such as WSN, the deployment area may be out of human reach. The challenges such as growing complexity, unreachable maintenance and unsecure communication demand for mechanism that can maintain the features of WSN such as multihop routing in dynamically changing environmental in a complete autonomous mode. In order to address autonomous capability for multihop ad-hoc network, it has been visualize that self-organized and self-secure network application can fully realize the network operational objectives.

Probabilistic methods that provide scalability and preventability can be found in nature and adapted to technology. Towards this vision, it is observed that various biological principles are capable to overcome the above adaptability issues. The most

Á. Herrero and E. Corchado (Eds.): CISIS 2011, LNCS 6694, pp. 118–126, 2011.

well-known bio-inspired mechanism is the swarm intelligence (ANT Colony, Particle swarm), AIS and intercellular information exchange (Molecular biology)[1-4]. Many of AIS based algorithms, bee inspired algorithms such as BeeAdHoc [5], BiSNET/e [3] have been reported. However, self-healable security is still an open issue. Widespread acceptance and adaptation of these protocols in real world wireless networks would not be possible until their security aspects have thoroughly investigated [4]. [4] propose misbehaviour detection in nature inspired MANET protocol, BeeAdHoc.

This paper introduces the architecture for implementing BIOlogical Inspired Secure Autonomous Routing Protocol (BIOSARP) consist an autonomous security management module on top of BIOARP [6].This paper is particularly on BIOSARP autonomous security module. The ACO based routing part BIOARP has been discussed in [6-8]. BIOSARP is based on the behaviour of human immune system (HIS). As HIS provides the complete security and protection to human body. The major aspect of HIS is to detect the anomalies by differentiating between self and non-self entities. The HIS security is used in the computer world with the name of artificial immune system (AIS).

General AIS algorithms are very complex and impracticable for WSN. The proposed AIS for BIOSARP algorithm is the extension of SRTLD [9] and SAID [10]. While implementing BIOSARP, the complexity factor is taken under consideration. Moreover, the blood brain barrier (BBB) system is enabled in BIOSARP in the initialization and learning period. These techniques will be accomplished by assigning each procedure to several groups of agents. These agents will work in a decentralized way to collect data and/or detect an event on individual nodes and carry data to the required destination. BIOSARP provides autonomous security, the mechanism overcomes the message alter, wormhole, sinkhole Sybil, selective forwarding and HELLO flood attacks.

The next section reviews the related research for self-security using AIS approaches. Section 3 describes the BIOSARP implementation. Section 4 shows the results and comparisons. The conclusion and future work are discussed in section 5.

2   Related Research

Wireless sensor nodes are mostly deployed in the unprotected/hostile environment. Therefore, it is easier for WSN to suffer with a number of attacks, due to sensor nodes resource constraints and vulnerabilities. These attacks involve signal jamming and eavesdropping, tempering, spoofing, resource exhaustion, altered or replayed routing information, selective forwarding, sinkhole attacks, Sybil attacks, wormhole attacks, flooding attacks and etc [11]. Many papers have proposed prevention countermeasures of these attacks and the majority of them are based on encryption and authentication. These prevention measures in WSN can reduce intrusion to some extent. In this case, intrusion detection system (IDS) can work as second secure defence of WSN to further reduce attacks and insulate attackers.

2.1 Overview of AIS Based Security in WSN

Overview of AIS based Security in WSN: In [10], the authors have proposed SAID with three-logic-layer architecture. SAID adopt the merits of local, distributive & cooperative IDS and is self-adaptive for intrusion detection of resource-constraint WSN. Knowledge base is deployed base station where the complex algorithm for agent evolution can be computed and intrusion rules can be stored.

2.2 Overview of Keying Based Security in WSN

Due to the factor of initialization phase, WSN need security mechanism to be in operation before the network deployment. As stated in [12] Node cloning attacks can be mounted only during deployment since a cloned node cannot initiate the protocol with success. It can be successfully connected only by acting as a responding node. Recent progress in implementation of elliptic curve cryptography (ECC) on sensors proves public key cryptography (PKC) is now feasible for resource constrained sensors [13]. The performance of PKC based security schemes is still not well investigated due to the special hardware characteristics.

In [9] the author presents the security enhancement which uses encryption and decryption with authentication of the packet header to supplement secure packet transfer. SRTLD solves the problem of producing real random number problem using random generator function encrypted with mathematical function. The output of random function is used to encrypt specific header fields in the packet such as source, destination addresses and packet ID. In this mechanism they assume that each sensor node is static, aware of its location and the sink is a trusted computing base.

Security in natural inspired routing protocols is still an open issue [4].

3 BIOSARP Security Architecture and Methodology

BIOARP is enriched with an autonomous security management; preliminary work is illustrated in [14]. We have divided the jobs among the agents. Agent works on two-layered architecture, agent layer on the top and wireless sensor network on bottom as shown in Figure 1.

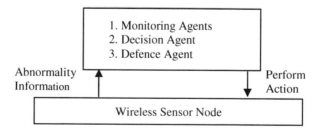

Fig. 1. Two layer BIOSARP Self-Security Architecture

The autonomous security module cooperates with the routing management, neighbour management and power management modules to provide secure autonomous routing protocol for WSN. Whenever the neighbour table is checked to select the optimal node, the neighbouring node behaviour is monitored in the routing management. As soon as the abnormal behaviour is detected, the information is passed to security management module. The security module then matches the neighbouring node characteristics with the given threshold. If any neighbouring node mismatches, the security module classifies it as non-self and remove entry from neighbour table.

The flow of the system is elaborated with the help of flowchart as shown in Figure 2. Whenever routing management module wants to select the next best node, the monitoring agent checks the behaviour of neighbouring nodes. First, the numbers of records are counted in neighbour table. If no record is found the checking process is deferred until the neighbours are discovered. Otherwise, the behaviour checking continues with the initialization of variables as shown in Table 1.

After initialization the correlation coefficient function is called which determines the relationship difference between x and y arrays. The correlation coefficient is a statistical function as shown by Equation 1 to calculate the relation between two groups of same entity. The statistical matching rule produces a number between -1 and 1 that relates how similar the two input sequences are.

$$x, y \in \{0...255\}^{N}, N = 1/8, \rho = \frac{\sum_{i=1}^{n}(X_i - \bar{X})(Y_i - \bar{Y})}{\sqrt{\sum_{i=1}^{n}(X_i - \bar{X})^2 \sum_{i=1}^{n}(Y_i - \bar{Y})^2}} \qquad [10] \qquad (1)$$

If the relation is having less or equal difference according to the given error rate, the process jumps to the selection criteria. Else, if the variation goes beyond detection agent is called to thoroughly check entry-by-entry in the current neighbour table. In the inspection, if any neighbouring nodes characteristics exceed the given threshold, the particular neighbour node is categorized as non-self by the decision agent. The decision based on the Equation 2 to classify node as self or non-self. After classification, the defence agent removes the non-self neighbouring nodes from the neighbouring table. Onwards ACO based routing procedure continues with $p^{k}_{ij}(t)$ as explained in [6].

$$\text{match } (f, \mathcal{E}, I, D) = \begin{cases} malicious, f\,(I, \alpha) \geq 1 - \\ benign, otherwise \end{cases} \qquad [10] \qquad (2)$$

where, I = Input string, D = Decision Agent's matching String, f = Matching Function, $\mathcal{E}$ = Matching Threshold.

Table 1. Security Parameters

	Packet Receiving Rate	*Energy*		*Packet Mismatch Rate*	*Packet Receiving Rate*
Tackled Attacks	Sink hole attack [15]	To make relationship with		Message alter attack[15]	To make relationship with
Node 1	x_1^{1}	y_1^{1}		x_2^{1}	y_2^{1}
Node 2	x_1^{2}	y_1^{2}		x_2^{2}	y_2^{2}
.	.	.		.	.
.	.	.		.	.
.	.	.		.	.
Node n	x_1^{n}	y_1^{n}		x_2^{n}	y_2^{n}

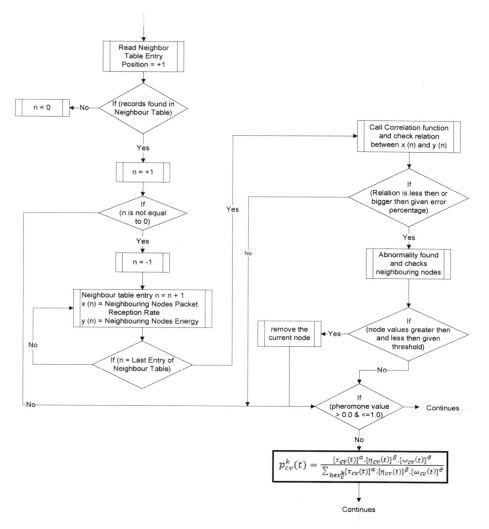

Fig. 2. Flow Chart of BIOSARP Autonomous Security Management

BIOSARP is additionally enhanced with BBB system that secures WSN communication even in the initialization and learning phase. BBB is based on packet encryption and decryption, the work done on SRTLD [9]. In addition, the output of random generator function is used to encrypt specific header fields in the packet such as source, destination addresses and packet ID.

4   Results and Comparisons

In the simulation study, NS-2 simulator is used to develop BIOSARP functional modules. Figure 3 shows the countermeasures against abnormalities found in WSN.

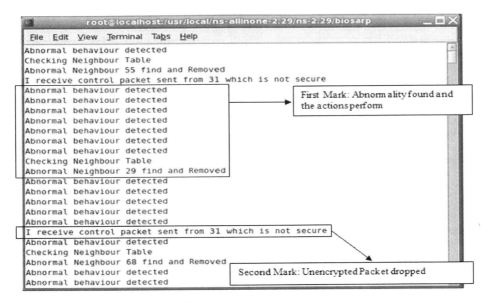

Fig. 3. NS-2 showing the Abnormality and actions taken against certain nodes

The simulation scenario is maintained as in [10] for BIOSARP and SAID comparison. When network has suffered attack by 10 malicious nodes, the power consumption value increased. Once the AIS self-security measure starts functioning, the energy consummation starts to reduce. And as soon as the malicious nodes stop attacking, the power consumption comes to the normal situation as observe at 450th sec in Figure 4.

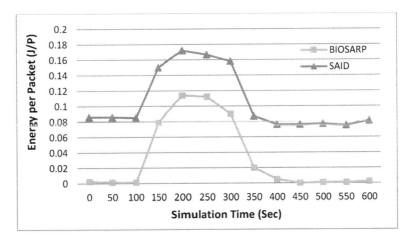

Fig. 4. BIOSARP & SAID Comparison in terms of Energy

Figure 5 shows the performance of BIOSARP as the number of compromised node increases from 4 to 20. In Figure 5, the power consumption increases as the number of compromised nodes increases in order to overcome the routing hole problem. Figure 6 shows the comparison of BIOSARP with SRTLD in terms on energy consumption. WSN simulator consists of 121 nodes are distributed in 80m x 80m region. Nodes numbered as 120, 110, 100 and 90 are the source nodes, node 0 is the sink node and 29, 25, 31 and 36 are adversary nodes.

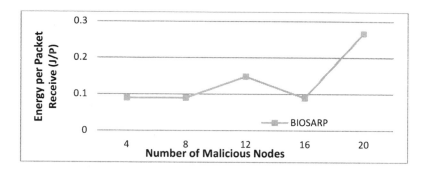

Fig. 5. Influence of increasing compromised nodes in network performance in terms of power consumption

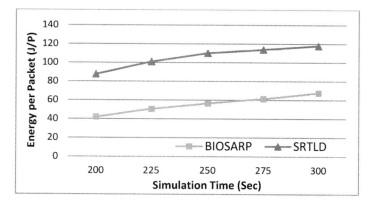

Fig. 6. Performance Comparisons between BIOSARP and SRTLD in Terms of Energy Consumption against Simulation Time

5   Conclusion

A biological inspired secure autonomous routing protocol is proposed named as BIOSARP for WSNs. The article elaborates the security process of finding the abnormality based on AIS. BIOSARP consumes 6% less energy as compared to SAID. In simulation BIOSARP consumes 48% less power than SRTLD. The result shows that BIOSARP outperforms SRTLD due to the several reasons. First is BIOSARP provides preventive measure using AIS that can detect abnormalities before real attacks happen. Thus additional attacks including, acknowledgement spoofing attack, altered attack, replayed routing information attack and sybil attack can be further mitigated. Other reasons include the less rediscoveries and replies in neighbour discovery, thus reduces power consumption and processing power.

Our immediate future work will involve building and testing the architecture by the implementation of proposed system in the real WSN test bed.

Acknowledgments. I wish to express my sincere appreciation, sincerest gratitude to Ministry of Higher Education Malaysia for their full support and to Research Management Center, Universiti Teknologi Malaysia (UTM) for their contribution and special thanks to researchers in Telematic Research Group, UTM.

References

1. Balasubramaniam, S., Botvich, D., Donnelly, W., Foghluh, M., Strassner, J.: Biologically Inspired Self-Governance and Self-Organisation for Autonomic Networks. In: Proceedings of the 1st International Conference on Bio Inspired Models of Network, Information and Computing Systems, vol. 275, p. 30. ACM, Cavalese (2006)
2. Balasubramaniam, S., Donnelly, W., Botvich, D., Agoulmine, N., Strassner, J.: Towards integrating principles of Molecular Biology for Autonomic Network Management. In: Hewlett Packard University Association (HPOVUA) Conference, Nice, France (2006)
3. Boonma, P., Suzuki, J.: MONSOON: A Coevolutionary Multiobjective Adaptation Framework for Dynamic Wireless Sensor Networks. In: Proc. of the 41st Hawaii International Conference on System Sciences (HICSS), Big Island, HI (2008)
4. Mazhar, N., Farooq, M.: BeeAIS: Artificial Immune System Security for Nature Inspired, MANET Routing Protocol, BeeAdHoc. In: de Castro, L.N., Von Zuben, F.J., Knidel, H. (eds.) ICARIS 2007. LNCS, vol. 4628, pp. 370–381. Springer, Heidelberg (2007)
5. Wedde, H.F., Farooq, M., Pannenbaecker, T., Vogel, B., Mueller, C., Meth, J., Jeruschkat, R.: BeeAdHoc: An Energy Efficient Routing Algorithm for Mobile Ad Hoc Networks Inspired by Bee Behavior. In: GECCO, vol. 1-59593-010-8/05/0006, ACM, Washington, DC (2005)
6. Saleem, K., Fisal, N., Baharudin, M.A., Ahmed, A.A., Hafizah, S., Kamilah, S.: Ant Colony Inspired Self-Optimized Routing Protocol based on Cross Layer Architecture for Wireless Sensor Networks. Wseas Transactions on Communications (WTOC) 9, 669–678 (2010)
7. Saleem, K., Fisal, N., Hafizah, S., Kamilah, S., Rashid, R., Baguda, Y.: Cross Layer based Biological Inspired Self-Organized Routing Protocol for Wireless Sensor Network. In: TENCON 2009. IEEE, Singapore (2009)
8. Saleem, K., Fisal, N., Hafizah, S., Kamilah, S., Rashid, R.: A Self-Optimized Multipath Routing Protocol for Wireless Sensor Networks. International Journal of Recent Trends in Engineering (IJRTE) 2 (2009)
9. Ali, A., Fisal, N.: Security enhancement for real-time routing protocol in wireless sensor networks. In: 5th IFIP International Conference on Wireless and Optical Communications Networks, WOCN 2008, pp. 1–5 (2008)
10. Ma, J., Zhang, S., Zhong, Y., Tong, X.: SAID: A Self-Adaptive Intrusion Detection System in Wireless Sensor Networks. Information Security Applications, 60–73 (2007)
11. Pathan, A.K., Lee, H.W., Hong, C.S.: Security in Wireless Sensor Networks: Issues and Challenges. In: Proceedings of 8th IEEE ICACT 2006, Phoenix Park, Korea, vol. II, pp. 1043–1048 (2006)

12. Lim, C.H.: LEAP++: A Robust Key Establishment Scheme forWireless Sensor Networks. In: The 28th International Conference on Distributed Computing Systems Workshops, vol. 1545-0678/08. IEEE, Beijing (2008)

13. Wang, H., Sheng, B., Tan, C.C., Li, Q.: Comparing Symmetric-key and Public-key based Security Schemes in Sensor Networks: A Case Study of User Access Control. In: The 28th International Conference on Distributed Computing Systems, vol. 1063-6927/08. IEEE, Beijing (2008)

14. Saleem, K., Fisal, N., Abdullah, M.S., Zulkarmwan, A.B., Hafizah, S., Kamilah, S.: Proposed Nature Inspired Self-Organized Secure Autonomous Mechanism for WSNs. In: Asian Conference on Intelligent Information and Database Systems, pp. 277–282. IEEE, Quang Binh University, Dong Hoi City (2009)

15. Li, G., He, J., Fu, Y.: A Distributed Intrusion Detection Scheme for Wireless Sensor Networks. In: The 28th International Conference on Distributed Computing Systems Workshops, pp. 309–314. IEEE, Beijing (2008)

Structural Properties of Cryptographic Sequences*

A. Fúster-Sabater

Institute of Applied Physics, C.S.I.C.
Serrano 144, 28006 Madrid, Spain
amparo@iec.csic.es

Abstract. In the present work, it is shown that the binary sequences obtained from a cryptographic generator, the so-called generalized self-shrinking generator, are just particular solutions of a type of linear difference equations. Cryptographic parameters e.g. period, linear complexity or balancedness of the previous sequences can be analyzed in terms of linear equation solutions. In brief, computing the solutions of linear difference equations is an easy method of generating new sequences with guaranteed cryptographic parameters.

Keywords: pseudorandom sequence, linear difference equation, sequence generator, stream cipher, cryptography.

1 Introduction

It is a well known fact that pseudorandom binary sequences are typically used in a wide variety of applications such as: spread spectrum communication systems, multiterminal system identification, global positioning systems, software testing, error-correcting codes or cryptography. This work deals specifically with this last application.

In order to keep the confidentiality of sensitive information, an encryption function currently called *cipher* converts the *plaintext* or original message into the so-called *ciphertext*. Symmetric key encryption functions are usually divided into two separated classes: stream ciphers and block-ciphers depending on whether the encryption function is applied either to each individual bit or to a block of bits of the plaintext, respectively. Stream ciphers are the fastest among the encryption procedures so they are implemented in many technological applications e.g. RC4 for encrypting Internet traffic [13] or the encryption function E0 in Bluetooth specifications [1]. Stream ciphers try to imitate the mythic *one-time pad cipher* or *Vernam cipher* [11] and are designed to generate a long sequence (the *keystream sequence*) of pseudorandom bits. See the most

---

* This work was supported in part by CDTI (Spain) and the companies INDRA, Unión Fenosa, Tecnobit, Visual Tools, Brainstorm, SAC and Technosafe under Project Cenit-HESPERIA; by Ministry of Science and Innovation and European FEDER Fund under Project TIN2008-02236/TSI.

Á. Herrero and E. Corchado (Eds.): CISIS 2011, LNCS 6694, pp. 127–134, 2011.

recent designs in stream ciphers [4], [14]. This keystream sequence is XORed with the plaintext (in emission) in order to obtain the ciphertext or with the ciphertext (in reception) in order to recover the plaintext.

Most keystream generators are based on maximal-length Linear Feedback Shift Registers (LFSRs) [7] whose output sequences, the so-called m-sequences, are combined in a non linear way (for instance, non linear filters or irregularly decimated generators) in order to produce pseudorandom sequences of cryptographic application [5], [11]. Inside the family of irregularly decimated generators, we can enumerate: a) the *shrinking generator* proposed by Coppersmith, Krawczyk and Mansour [2] that includes two LFSRs, b) the *self-shrinking generator* designed by Meier and Staffelbach [10] involving only one LFSR and c) the *generalized self-shrinking generator* proposed by Hu and Xiao [8] that includes the self-shrinking generator. Irregularly decimated generators produce good cryptographic sequences ([6], [11], [12]) characterized by long periods, good correlation features, excellent run distribution, balancedness, simplicity of implementation, etc. The underlying idea of this kind of generators is the irregular decimation of an m-sequence according to the bits of another one. The decimation result is the output sequence that will be used as keystream sequence in the cryptographic procedure.

In this work, it is shown that the generalized self-shrinking sequences are particular solutions of a type of linear difference equations. At the same time, other solution sequences not included in the previous family also exhibit good properties for their application in cryptography. In brief, computing the solutions of linear difference equations provides one with new binary sequences whose cryptographic parameters can be easily guaranteed. That is to say, linear difference equations can contribute very efficiently to the generation of keystream sequences for stream cipher.

2   Cryptographic Generators Based on Decimations: The Generalized Self-shrinking Generator

The more general and representative of the irregularly decimated generators is the generalized self-shrinking generator [8]. It can be described as follows:

1. It makes use of two sequences: an m-sequence $\{a_n\}$ and a shifted version of such a sequence denoted by $\{v_n\}$.
2. It relates both sequences by means of a simple decimation rule to generate the output sequence.

The result of the previous steps is a family of generalized self-shrinking sequences that can be defined in a more formal way as follows [8]:

Definition 1. *Let $\{a_n\}$ be an m-sequence over $GF(2)$ with period $2^L - 1$ generated from a LFSR of primitive characteristic polynomial of degree L. Let G be an L-dimensional binary vector defined as:*

$$G = (g_0, g_1, g_2, \ldots, g_{L-1}) \in GF(2)^L. \tag{1}$$

The n-th element of the sequence $\{v_n\}$ is defined as:

$$v_n = g_0 a_n \oplus g_1 a_{n+1} \oplus g_2 a_{n+2} \oplus \ldots \oplus g_{L-1} a_{n+L-1}, \tag{2}$$

where the sub-indexes of the sequence $\{a_n\}$ are reduced mod $2^L - 1$ and the symbol $\oplus$ represents the XOR logic operation. For $n \geq 0$ the decimation rule is very simple:

1. *If $a_n = 1$, then v_n is output.*
2. *If $a_n = 0$, then v_n is discarded and there is no output bit.*

In this way, a balanced output sequence $b_0 \, b_1 \, b_2 \ldots$ denoted by $\{b_n\}$ or $\{b(G)\}$ is generated. Such a sequence is called the generalized self-shrinking sequence associated with G.

Let us see a simple example. For the 4-degree m-sequence $\{a_n\} = \{011110101$ $100100\}$ whose characteristic polynomial is $x^4 + x^3 + 1$, we get 16 generalized self-shrinking sequences based on $\{a_n\}$:

$$
\begin{aligned}
&0. \quad G = (0000), \{b(G)\} = 00000000 \sim \\
&1. \quad G = (1000), \{b(G)\} = 11111111 \sim \\
&2. \quad G = (0100), \{b(G)\} = 11100100 \sim \\
&3. \quad G = (0010), \{b(G)\} = 11011000 \sim \\
&4. \quad G = (0001), \{b(G)\} = 10101010 \sim \\
&5. \quad G = (1001), \{b(G)\} = 01010101 \sim \\
&6. \quad G = (1101), \{b(G)\} = 10110001 \sim \\
&7. \quad G = (1111), \{b(G)\} = 01101001 \sim \\
&8. \quad G = (1110), \{b(G)\} = 11000011 \sim \\
&9. \quad G = (0111), \{b(G)\} = 10010110 \sim \\
&10. \, G = (1010), \{b(G)\} = 00100111 \sim \\
&11. \, G = (0101), \{b(G)\} = 01001110 \sim \\
&12. \, G = (1101), \{b(G)\} = 10110001 \sim \\
&13. \, G = (1100), \{b(G)\} = 00011011 \sim \\
&14. \, G = (0110), \{b(G)\} = 00111100 \sim \\
&15. \, G = (0011), \{b(G)\} = 01110010 \sim
\end{aligned}
$$

Notice that the generated sequences are not 16 different sequences as some of them are shifted versions of the others.

3 Cryptographic Sequences as Solutions of Linear Difference Equations

In this section, structural properties of the previous sequences will be studied in terms of solutions of linear difference equations.

In this work, the following homogeneous linear difference equations with binary coefficients will be considered:

$$\left(E^r \oplus \sum_{j=1}^{r} c_j \, E^{r-j}\right) z_n = 0, \qquad n \geq 0 \tag{3}$$

where $z_n \in GF(2)$ is the n-th term of a binary sequence $\{z_n\}$ that satisfies the previous equation. The symbol E denotes the shifting operator that operates on the terms z_n of a solution sequence, i.e. $E^j z_n = z_{n+j}$. The coefficients c_j are binary coefficients $c_j \in GF(2)$, r is an integer and the symbol $\oplus$ represents the XOR logic operation. The r-degree characteristic polynomial of (3) is:

$$P(x) = x^r + \sum_{j=1}^{r} c_j \, x^{r-j}. \tag{4}$$

If $P(x)$ is a primitive polynomial [9] and α is one of its roots, then

$$\alpha, \, \alpha^2, \, \alpha^{2^2}, \ldots, \, \alpha^{2^{(r-1)}} \in GF(2)^r \tag{5}$$

are the r different roots of such a polynomial. In this case, it can be proved [3] that the solution of (3) is a sequence of the form:

$$z_n = \sum_{j=0}^{r-1} A^{2^j} \alpha^{2^j n}, \qquad n \geq 0 \tag{6}$$

where A is an arbitrary element in $GF(2)^r$. That is $\{z_n\}$ is an m-sequence [7] of characteristic polynomial $P(x)$ and period $2^r - 1$ whose starting point is determined by the value of A.

Let us generalize the previous difference equations to a more complex type of linear difference equations whose roots have a multiplicity greater than 1. In fact, we are going to consider difference equations of the form:

$$(E^r \oplus \sum_{j=1}^{r} c_j \, E^{r-j})^p \, z_n = 0, \qquad n \geq 0 \tag{7}$$

p being an integer $p > 1$. The characteristic polynomial $P_M(x)$ of this type of equations is:

$$P_M(x) = P(x)^p = (x^r + \sum_{j=1}^{r} c_j \, x^{r-j})^p. \tag{8}$$

In this case, the roots of $P_M(x)$ are the same as those of the polynomial $P(x)$, that is $(\alpha, \alpha^2, \alpha^{2^2}, \ldots, \alpha^{2^{(r-1)}})$, but with multiplicity p. Now the solutions of (7) are [3]:

$$z_n = \sum_{i=0}^{p-1} \left(\binom{n}{i} \sum_{j=0}^{r-1} A_i^{2^j} \alpha^{2^j n} \right), \qquad n \geq 0 \tag{9}$$

where $A_i \in GF(2)^r$ and the $\binom{n}{i}$ are binomial coefficients modulo 2.

In brief, the n-th term of a solution sequence $\{z_n\}$ is the bit-wise XOR logic operation of the n-th term of p sequences $\{\sum_{j=0}^{r-1} A_i^{2^j} \alpha^{2^j n}\}$ $(0 \leq i < p)$ weighted by binomial coefficients.

Table 1. Binomial coefficients, primary sequences and periods T_i

Binomial coeff.	Primary sequences	T_i
$\binom{n}{0}$	$S_0 = \{1, 1, 1, 1, 1, 1, 1, 1 \sim\}$	$T_0 = 1$
$\binom{n}{1}$	$S_1 = \{0, 1, 0, 1, 0, 1, 0, 1 \sim\}$	$T_1 = 2$
$\binom{n}{2}$	$S_2 = \{0, 0, 1, 1, 0, 0, 1, 1 \sim\}$	$T_2 = 4$
$\binom{n}{3}$	$S_3 = \{0, 0, 0, 1, 0, 0, 0, 1 \sim\}$	$T_3 = 4$
$\binom{n}{4}$	$S_4 = \{0, 0, 0, 0, 1, 1, 1, 1 \sim\}$	$T_4 = 8$
$\binom{n}{5}$	$S_5 = \{0, 0, 0, 0, 0, 1, 0, 1 \sim\}$	$T_5 = 8$
$\binom{n}{6}$	$S_6 = \{0, 0, 0, 0, 0, 0, 1, 1 \sim\}$	$T_6 = 8$
$\binom{n}{7}$	$S_7 = \{0, 0, 0, 0, 0, 0, 0, 1 \sim\}$	$T_7 = 8$
$\ldots$	$\ldots$	$\ldots$

In fact, when n takes successive values each binomial coefficient $\binom{n}{i}$ $(n \geq i \geq 0)$ defines a *primary sequence* with constant period T_i. In Table 1, the first binomial coefficients with their corresponding primary sequences and periods are depicted.

Now the main results concerning generalized self-shrinking sequences and linear difference equations are introduced.

Theorem 1. *The family of generalized self-shrinking sequences B(a) based on the m-sequence $\{a_n\}$ are particular solutions of the homogeneous linear difference equation:*

$$(E \oplus 1)^p z_n = 0, \qquad p = 2^{L-1}, \tag{10}$$

whose characteristic polynomial is $(x + 1)^p$.

Sketch of proof: According to [8], the periods of the generalized self-shrinking sequences $B(a)$ are $T \in \{1, 2, 2^{L-1}\}$. It is a well known fact in binary sequences [9] that if the period T of a binary sequence is a power of 2, then its characteristic polynomial $f(x)$ is a power of $(x + 1)$. Thus,

$$f(x) = (x + 1)^{LC} \tag{11}$$

where LC is its linear complexity (the shortest linear recursion satisfied by such a sequence). At the same time, the linear complexity of a periodic sequence is less than or equal to its period that is $LC \leq T$. Therefore, the characteristic polynomial $f(x)$ of any generalized self-shrinking sequence divides the characteristic polynomial of (10). In addition, the generalized self-shrinking sequences satisfied (10) and consequently they are particular solutions of such an homogeneous linear difference equation. □

Now the characteristics of the sequences that satisfy the previous linear difference equation are analyzed in detail. According to (9), the solutions of the difference equation given in (10) are of the form:

$$z_n = \binom{n}{0} A_0 \oplus \binom{n}{1} A_1 \oplus \ldots \oplus \binom{n}{p-1} A_{p-1}, \qquad n \geq 0 \tag{12}$$

where $A_i \in GF(2)$ are binary coefficients, $\alpha = 1$ is the unique root with multiplicity p of the polynomial $(x + 1)$ of degree $r = 1$ and the $\binom{n}{i}$ $(0 \le i < p)$ are binomial coefficients mod 2. Remark that the sequence $\{z_n\}$ is just the bit-wise XOR logic operation of primary sequences weighted by the corresponding coefficients A_i.

It must be noticed that not all the solutions $\{z_n\}$ of (10) are generalized self-shrinking sequences although all generalized self-shrinking sequences are solutions of (10). From (12), particular features of the solution sequences and consequently of the generalized self-shrinking sequences can be easily determined. All of them are related with the choice of the p-tuple $(A_0, A_1, A_2, \ldots, A_{p-1})$ of binary coefficients.

Periods of the Solution Sequences

According to Table 1, the periods of the primary sequences are just powers of 2. Moreover, according to (12) $\{z_n\}$ is the bit-wise XOR of sequences with different periods all of them powers of 2. Thus, the period of $\{z_n\}$ is the maximum period of the primary sequences involved in (12), that is the T_i corresponding to the primary sequence with the greatest index i such that $A_i \neq 0$.

Concerning the generalized self-shrinking sequences, we have:

- A generalized self-shrinking sequence:

$$\{b(G)\} = 11111111 \sim,$$

with period $T = 1$ corresponding to $A_0 \neq 0$, $A_i = 0$ $\forall\, i > 0$ in (12).
- A generalized self-shrinking sequence:

$$\{b(G)\} = 01010101 \sim,$$

with period $T = 2$ corresponding to $A_1 \neq 0$, $A_i = 0$ $\forall\, i > 1$ in (12).
- Different generalized self-shrinking sequences with period $T = 2^{L-1}$ corresponding to any $A_i \neq 0$ $(2^{L-2} \le i < 2^{L-1})$, $A_j = 0$ $\forall\, j \ge 2^{L-1}$ in (12).

Linear Complexity of the Solution Sequences

According to [9], the linear complexity of a sequence equals the number and multiplicity of the characteristic polynomial roots that appears in its linear recurrence relationship. Therefore coming back to (12) and analyzing the coefficients A_i, the linear complexity of $\{z_n\}$ can be computed. In fact, we have a unique root 1 with maximal multiplicity p. Thus, if i is the greatest index $(0 \le i < p)$ for which $A_i \neq 0$, then the linear complexity LC of the sequence $\{z_n\}$ will be:

$$LC = i + 1 \tag{13}$$

as it will be the multiplicity of the root 1.

Concerning the generalized self-shrinking sequences, the main result related to their linear complexity can be stated as follows:

Theorem 2. *The linear complexity LC of the generalized self-shrinking sequences with period $T_i = 2^{L-1}$ satisfies:*

$$2^{L-2} < LC \le 2^{L-1}. \tag{14}$$

Sketch of proof: The result follows from the fact that those generalized self-shrinking sequences involve primary sequences $\binom{n}{i}$ for $A_i \neq 0$ with i in the range $2^{L-2} \leq i < 2^{L-1}$, that is precisely the range of values of their corresponding linear complexity.   □

4   Generation of Cryptographic Sequences in Terms of Primary Sequences

From the previous section, it can be deduced that the bit-wise addition of correct primary sequences (or equivalently a correct choice of the p-tuple $(A_0, A_1, A_2, \ldots, A_{p-1})$) results in the generation of sequences with controllable period and linear complexity. Nevertheless, from a cryptographic point of view balancedness must be taken into account.

In this sense, it must be noticed that the complementation of the last bit of a generalized self-shrinking sequence with period 2^{L-1} means that the resulting sequence includes the primary sequence

$$\binom{n}{2^{L-1}-1} \qquad (n \geq 2^{L-1}-1) \tag{15}$$

That is the identically null sequence except for the last element that is 1. This implies that the obtained sequence will have period $T = 2^{L-1}$, maximum linear complexity $LC = 2^{L-1}$ and quasi-balancedness as the difference between the number of 1's and 0's will be just one. For a cryptographic range $L = 128$, this difference is negligible. In brief, the selection of coefficients A_i allows one to control period, linear complexity and balancedness of the solution sequences.

5   Conclusions

In this work, it is shown that generalized self-shrinking sequences are particular solutions of homogeneous linear difference equations with binary coefficients. At the same time, there are other many solution sequences not included in the previous class that can be used for cryptographic purposes. The choice of the p-tuple $(A_0, A_1, A_2, \ldots, A_{p-1})$ of binary coefficients allows one:

1. To get all the solutions of the above linear difference equation (12), among them there are sequences with application in stream cipher.
2. To obtain sequences with controllable period, linear complexity and balancedness.

It must be noticed that, although generalized self-shrinking sequences and self-shrinking sequences are generated from LFSRs by irregular decimation, in practice they are simple solutions of linear equations. Thus, the solutions of linear difference equations with binary coefficients appear as excellent binary sequences with cryptographic application. An efficient computation of such sequences seems to be a good tool for the generation of keystream sequences in stream ciphers.

References

1. Bluetooth, Specifications of the Bluetooth system,Version 1.1, http://www.bluetooth.com/
2. Coppersmith, D., Krawczyk, H., Mansour, Y.: The Shrinking Generator. In: Stinson, D.R. (ed.) CRYPTO 1993. LNCS, vol. 773, pp. 22–39. Springer, Heidelberg (1994)
3. Dickson, L.E.: Linear Groups with an Exposition of the Galois Field Theory, pp. 3–71. Dover, New York (1958); An updated reprint can be found at, http://www-math.cudenver.edu/~wcherowi/courses/finflds.html
4. eSTREAM, the ECRYPT Stream Cipher Project, Call for Primitives, http://www.ecrypt.eu.org/stream/
5. Fúster-Sabater, A., Caballero-Gil, P.: Strategic Attack on the Shrinking Generator. Theoretical Computer Science 409(3), 530–536 (2008)
6. Fúster-Sabater, A., Caballero-Gil, P., Delgado-Mohatar, O.: Deterministic Computation of Pseudorandomness in Sequences of Cryptographic Application. In: Allen, G., Nabrzyski, J., Seidel, E., van Albada, G.D., Dongarra, J., Sloot, P.M.A. (eds.) ICCS 2009. LNCS, vol. 5544, pp. 621–630. Springer, Heidelberg (2009)
7. Golomb, S.W.: Shift Register-Sequences. Aegean Park Press, Laguna Hill (1982)
8. Hu, Y., Xiao, G.: Generalized Self-Shrinking Generator. IEEE Trans. Inform. Theory 50, 714–719 (2004)
9. Lidl, R., Niederreiter, H.: Introduction to Finite Fields and Their Applications. Cambridge University Press, Cambridge (1986)
10. Meier, W., Staffelbach, O.: The Self-shrinking Generator. In: De Santis, A. (ed.) EUROCRYPT 1994. LNCS, vol. 950, pp. 205–214. Springer, Heidelberg (1995)
11. Menezes, A.J., et al.: Handbook of Applied Cryptography. CRC Press, New York (1997)
12. NIST Test suite for random numbers, http://csrc.nist.gov/rng/
13. Rivest, R.L.: The RC4 Encryption Algorithm. RSA Data Sec., Inc., March 98, http://www.rsasecurity.com
14. Robshaw, M., Billet, O.: New Stream Cipher Designs. LNCS, vol. 4986. Springer, Heidelberg (2008)

A Multisignature Scheme Based on the SDLP and on the IFP

R. Durán Díaz[1], L. Hernández Encinas[2], and J. Muñoz Masqué[2]

[1] Universidad de Alcalá, 28871-Alcalá de Henares, Spain
raul.duran@uah.es
[2] Instituto de Física Aplicada, CSIC, C/ Serrano 144, 28006-Madrid, Spain
{luis,jaime}@iec.csic.es

Abstract. Multisignature schemes are digital signature schemes that permit one to determine a unique signature for a given message, depending on the signatures of all the members of a specific group. In this work, we present a new semi-short multisignature scheme based on the Subgroup Discrete Logarithm Problem (SDLP) and on the Integer Factorization Problem (IFP). The scheme can be carried out in an on- and off-line basis, is efficient, and the bitlength of the multisignature does not depend on the number of signers.

Keywords: Digital signature, Multisignature, Public key cryptography.

1   Introduction

There are currently different methods and algorithms to perform, in a safe way, digital signatures. Most of these protocols are based on Public Key Cryptography [1]. The main feature of this kind of cryptography is that each individual has two keys, one public key and one private key. Additionally, to make more efficient the procedures of digital signatures and their electronic transmission, hash functions are used [2]. These functions are publicly known and allow signing a digest of the original document instead of the whole document.

Multisignature schemes are protocols of digital signature whereby a group of users, $G = \{U_1, \ldots, U_t\}$, signs a document such that the signature is valid if and only if all members of the group take part in the protocol and the signature verifies a specific condition of validity. These schemes have application in settings such us, for example, corporate scenarios for signing contracts between companies, the government and public administrations, agreements between different organization, etc. The easiest way to carry out a multisignature for a message is to consider as such signature the list formed by all the partial signatures of each one of the signers. However, this signature is not practical since its length is proportional to the number of signers [3,4].

In general, most of the multisignature protocols are performed as follows:

1. The signer U_1 signs the original message by using the signer private key.

Á. Herrero and E. Corchado (Eds.): CISIS 2011, LNCS 6694, pp. 135–142, 2011.
© Springer-Verlag Berlin Heidelberg 2011

2. Each one of the following signers, in an ordered way, signs the document, already signed by the one who is previous in the group.
3. The last member of G, U_t, signs the signed document that the previous signer has sent to him and sends to the verifier the original message and the multisignature calculated by the group of signers.

The verifier performs the verification of the multisignature by checking each one of the partial signatures of the group of signers, following the protocol and keeping the order in which they were signed.

The first multisignature scheme was proposed in [5], where a modification of the RSA cryptosystem was performed in such a way that the module considered was the product of three primes instead of just two. In [6] a scheme was proposed where the signature length is similar to the length of a simple signature and shorter than the signature obtained from the scheme proposed in [5]. This proposal can be used only if the cryptosystem is bijective. Other proposals based on the RSA cryptosystems have been proposed [7,8,9,10,11].

Regarding multisignature schemes based on the discrete logarithm problem, in [12] the group of signers must cooperate to sign the message and send the signature to a given group of verifiers. Only the union of all verifiers is able to validate the multisignature. Additionally, the signers must use not only their own private keys, but also the public key of all the verifiers. However, this scheme has some weaknesses [13,14]. The scheme proposed in [15] allows to perform a multisignature if the verifiers of the signature belong to a previously specified group.This scheme has some weaknesses as well [16,17].

In [18] a multisignature scheme for a generic model of public key is presented. The model requires some properties: Each one of the signers must have a certified public key with its corresponding private key, which must be generated by the signer himself. The signers must interact in a given number of rounds. In each round each signer receives a message, performs several calculations and sends another message to the next signer. It must be computationally infeasible to forge a multisignature if there exists one honest signer.

Our multisignature scheme has the property and advantage that each signer has his own private key, but all of them share the same public key. In this sense, the new scheme does not match exactly the model proposed in [18] since the procedure is carried out in just one round in which all the signers participate. Moreover, each signer does not need to have his own certified pair of keys (public and private). In fact, in the protocol all the signers share the same public key, but each one has his own private key. This fact simplifies and spares some of the problems related to the computational effort for computation, bandwidth, and, therefore, the overall efficiency of the proposed protocol.

Our proposal verifies several properties: It is secure, efficient, independent of the number of signers, the signature is determined by all the signers in any previously given order, allows adding new signers, and the verification procedure does require the verification of the partial signature of each member of G.

2   A Multisignature Scheme Based on SDLP and IFP

We propose a new multisignature scheme whereby each member of a given group, G, signs a document making use of his private key. The verifier of the signature checks whether the signature corresponds to the multisignature of the group, by using the public key that all the members of the group share [19].

We suppose that $G = \{U_1, U_2, \ldots, U_t\}$ is the group of signer and $\mathcal{T}$ is the Trusted Third Party which computes its own private key, the unique public key associated to all private keys, as well as helps the members of G to generate their private key.

2.1   Key Generation

First of all, $\mathcal{T}$ generates its own private key:

1. $\mathcal{T}$ chooses two large primes p and q such that

$$p = u_1 \cdot r \cdot p_1 + 1, \quad q = u_2 \cdot r \cdot q_1 + 1,$$

with r, p_1, q_1 primes, $u_1, u_2 \in \mathbb{Z}$, with $\gcd(u_1, u_2) = 2$, $i.e.$, $u_1 = 2v_1$, $v_2 = 2v_2$, and $\gcd(v_1, v_2) = 1$. To guarantee the security of the scheme, the bitlength of r is chosen so that the Discrete Logarithm Problem in a Subgroup of $\mathbb{Z}_n^*$, of order r, be computationally infeasible. Although the factors of n are of a particular form, they can be efficiently generated and to our knowledge there is no known efficient algorithm to factorize n ([20], [21]).

2. $\mathcal{T}$ computes

$$n = p \cdot q,$$
$$\phi(n) = (p-1)(q-1) = u_1 \cdot u_2 \cdot r^2 \cdot p_1 \cdot q_1,$$
$$\lambda(n) = \operatorname{lcm}(p-1, q-1) = \frac{\phi(n)}{\gcd(p-1, q-1)} = 2v_1 \cdot v_2 \cdot r \cdot p_1 \cdot q_1,$$

where $\phi(n)$ is the Euler function and $\lambda(n)$ is the Carmichael function.

3. Next, $\mathcal{T}$ selects an element $\alpha \in \mathbb{Z}_n^*$ of order r modulo n, verifying

$$\gcd(\alpha, \phi(n)) = \gcd(\alpha, u_1 \cdot u_2 \cdot r^2 \cdot p_1 \cdot q_1) = 1.$$

The element α can be efficiently computed due to the fact that $\mathcal{T}$ knows the factorization of n, $\phi(n)$, and $\lambda(n)$ [21, Lemma 3.1]. We denote by S_r the multiplicative subgroup of $\mathbb{Z}_n^*$ generated by α.

4. $\mathcal{T}$ generates a secret random number $s \in \mathbb{Z}_r^*$ and computes

$$\beta \equiv \alpha^s \pmod{n}. \tag{1}$$

5. The values (α, r, β, n) are made public; whereas $\mathcal{T}$ keeps secret (p, q, s).

Remark that breaking the key generation protocol amounts to solving the Integer factorization Problem (IFP). Moreover, to determine s from β in the expression (1) the Subgroup Discrete Logarithm Problem (SDLP) must be solved.

Before generating the private key of each signer, $\mathcal{T}$ generates its private key and the shared public key as follows:

1. $\mathcal{T}$ determines its private key by generating four random integer numbers $a_0, b_0, c_0, d_0 \in \mathbb{Z}_r^*$.
2. $\mathcal{T}$ obtains the common public key by computing

$$P \equiv \alpha^{a_0} \cdot \beta^{b_0} \pmod{n} \equiv \alpha^{a_0 + s \cdot b_0} \equiv \alpha^h,$$
$$Q \equiv \alpha^{c_0} \cdot \beta^{d_0} \pmod{n} \equiv \alpha^{c_0 + s \cdot d_0} \equiv \alpha^k.$$

where $h \equiv (a_0 + s \cdot b_0) \pmod{r}$ and $k \equiv (c_0 + s \cdot d_0) \pmod{r}$.

For avoiding $\mathcal{T}$ can impersonate any signer of G, an interactive session between each user U_i and $\mathcal{T}$ is developed to compute U_i's private key, $i = 1, \ldots, t$:

1. U_i generates two secret integers $b_i, d_i \in \mathbb{Z}_r$ at random and sends the values of $\alpha^{b_i}, \alpha^{d_i}$ to $\mathcal{T}$ in a secure way, in order to protect both secret integers. Note that $\mathcal{T}$ can determine A_i and C_i since it knows h, k, α^{b_i}, and α^{d_i}, but it cannot compute a_i, c_i because it cannot solve the SDLP. In short, each party gets access to only 2 out of the 4 key parameters.
2. $\mathcal{T}$ computes

$$A_i \equiv \alpha^h \cdot (\alpha^{b_i})^{-s} \pmod{n} \equiv \alpha^{a_i},$$
$$C_i \equiv \alpha^k \cdot (\alpha^{d_i})^{-s} \pmod{n} \equiv \alpha^{c_i}.$$

Then $\mathcal{T}$ sends to U_i the values of A_i, C_i by using a secure channel.
3. The private key of U_i is the set (b_i, d_i, A_i, C_i). Remark that for U_i it is also impossible to compute the values of a_i and c_i.

2.2   Key Verification

To verify the correctness of $\mathcal{T}$'s key, each signer, $U_i \in G$, $i = 1, \ldots, t$, tests if

$$\alpha \not\equiv 1 \pmod{n}, \quad \alpha^r \equiv 1 \pmod{n}.$$

Moreover, each signer must verify that his private key corresponds to the public key (P, Q) by checking the correctness of the following expressions:

$$P \equiv A_i \cdot \beta^{b_i} \pmod{n}, \quad Q \equiv C_i \cdot \beta^{d_i} \pmod{n}.$$

In fact, we have:

$$A_i \cdot \beta^{b_i} \pmod{n} \equiv \alpha^{a_i} \cdot \beta^{b_i} \equiv \alpha^{a_i + s \cdot b_i} \equiv \alpha^h \equiv P,$$
$$C_i \cdot \beta^{d_i} \pmod{n} \equiv \alpha^{c_i} \cdot \beta^{d_i} \equiv \alpha^{c_i + s \cdot d_i} \equiv \alpha^k \equiv Q.$$

2.3   Signing a Message

We will present a protocol to determine a multisignature of the group G for a given message M, where only the signers participate.

We suppose a secure hash function, $\mathfrak{h}$, has been selected (for example, one of the SHA-2 family) with $\mathfrak{h}(M) = m$. Moreover, it is assumed that the set of signers has been ordered, due to the fact that each signer will sign the signature determined by the previous signer.

The process is as follows: Each signer verifies the *partial signature* determined by the previous signer, computes his own signature by using the received signature, and sends the new partial signature to the next signer.

1. The first signer, U_1, computes his partial signature for the message M by using his private key, (b_1, d_1, A_1, C_1), and $m = \mathfrak{h}(M)$:

$$F_1 \equiv A_1 \cdot C_1^m \pmod{n},$$
$$g_1 \equiv b_1 + m \cdot d_1 \pmod{r}$$

and sends (F_1, g_1) to the second signer, U_2.

2. The second signer, U_2, verifies U_1's signature checking if

$$P \cdot Q^m \equiv F_1 \cdot \beta^{g_1} \pmod{n}.$$

U_2 computes his partial signature for the message:

$$F_2 \equiv F_1 \cdot A_2 \cdot C_2^m \pmod{n} \equiv \alpha^{a_1 + a_2 + m(c_1 + c_2)},$$
$$g_2 \equiv g_1 + b_2 + m \cdot d_2 \pmod{r} \equiv b_1 + b_2 + m(d_1 + d_2).$$

U_2 sends (F_2, g_2) as his partial signature to the third signer.

$\cdots$

i. The signer U_i receives the U_{i-1}'s partial signature (F_{i-1}, g_{i-1}) and then verifies this partial signature checking if

$$P^{i-1} \cdot Q^{(i-1) \cdot m} = F_{i-1} \cdot \beta^{g_{i-1}} \pmod{n}.$$

U_i computes his partial signature:

$$F_i \equiv F_{i-1} \cdot A_i \cdot C_i^m \pmod{n} \equiv \alpha^{a_1 + \cdots + a_i + m(c_1 + \cdots + c_i)},$$
$$g_i \equiv g_{i-1} + b_i + m \cdot d_i \pmod{r} \equiv b_1 + \cdots + b_i + m(d_1 + \cdots + d_i).$$

U_i sends (F_i, g_i) to the next signer.

$\cdots$

t. The last signer in the group, U_t, receives the U_{t-1}'s partial signature and verifies that signature testing if

$$P^{t-1} \cdot Q^{(t-1) \cdot m} \equiv F_{t-1} \cdot \beta^{g_{t-1}} \pmod{n}.$$

U_t computes his partial signature for the message:

$$F_t \equiv F_{t-1} \cdot A_t \cdot C_t^m \pmod{n} \equiv \alpha^{a_1 + \cdots + a_t + m(c_1 + \cdots + c_t)},$$
$$g_t \equiv g_{t-1} + b_t + d_t \cdot m \pmod{r} \equiv b_1 + \cdots + b_t + m(d_1 + \cdots + d_t).$$

U_t makes public the multisignature for M: $(F, g) = (F_t, g_t)$.

The verification of each partial signature carried out by each signer (but the first one) is necessary in order to avoid that a signer signs a non-valid message. Moreover, the verification of the U_i's partial signature is correct because it is

$$
\begin{aligned}
F_i \cdot \beta^{g_i} \pmod{n} &\equiv \alpha^{a_1 + \cdots + a_i + m(c_1 + \cdots + c_i)} \beta^{b_1 + \cdots + b_i + m(d_1 + \cdots + d_i)} \\
&\equiv \alpha^{a_1 + \cdots + a_i} (\alpha^{c_1 + \cdots + c_i})^m \beta^{b_1 + \cdots + b_i} (\beta^{d_1 + \cdots + d_i})^m \\
&\equiv \prod_{j=1}^{i} \alpha^{a_j} \cdot \beta^{b_j} (\alpha^{c_j} \cdot \beta^{d_j})^m \equiv \prod_{j=1}^{i} P \cdot Q^m = P^i \cdot Q^{i \cdot m}.
\end{aligned}
$$

2.4   Verifying the Multisignature

Let (F, g) be the multisignature for a message M computed by the group of t signers, G. In order to verify such signature, a verifier must to check if

$$
P^t \cdot Q^{t \cdot m} \equiv F \cdot \beta^g \pmod{n}. \tag{2}
$$

This verification equation is correct as

$$
\begin{aligned}
F \cdot \beta^g \pmod{n} &\equiv \alpha^{a_1 + \cdots + a_t + m(c_1 + \cdots + c_t)} \beta^{b_1 + \cdots + b_t + m(d_1 + \cdots + d_t)} \\
&\equiv \prod_{j=1}^{t} \alpha^{a_j} \cdot \beta^{b_j} (\alpha^{c_j} \cdot \beta^{d_j})^m \equiv \prod_{j=1}^{t} P \cdot Q^m = P^t \cdot Q^{t \cdot m}.
\end{aligned}
$$

2.5   Properties and Security Analysis

The proposed multisignature scheme has the following properties:

1. The scheme has a fixed size, *i.e.*, it does not depend on the number of signers.
2. The multisignature is a semi-short signature in the sense that the pair (F, g) is composed by two elements belonging to $\mathbb{Z}_n^*$ and to $\mathbb{Z}_r^*$, respectively.
3. The multisignature is efficient as all computations require polynomial time.
4. It is possible to include new signers in the group G without re-execution of the protocol by the rest of the signers. It is possible to place the new signers at the end of the signer group so that each one of them follows the protocol by computing his partial signature from the previously computed multisignature.
5. The multisignature verification process is easy and efficient.

The proposed multisignature scheme is secure since to break the proposed scheme an attacker needs to solve three difficult problems: IFP, DLP, and SDLP. Hence, a signer knowing only his private key cannot determine neither $\mathcal{T}$'s private key nor its secret value s.

In the scheme it is impossible for two signers to compute a forged signature because each signer verifies the signatures of all the previous signers.

Moreover, two or more signers could try to conspire with the goal of obtaining the secret value s of $\mathcal{T}$, and then computing new private keys.

In this attack, if the signers U_i and U_j, $j > i$, share their signatures (F_i, g_i) and (F_j, g_j), they know that the following holds

$$F_i \cdot \beta^{g_i} \equiv F_j \cdot \beta^{g_j} \pmod{n},$$

$$A_i \cdot \beta^{b_i} \cdot C_i^m \cdot \beta^{md_i} \equiv A_j \cdot \beta^{b_j} \cdot C_j^m \cdot \beta^{md_j} \pmod{n},$$

$$\alpha^{a_i + s \cdot b_i + m \cdot c_i + s \cdot m \cdot d_i} \equiv \alpha^{a_j + s \cdot b_j + m \cdot c_j + s \cdot m \cdot d_j} \pmod{n}.$$

Then, they can suppose that the exponents verify the following equations:

$$a_i + s \cdot b_i + m \cdot c_i + s \cdot m \cdot d_i \equiv a_j + s \cdot b_j + m \cdot c_j + s \cdot m \cdot d_j \pmod{r},$$

$$a_i - a_j + m(c_i - c_j) \equiv s((b_j - b_i) + m(d_j - d_i)) \pmod{r},$$

$$s \equiv (a_i - a_j + m(c_i - c_j))((b_j - b_i) + m(d_j - d_i))^{-1} \pmod{r}.$$

But, none of them can solve this equation because they do not know a_i, a_j, c_i, c_j.

The scheme is secure even if a user has access to the signatures of two distinct messages signed with the same keys because it implies solving IFP and DLP.

Finally, nobody can determine a forged multisignature for the message M without being detected by $\mathcal{T}$. In fact, a forger could know the public key, (P, Q), the message, M, its hash, m, the number of signers, t, and the values (α, r, β, n). From these data, he can choose an integer $\bar{g}$ and determine the element $\beta^{\bar{g}} = \alpha^{s \cdot \bar{g}} \in S_r$. Moreover, he can compute

$$\overline{F} \equiv P^t \cdot Q^{t \cdot m} \cdot (\beta^{\bar{g}})^{-1} \pmod{n}$$

and publish the pair $(\overline{F}, \bar{g})$ as a multisignature of the signer group G for the message M, that passes the verification equation (2).

Nevertheless, $\mathcal{T}$ can prove that this multisignature is a forgery. It is sufficient that it calculates

$$\widetilde{F} \equiv \prod_{i=1}^{t} A_i \cdot C_i^m \pmod{n},$$

and shows that $\widetilde{F}^{-1} \cdot F \not\equiv 1 \pmod{n}$.

3   Conclusions

A new semi-short multisignature scheme based on three difficult problems from Number Theory, namely, integer factorization, discrete logarithms, and subgroup discrete logarithms has been proposed. A multisignature (F, g) is semi-short in the sense that $F \in \mathbb{Z}_n^*$ and $g \in \mathbb{Z}_r^*$, where the bitlength of n is much bigger than the the bitlength of r.

This scheme permits one to obtain a semi-short signature with a fixed bitlength, which is independent of the number of signers.

The multisignature scheme is efficient since the computations only require polynomial time, verifies the conditions of multisignature schemes, and moreover it is secure both against conspiracy attacks and against forgery.

Acknowledgment. This work has been partially supported by the "Fundación Memoria D. Samuel Solórzano Barruso" under the Project FS/7-2010.

References

1. Menezes, A., van Oorschot, P., Vanstone, S.: Handbook of applied cryptography. CRC Press, Boca Raton (1997)
2. National Institute of Standards and Technology: Secure Hash Standard (SHS). Federal Information Processing Standard Publication 180-2 (2002)
3. Aboud, S.J.: Two efficient digital multisignature schemes. Int. J. Soft. Comput. 2, 113–117 (2007)
4. Boyd, C.: Some applications of multiple key ciphers. In: Günther, C.G. (ed.) EUROCRYPT 1988. LNCS, vol. 330, pp. 455–467. Springer, Heidelberg (1988)
5. Itakura, K., Nakamura, K.: A public-key cryptosystem suitable for digital multisignatures. NEC Res. Development 71, 1–8 (1983)
6. Okamoto, T.: A digital multisignature scheme using bijective public-key cryptosystems. Commun. ACM Trans. Computer Systems 6, 432–441 (1988)
7. Aboud, S.J., Al-Fayoumi, M.A.: A new multisignature scheme using re-encryption technique. J. Applied Sci. 7, 1813–1817 (2007)
8. Harn, L., Kiesler, T.: New scheme for digital multisignature. Elect. Lett. 25, 1002–1003 (1989)
9. Kiesler, T., Harn, L.: RSA blocking and multisignature schemes with no bit expansion. Elect. Lett. 26, 1490–1491 (1990)
10. Park, S., Park, S., Kim, K., Won, D.: Two efficient RSA multisignature schemes. In: Han, Y., Quing, S. (eds.) ICICS 1997. LNCS, vol. 1334, pp. 217–222. Springer, Heidelberg (1997)
11. Pon, S.F., Lu, E.H., Lee, J.Y.: Dynamic reblocking RSA-based multisignatures scheme for computer and communication networks. IEEE Comm. Let. 6, 43–44 (2002)
12. Laih, C.S., Yen, S.M.: Multisignature for specified group of verifiers. J. Inform. Sci. Engrg. 12(1), 143–152 (1996)
13. He, W.H.: Weakness in some multisignature schemes for specified group of verifiers. Inform. Proc. Lett. 83, 95–99 (2002)
14. Yen, S.M.: Cryptanalysis and repair of the multi-verifier signature with verifier specification. Computers & Security 15(6), 537–544 (1996)
15. Zhang, Z., Xiao, G.: New multisignature scheme for specified group of verifiers. Appl. Math. Comput. 157, 425–431 (2004)
16. Lv, J., Wang, X., Kim, K.: Security of a multisignature scheme for specified group of verifiers. Appl. Math. Comput. 166, 58–63 (2005)
17. Yoon, E.J., Yoo, K.Y.: Cryptanalysis of Zhang-Xiao's multisignature scheme for specified group of verifiers. Appl. Math. Comput. 170, 226–229 (2005)
18. Bellare, M., Neven, G.: Multi-signatures in the plain public-key model and a general forking lemma. In: Proc. 13th ACM Conference on Computer and Communications Security (CCS 2006), pp. 390–399. ACM Press, New York (2006)
19. Pedersen, T.P., Pfitzmann, B.: Fail-stop signatures. SIAM J. Comput. 26, 291–330 (1997)
20. Maurer, U.: Some number-theoretic conjectures and their relation to the generation of cryptographic primes. In: Proc. Cryptography and Coding 1992, pp. 173–191. Oxford University Press, New York (1992)
21. Susilo, W.: Short fail-stop signature scheme based on factorization and discrete logarithm assumptions. Theor. Comput. Sci. 410, 736–744 (2009)

A Group Signature Scheme Based on the Integer Factorization and the Subgroup Discrete Logarithm Problems

R. Durán Díaz[1], L. Hernández Encinas[2], and J. Muñoz Masqué[2]

[1] Universidad de Alcalá, 28871-Alcalá de Henares, Spain
raul.duran@uah.es
[2] Instituto de Física Aplicada, CSIC, 28006-Madrid, Spain
{luis,jaime}@iec.csic.es

Abstract. Group signature schemes allow a user, belonging to a specific group of users, to sign a message in an anonymous way on behalf of the group. In general, these schemes need the collaboration of a Trusted Third Party which, in case of a dispute, can reveal the identity of the real signer. A new group signature scheme is presented whose security is based on the Integer Factorization Problem (IFP) and on the Subgroup Discrete Logarithm Problem (SDLP).

Keywords: Digital signature, Group signature, Public key cryptography.

1 Introduction

As it is well-known, there are different protocols to determine digital signatures. In general, these protocols are based on public key cryptosystems [1,2,3]. The main characteristic of this signature schemes is that each signer has one public key and one private key.

Moreover, the procedures of digital signatures are made more efficient if hash functions are used [4]. The hash functions are public and they allow to sign a digest or hash of the message.

Group signature schemes were proposed by Chaum and van Heyst in 1991 [5]. These schemes permit a signer group to sign a given message such that only a member of the group computes the signature on behalf of the whole group. A Trusted Third Party ($\mathcal{T}$) collaborates in the generation of the keys and is able to reveal the identity of the user who signed the message, if a dispute arises.

The main characteristics defining the group signatures are the following:

1. Only a member of the signer group signs the message.
2. The receiver of the message can verify that the signature of the message was generated by a member of the signer group, but he cannot determine which member of the group was the signer.
3. If a dispute arises, it is possible to open the signature in order to determine who was the actual signer of the message.

Á. Herrero and E. Corchado (Eds.): CISIS 2011, LNCS 6694, pp. 143–150, 2011.

Group signatures can be understood as an extension of credential authentication and membership authentication schemes. In the first schemes, a user proves that he belongs to a specific group [6]; whereas in the second ones, a member of a group can convince a verifier that he belongs to that group without revealing him his identity [7,8].

There exist several proposals for group signatures, which use a number of cryptographic primitives. Some of these proposals need a Trusted Third Party (TTP), $\mathcal{T}$, at least for the initialization process. Other schemes, however, allow any user to create the group he chooses to belong to.

As a general rule, group signatures make use of schemes whose security is based on computationally-intractable mathematical problems [9,10,11]. Typically, such problems are the Integer Factorization Problem (IFP) and the Discrete Logarithm Problem (DLP).

Nevertheless, most of these protocols show some limitations. For example, the schemes described in [12,13,14] have a security problem [15]. Moreover, the security of the schemes presented in [16,17] is tested under artificial and unlikely conditions [18].

The proposed group signature scheme presented here guarantees that a true group signature is generated for a given message. Moreover, the scheme improves existing protocols in terms of user friendliness, computational efficiency, time and band-width saving. Moreover, this proposal verifies the properties required for group signature schemes: Only a group member can validly sign a document or message. The signed-message receiver is able to verify that the signature is a valid group signature, $i.e.$, it has been carried out by one legitimate member of the group. However, the receiver will not be able to determine which particular group member actually signed the message. Finally, if required (in case of a dispute, for example) it is possible to disclose the signer, $i.e.$, to reveal which user actually signed the message.

The rest of this paper is organized as follows: In section 2 a group signature scheme based on the Integer Factorization and Subgroup Discrete Logarithm Problems is proposed. In section 3, the main properties of the new scheme are shown. The security analysis of the proposal is performed in section 4, and finally, the conclusions are presented in section 5.

2   A Group Signature Scheme Based on IFP and SDLP

In this section we propose a group signature scheme for which a randomly chosen member of a given group signs a document, on behalf of the whole group, making use of his private key. The verifier of the signature checks whether or not the signature corresponds to one of them, using the public key that all the members of the group share. Moreover, the verifier will not be able to decide who was the original signer.

Let $G = \{U_1, U_2, \ldots, U_t\}$ be the signer group and let $\mathcal{T}$ be the Trusted Third Party.

2.1 Setup Phase

In this phase, $\mathcal{T}$ generates its pre-key, the public key shared by the group, as well as helps the members of G to generate their private keys [19].

Pre-key generation. $\mathcal{T}$ generates its pre-key as follows:

1. $\mathcal{T}$ chooses two large primes p and q, such that

$$p = u_1 \cdot r \cdot p_1 + 1,$$
$$q = u_2 \cdot r \cdot q_1 + 1,$$

   where r, p_1, q_1 are prime numbers, $u_1, u_2 \in \mathbb{Z}$ with $\gcd(u_1, u_2) = 2$, that is, $u_1 = 2v_1$, $u_2 = 2v_2$, and $\gcd(v_1, v_2) = 1$.
   In order to guarantee the security of the scheme, the bitlength of r is selected so that the Subgroup Discrete Logarithm Problem (SDLP) of order r in $\mathbb{Z}_n^*$ be computationally infeasible.
2. $\mathcal{T}$ computes

$$n = p \cdot q,$$
$$\phi(n) = (p-1)(q-1) = u_1 \cdot u_2 \cdot r^2 \cdot p_1 \cdot q_1,$$
$$\lambda(n) = \mathrm{lcm}(p-1, q-1) = \frac{\phi(n)}{\gcd(p-1, q-1)} = 2v_1 \cdot v_2 \cdot r \cdot p_1 \cdot q_1,$$

   where $\phi(n)$ is the Euler function, $\lambda(n)$ is the Carmichael function, and lcm represents the least common multiple.
   Then, $\mathcal{T}$ selects an element $\alpha \in \mathbb{Z}_n^*$ with multiplicative order r modulo n, such that

$$\gcd(\alpha, \phi(n)) = \gcd(\alpha, u_1 \cdot u_2 \cdot r^2 \cdot p_1 \cdot q_1) = 1.$$

   Note that this element, α, can be efficiently computed as $\mathcal{T}$ knows the factorization of n and consequently it knows $\phi(n)$ and $\lambda(n)$ [19, Lemma 3.1].
   We denote by S_r the subgroup of $\mathbb{Z}_n^*$ generated by α.
3. $\mathcal{T}$ generates a secret random number $s \in \mathbb{Z}_r^*$ and determines

$$\beta = \alpha^s \pmod{n}. \tag{1}$$

4. $\mathcal{T}$ publishes the values (α, r, β, n); whereas it keeps secret the values of (p, q, s).

With the previous hypothesis, the security of $\mathcal{T}$'s secret, s, is based on the Integer Factorization Problem (IFP) and on the Subgroup Discrete Logarithm Problem (SDLP).

Key generation. In order to determine the private keys of the members of G, $\mathcal{T}$ computes its private key and the public key which will be shared by all the signers of G.

To do this, $\mathcal{T}$ generates four random numbers $a_0, b_0, c_0, d_0 \in \mathbb{Z}_r^*$ as its private key and determines the shared public key for G by computing

$$\left. \begin{array}{l} P = \alpha^{a_0} \cdot \beta^{b_0} \quad (\text{mod } n) \\ Q = \beta^{c_0} \cdot \alpha^{d_0} \quad (\text{mod } n) \end{array} \right\} \tag{2}$$

From (2), we have

$$P \equiv \alpha^{a_0} (\alpha^s)^{b_0} \quad (\text{mod } n) \equiv \alpha^{a_0 + s \cdot b_0} \quad (\text{mod } n),$$
$$Q \equiv (\alpha^s)^{c_0} \alpha^{d_0} \quad (\text{mod } n) \equiv \alpha^{s \cdot c_0 + d_0} \quad (\text{mod } n).$$

Hence, $P, Q \in S_r$, that is, there exist integers $h, k \in \mathbb{Z}_r$ such that

$$\left. \begin{array}{l} h = (a_0 + s \cdot b_0) \quad (\text{mod } r) \\ k = (s \cdot c_0 + d_0) \quad (\text{mod } r) \end{array} \right\} \tag{3}$$

In order to guarantee that $\mathcal{T}$ cannot impersonate any user of G, an interactive session between each user U_i and $\mathcal{T}$ is necessary to determine the private key of U_i, $1 \leq i \leq t$. Hence, the following interactive protocol is developed:

1. U_i generates two secret integers $b_i, d_i \in \mathbb{Z}_r$ at random and sends to $\mathcal{T}$ the values of $\alpha^{b_i}, \alpha^{d_i}$, in a secure way for protecting both secret integers.
2. $\mathcal{T}$ computes

$$A_i = \alpha^h \cdot (\alpha^{b_i})^{-s} \quad (\text{mod } n) = \alpha^{a_i},$$
$$C_i = \alpha^k \cdot (\alpha^{d_i})^{-1} \quad (\text{mod } n) = \beta^{c_i}.$$

From (3), $\mathcal{T}$ can compute A_i, C_i since it knows h, k, α^{b_i}, and α^{d_i}, but it cannot compute a_i, c_i because it cannot solve the SDLP. Then $\mathcal{T}$ sends to U_i the values of A_i, C_i by using a secure channel.
3. The private key of U_i is the set (b_i, d_i, A_i, C_i). Note that for U_i is also impossible to compute the values of a_i, c_i.

Remark. Note that $\mathcal{T}$ knows two values of the U_i's private, A_i, C_i, but it is impossible for it to know the rest of that key. Moreover, for both U_i and $\mathcal{T}$ it is impossible to compute the values a_i, c_i because they are protected by the SDLP.

Key verification. For verifying the pre-key of $\mathcal{T}$, each members of the signer group, U_i, $1 \leq i \leq t$, must check

$$\alpha \not\equiv 1 \quad (\text{mod } n),$$
$$\alpha^r \equiv 1 \quad (\text{mod } n).$$

Moreover, each signer, U_i, $1 \leq i \leq t$, must verify that his private key corresponds to the shared public key, i.e., must check if it holds:

$$P \equiv A_i \cdot \beta^{b_i} \quad (\text{mod } n), \tag{4}$$
$$Q \equiv C_i \cdot \alpha^{d_i} \quad (\text{mod } n). \tag{5}$$

In fact:

$$A_i \cdot \beta^{b_i} \quad (\text{mod } n) \equiv \alpha^{a_i} \cdot \beta^{b_i} = \alpha^{a_i + s \cdot b_i} = \alpha^h = P,$$
$$C_i \cdot \alpha^{d_i} \quad (\text{mod } n) \equiv \beta^{c_i} \cdot \alpha^{d_i} = \alpha^{s \cdot c_i + d_i} = \alpha^k = Q.$$

2.2   Group Signature Generation

Let M be the message to be signed by a member of G. We can assume that after computing its hash value (by using, for example, a public hash function from the SHA-2 family), we have $\mathfrak{h}(M) = m$. For signing M on behalf of the group G, a random and anonymous member of G is chosen, for example, U_i. Next, U_i does the following.

1. U_i generates a secret integer $\lambda_i \in \mathbb{Z}_r$ at random. This value must be generated each time a message is signed.
2. U_i determines his signature, (F_i, G_i, H_i), for M, computing the following values:

$$\left. \begin{array}{l} F_i = A_i \cdot C_i^m \cdot \alpha^{\lambda_i} \quad (\text{mod } n) \\ G_i = \beta^{b_i} \cdot (\alpha^{d_i})^m \cdot \alpha^{-\lambda_i} \quad (\text{mod } n) \\ H_i = \mathfrak{h}(\alpha^{\lambda_i}) \end{array} \right\} \tag{6}$$

3. Finally, $\mathcal{T}$ publishes the group signature for the message M: $(F, G, H) = (F_i, G_i, H_i)$.

Remark. Nobody can impersonate the user U_i because he is the only one knowing the values $b_i, d_i,$ and λ_i.

2.3   Group Signature Verification

Let (F, G, H) be a group signature of G for the message M. In order to verify this signature, any verifier knowing the public key of the group G, (P, Q), can check that

$$P \cdot Q^m \equiv F \cdot G \quad (\text{mod } n). \tag{7}$$

The equation (7) can be immediately justified from expressions (4)-(6) as follows:

$$\begin{aligned} F \cdot G \quad (\text{mod } n) &\equiv A_i \cdot C_i^m \cdot \alpha^{\lambda_i} \cdot \beta^{b_i} \cdot \alpha^{m \cdot d_i} \cdot \alpha^{-\lambda_i} \quad (\text{mod } n) \\ &= A_i \cdot \beta^{b_i} \cdot C_i^m \cdot \alpha^{m \cdot d_i} \\ &= P \cdot Q^m. \end{aligned}$$

3   Properties of the New Scheme

The proposed scheme has the following properties:

1. All the operations involved in the different phases described in the previous paragraphs can be efficiently computed in polynomial time.
2. Despite $\mathcal{T}$ knows part of U_i's private key, it cannot forge the signature determined by U_i as the signer has generated at random the value: λ_i. Nevertheless, it can generate a valid group signature.
3. The verifier is only able to test whether the signature was generated by a member of the signer group and it is not able to ascertain the identity of the actual signer.

4. In case of dispute, $\mathcal{T}$ can disclose the signer since it knows part of the private key of each member of G.

In fact, as $\mathcal{T}$ knows the values of A_i and C_i of the signer U_i, by using the equations in (6) defining the group signature, it can compute

$$\frac{F}{A_i \cdot C_i^m} \pmod{n} \equiv \frac{A_i \cdot C_i^m \cdot \alpha^{\lambda_i}}{A_i \cdot C_i^m} = \alpha^{\lambda_i}.$$

Then, $\mathcal{T}$ can prove, without the collaboration of U_i, that

$$\mathfrak{h}\left(\frac{F}{A_i \cdot C_i^m} \pmod{n}\right) = \mathfrak{h}(\alpha^{\lambda_i}) = H_i.$$

4   Security Analysis

Moreover, the scheme is secure as no member of G, say U_i, knowing only his own private key, (b_i, d_i, A_i, C_i), and the shared public key, $(P = \alpha^{a_0 + s \cdot b_0}, Q = \alpha^{s \cdot c_0 + d_0})$, can determine neither the secret value s of $\mathcal{T}$, nor its private key (a_0, b_0, c_0, d_0).

In fact, determining s from α and $\beta \equiv \alpha^s \pmod{n}$, see formula (1), means solving the discrete logarithm problem in the subgroup S_r, of order r generated by α, which is impossible as the size of r was chosen such that the SDLP was unfeasible to solve, and moreover, the factorization of n is infeasible as well.

Moreover, the private key of $\mathcal{T}$ was generated at random and it is only known that it verifies the equation (2), but computing any of the values of this key implies solving the DLP in $\mathbb{Z}_n^*$.

It is also impossible for any U_i to determine the values of $h = a_i + s \cdot b_i$, and $k = s \cdot c_i + d_i$, as he only knows $b_i, d_i, \alpha^{a_i}, \beta^{c_i}$. In all cases, it is necessary to solve a discrete logarithm problem.

Furthermore, two members of G, say U_i and U_j, could conspire and try to compute any of the secret values of $\mathcal{T}$: $s, h, k, a_0, b_0, c_0, d_0$, or generate a false signature for the group. To carry out any of these attacks, both could generate their signatures for a message, say (F_i, G_i, H_i) and (F_j, G_j, H_j), respectively. Then, from the verification identity (7), they have

$$F_i \cdot G_i \pmod{n} \equiv F_j \cdot G_j = P \cdot Q^m.$$

Hence, they obtain

$$A_i \cdot C_i^m \cdot \beta^{b_i} \cdot \alpha^{m \cdot d_i} \equiv A_j \cdot C_j^m \cdot \beta^{b_j} \cdot \alpha^{m \cdot d_j} \pmod{n},$$

or equivalently,

$$\alpha^{a_i} \cdot \beta^{m \cdot c_i} \cdot \beta^{b_i} \cdot \alpha^{m \cdot d_i} \equiv \alpha^{a_j} \cdot \beta^{m \cdot c_j} \cdot \beta^{b_j} \cdot \alpha^{m \cdot d_j} \pmod{n},$$

and as α has order r modulo n, it results

$$(a_i + m \cdot d_i) + s(b_i + m \cdot c_i) \equiv (a_j + m \cdot d_j) + s(b_j + m \cdot c_j) \pmod{r}.$$

that is, they could obtain

$$s \equiv (a_i - a_j + m(d_i - d_j)) \cdot (b_j - b_i + m(c_j - c_i))^{-1} \pmod{r}.$$

Nevertheless, none of them know the values of a_i, a_j, c_i, c_j, so they cannot compute s.

Finally, nobody is able to forge a group signature for the message M without this fact being detected and proved by $\mathcal{T}$. In fact, a forger could know the public key, (P, Q), the message, M, its hash, m, and the values (α, r, β, n). From these data, the forger can choose an element $\widetilde{G} \in S_r$, determine the value

$$\widetilde{F} = P \cdot Q^m \cdot \widetilde{G}^{-1} \pmod{n},$$

and publish the set $(\widetilde{F}, \widetilde{G}, \widetilde{H})$, for a hash value $\widetilde{H}$, as a group signature for the message M, that passes the verification equation (7).

Nevertheless, $\mathcal{T}$ can prove that this group signature is a forgery by computing

$$\overline{H}_i = \mathfrak{h}\left(\frac{\widetilde{F}}{A_i \cdot C_i^m} \pmod{n} \right), \quad 1 \leq i \leq t,$$

and showing that $\overline{H}_i \neq \widetilde{H}, \forall i$.

5   Conclusions

A new group signature scheme has been proposed. The security of the scheme is based on two difficult problems from Number Theory: Integer factorization and subgroup discrete logarithms (and the DLP in the key generation).

The scheme verifies the properties required for general group signature schemes. Any single member of the signer group is able to sign the message. The receiver of the message can verify that the signature of the message was generated by a actual member of the signer group, but he cannot determine which member of the group was the signer. If a dispute arises, a Trusted Third Party can open the signature and determine who was the signer of the message.

The group signature scheme is efficient since the computations only require polynomial time and moreover it is secure against conspiracy attacks and against forgery.

Acknowledgment. This work has been partially supported by the "Fundación Memoria D. Samuel Solórzano Barruso" under the Project FS/7-2010.

References

1. ElGamal, T.: A public-key cryptosystem and a signature scheme based on discrete logarithm. IEEE Trans. Inform. Theory 31, 469–472 (1985)
2. Menezes, A., van Oorschot, P., Vanstone, S.: Handbook of applied cryptography. CRC Press, Boca Raton (1997)

3. Rivest, R.L., Shamir, A., Adleman, L.: A method for obtaining digital signatures and public-key cryptosystems. Comm. ACM 21, 120–126 (1978)
4. National Institute of Standards and Technology: Secure Hash Standard (SHS). Federal Information Processing Standard Publication 180-2 (2002)
5. Chaum, D., van Heyst, E.: Group signatures. In: Davies, D.W. (ed.) EUROCRYPT 1991. LNCS, vol. 547, pp. 257–265. Springer, Heidelberg (1991)
6. Chaum, D.: Showing credentials without identification. In: Pichler, F. (ed.) EUROCRYPT 1985. LNCS, vol. 219, pp. 241–244. Springer, Heidelberg (1986)
7. Ohta, K., Okamoto, T., Koyama, K.: Membership authentication for hierarchical multigroups using the extended fiat-shamir scheme. In: Damgård, I.B. (ed.) EUROCRYPT 1990. LNCS, vol. 473, pp. 446–457. Springer, Heidelberg (1991)
8. Shizuya, H., Koyama, S., Itoh, T.: Demonstrating possession without revelating factors and its applications. In: Seberry, J., Pieprzyk, J.P. (eds.) AUSCRYPT 1990. LNCS, vol. 453, pp. 273–293. Springer, Heidelberg (1990)
9. Bresson, E., Stern, J.: Efficient revocation in group signature. In: Kim, K.C. (ed.) PKC 2001. LNCS, vol. 1992, pp. 190–206. Springer, Heidelberg (2001)
10. Camenish, J., Michels, M.: Separability and efficiency for generic group signature schemes (Extended abstract). In: Wiener, M. (ed.) CRYPTO 1999. LNCS, vol. 1666, pp. 413–430. Springer, Heidelberg (1999)
11. Camenish, J., Stadler, M.: Efficient group signature schemes for large groups. In: Kaliski Jr., B.S. (ed.) CRYPTO 1997. LNCS, vol. 1294, pp. 410–424. Springer, Heidelberg (1997)
12. Ateniese, G., Camenish, J., Joye, M., Tsudik, G.: A practical and provably secure coalition-resistant group signature scheme. In: Bellare, M. (ed.) CRYPTO 2000. LNCS, vol. 1880, pp. 255–270. Springer, Heidelberg (2000)
13. Ateniese, G., de Medeiros, B.: Efficient group signatures without trapdoors. In: Laih, C.-S. (ed.) ASIACRYPT 2003. LNCS, vol. 2894, pp. 246–268. Springer, Heidelberg (2003)
14. Nguyen, L., Safavi-Naini, R.: Efficient and provably secure trapdoor-free group signature schemes from bilinear pairings. In: Lee, P.J. (ed.) ASIACRYPT 2004. LNCS, vol. 3329, pp. 372–386. Springer, Heidelberg (2004)
15. Shoup, V., Gennaro, R.: Securing threshold cryptosystems against chosen ciphertext attack. J. Cryptology 15(2), 75–96 (2002)
16. Boneh, D., Boyen, X., Shacham, H.: Short group signatures. In: Franklin, M. (ed.) CRYPTO 2004. LNCS, vol. 3152, pp. 41–55. Springer, Heidelberg (2004)
17. Camenich, J., Lysyanskaya, A.: Signature schemes and anonymous credentials from bilinear maps. In: Franklin, M. (ed.) CRYPTO 2004. LNCS, vol. 3152, pp. 56 72. Springer, Heidelberg (2004)
18. Boneh, D., Boyen, X.: Short signatures without random oracles. In: Cachin, C., Camenish, J. (eds.) EUROCRYPT 2004. LNCS, vol. 3027, pp. 56–73. Springer, Heidelberg (2004)
19. Susilo, W.: Short fail-stop signature scheme based on factorization and discrete logarithm assumptions. Theor. Comput. Sci. 410, 736–744 (2009)

Keeping Group Communications Private: An Up-to-Date Review on Centralized Secure Multicast

J.A.M. Naranjo and L.G. Casado*

Dpt. of Computer Architecture and Electronics,
University of Almería, Spain
{jmn843,leo}@ual.es

Abstract. The secure multicast field has been extensively studied for more than a decade now and there exist numerous proposals throughout academic literature. This paper presents a selection of those most important and popular to the date, focusing on centralized schemes due to their high popularity and the recent publication of alternatives that do not appear in previous revisions. Comparisons are provided and special attention is paid to communications and storage overhead.

Keywords: key distribution, secure group communication, centralized secure multicast.

1 Introduction

Secure multicast communications imply establishing a common encryption key that can be used to cipher the transmitted information. The first and trivial approach for achieving that is to establish n secure channels (one for each recipient), which obviously soon becomes impractical as the number of recipients scales. Therefore a wide variety of schemes have appeared in the last decade. Regardless of their nature, schemes must provide: information privacy while in transit, an efficient and fault-tolerant rekeying process so an acceptable quality of service (QoS) is guaranteed, and *forward* and *backward secrecy*. The former implies that a member which leaves the network (i.e., her membership expires) should not be able to decrypt any ciphered information transmitted thereafter, while the latter implies that an arriving member should not be able to decrypt any ciphered information transmitted before her arrival. Both impose a refreshment of the encryption key used to cipher the transmitted information. These two restrictions may become an efficiency problem at high churn rates (avalanches of members joining and/or leaving). Some less restrictive scenarios may not require backward secrecy. Additionally, schemes must be resistant to *collusion*, i.e., old recipients allying together to use their expired key material in order to illegally

* J.A.M. Naranjo and L. G. Casado are supported by the Spanish Ministry of Science and Innovation (TIN2008-01117). L. G. Casado is also supported by funds of Junta de Andalucía (P08-TIC-3518).

Á. Herrero and E. Corchado (Eds.): CISIS 2011, LNCS 6694, pp. 151–159, 2011.

decrypt new information. There are other features of schemes that are directly related to reliability. One of them is the *self-healing* property: in some schemes members are able to obtain lost keying material without needing to make new requests to the Key Server. Finally, secure multicast protocols can be divided into *stateful* and *stateless*. In the former, re-key messages contain modifications on the previous keying states and thus users must be aware of all re-key operations performed since their arrival. In the latter, members may obtain all the keying material from scratch at every re-key operation, which clearly makes them more resilient against faulty networks. Addressing these reliability issues has become the trend in the last years due to the popularization of mobile and ad-hoc networks.

Centralized secure multicast schemes are of great use thanks to its simplicity and the popularization of services like IPTV [1] and ad-hoc networks. Even in decentralized architectures for huge audiences they appear at the core of every separate group. Therefore, centralized schemes are an important part of the secure multicast global field. This paper presents a selection of the most important centralized secure multicast protocols to the date, due to the recent appearance of new proposals that, for obvious reasons, were not included in previous surveys [2][3] (another interesting, updated survey is [4]). Schemes are discussed and compared attending to the properties mentioned above, and divided into three main categories attending to the scenario they are addressed to: (1) general-purpose schemes, suitable for a wide range of applications, (2) multi-group schemes, specially useful in scenarios that involve several different information channels (such as IPTV platforms) and (3) self-healing schemes for ad-hoc networks. The following notation will be used along the paper. The single entity that manages the re-keying process receives the name *Key Server*. Hosts that conform the main body of the network are named *members*. h and d denote trees height and degree, respectively. The total number of members is given by n. b is the bitlength of a symmetric key. Additional specific notation will be indicated where needed. Sections 2, 3 and 4 review the three categories respectively, discuss them and show comparisons. Section 5 concludes the survey and gives a global vision of the field.

2 General-Purpose Schemes: LKH and Extensions

General purpose schemes were the first ones to appear and have been around for more than ten years now. One of the earliest is the Group Key Management Protocol (GKMP) [5], in which the Key Server shares a key with every member in the audience and a common group key. Some re-key operations require a unicast connection with each member, hence the scheme scales poorly. Among the different existing approaches, the hierarchical tree of keys is clearly the preferred one, due to its smart arrangement of users and keys. The first scheme of that kind was the Logical Key Hierarchy (LKH) [6] [7]. In order to reduce the number of re-key messages per join/leave operation of the trivial approach, a logical tree is built with randomly chosen *user keys* at the leaves. Figure 1(a) depicts such a tree. Every user key is only known by its owner and the Key Server. A Data Encryption Key (DEK), namely *group key*, is placed at the root node: it encrypts the actual broadcast information, while intermediate tree nodes keep Key Encryption Keys (KEKs), used in the re-key process. A user knows only the keys in her *key path*, i.e., the keys in the path from its leave to the root. The arrival or departure of a member implies that the group key, the member's keypath and those nodes that are siblings to the keypath must be refreshed. For balanced trees, the number of required multicast messages for a single join operation is $2h - 1$ while the new member must receive $h + 1$ keys. A leave requires $2h$ keys updated. Appropriate tree configurations for optimal bandwidth usage are discussed in [8] and [9]. Subsequent efforts seek to reduce the number of messages sent by LKH. A widely adopted approach is to use one-way functions or combinations of one-way functions with pseudo-random number generators (PRNGs). LKH+ [10], LKH++ [11] and the recent SKD [12] use this approach in a temporary manner: new keys are derived from old ones by means of a one-way function, independently of their position within the tree. LKH++ and SKD approximately halve LKH's bandwidth usage in join operations. Additionally, SKD claims a large reduction of the computation effort required at the Key Server. One-way Function Trees (OFT) [13], One-way Function Chain Trees (OFCT) [14] and ELK [15] use the one-way function approach in a spatial manner: every key in the tree is derived from its children, therefore the tree is built in a bottom-up fashion, starting at user keys (which are randomly picked by the Key Server). These schemes assume one-way functions to be perfect, but Horng proposed a collusion attack against OFT in [16] which was taken into account by Ku and Chen in order to develop an improved collusion resistant version of that protocol [17]. ELK addresses bandwidth reduction and reliability simultaneously: a communication-computation tradeoff is introduced, and some degree of tolerance against message losses is achieved. Members need no aid from the Key Server to derive their key path and, with the use of batch and scheduled re-keys, no multicast messages are required in joins.

The Flat Table (FT) approach [18] (contemporary to LKH) also uses a hierarchical key tree arrangement though there are subtle differences which allow *storage-communication-optimality* [19]. However, vulnerabilities against collusion attacks were soon discovered [20]. The recent EGK scheme [20] retakes the Flat Table idea and smartly solves the collusion problem. Its authors claim to obtain storage-communication-optimality and constant small message sizes. The Clustering approach [21] groups members within clusters of fixed size (say c). Every cluster is placed at a tree leave and assigned a KEK. The storage overhead at the Key Server is reduced, but leaves require one by one key encryptions within the affected cluster.

SecureLock [22], and the scheme proposed in [23] may be also included in the general-purpose category although their approach is mainly focused on using the computational capabilities of the Key Server rather than arranging members in a given structure. The scheme in [23] is stateless but needs large re-key messages which prevent it from being used in very large networks. The SecureLock is also

Table 1. General-purpose secure multicast schemes comparison

| | Storage overhead | | Communications overhead | | |
| | Key Server | Member | Join | | Leave |
			Multicast	Unicast	Multicast
GKMP [5], 1997	$2b$	$2b$	$2b$	$2b$	$(n-1)b$
Clusters [21], 1999	$\frac{n}{c}\frac{d}{d-1}+\frac{n}{c}$	$log_d(\frac{n}{c})+2$	$c-1+d\,log_d(\frac{n}{c})$	$log_d(\frac{n}{c})+2$	$c-1+d\,log_d(\frac{n}{c})$
LKH [6][7], 1999	$(2n-1)b$	$(h+1)b$	$(2h-1)b$	$(h+1)b$	$2hb$
ELK [15], 2001	$(2n-1)b$	$(h+1)b$	0	$(h+1)b$	$h(b_1+b_2)$
LKH++ [11], 2002	$(2n-1)b$	$(h+1)b$	$b+log_2 n$	$(h+1)b$	$log_2 n+(h-1)b$
OFT [13], 2003	$(2n-1)b$	$(h+1)b$	$(h+1)b$	$(h+1)b$	$(h+1)b$
SKD [12], 2009	$\frac{(dn-1)b}{d-1}$	hb	h	hb	$(d-1)hb$
EGK [20], 2010	$log_2 n$	$log_2 n$	b	$2b$	$log_2 n$

stateless but its computation complexity becomes excessive when increasing the number of members. To alleviate that problem, Scheikl et al. combine it with the LKH approach, thus obtaining a stateful protocol [24].

Most of the protocols reviewed above can handle large, dynamic audiences in many multicast services that demand privacy. Regarding security, they are mainly collusion free except for OFT and FT. Finally, and regarding reliability, we must remark that LKH was introduced in the late 90's, a time when the main part of communications were held on reliable links. That is the main reason why these schemes normally do not address reliability issues and therefore they are statefull and not self-healing. Probably ELK is the most reliable protocol in this family. Table 1 shows a comparison in terms of storage and communication costs of the most important schemes along with recent proposals (SKD and EGK). Data are expressed in bits. There are small but subtle variations in the results shown. It can be seen that older schemes focus on reducing communications in re-key operations, while acquiescing in linear storage needs. More recent proposals focus on the latter, given that acceptable bandwidth usage results were already obtained. Other reasons for storage reduction are the popularization of smart devices (with low storage capabilities) and the ever increasing audiences as multimedia multicast services become more and more popular. As a last remark we note that statistical improvements can be applied to member arrangement in tree-based schemes in order to gain efficiency and scalability [25].

3   Multi-group Schemes

There exist scenarios in which several, different information channels are encrypted separately and reach different, not disjoint groups of members. Typical examples are multimedia platforms with several pay-per-view channels and communications in hierarchically managed networks. Schemes shown next can be seen as an extension of the tree approach: multiple trees are built from a single, global set of leaves, thus obtaining several roots. Figure 1(b) shows an arrangement example. Since a single member may now belong to more than one group, her key path includes all keys from her leaf to the different roots she is connected to, therefore re-key operations will normally affect more than one tree (however, note that not all users are always connected to all roots). The pioneer proposal,

Table 2. Multi-group secure multicast schemes comparison

	Storage overhead		Communications overhead		
	Key Server	Member	Join		Leave
			Multicast	Unicast	Multicast
MG[26][27]	$O(\log n)$	$O(Mn)$	$O(d \log n)$	$O(Md \log n)$	$O(Md \log n)$
HAC[28]	$O(\frac{d}{d-1}Mn_0)$	$O(\log n_0)$	0	$O(1)$	$O(d \log n_0)$
Zhang et al.[29]	$O(n)$	$O(1)$	0	$O(M)$	$O(M)$

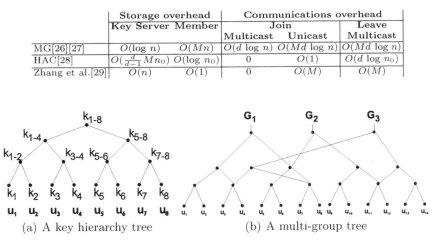

(a) A key hierarchy tree   (b) A multi-group tree

Fig. 1. Tree hierarchies of keys

the MG scheme, appears in [26] and [27]. Due to the intricate resultant network, single re-key operations become significantly complex in terms of overhead and therefore batch re-keyings are used. The HAC scheme [28] reduces both bandwidth and communications overhead by improving the multi-tree arrangement and using one-way functions. Both schemes are statefull. Zhang et al. present a stateless protocol based on the bilinear Diffie-Hellman Problem [29]. Table 2 shows a comparison of [27], [28] and [29] in big$-O$ notation terms. M is the number of groups/trees and n_0 the average number of members in a subgroup. Other multi-group schemes are [30] and [31]. To the best of our knowledge, it is the first time this kind of schemes is included in a survey.

4   Self-healing Schemes for Ad-Hoc Networks

Last decade advances on smart devices have led to the development and massive use of MANETS: mobile ad-hoc networks with unreliable links, limited bandwidth, highly dynamic topologies and unpredictable member behavior (there is no guarantee that members will be online at a given time or for a given period of time). What's more, most of the devices used in these networks have low computational capacities given their need to manage energy efficiently. Due to the specific restrictions that MANETS impose, re-keying is usually performed on a batch manner. An interval between two batch re-keys is called a *session*. Zhu et al. present one of the earliests schemes in [32]. They add reliability and self-healing to a traditional scheme in order to obtain *m-recoverability* at a low additional bandwidth overhead. m-recoverability implies that a member may still recover the current keying material after missing a maximum of m key updates.

An important family within self-healing schemes are those based on polynomials and secret sharing techniques. The scheme in [33] by Staddon et al. also achieves m-recoverability. It combines the transmission to members of an initial set of shares with the transmission of additional, redundant shares at every update round. With that information, members are able to recover a given key even if they miss its corresponding update. The price for that is an increase in bandwidth overhead, up to $O(mt^2)$: m is the maximum number of updates a member can miss, while t is both the polynomial degree and the minimum number of ex-members that must collude in order to break the system. The protocol presented in [34] by Liu et al. goes further by reducing the bandwidth overhead to $O(tj)$. The value j is the current session within the interval m: note that the re-key information transmitted is a multiple of j and therefore increases depending on the current session, to a maximum of m times. More recent schemes involve the use of one way functions. The scheme in [35] by Dutta et al. achieves a better bandwidth usage, constant member storage requirements, presumably unconditional security and is not restricted to only m sessions recoverability. However, Du et al. reveal security weaknesses of [35] and propose an improved, collusion-free protocol [36]. Finally, the same authors propose another constant storage scheme [37] but they do not guarantee its resistance to collusion.

Table 3 compares the schemes found in [33], [34], [35] and [37], focusing on the storage requirements at the member and the communication overhead per key update (q is a large prime involved in calculations, greater than n). Data are expressed in terms of bits. Given the limited memory space of smart devices, constant storage requirements are desirable. As we see, Dutta et al. [35] and Du et al. [37] offer the best results in those terms. Regarding the communication overhead, Dutta et al. [35] shows the best results again. However, its vulnerability to collusion attacks makes it a weak option to choose. Du et al. [37] and Liu

Table 3. Self-healing secure multicast schemes comparison

	Storage at member	Communication overhead	Collusion resistant	Key long life-span
Staddon et al. [33]	$(m-j+1)^2 \log q$	$(mt^2 + 2mt + m + t) \log q$	Yes	No
Liu et al. [34]	$(m-j+1) \log q$	$(2tj+j) \log q$	Yes	No
Dutta et al. [35]	$3 \log q$	$(t+1+j) \log q$	No	Yes
Du et al. [37]	$3 \log q$	$(3t+2+j) \log q$	Yes	Yes

Table 4. Feature comparison for the different schemes reviewed

	Cat.	Stful/Stless	Coll. Res.	Rel.	Keys tree		Cat.	Stful/Stless	Coll. Res.	Rel.	Keys tree
SL [22], 1989	1	Stless	✓			SKD [12], 2009	1	Stful	✓		✓
GKMP [5], 1997	1	Stful	✓			EGK [20], 2010	1	Stful	✓		✓
Cluster [21], 1997	1	Stful	✓		✓	Naranjo [23], 2010	1	Stless	✓		
LKH [6][7], 1999	1	Stful	✓		✓	Zhang [29], 2006	2	Stless	✓	✓	✓
LKH+ [10], 1999	1	Stful	✓		✓	MG [26][27], 2007	2	Stful	✓		✓
OFCT [14], 1999	1	Stful	✓		✓	HAC [28], 2008	2	Stful	✓		✓
FT [18], 1999	1	Stful				Staddon [33], 2002	3	Stless			✓
ELK [15], 2001	1	Stful	✓	✓	✓	Zhu [32], 2003	3	Stless		✓	✓
LKH++ [11], 2002	1	Stful	✓		✓	Liu [34], 2003	3	Stless	✓	✓	
SL+HTA[24],2002	1	Stful	✓		✓	Dutta [35], 2007	3	Stless		✓	
OFT [13], 2003	1	Stful			✓	Du [36], 2008	3	Stless	✓	✓	
Ku [17], 2003	1	Stful	✓		✓	Du [37], 2009	3	Stless		✓	

et al. [34] show good results and achieve resistance against collusion. Note that overhead depends, among other values, on the security parameter, which results in a tradeoff between security and bandwidth usage. Key life-span refers to user keys lifetime: some schemes, such as Staddon et al. [33] and Liu et al. [34], require the user key to be renewed after m sessions. That is clearly a drawback since it increases the workload at the Key Server side and bandwidth usage, specially in faulty networks which is the case. To conclude, we believe that self-healing schemes still have several challenges to overcome, mainly: costly setup phases that must be repeated after m sessions, generalizing a constant use of storage, going further on bandwidth usage reduction and overcoming the usual security-communication overhead tradeoff.

5   Conclusions

This paper shows a survey on the field that includes some of the latest proposals. Table 4 compares the different schemes introduced along the paper according to their features: "Cat.", category, either (1) general-purpose, (2) multi-group or (3) ad-hoc oriented; "Stful/Stless", stateful or stateless; "Coll.Res.", collusion resistant; and "Keys tree", use of the hierarchical tree approach. Still new proposals appear each year and, with the popularization of new scenarios like IPTV and specially ad-hoc networks, the desirable features for a secure multicast scheme are evolving: low bandwidth and faulty links demand to reduce the number and frequency of communications with the Key Server and the possibility to recover from information loss. It seems clear that this trend will increase in the foreseeable future.

References

1. Cisco IOS Secure Multicast, http://www.cisco.com/en/US/prod/collateral/iosswrel/ps6537/ps6552/prod_white_paper0900aecd8047191e.html
2. Rafaeli, S., Hutchison, D.: A survey of key management for secure group communication. ACM Comput. Surv. 35(3), 309–329 (2003)
3. Chan, K.-C., Chan, S.-H.G.: Key management approaches to offer data confidentiality for secure multicast. IEEE Network 17(5), 30–39 (2003)
4. Zhu, S., Jajodia, S.: Scalable group key management for secure multicast: A taxonomy and new directions. In: Huang, H., MacCallum, D., Du, D.-Z. (eds.) Network Security, pp. 57–75. Springer, US (2010)
5. Harney, H., Muckenhirn, C.: Group key management protocol (GKMP) specification. RFC 2093 (1997)
6. Wallner, D., Harder, E., Agee, R.: Key management for multicast: Issues and architectures. RFC 2627 (1999)
7. Wong, C.K., Gouda, M., Lam, S.S.: Secure group communications using key graphs. IEEE/ACM Transactions on Networking 8(1), 16–30 (2000)
8. Chan, K.-C., Chan, S.-H.G.: Distributed servers approach for large-scale secure multicast. IEEE JSAC 20(8) (October 2002)
9. Chan, K.-C., Chan, S.-H.G.: Distributed servers networks for secure multicast. In: Proc. IEEE Globecom 2001, San Antonio, TX, pp. 25–29 (2001)

10. Waldvogel, M., Caronni, G., Sun, D., Weiler, N., Plattner, B.: The VersaKey framework: versatile group key management. IEEE Journal on Selected Areas in Communications 17(9), 1614–1631 (1999)
11. Di Pietro, R., Mancini, L.V., Jajodia, S.: Efficient and secure keys management for wireless mobile communications. In: Proceedings of POMC 2002, pp. 66–73 (2002)
12. Lin, J.-C., Huang, K.-H., Lai, F., Lee, H.-C.: Secure and efficient group key management with shared key derivation. Comput. Stand. Inter. 31(1), 192–208 (2009)
13. Sherman, A.T., McGrew, D.A.: Key establishment in large dynamic groups using one-way function trees. IEEE Trans. Software 29, 444–458 (2003)
14. Canetti, R., Garay, J., Itkis, G., Micciancio, D., Naor, M., Pinkas, B.: Multicast security: A taxonomy and some efficient constructions. In: Proceedings of INFOCOM 1999, pp. 708–716. IEEE, Los Alamitos (1999)
15. Perrig, A., Song, D., Tygar, J.D.: Elk, a new protocol for efficient large-group key distribution. Proceedings of IEEE S&P, 247–262 (2001)
16. Horng, G.: Cryptanalysis of a key management scheme for secure multicast communications. IEICE Transactions on Communications E85-B(5), 1050–1051 (2002)
17. Ku, W.-C., Chen, S.-M.: An improved key management scheme for large dynamic groups using one-way function trees. In: Proceedings 2003 International Conference on Parallel Processing Workshops, pp. 391–396 (October 2003)
18. Chang, I., Engel, R., Kandlur, D., Pendarakis, D., Saha, D.: Key management for secure internet multicast using boolean function minimization techniques. In: Proceedings of INFOCOM 1999, pp. 689–698. IEEE, Los Alamitos (1999)
19. Poovendran, R., Baras, J.S.: An information-theoretic approach for design and analysis of rooted-tree-based multicast key management schemes. IEEE Transactions on Information Theory, 2824–2834 (2001)
20. Zhou, Z., Huang, D.: An optimal key distribution scheme for secure multicast group communication. In: INFOCOM 2010, pp. 331–335 (2010)
21. Canetti, R., Malkin, T., Nissim, K.: Efficient communication-storage tradeoffs for multicast encryption, pp. 459–474. Springer, Heidelberg (1999)
22. Chiou, G.-h., Chen, W.-T.: Secure broadcasting using the secure lock. IEEE Trans. Softw. Eng. 15(8), 929–934 (1989)
23. Naranjo, J.A.M., López-Ramos, J.A., Casado, L.G.: Applications of the Extended Euclidean Algorithm to privacy and secure communications. In: Proceedings of CMMSE (2010)
24. Scheikl, O., Lane, J., Boyer, R., Eltoweissy, M.: Multi-level secure multicast: the rethinking of secure locks. In: Proceedings International Conference on Parallel Processing Workshops, pp. 17–24 (2002)
25. Pais, A.R., Joshi, S.: A new probabilistic rekeying method for secure multicast groups. Int. J. Inf. Secur. 9, 275–286 (2010)
26. Sun, Y., Liu, K.J.R.: Scalable hierarchical access control in secure group communications. In: INFOCOM 2004, vol. 2, pp. 1296–1306 (2004)
27. Sun, Y., Liu, K.J.R.: Hierarchical group access control for secure multicast communications. IEEE/ACM Trans. Netw. 15, 1514–1526 (2007)
28. Zhang, Q., Wang, Y., Jue, J.P.: A key management scheme for hierarchical access control in group communication. International Journal of Network Security 7(3), 323–334 (2008)
29. Zhang, J., Varadharajan, V., Mu, Y.: A scalable multi-service group key management scheme. In: Proceedings of AICT-ICIW 2006, pp. 172–177 (2006)
30. Yan, J., Ma, J., Liu, H.: Key hierarchies for hierarchical access control in secure group communications. Computer Networks 53(3), 353–364 (2009)

31. Hur, J., Yoon, H.: A multi-service group key management scheme for stateless receivers in wireless mesh networks. Mob. Netw. Appl. 15, 680–692 (2010)
32. Zhu, S., Setia, S., Jajodia, S.: Adding reliable and self-healing key distribution to the subset difference group rekeying method for secure multicast. In: Stiller, B., Carle, G., Karsten, M., Reichl, P. (eds.) NGC 2003 and ICQT 2003. LNCS, vol. 2816, pp. 107–118. Springer, Heidelberg (2003)
33. Staddon, J., Miner, S., Franklin, M., Balfanz, D., Malkin, M., Dean, D.: Self-healing key distribution with revocation. In: Proceedings of IEEE Symposium on Security and Privacy, pp. 241–257 (2002)
34. Liu, D., Ning, P., Sun, K.: Efficient self-healing group key distribution with revocation capability. In: Proceedings of the 10th ACM conference on Computer and Communications Security, CCS 2003, pp. 231–240 (2003)
35. Dutta, R., Dong, Y., Mukhopadhyay, W.S.: Constant storage self-healing key distribution with revocation in wireless sensor network (2007)
36. Du, W., He, M.: Self-healing key distribution with revocation and resistance to the collusion attack in wireless sensor networks. In: Baek, J., Bao, F., Chen, K., Lai, X. (eds.) ProvSec 2008. LNCS, vol. 5324, pp. 345–359. Springer, Heidelberg (2008)
37. Du, W., He, M., Li, X.: A new constant storage self-healing key distribution with revocation in wireless sensor networks. In: Hua, A., Chang, S.-L. (eds.) ICA3PP 2009. LNCS, vol. 5574, pp. 832–843. Springer, Heidelberg (2009)

Java Card Implementation of the Elliptic Curve Integrated Encryption Scheme Using Prime and Binary Finite Fields

V. Gayoso Martínez[1], L. Hernández Encinas[2], and C. Sánchez Ávila[3]

[1] Universidad Francisco de Vitoria, Pozuelo de Alarcón (Madrid), Spain
v.gayoso.prof@ufv.es
[2] Department of Information Processing and Coding, Applied Physics Institute,
CSIC, Madrid, Spain
luis@iec.csic.es
[3] Department of Applied Mathematics to Information Technologies,
Polytechnic University, Madrid, Spain
carmen.sanchez.avila@upm.es

Abstract. Elliptic Curve Cryptography (ECC) can be considered an approach to public-key cryptography based on the arithmetic of elliptic curves and the Elliptic Curve Discrete Logarithm Problem (ECDLP). Regarding encryption, the best-known scheme based on ECC is the Elliptic Curve Integrated Encryption Scheme (ECIES), included in standards from ANSI, IEEE, and also ISO/IEC. In the present work, we provide a comparison of two Java Card implementations of ECIES that we have developed using prime and binary fields, respectively.

Keywords: Java Card, elliptic curves, public key encryption schemes.

1 Introduction

In the current world, cryptography is essential for the protection of data and communication systems. Whitfield Diffie and Martin Hellman sparked off a revolution when they introduced the concept of public-key cryptography in 1976. Since that year, a great number of cryptosystems have been proposed, though many have been proved to be unsuitable for commercial purposes due to vulnerabilities in their designs or to their high complexity. The best-known successful public-key cryptosystem is RSA [1,2], which was the first algorithm known to be suitable for signing as well as encrypting data.

In 1985, Victor Miller [3] and Neil Koblitz [4] independently suggested the usage of elliptic curves defined over finite fields in cryptography [5]. In comparison with other public-key cryptosystems, Elliptic Curve Cryptography (ECC) uses significantly shorter keys. The reason for this fact is related to the hardness of the ECDLP, which is considered to be more difficult to solve than the Integer Factorization Problem (IFP) used by RSA or the Discrete Logarithm Problem (DLP) which is the basis of the ElGamal encryption scheme [6].

Á. Herrero and E. Corchado (Eds.): CISIS 2011, LNCS 6694, pp. 160–167, 2011.

Smart cards are small, portable, tamper-resistant devices offering users convenient storage and processing capabilities, and as such they play a prominent role in providing the required security level in banking transactions, the GSM and UMTS cellular systems or pay TV environments, to put only a few examples. Smart cards are amenable to cryptographic implementations, as they contain multiple software and hardware countermeasures designed to protect sensible information such as the keying material [7].

The two most widely used smart card platforms are Java Card [8], developed by Sun with the support from several leading smart card providers during the 1990s, and MULTOS (a multi-application operating system controlled by the MULTOS Consortium) [9]. Though both platforms implement cryptographic capabilities, the public-key cryptography capabilities provided by Java Card are more complete, specially regarding ECC functionality.

In the present work, we describe two implementations, using prime and binary fields, of the best known encryption scheme using elliptic curves, the Elliptic Curve Integrated Encryption Scheme (ECIES). To our knowledge, there are no smart card implementations of this encryption scheme, so this is the first time that ECIES is implemented, and its performance is analysed, in Java Cards. We also provide a performance comparison of both implementations using different combinations of plaintext lengths and key sizes.

This paper is organized as follows: Section 2 presents a brief introduction to ECC and ECIES. Section 3 includes a summary of the ECIES support in Java Card. Section 4 provides the main characteristics of the smart cards used in the tests and offers some details about the applet development phase. Finally, in Section 5 we present the experimental results of the tests along with the most important findings and conclusions.

2   Elliptic Curve Cryptography and ECIES

An elliptic curve E defined over a finite field $\mathbb{F}$ is a plane non-singular cubic curve with at least a rational point [10]. In practice, generic elliptic curves are managed using the following equation, known as the Weierstrass equation in non-homogeneous form [11], where the elements $a_1, a_2, a_3, a_4, a_6 \in \mathbb{F}$ and $\Delta \neq 0$, being Δ the discriminant of the curve E [12]:

$$E : y^2 + a_1 xy + a_3 y = x^3 + a_2 x^2 + a_4 x + a_6. \tag{1}$$

The homogeneous version of the Weierstrass equation implies the existence of a special point, called the point at infinity, which is denoted as $\mathcal{O}$ and does not have a counterpart in the affine plane.

When working with finite fields, it is possible to obtain simplified versions of the Weierstrass equation. If the finite field is a prime field, i.e. $\mathbb{F} = \mathbb{F}_p$, where $p > 3$ is a prime number, the equation defining the elliptic curve becomes:

$$y^2 = x^3 + ax + b. \tag{2}$$

On the other hand, if the finite field is a binary field, i.e. $\mathbb{F} = \mathbb{F}_{2^m}$, where m is a positive integer number, then the equation of the elliptic curve is:

$$y^2 + xy = x^3 + ax^2 + b. \tag{3}$$

Typical applications in security are key exchange, digital signatures and data encryption. For those three applications, there are lots of standards, some of them implemented through ECC. The best known ECC schemes and protocols are the Elliptic Curve Diffie Hellman (ECDH), a key agreement protocol [3,4]; the Elliptic Curve Digital Signature Algorithm (ECDSA), equivalent to the DSA algorithm [13]; and the Elliptic Curve Integrated Encryption Scheme, the most extended ECC encryption scheme, defined in ANSI X9.63 [14], IEEE 1363a [15], and ISO/IEC 18033-2 [16].

As its name properly indicates, ECIES is an integrated encryption scheme which uses the following functions:

- Key Agreement (KA): Function used for the generation of a shared secret by two parties.
- Key Derivation Function (KDF): Mechanism that produces a set of keys from keying material and some optional parameters.
- Encryption (ENC): Symmetric encryption algorithm.
- Message Authentication Code (MAC): The output of the MAC function is the data used to authenticate a message.
- Hash (HASH): Digest function, used within the KDF and the MAC function.

3   ECIES Support in Java Card

Java Card is a framework for programming and executing applications in smart cards developed by Sun and several smart card providers. Java Card version 2.1 already presented some cryptographic capabilities (e.g. DES, RSA, SHA-1, etc.), but the support for ECC was not included until version 2.2.

Even though ECDH and ECDSA are available in several versions of Java Card, and thus a programmer can use both ECC schemes by calling the proper methods of the Java Card API, this is not the case for ECIES. In fact, not only ECIES is not directly implemented as a single primitive in Java Card, but some of the functionality needed (e.g. the KDF and some MAC functions) must be developed by the programmer. To our knowledge, no ECIES implementation has been developed in Java Card prior to ours.

Java Card 2.2.1 implements the following functionality related to ECIES:

- KA function: Both Diffie-Hellman (DH) and the related Diffie-Hellman with cofactor (DHC), with the peculiarity that, instead of the product of the sender's ephemeral private key and the recipient's public key, both functions provide the SHA-1 output of that result.
- ENC function: AES with key length 128, 192, and 256 bits in modes CBC and ECB (in both cases without padding).

- HASH function: SHA-1.
- ECC key length: 113, 131, 163, and 193 bits in binary fields, and 112, 128, 160, and 192 bits in prime fields.

In comparison to the previous version, Java Card 2.2.2 included new MAC and hash functions. More precisely, in this version programmers were able to use the following functions that were not previously available: SHA-256, SHA-384, SHA-512, HMAC-SHA-1, HMAC-SHA-256, HMAC-SHA-384, and HMAC-SHA-512.

4   Smart Cards Used in the Tests and Applet Development

The smart card models used in the tests presented in this contribution, namely JCOP 41 and JCOP J3A, have been kindly provided by NXP Semiconductors. All the information presented in this section is publicly available at the NXP web site [17,18,19].

Table 1 summarizes the main characteristics of JCOP 41 [17,18] and JCOP J3A cards [17,19]:

It must be clarified at this point that the JCOP 41 product implements ECC for curves defined over $\mathbb{F}_{2^m}$, while the JCOP J3A model allows to use elliptic curves defined over $\mathbb{F}_p$. This is the reason why the available key sizes are not the same in those cards (131, 163, and 193 bits in JCOP 41 cards, and 128, 160, and 192 in JCOP J3A cards). For comparison purposes, in practice we will treat keys of similar lengths as if they were of the same size, as the difference in bits is not significant (131 vs 128, 163 vs 160, and 193 vs 192).

The applets for the JCOP 41 and JCOP J3A products have been developed by us using the Eclipse software (version 3.2) and the JCOP Tools plug-in for Eclipse kindly provided by NXP Semiconductors. This plug-in allows to easily compile, download and install Java Card applets in the JCOP smart cards.

With the goal of producing a valid comparison, we decided to implement the same ECIES functionality in both platforms, with the sole exception of the finite fields and the key lengths used (binary finite fields with key lengths of 131, 163, and 193 bits in JCOP 41 cards, and prime finite fields with key lengths of 128, 160, and 192 in JCOP J3A cards).

Table 1. JCOP 41 and JCOP J3A features

	JCOP 41	JCOP J3A
Hardware module	P5CT072	P5CD080
CPU	Secure MX51	Secure MX51
Operating system	JCOP 2.2.1	JCOP 2.4.1
Java Card version	2.2.1	2.2.2
GlobalPlatform version	2.1.1	2.1.1
ROM	160 Kbytes	200 Kbytes
EEPROM	72 Kbytes	80 Kbytes
RAM	4608 bytes	6144 bytes
Cryptographic coprocessors	3DES and PKI	3DES, AES, and PKI

The most important common features of the applets for both platforms are the following:

- KA function: DH, where the output of the function is the SHA-1 value of the shared secret.
- KDF function: KDF1 [16].
- ENC algorithm: 3DES with two keys, in CBC mode, and without padding.
- MAC function: HMAC-SHA-1 [20].
- HASH function: SHA-1.

As the maximum length for the APDUs transmitted to and from the smart cards using the T=0 protocol is 255 bytes [21], the plaintexts managed in the tests performed in this contribution have a maximum size of 160 bytes, so both the cryptogram provided by the smart card during the encryption process and the cryptogram sent to the smart card in the decryption process can be inserted in a single APDU.

The application code size in EEPROM is 4940 bytes for the JCOP 41 card and 4328 bytes in the case of the JCOP J3A card, as informed by Eclipse. The reason for this difference is that the JCOP 41 implementation manages keys of 4 possible sizes (113, 131, 163, and 193 bits) whilst the JCOP J3A manages only three types of keys (128, 160, and 192 bits). Regarding the keys of 113 bits available at the JCOP 41 cards, though implemented, we decided not to use them in this comparison, as that key size does not have a counterpart of a similar length in the JCOP J3A model.

Finally, it is worth mentioning that the elliptic curves implemented by the JCOP cards are standard curves published by SECG (sect131r1, sect193r1, secp128r1, and secp160r1), WAP Forum (c2pnb163v1), and ANSI (P-192).

5   Experimental Results and Conclusions

In order to be able to measure the encryption and decryption time, we developed a Java application using the Java Smartcard I/O API [22], available since Java SE 6, and the `System.nanoTime()` method included in that API, which returns the current value in nanoseconds of the most precise available system timer.

Using that timing function, the starting time has been taken exactly before sending the command APDU with the encryption/decryption request to the smart card, while the finishing time for each measurement has been obtained just after receiving the response APDU with the output of the encryption/decryption process from the smart card.

All the tests have been performed 20 times for each combination of message length (64, 96, 128, and 160 bytes) and key length (131, 163, and 193 bits when using the prime curves of JCOP 41, and 128, 160, and 192 bits in the case of the prime curves included in JCOP J3A).

The data included in Table 2 show the mean value of the 20 tests performed for every encryption and decryption combination in JCOP 41 and JCOP J3A cards. Taking into account all the tests, the maximum standard deviation computed

Table 2. JCOP 41 encryption and decryption time in milliseconds

			Encryption				Decryption		
			Message length (bytes)				Message length (bytes)		
		64	96	128	160	64	96	128	160
JCOP 41	Key	131	433.79	463.97	498.25	531.29	279.02	280.32	296.01	297.87
	length	163	461.07	491.89	525.60	554.59	291.71	293.15	309.11	310.76
	(bits)	193	499.28	529.95	563.75	593.98	311.19	313.08	328.78	331.00
JCOP J3A	Key	128	489.58	498.19	517.37	520.19	436.72	439.72	453.35	455.42
	length	160	532.51	535.03	549.06	551.17	459.89	462.83	476.58	479.01
	(bits)	192	597.85	601.28	615.44	617.52	523.09	525.75	539.93	542.82

is 0.81 milliseconds, which provides useful information about the stability of the smart card performance. Due to this stability, we decided that it was not necessary to perform additional tests, as the measures taken are concentrated around each average value and the CV in the worst-case scenario is 0.00286.

The results depend on the Java Card applet and the particular software optimizations applied (size of the arrays, variable usage and sharing, etc.), which means that a different applet could produce different values.

Figures 1 and 2 present the performance of JCOP 41 and JCOP J3A when encrypting and decrypting messages of 64 and 160 bytes, respectively. Those figures include the processing results for key lengths of 131, 163, and 193 bits (JCOP 41), and 128, 160, and 192 bits (JCOP J3A).

After reviewing the data, it can be stated that the encryption time is relatively similar in JCOP 41 and JCOP J3A cards. However, it seems that the JCOP J3A implementation is more sensible to an increase in the key size than the JCOP 41 applet when maintaining the length of the plaintext.

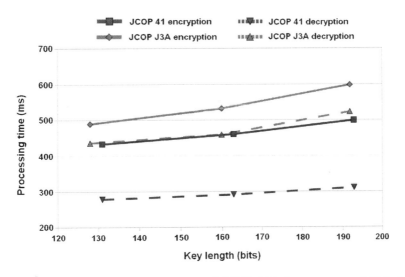

Fig. 1. Processing time in JCOP 41 and JCOP J3A for messages of 64 bytes

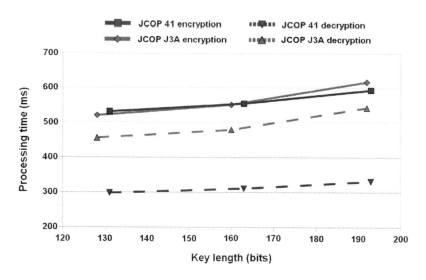

Fig. 2. Processing time in JCOP 41 and JCOP J3A for messages of 160 bytes

Observing the decryption time, it is clear that there is an important gap (approximately 150-200 milliseconds, depending on the key length and message size) regarding the decryption process in both smart cards. Given that the applet functionality is basically the same (all the variables are located in RAM, the arrays have the same length in all the cases, etc.) this difference can be only explained due to a difference in the DES cryptoprocessor used in those models or to the countermeasures put in place in each card to protect them against side channel attacks.

In both smart cards, the decryption process is faster than the encryption procedure, basically because in the encryption process there is one step (the generation of the ephemeral key pair) which is not performed during the decryption process.

The quite noticeable increase in the encryption processing time for the JCOP 41 cards can be also visualized in Figure 1, where it can be seen how the encryption time gap existing between JCOP 41 and JCOP J3A almost dissapears when passing from plaintexts of 64 bytes to clear messages of 160 bytes. This result suggests that, when encrypting plaintexts of more than 160 bytes, JCOP 41 cards will be slower than the JCOP J3A model using the same configuration.

Another consequence of the increase in the relative difference of the encryption and decryption time in the JCOP 41 cards is that, when encrypting messages of 160 bytes, the time needed to encrypt the plaintext nearly doubles the time needed to decrypt the cryptogram.

Acknowledgement. This work has been partially supported by the "Fundación Memoria D. Samuel Solórzano Barruso" under the Project FS/7-2010.

References

1. Rivest, R., Shamir, A., Adleman, L.: A method for obtaining digital signatures and public-key cryptosystems. ACM Commun. 26, 96–99 (1983)
2. Menezes, A.J., Oorschot, P., Vanstone, S.: Handbook of applied cryptography. CRC Press, Florida (1996)
3. Miller, V.S.: Use of elliptic curves in cryptography. In: Williams, H.C. (ed.) CRYPTO 1985. LNCS, vol. 218, pp. 417–426. Springer, Heidelberg (1986)
4. Koblitz, N.: Elliptic curve cryptosystems. Math. Comput. 48, 203–209 (1987)
5. Menezes, A.J.: Elliptic curve public key cryptosystems. Kluwer Academic Publishers, Boston (1993)
6. ElGamal, T.: A public-key cryptosystem and a signature scheme based on discrete logarithm. IEEE Trans. Inform. Theory 31, 469–472 (1985)
7. Preneel, B.: A survey of recent developments in cryptographic algorithms for smart cards. Comput. Netw. 51, 2223–2233 (2007)
8. Oracle Corporation. Java Card Technology, http://java.sun.com/javacard/
9. MAOSCO Limited. MULTOS smart card technology, http://www.multos.com
10. Cohen, H., Frey, G.: Handbook of elliptic and hyperelliptic curve cryptography. Chapman and Hall, Florida (2006)
11. Silverman, J.H.: The arithmetic of elliptic curves. Springer, New York (1986)
12. Hankerson, D., Menezes, A.J., Vanstone, S.: Guide to elliptic curve cryptography. Springer, New York (2004)
13. NIST FIPS 186-3. Digital Signature Standard (DSS). National Institute of Standards and Technology (2009)
14. ANSI X9.63. Public Key Cryptography for the Financial Services Industry: Key Agreement and Key Transport Using Elliptic Curve Cryptography. American National Standards Institute (2001)
15. IEEE 1363a. Standard Specifications for Public Key Cryptography - Amendment 1: Additional Techniques. Institute of Electrical and Electronics Engineers (2004)
16. ISO/IEC 18033-2. Information Technology – Security Techniques – Encryption Algorithms – Part 2: Asymmetric Ciphers. International Organization for Standardization / International Electrotechnical Commission (2006)
17. NXP Semiconductors. Smart Solutions for Smart Services, http://www.nxp.com/acrobat_download2/literature/9397/75016728.pdf
18. NXP Semiconductors. P5CT072 - Secure Dual Interface PKI Smart Card Controller (2004), http://www.nxp.com/acrobat_download2/other/identification/sfs085512.pdf
19. NXP Semiconductors. P5Cx012/02x/40/73/80/144 family - Secure Dual Interface and Contact PKI Smart Card Controller (2008), http://www.nxp.com/documents/data_sheet/P5CX012_02X_40_73_80_144_FAM_SDS.pdf
20. IETF RFC 2104. HMAC: Keyed Hashing for Message Authentication. Internet Engineering Task Force (1997), http://www.ietf.org/rfc/rfc2104
21. Rankl, W., Effing, W.: Smart card handbook. John Wiley & Sons, West Sussex (2003)
22. Oracle Corporation. Java smart card I/O API, http://jcp.org/en/jsr/detail?id=268

Comprehensive Protection of RFID Traceability Information Systems Using Aggregate Signatures

Guillermo Azuara and José Luis Salazar

University of Zaragoza, C/ Maria de Luna 3, 50018, Zaragoza, Spain
{gazuara,jsalazar}@unizar.es

Abstract. This work describes how the use of aggregate signatures can contribute to the comprehensive protection of RFID systems. Following a brief description of a product traceability system based on RFID technology and made secure by the use of aggregate signatures, a review is given of the main security threats to such systems and it is shown how the properties of aggregate signatures can provide comprehensive protection. Throughout the paper the protection measures adopted against the threats described for a real prototype are explained.

Keywords: RFID, Virus, Aggregate signatures.

1 Introduction

RFID technology is increasingly present in many areas of our daily lives and also in industrial processes. The advances in ubiquitous computing, where the use of RFID for marking objects is becoming common, has numerous advantages. However, there are new challenges on the horizon such as the proliferation of attacks and specific malware in RFID environments [1]. This work concentrates on how these threats can affect an RFID-based traceability system and how the use of aggregate signatures can contribute to preventing or mitigating these effects. The use of the proposed system protects it against new risks that can have an impact on automated systems of information capture, providing an interesting novelty to traceability systems and quality management.

In the following section we briefly describe a system of RFID secured traceability on which the impact of various threats will be studied.

Section three outlines the security risks and basic characteristics of the threats that may affect RFID systems and their execution.

Section four provides an evaluation of which of these threats affect the system and how aggregate signatures and other counter-measures can contribute to minimising their impact.

The conclusions are set out in the final section.

2 RFID Traceability

RFID technology enables objects or persons to be identified with a unique identifier, the information being transmitted with a specific protocol to a receiving device, called

Á. Herrero and E. Corchado (Eds.): CISIS 2011, LNCS 6694, pp. 168–176, 2011.
© Springer-Verlag Berlin Heidelberg 2011

a reader, by means of radio waves [2]. The simplest form of RFID consists of a tag (containing a minute integrated circuit with its corresponding antenna) and a RFID reader, although in most cases this basic system is also connected to an information system (back-end) with a database that stores all the information relating to the object. Here, this technology can show its full potential, but it is also the most vulnerable point from the security aspect.

Traceability is defined, according to the International Standards Organization (ISO) [3], as "The property of the result of a measurement or the value of a standard whereby it can be related to stated references, usually national or international standards, through an unbroken chain of comparisons all having stated uncertainties".

Traceability systems based on RFID technology are increasingly common and they provide many advantages over other systems (bar codes, for example). In [4] a RFID-based traceability system was proposed that, in addition to traceability, facilitates control of the requirements at every stage the product must pass through and the locating of the entity responsible for certification at every checkpoint. This involved the use of aggregate signatures, defined in [5] as "a function in which given a set of U users, each one with a public and private key (K_{u+} and K_{u-}), and a subset $V \subseteq U$, if each user $u \in V$ produces a signature σ_u of a message M_u these signatures can be compacted into an aggregated signature σ by an untrusted third party different from the users of V".

The use of aggregate signatures allows the validity of the data held in a tag to be verified in one cryptographic operation. This takes place at every checkpoint before new data is introduced and the new aggregate signature is updated. If everything is correct, the corresponding computations are done and the data recorded in both the RFID label and the information system.

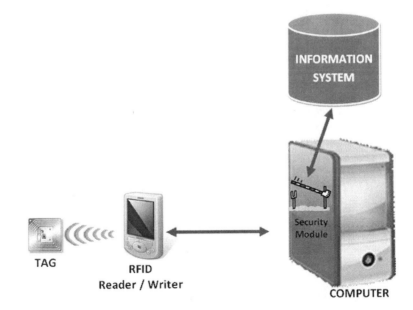

Fig. 1. Checkpoint Architecture

In the process for which product traceability is required, are several checkpoints to be entrusted with guaranteeing the system under study.

At each checkpoint the reader takes the data from the tag. This one checks the aggregate signature and, if it is correct, checkpoint generates a new signature that encompasses the data input at this point and passes the new data and signature to the information system. This operation is executed by the "security module", meaning the part of the system responsible for generating and verifying the aggregate signatures at each point. Thus, the system works as a data filter, preventing those items not correctly signed can reach the information system. An extensive description of our system is in [6] and [7].

Figure 1 (in next page) shows the architecture of the system, where each computer connected to an RFID reader has a "Security Module".

3   RFID Security Risks

RFID systems are susceptible to various types of attacks. This technology is not immune to risks, and some authors have classified the most significant threats into several categories. Many of these threats are related to privacy ([8], [9] and [10]). In our system, privacy is not something that we need to safeguard, because traceability is, in this case, the objective of the process as a whole. On the other hand, taxonomy proposal in [11] adds three more risk groups to that of privacy is proposed: Business Process Risks, related to the impact of RFID system failures on automatic systems based on them, Business Intelligence Risks, and finally "external" risks. Although this perspective is more extensive and closer to reality than previous ones, we are going to use as a base the structure proposed in [1], where types of attacks and threats are classified and related to a model with four layers: physical, network and transport, application, and strategy. The first three ones correspond quite closely to the layers given in the OSI model, while the fourth one encompasses the risks associated with logistic factors and also contemplates the possibility that attacks may be multilayer, in other words they affect several of the basic layers.

As developed in [1] and [12], the main risks for each layer are as follows:

- Physical layer: permanent or temporary tag disablement, relay attacks and removal or destruction of RFID readers.
- Network and transport layer: identity, cloning and spoofing (affecting tags), impersonation and eavesdropping (both mainly affecting readers), and network protocol attacks.
- Application layer: unauthorized tag reading, modification of tag details, attacks in the middleware (such as buffer overflows and malicious code injection).
- Strategic layer: industrial espionage, social engineering, privacy threats, targeting objects (for example targeting people with valuable items with intention to rob).

Furthermore, there are multilayer attacks which may include denial of service attacks, reading / writing of information in the free space of the tag without the user's knowledge, traffic analysis, attacks on the cryptographic information algorithms, attacks based on monitoring the physical working parameters (energy consumption, variation in electromagnetic fields, etc...) and relay attacks (recording of a password of a previous transaction and repeating it when presented with the same challenge).

4 Robustness of the System Against Threats

In view of these various threats, we will examine those that probably affect most the system and the protection measures adopted, some of them based on the guidelines suggested in [1] and [13].

4.1 Physical Layer

It is quite likely that a tag may become detached or damaged during the process. In such a case, at the first point at which the tag fault or absence is detected, the product is withdrawn from the production chain, the database is checked to confirm up to what point the process has been recorded, a new tag is issued with all the information and the process continues from that point.

The KILL [14], [15] and DESTROY [16] command, created to defend the privacy of the future buyer once the product is acquired [17] and which permanently disables the tag, is not relevant in this process because the tag is only for internal use and is not supposed to reach the final user. Note that some works like [18] suggest that kill tag state may be reversible. For more information about attacks based on the use of these commands is recommended reading [19].

It seems unlikely that active interference could be carried out by a supposed attacker given that the process always takes place in private installations, so that it should be enough to observe the physical protection measures proposed in [13] which are: access control, security cameras, security guards and similar precautions. Nevertheless, there should also be a contingency plan in case a checkpoint in the traceability system fails so that the productive process can continue and data continue to be taken.

The possibility of relay attacks, as suggested in [20], is remote due to the nature of the installations and the short communication distances between tags and readers. Moreover, the use of aggregate signatures protects the system from possible malicious alterations of the data as it is all protected by the signature and a temporary seal. In these circumstances it is highly unlikely that the system does not realise data is tampered with.

The most worrying risk from the point of view of its impact would be tag cloning. However, cloning a tag with the same physical appearance is difficult given that this would involve manufacturing an identical model of tag. Furthermore, these cloned tags would have to be introduced into the market when the production process of the product has finished, otherwise they would be easily detected by the system. Even so, if an increase in the level of security was required, it would be possible to turn to hardware solutions based on the use of physically unclonable functions (PUFs) [21-23]. In the case of similar tags being cloned but with a different unique identification number, this would immediately be detected because the aggregate signature includes the unique identifier, and therefore if the card is not the same the identifier changes and it is automatically detected that the signature is not correct. Moreover, other tag data as weight or identification number that looks at first glance, it is easy check that the weight has changed or the number does not match or is repeated. For more information about avoiding tag cloning recommended reading [19], [23-28] and [29-31] about detecting it.

4.2 Network and Transport Layer

There is no encrypted data in the tag, so there would be no problem if someone read the content of the card with a legitimate reader. Similarly, if a fraudulent reader wrote a tag, this would be detected at the next checkpoint since it would not be able to provide a valid signature.

4.3 Application Layer

As mentioned in the previous point, there is no problem about unauthorized readings as all the information is plaintext and, as it has also been pointed out, modification of the data is automatically detected by the security module.

Although the risk classification we are using deals only with buffer overflows and malicious code injection, it is also possible to speak in general terms about malware specifically designed to attack RFID systems [12], i.e. software designed to cause damage in the systems. There are three main types of malware: RFID exploits, RFID worms and RFID viruses [12].

Starting with the main threats, the greatest danger of the exploits in RFID is precisely that they are frequently unexpected and their processing can exploit vulnerabilities both in the RFID system and in the information system itself or the entire network. Normally these attacks are aimed at specific components of the system, such as databases, web interfaces or APIs managing readers. One of the simplest attacks would be the injection of SQL commands such as shutdown or drop table that cause serious damage to the system (switching off or deleting tables) or even data theft. For example, some databases such as Microsoft SQL Server allow administrators to execute system commands, so that if the database is functioning as root all the system can be jeopardised. The use of aggregate signatures guarantees that data have been input by authorised entities, so that if the signature is not correct data is not passed to the information system, and the security module discards the data and therefore does not execute the command.

Another type of attack within the exploits category would be the insertion of code. If the RFID applications use web protocols to consult the database, it is very likely that clients will be able to interpret scripts, in which case they could be vulnerable to this type of attack in the same way as web navigators but with a higher degree of danger given that navigators normally have limited access to the host. To prevent this, and as the cited codes habitually use non alphanumeric characters, a first measure is the system cannot process any input that has any element of this kind. Additionally, as in the previous case, the security module will filter the data reaching the information system. If possible it would be advantageous not to allow the execution of script languages in the back-end system.

No less dangerous is a buffer overflow [1] that occurs when an area of the memory writes more data than it can contain, and these extra data overwrites areas of the adjacent memory. The greatest danger is that an attacker intentionally producing an overflow can execute arbitrary code. Although the majority of compilers, navigators and systems are already protected against these attacks, an example of overflow in an RFID system is presented in [12]. In this case, the previous filtering of the security module through the confirmation of the validity of the signature meant that the malicious data did not pass to the system. Special care should also be taken in the programming, and it should be ensured that only the areas of the memory where there are data should be read.

RFID worms exploit system faults to introduce malicious code into the reader that overwrites the tags with a code that causes the infection of a new reader and so on. Again, the previous checking of the signatures will obstruct the propagation of the infection through the tags, but the security of the system should be audited to find out how the reader has been infected (probably via the network). In this case, it is important to emphasise again the importance of an appropriate security policy for all the systems involved in the process.

The first RFID virus was presented and explained at length in [12]. It carries out an SQL code injection when the tag is read, copying the instructions of the injection in the database so that when a new tag is written it becomes infected and also propagates the virus. From this initial idea, it is possible to programme payloads to cause more dangerous effects.

Even if dealing with a virus with the improvements described, applying the basic general norms such as limiting the permissions for the database and the number of users, isolating the middleware server from the rest of the network and reviewing the middleware code to avoid security gaps [32], [33], we can count on a high degree of protection against these threats (at least at the moment). Also, the implementation of the "security module" enables the propagation of the virus through the tags to be limited, given that the data will not be processed by the information system.

4.4 Strategic Layer

Of the risks cited (industrial espionage, social engineering, threats to privacy, targeting of objects), we could only be affected to some extent by the possibility that through social engineering techniques some person, in some position of privilege, could perform an action that might compromise the security of the system. The countermeasures proposed are appropriate training of personnel and implementing a general security policy, as well as the impossibility of users having direct access to the private keys of the devices. In other words, when a legitimate user starts a session, the authenticity of the user should be verified for the system, after which the system will be responsible to carry out the calculations, without the user having direct access to the private key used in the operation.

4.5 Multilayer Attacks

We consider that attacks that could affect our system are: denial of service, reading / writing of information in the free space of the tag without the knowledge of the user, and relay attacks. The others do not affect us since privacy is not an issue.

Denial of service attacks could affect the production chain. However, for their execution physical access to the premises is necessary so that the physical measures proposed in Subsection 4.1 should be sufficient. It should not be forgotten that there are communication networks in the system which could be vulnerable to external DoS attacks, so that the usual security measures should be taken to prevent these from occurring.

Unauthorised reading, as already mentioned, is not a problem given that there is no secret data involved. Unauthorised writing has been dealt with in Subsections 4.2 and 4.3.

As regards relay attacks, these have also been dealt with, specifically in Subsection 4.1.

5 Conclusions

As explained in the previous sections, the security of an RFID system depends on the security of all layers integrated into the system, none of which should be ignored.

Given that in the present case the system will always be located in private installations without public access, many of the potential problems will not affect us. Furthermore, as privacy is not a requirement, attacks directed at finding secret data will not be of concern.

The use of aggregate signatures in the system, in addition to the initial step of ensuring the veracity of the data, the time of its introduction and the fact that only authorised entities may carry out the writing also provides protection against other types of threat as has been pointed out in the previous paragraphs: relay attacks, cloning, unauthorised writing, modification of tag data, SQL injection, insertion of codes, buffer overflow, RFID worms, RFID viruses, and social engineering.

The worst threat hanging over RFID security is the idea that the system is secure merely because of the use of RFID technology. A knowledge of the risks and the implementation of all possible safeguards is fundamentally important, both in respect of the RFID and of the other systems used in the process.

Since this scenario of aggregate signatures can be implemented in an information system, independently from used technology, it allows its use in any process in which there is a chain of steps, and to be able to know who takes responsibility of the data introduced in each point (either a human agent or an autonomous system) and to protect the system, if a signature verification is performed before entering data into it.

Acknowledgments

This work has been partially financed by CPUFLIPI Project (MICINN TIN2010-17298) of Spanish Government.

References

1. Mitrokotsa, A., Rieback, M.R., Tanenbaum, A.S.: Classifying RFID Attacks and Defenses. Inf. Syst. Front. 12, 491–505 (2010)
2. Landt, J.: The History of RFID. IEEE Potentials 24, 8–11 (2005)

3. ISO/IEC Guide, I.S.O.: 99:2007 - International Vocabulary of Metrology – Basic and General Concepts and Associated Terms, VIM (2007)
4. Azuara, G., Salazar, J.L., Tornos, J.L., et al.: Reliable Food Traceability Using RFID Tagging. In: Sion, R., Curtmola, R., Dietrich, S., Kiayias, A., Miret, J.M., Sako, K., Sebé, F. (eds.) RLCPS, WECSR, and WLC 2010. LNCS, vol. 6054, pp. 57–67. Springer, Heidelberg (2010)
5. Boneh, D., Gentry, C., Lynn, B., et al.: Aggregate and Verifiably Encrypted Signatures from Bilinear Maps. In: Biham, E. (ed.) EUROCRYPT 2003. LNCS, vol. 2656, pp. 416–432. Springer, Heidelberg (2003)
6. Garrido, P., Naranjo, F., Tramullas, J., et al.: Free Traceability Management using RFID and Topic Maps. In: Proceedings of the 4th European Conference on Information Management and Evaluation, pp. 93–103 (2010)
7. López, A.M., Pascual, E., Salinas, A.M., et al.: Design of a RFID Based Traceability System in a Slaughterhause. In: Workshops Proceedings of the 5th International Conference on Intelligent Environments, vol. 4, pp. 67–68 (2009)
8. Avoine, G., Oechslin, P.: RFID traceability: A multilayer problem. In: S. Patrick, A., Yung, M. (eds.) FC 2005. LNCS, vol. 3570, pp. 125–140. Springer, Heidelberg (2005)
9. Ayoade, J.: Roadmap to Solving Security and Privacy Concerns in RFID Systems. Computer Law & Security Report 23, 555–561 (2007)
10. Garfinkel, S.L., Juels, A., Pappu, R.: RFID Privacy: An Overview of Problems and Proposed Solutions. IEEE Security & Privacy 3, 34–43 (2005)
11. Karygicmnis, A., Phillips, T., Tsibertzopoulos, A.: RFID Security: A Taxonomy of Risk. In: First International Conference on Communications and Networking in China, pp. 1–8 (2006)
12. Rieback, M.: Security and Privacy of Radio Frecuency Identification. Vrije Universiteit, Amsterdam (2008)
13. Karygiannis, A. T., Eydt, B., Barber, G., et al.: Guidelines for Securing Radio Frequency Identification (RFID) Systems. NIST SP - 800-98 (2007)
14. Auto-ID Center: 860MHz – 930 MHz Class 1 Radio Frequency (RF) Identification Tag Radio Frequency & Logical Communication Interface Specification Defines Communications Interface and Protocol, RF, and Tag Requirements (2003)
15. Auto-ID Center: 900 MHz Class 0 Radio Frequency (RF) Identification Tag Specification Communications Interface and Protocol, RF, and Tag Requirements, Operational Algorithms for 900MHz Communications (2003)
16. Auto-ID Center: 13.56 MHz ISM Band Class 1 Radio Frequency (RF) Identification Tag Interface Specification Defines Communications Interface and Protocol, RF, and Tag Requirements (2003)
17. Juels, A., Rivest, R. L., Szydlo, M.: The Blocker Tag: Selective Blocking of RFID Tags for Consumer Privacy. pp.103-111 (2003)
18. Bolan, C.: The Lazarus Effect: Resurrecting Killed RFID Tags (2006)
19. El-Said, M.M., Woodring, I.: An Empirical Study for Protecting Passive RFID Systems Against Cloning. In: Sixth International Conference on Information Technology: New Generations, pp. 558–563 (2009)
20. Kfir, Z., Wool, A.: Picking Virtual Pockets using Relay Attacks on Contactless Smartcard. In: Security and Privacy for Emerging Areas in Communications Networks, pp. 47–58 (2005)
21. Bolotnyy, L., Robins, G.: Physically Unclonable Function-Based Security and Privacy in RFID Systems. In: Fifth Annual IEEE International Conference on Pervasive Computing and Communications, pp. 211–220 (2007)

22. Devadas, S., Suh, E., Paral, S., et al.: Design and Implementation of PUF-Based "Unclonable" RFID ICs for Anti-Counterfeiting and Security Applications. In: IEEE International Conference on RFID, pp. 58–64 (2008)
23. Jeng, A.B., Chang, L.-C., Wei, T.-E.: Survey and Remedy of the Technologies used for RFID Tags Against Counterfeiting. International Conference on Machine Learning and Cybernetics 5, 2975–2981 (2009)
24. Abawajy, J.: Enhancing RFID Tag Resistance Against Cloning Attack. In: Third International Conference on Network and System Security, pp. 18–23 (2009)
25. Tuyls, P., Batina, L.: RFID-tags for anti-counterfeiting. In: Pointcheval, D. (ed.) CT-RSA 2006. LNCS, vol. 3860, pp. 115–131. Springer, Heidelberg (2006)
26. Juels, A.: Strengthening EPC Tags Against Cloning. In: Proceedings of the 4th ACM Workshop on Wireless Security, pp. 67–76 (2005)
27. Duc, D.N., Park, J., Lee, H., et al.: Enhancing Security of EPCglobal Gen-2 RFID Tag Against Traceability and Cloning (2006)
28. Laurie, A.: Practical Attacks Against RFID. Network Security 2007, 4–7 (2007)
29. Mirowski, L.T., Hartnett, J.: Deckard: A System to Detect Change of RFID Tag Ownership. IJCSNS International Journal of Computer Science and Network Security 7, 87–98 (2007)
30. Zanetti, D., Fellmann, L., Capkun, S.: Privacy-Preserving Clone Detection for RFID-Enabled Supply Chains. In: IEEE International Conference on RFID 2010, pp. 37–44 (2010)
31. Khor, J.H., Ismail, W., Younis, M.I., et al.: Security Problems in an RFID System. Wireless Pers. Commun. 1(10) (2010)
32. Clarke, J.: Platform-Level Defenses. In: Anonymous SQL Injection Attacks and Defense, pp. 377–413. Syngress, Boston (2009)
33. Clarke, J.: Code-Level Defenses. In: Anonymous SQL Injection Attacks and Defense, pp. 341–376. Syngress, Boston (2009)

Cryptanalysis of Multicast Protocols
with Key Refreshment
Based on the Extended Euclidean Algorithm

Alberto Peinado and Andrés Ortiz

Dept. Ingeniería de Comunicaciones,
E.T.S.I. Telecomunicación, Universidad de Málaga,
Campus de Teatinos, 29071 Málaga, Spain
{apeinado,aortiz}@ic.uma.es

Abstract. Recently, Naranjo, López-Ramos and Casado have proposed a key refreshment for multicast schemes based on the extended Euclidean algorithm. We show in this paper that the key refreshment is not secure, describing several weaknesses and the algorithm to obtain the private key of any user. Hence, every system in which the key refreshment is applied will be compromised.

Keywords: Cryptanalysis, Key refreshment, Key Distribution, Multicast.

1 Introduction

In 2010, Naranjo *et al* proposed a key refreshment [1] based on the extended Euclidean algorithm to be applied over multicast networks. The scheme was presented as a solution to one of the most important aspects related to multicast security.

The scenario can be described as a Key server and a set of members that either send or receive multicast messages. Although the data communications can be *one-to-many* or *many-to-many*, the communications related to key refreshment corresponds to the *one-to-many* type, and they are always originated at the Key server.

Members can enter and leave to the system at any time. Therefore, the key must be refreshed every time an arrival or departure is performed. This is mandatory to achieve backward and forward security. On the other hand, the key refreshment must be applied periodically to avoid, prevent or minimize statistical or brute force attacks.

Next section describes the key refreshment defined in [1]. Section 3 deals with the cryptanalysis showing the main weakness of the scheme. Section 4 describes the authentication protocol defined in [1] to detect forged refreshments. In section 5, the cryptanalysis of the authentication mechanism is presented. Section 6 described the zero-knowledge protocol also defined in [1] to complement and increase the global security of the system. In section 7, we present the cryptanalysis of this zero-knowledge protocol, in such a way that user's key is easily recovered. Finally, conclusions appear in section 8.

Á. Herrero and E. Corchado (Eds.): CISIS 2011, LNCS 6694, pp. 177–182, 2011.
© Springer-Verlag Berlin Heidelberg 2011

2 Key Refreshment

Let r be the symmetric encryption key to be multicast, and let n be the number of members at a given time. The process can be divided in several phases.

Phase 1. Member ticket assignment. When a member i enters the system, he joins the group and a member ticket x_i is assigned by the Key server. Every ticket x_i is a large prime and is transmitted to the corresponding member under a secure channel. It is important to note that this communication is performed once per member only, in such a way that the ticket x_i is used by the member i for the whole time he is in the group. Furthermore, all tickets must be different from each other.

Therefore, x_i is only known by its owner and the Key server, while r will be shared by all group members and the Key server.

Phase 2. Distribution. This phase is performed by several steps.
Step 1. The Key server selects the parameters of the system to generate the encryption key r. It selects:

- Two large prime numbers, m and p, such that p divides $m - 1$.
- $\delta < x_i$ for every $i = 1, ..., n$
- k such that $\delta = k + p$.
- g such that $g^p = 1 \bmod m$.

The encryption key r is computed as $r = g^k \bmod m$.
Step 2. The Key server calculates

$$L = \prod_{i=1}^{n} x_i .$$
(1)

The parameter L is kept private in the Key server.
Step 3. The Key server computes u and v by means of the Extended Euclidean algorithm [4], such that

$$u \cdot \delta + v \cdot L = 1 .$$
(2)

Step 4. The Key server multicasts g, m and u as plain text.
Step 5. Each member i calculates $\delta = u^{-1} \bmod x_i$ to obtain the encryption key r by means of the equation

$$g^{\delta} \bmod m = g^k \bmod m = r .$$
(3)

Each refreshment of the encryption key r, implies the generation of new values for m, g, p and/or k. As a consequence, δ, u and v will be also refreshed.

Phase 3. Arrival of a member j. In this case, the ticket x_j is assigned to member j by the Key server. Then, the ticket is included in the encryption key generation by means of equation 1, since the parameter L is the product of all the tickets. In this way, the encryption key r does not change, and thus the rest of the members do not need to refresh the key. The only operation the Key server must perform is a multiplication to obtain the new value for L.

Phase 4. Departure of a member j. When a member leaves the group, he should not be able to decrypt contents anymore. Hence, a key refreshment is mandatory. This is achieved by dividing L by the ticket x_j, and generating a new encryption key afterwards. In this case, the new key must be distributed to every member using the procedure of phase 2.

Phase 5. Other refreshments. For security reasons, the Key server might decide to refresh the encryption key r after a given period of time with no arrivals or departures. This refreshment is performed by the procedure of phase 2.

3 Main Weakness of the Scheme

In this section, the main weakness of the key refreshment scheme, described in the previous section, is presented. This weakness allows the legal members to obtain the parameter L (or a multiple of L), kept private by the Key server. If a user knows L or a multiple of L, then he can impersonate the server and generate fake refreshments. Next, we show how to recover L or a multiple of L.

Let us consider a legal member h which receives the key refreshment parameters $(g, m$ and $u)$ in a regular way. He performs the distribution phase, as described in section 2. Since the member h computes $\delta = u^{-1} \bmod x_h$, he can obtain a multiple of L by the following equation

$$v \cdot L = 1 - u \cdot \delta . \tag{4}$$

The knowledge of that multiple allows the member h to impersonate the server. The only thing he has to do is the following.

Step 1. Member h generates a new value $\delta' < \delta$, and computes u' and v' applying the extended Euclidean algorithm, such that

$$u' \cdot \delta' + v' \cdot (v \cdot L) = 1 . \tag{5}$$

Step 2. Member h sends g, m and u' to the other members. Those members will obtain the new value $\delta' = u'^{-1} \bmod x_i$, and compute the refreshed key by equation 3. The effect of this fake refreshment is a malfunctioning of the system, since the legal members cannot identify legal refreshments.

Although the knowledge of a multiple of L is enough to impersonate the server, the member h could obtain the parameter L when a new refreshment arrive. Two cases are considered.

Case 1. Let us suppose that the number of members does not change in a given time interval, and the server performs a new refreshment. This situation corresponds to phase 5 described in section 2. In this case, the server generates g', m' and u'. However, the parameter L is the same, as it is derived from equation 1. The member h applies the key recovering process, obtaining $\delta' = u'^{-1} \bmod x_h$, and a multiple of L by the equation

$$v' \cdot L = 1 - u' \cdot \delta' . \tag{6}$$

The member h knows two different multiples of L, $v \cdot L$ and $v' \cdot L$. The greatest common divisor (gcd) of these multiples gives L with high probability. In the case L is not recovered from the gcd, a lower multiple is obtained. Anyway, the member h could try it again in the next refreshment.

Example. This is an example performed with the help of MapleV software. Let us consider a group of 10 member. The tickets could be the following primes: $x_1 = 71$, $x_2 = 73$, $x_3 = 79$, $x_4 = 83$, $x_5 = 89$, $x_6 = 97$, $x_7 = 101$, $x_8 = 103$, $x_9 = 107$ and $x_{10}=109$. Hence, $L = 35597295809230452047$.

The server establishes the following parameters: $m = 1259$, $p = 37$ and $g = 698$. If $k = 32$ is considered, then $\delta = k + p = 69$. Applying the extended Euclidean algorithm, $u = -5674931215964274964$ and $v = 11$. Finally, the key $r = g^k \bmod m = 1123$.

When member 1 receives g, m and u, he obtains $\delta = u^{-1} \bmod x_1 = 69$, and the key $r = g^{69} \bmod m = 1123$. He also computes a multiple of L applying equation 6 and obtains $vL = 39157025390153497251 7$. The other members act in the same way and recover the same value of r and vL.

A given time later, the server refresh the values: $m' = 3539$, $p' = 61$, $g' = 2036$, and $k' = 3$. This determines $\delta' = 64$. Since no arrival or departure has been produced, L has the same value. Hence, $u = 9455531699326838825$, $v = -17$ and $r = 1300$.

When the members receive the new values m', g' and u', they compute the values $\delta' = u'^{-1} \bmod x_i = 64$ and the multiple $v'L = -605154028756917684799$.

They obtain $L = \gcd(39157025390153497251 7, -605154028756917684799) = 35597295809230452047$.

Case 2. Let us suppose that the number of members changes, thus originating a key refreshment. In this situation, the parameter L has changed, but maintains many common factors with the previous value, as it is derived from equation 1. The server sends g', m' and u', computed from the new value L'. When the member h obtain $\delta' = u'^{-1} \bmod x_h$, he also obtains a multiple of L',

$$v' \cdot L' = 1 - u' \cdot \delta'. \tag{7}$$

The member h could employ $v'L'$ to impersonate the server, as it is previously described in this section. Furthermore, if he computes the gcd to the multiples computed from different refreshments, he could obtain a new parameter L_{sub} that corresponds to the product of the tickets of members still in the group.

Therefore, if member h applies this procedure at every refreshment he could obtain the product of tickets belonging to the members that arrive to the group at the same time that member h. This fact could help the cryptanalyst to recover the tickets because the gcd decrease progressively the multiple size.

4   Key Refreshment Message Authentication

In [1], the authors propose a message authentication protocol to authenticate the refreshment messages from the Key server, trying to protect the system against forged refreshment messages. Since the only two entities in the system that know the ticket are its owner and the Key server, the protocol tries to prove that the sender of the messages knows the recipient's ticket. It is as follows:

Step 1. The Key server computes $s = (g^k)^{-1} \bmod L$. Then the server chooses a random number a, such that $a < x_i$, for every x_i, and multicasts $a \cdot s$ and $h(a)$, where $h(a)$ is the output of a hash operation not specified in [1].

Step 2. Every member i receives the authentication message and computes the value $h(a \cdot s \cdot r \bmod x_i)$ which should be equal to the value $h(a)$ received if x_i is a factor of L.

5 Breaking the Authentication Protocol

As it is described in section 3, the main weakness of the key refreshment scheme proposed in [1] resides on the fact that any user could impersonate the server, generating forged refreshment messages, from the knowledge of a multiple of L.

The protocol described in previous section tries to avoid this situation. However, the same weakness described in section 3, allows the members to break the authentication protocol in such a way that they could generate forged refreshment that will be considered as authentic by the recipients.

The procedure to break the protocol is the following.

Step 1. Let us consider that the member h wants to impersonate the Key server. The member h knows a multiple of L, computed as it is described in section 3. He generates new values for the system parameters, that is, m', p', g', δ' and k'. Then, he computes u', v' applying the extended Euclidean algorithm to δ' and the multiple of L, $v \cdot L$. In this point, the member h begins with the authentication protocol described in section 4 using $v \cdot L$ instead of L, that is, he generates $s' = (g'^{k'})^{-1} \bmod vL$, and chooses a' at random. Then, he sends the forged refreshment (m', g', u') and the authentication message $(a' \cdot s', h(a'))$.

Step 2. The member i receives the message and computes $\delta' = u'^{-1} \bmod x_i$, and the refreshed key $r' = g'^{\delta'} \bmod m'$. Then, in order to authenticate the refreshment, he computes $h(a' \cdot s' \cdot r' \bmod x_i)$. As one can easily observe, $h(a' \cdot s' \cdot r' \bmod x_i) = h(a)$ since the system parameters have been selected in the same way as the server does, and x_i is a factor of L, and a factor of any multiple of L.

6 Zero-Knowledge Protocol

In [1], a zero knowledge protocol is proposed to verify that the information is distributed over legal peers. In other words, the aim of the protocol is to verify that a given peer j holds a valid ticket x_j. It is supposed that the two peers involved in this protocol have previously obtain key r using the key refreshment scheme described in section 2. The protocol is as follows:

Step 1. Peer i chooses a random integer r such that $1 < r < m$ and sends it to the Key server.

Step 2. The Key server computes $inv = r^{-1} \bmod L$ and sends it to i.

Step 3. Peer i sends $(inv, g^{xi} \bmod m)$ to peer j.

Step 4. Peer j calculates $r_j = inv^{-1} \bmod x_j$, $\beta_j = r_j \cdot (g^{xi})^{xj} \bmod m$ and sends (β_j, g^{xj}) to peer i.

Step 5. Peer i computes $\beta_i = r \cdot (g^{xj})^{xi}$, which should be equal to β_j.

7 Discovering User's Key

Although the zero-knowledge protocol described in section 6 is inspired on the Diffie-Hellman [4] key agreement scheme, it does not satisfy the objectives. Instead of verifying if a given peer is a legal one, the protocol allows the extraction of the secret key, *i.e.* the ticket x_j, of the peer j under verification.

Let us consider that the peer i is a legal peer and he runs the protocol to verify the legal peer j. Then, peer i can obtain the ticket x_j, thus breaking completely the security of the system. The process is as follows.

Step 1. Peer i computes his part of the Diffie-Hellman challenge, that is, $dh_i = g^{xi}$ mod m, chooses inv at random and sends dh_i and inv to the peer j. Note that the original protocol described in section 6 establishes that peer i sends an integer inv and dh_i. Peer i has not established any communication with the server.

Step 2. Peer j computes $r_j = inv^{-1}$ mod x_j, $dh_j = g^{xj}$ mod m, and $\beta_j = r_j(dh_i)^{xj}$ mod m. He sends dh_j and β_j to the peer i.

Step 3. Peer i computes the complete Diffie-Hellman key as $dh = (dh_j)^{xi}$ mod m. Then, he recovers the value r_j mod $m = \beta_j \cdot dh^{-1}$ mod m. If m is greater or equal than x_j, then $r_j = r_j$ mod m and $(inv \cdot r_j - 1)$ is a multiple of x_j. Therefore, x_j could be computed as $x_j = \gcd(inv \cdot r_j - 1, vL)$ with high probability. If m is lower then x_j, then x_j can be recovered $r_j < m$.

8 Conclusions

The key refreshing scheme proposed in [1], and applied later in [2] and [3], has an important security weakness. Therefore, the legal members can impersonate the Key server against the rest of users. Furthermore, the authentication protocol fails because forged refreshments are not detected. Finally, the secret keys (tickets) of the members can be recovered by another members using the zero-knowledge protocol proposed in [1] to detect illegal peers.

Acknowledgments. This work was supported by Ministry of Science and Innovation and European FEDER Fund under Project TIN2008-02236/TSI.

References

1. Naranjo, J.A.M., López-Ramos, J.A., Casado, L.G.: Applications of the Extended Euclidean Algorithm to Privacy and Secure Communications. In: Proc. of 10th International Conference on Computational and Mathematical Methods in Science and Engineering (2010)
2. Naranjo, J.A.M., López-Ramos, J.A., Casado, L.G.: Key Refreshment in overlay networks: a centralized secure multicast scheme proposal. In: XXI Jornadas de Paralelismo, Valencia, Spain, pp. 931–938 (2010)
3. Naranjo, J.A.M., López-Ramos, J.A., Casado, L.G.: A Key Distribution scheme for Live Streaming Multi-tree Overlays. In: 3rd International Conference on Computational Intelligence in Security for Information Systems, CISIS 2010, pp. 223–230 (2010), doi:10.1007/978-3-642-16626-6-24
4. Menezes, A., Oorschot, P., Vanstone, S.: Handbook of applied cryptography. CRC Press, Boca Raton (1996)

Improving the Message Expansion of the Tangle Hash Function[*]

Rafael Álvarez, José-Francisco Vicent, and Antonio Zamora

Dpto. de Ciencia de la Computación e Inteligencia Artificial
Universidad de Alicante (Campus de San Vicente)
Ap. Correos 99, E–03080, Alicante, Spain
{ralvarez,jvicent,zamora}@dccia.ua.es

Abstract. Tangle is an iterative one-way hash function based on the Merkle-Damgard scheme strengthened by a message dependent round function. It was submitted to the NIST SHA-3 competition, being accepted for first round evaluation. We propose an alternative message expansion scheme for Tangle in order to thwart the collision attacks found during such evaluation. Based on the fact that differences at the beginning of the expanded message contribute to better avalanche, the improved message expansion scheme presents much better properties than the original version while maintaining very good performance characteristics.

Keywords: hash cryptography digest sha-3 expansion avalanche tangle.

1 Introduction

Tangle is an iterative one-way hash function based on the Merkle-Damgard scheme (see [3]) strengthened by a message dependent round function combined with an 8×8 Sbox look-up (see [1]) and a matrix pseudorandom generator based message expansion function.

With a compression function that natively accepts a 4096 bit long message block as input and produces a 1024 bit digest as output, it supports six different digest sizes (224, 256, 384, 512, 768 and 1024 bits) through output truncation; differing in the number of rounds and the initial values but sharing the same compression function.

It supports the same interface as SHA-2 (see [7]), accepting messages up to 2128 bits in length and padding the message in a similar way to obtain a message with a length multiple of 4096 bits.

The design is primarily for 32-bit microprocessors and little-endian memory organization since they were the most common scenario at that time but meant to be satisfactorily implementable in different architectures.

It was submitted to the NIST's SHA-3 (see [8]) competition and accepted for first round evaluation, appearing to have relatively high performance in relation to many other contestants. Unfortunately, collisions were found for all hash sizes ([9]) and was not suitable for second round evaluation.

[*] Partially supported by the grant GRE09-02 of the University of Alicante.

Á. Herrero and E. Corchado (Eds.): CISIS 2011, LNCS 6694, pp. 183–189, 2011.
© Springer-Verlag Berlin Heidelberg 2011

In this paper we propose a modified expansion scheme for Tangle that improves security, specifically directed to prevent the attacks that were successful against the original version of this hash function. First, we describe the original message expansion scheme submitted to NIST and analyze its main flaws in section 2. Then we describe and analyze the proposed alternative scheme (section 3). Finally we present some open problems (section 4) and conclusions (section 5).

2   Preliminaries

The original message expansion function of Tangle is described in the following. It is based on a simple matrix based pseudorandom generator that is seeded with the input message and creates a sequence of words of the length required by the compression function (4096 bits). A description of Tangle in greater detail can be found on the submission documentation ([2]).

2.1   Original Message Expansion

The message expansion function expands the 128 words of message block M into $2R$ words (two words per round of the compression function, as required by each digest size). For this purpose a small matrix based pseudorandom generator is used.

The following non-linear functions are used in the specification:

$$F_1(x, y, z) = (x \wedge (y \vee z)) \vee (y \wedge z)$$
$$F_2(x, y, z) = (\neg y \wedge (x \vee z)) \vee (x \wedge z)$$
$$FR_1(x) = \text{rotl}(x, 3) \oplus \text{rotl}(x, 13) \oplus \text{rotl}(x, 29)$$
$$FR_2(x) = \text{rotl}(x, 5) \oplus \text{rotl}(x, 19) \oplus \text{rotl}(x, 27)$$
$$S_{box}(x) = \text{S-box lookup of } x, \text{ multiplicative inverse in } GF(2^8)$$

Generator Description. The generator has 8 state words, $X_0, X_1, \ldots, X_7$, and is iterated $X^i = A' X^{i-1}$ and $A' = PAP^{-1}$, where

$$A = \begin{pmatrix} 0\,1\,0\,0\,0\,0\,0\,0 \\ 0\,0\,1\,0\,0\,0\,0\,0 \\ 0\,0\,0\,1\,0\,0\,0\,0 \\ 0\,0\,0\,0\,1\,0\,0\,0 \\ 0\,0\,0\,0\,0\,1\,0\,0 \\ 0\,0\,0\,0\,0\,0\,1\,0 \\ 0\,0\,0\,0\,0\,0\,0\,1 \\ 1\,0\,1\,1\,1\,0\,0\,0 \end{pmatrix},$$

$$P = \begin{pmatrix} 1 1 0 1 1 0 1 0 \\ 0 0 1 0 1 0 0 0 \\ 0 0 1 1 1 1 1 1 \\ 1 0 1 1 0 1 0 1 \\ 0 0 0 1 1 0 0 1 \\ 1 1 1 1 1 0 0 1 \\ 0 1 0 1 0 0 1 1 \\ 0 1 0 1 0 0 0 1 \end{pmatrix}, \quad P^{-1} = \begin{pmatrix} 0 1 0 0 0 1 0 1 \\ 0 1 1 1 1 1 1 1 \\ 0 0 1 1 0 1 1 0 \\ 1 1 0 0 1 1 1 1 \\ 0 1 1 1 0 1 1 0 \\ 0 0 0 1 1 1 0 1 \\ 0 0 0 0 0 0 1 1 \\ 1 0 1 1 0 0 0 1 \end{pmatrix}.$$

Since matrix A is constructed as a companion matrix of a primitive polynomial, its period is guaranteed to be $2^8 - 1$ or 255 iterations [6].

Generator Seeding. The initial state of the generator, X_j^0, with $j = 0, 1, \ldots, 7$, is a function of the whole message block M (with words M_1 to M_{128}) and the hash working variables $h_0, h_1, \ldots, h_{31}$.
For $j = 0$ to 7:

$$g_1 = h_j + h_{j+8}$$
$$g_2 = M_j + M_{j+8} + M_{j+16} + M_{j+24}$$
$$g_3 = M_{j+32} + M_{j+40} + M_{j+48} + M_{j+56}$$
$$g_4 - h_{j+16} + h_{j+24}$$
$$g_5 = M_{j+64} + M_{j+72} + M_{j+80} + M_{j+88}$$
$$g_6 = M_{j+96} + M_{j+104} + M_{j+112} + M_{j+120}$$
$$X_j = FR_1(g_1 + g_2 + g_3) + FR_2(g_4 + g_5 + g_6)$$

Iteration and Extraction. The generator is iterated $R/2$ times using the following expression and, on each iteration of the generator, 4 message expansion words (W_t) are extracted using a nonlinear output function. K_i is constant i as defined in the original specification of Tangle (see [2])
For $k = 1$ to $R/2$:

$$X_0^k = X_0^{k-1} \oplus X_3^{k-1} \oplus X_6^{k-1} \oplus X_7^{k-1}$$
$$X_1^k = X_0^{k-1} \oplus X_1^{k-1} \oplus X_3^{k-1} \oplus X_6^{k-1}$$
$$X_2^k = X_0^{k-1} \oplus X_1^{k-1} \oplus X_3^{k-1} \oplus X_4^{k-1} \oplus X_5^{k-1}$$
$$X_3^k = X_4^{k-1} \oplus X_5^{k-1} \oplus X_6^{k-1} \oplus X_7^{k-1}$$
$$X_4^k = X_0^{k-1} \oplus X_2^{k-1} \oplus X_7^{k-1}$$
$$X_5^k = X_2^{k-1} \oplus X_5^{k-1} \oplus X_6^{k-1} \oplus X_7^{k-1}$$
$$X_6^k = X_2^{k-1} \oplus X_3^{k-1} \oplus X_4^{k-1} \oplus X_6^{k-1} \oplus X_7^{k-1}$$
$$X_7^k = X_0^{k-1} \oplus X_4^{k-1} \oplus X_6^{k-1}$$

$$t = 4(k-1)$$
$$W_t = F_1(X_0^k, X_1^k, K_{(t \bmod 256)}) + M_{(t \bmod 128)}$$
$$W_{(t+1)} = F_2(X_2^k, X_3^k, K_{(t+1 \bmod 256)}) + M_{(t+1 \bmod 128)}$$
$$W_{(t+2)} = F_1(X_4^k, X_5^k, K_{(t+2 \bmod 256)}) + M_{(t+2 \bmod 128)}$$
$$W_{(t+3)} = F_2(X_6^k, X_7^k, K_{(t+3 \bmod 256)}) + M_{(t+3 \bmod 128)}$$

2.2 Cryptanalysis

This pseudorandom generator based expansion scheme presents the following flaws in terms of security:

- It does not contain the original message. most hash functions include the message within the message expansion; that way it is certain that any two different messages will produce different message expansions.
- It has a very poor avalanche. The number of bits changed in the produced expansion when changing a single bit in the input message is very low. A proper message expansion scheme should cause, on average, 50% of the output bits to change when one input bit is flipped.
- It does not take advantage of the fact that differences at the beginning of the message expansion cause a bigger change (avalanche) than those at the end; mainly because they affect more rounds.

These three criteria are, certainly, very important since they can create an avenue for a successful collision attack.

- If an expansion scheme does not include the original message, then two different messages could possibly be expanded to the same message expansion, causing an instant collision.
- On the other hand a message expansion scheme with poor avalanche, allows greater control of the expanded message simplifying the task of causing a collision in the compression function.
- Finally, an expansion scheme must place the biggest differences at the beginning so they are processed in as many rounds as possible, maximizing the avalanche of the compression function too.

These flaws were observed by Esmaeili ([4]) and collisions were found by Thomsen ([9]) for all digest sizes with a minor computational overhead.

The improved message expansion scheme, described in the following section, is motivated by these same criteria: including the message in the message expansion and maximizing differences at the beginning of the expanded message.

3   Improved Message Expansion

3.1   Description

Tangle divides the input message in 4096bit blocks, consisting of 128 message words of 32 bits each (M) available to the hash function. The round function uses 2 expanded words per round so it requires as many expanded message words (W) as twice the number of rounds per each different digest size. In order to maximize differences in similar messages, two 32bit pseudo-CRC words are included that act as mini-hashes making collision attacks more difficult. In this way, the expanded message is formed by:

$$\text{PCRC}_1|\text{PCRC}_2|W_0|W_1|\ldots|W_n|M_0|M_1|\ldots|M_{127}$$

3.2   Pseudo-CRCs

The first pseudo 32bit CRC is computed using a weighted sum code applied to error detection using the algorithm for WSC-1 described by [5]. This is similar to a normal CRC but faster, acting as a small hash of the message.

$$\text{PCRC}_1 = \text{WSC-1}(M_0 \ldots M_{127})$$

The second pseudo CRC is a derivation of the message expansion scheme and is calculated together with the message expansion:

$$A = \text{PCRC}_1;$$

For each required expansion word W_i with $i = n$ to 0 do:

$$W_i = \text{ROTL}((W_{i+5} \oplus W_{i+9} \oplus W_{i+17} \oplus W_{i+128}), 1)$$
$$\oplus K_{S_{box}(A \oplus (A>>8) \oplus (A>>16) \oplus (A>>24))}$$
$$A = A \oplus W_i$$

The expansion words W_i are generated backwards, last to first; and in the end, $PCRC_2$ is the last A. The $\oplus$ symbol denotes binary XOR, the $>>$ symbol denotes bit shift to the right and ROTL means left bit rotation. The $K_{S_{BOX}}()$ expression implies that the constant K is chosen as the output of the SBOX.

3.3   Results

This expansion scheme achieves good results in terms of avalanche as shown in Table 1 and prevents known collision attacks against the original version of Tangle.

Where expanded size is the total size of the expanded message in 32 bit words, while the number of actual expanded W words is in parenthesis; expanded ratio is the percentage of expanded words in relation to the message size; and avalanche means the number of bits changing in the expanded message for a single bit change in the message. The expected avalanche value is 50% and the actual message words embedded in the expanded message are not taken into account when computing avalanche.

Regarding performance, the proposed message expansion does not add a significant overhead to the original version obtaining equally good results, as shown in Table 2.

Table 1. Avalanche results for the proposed expansion scheme

Digest Size	Rounds	Expanded Size	Expanded Ratio	Avalanche
224	72	144(14)	10.9%	49%
256	80	160(30)	23.4%	50%
384	96	192(62)	48.4%	50%
512	112	224(94)	73.4%	50%
768	128	256(126)	98.4%	50%
1024	144	288(158)	123.4%	50%

Table 2. Performance values in cycles per byte

Digest	Speed
224	10.79 cpb
256	12.53 cpb
384	15.94 cpb
512	19.36 cpb
768	22.69 cpb
1024	26.06 cpb

4 Future Work

Although the proposed message expansion presents many favorable properties and is designed to prevent known collision attacks against Tangle, there are still other areas were Tangle can be improved:

- In the smaller digest sizes, the expansion ratio is very small and not all message words are used as input to generate the expanded message words. This implies that the actual expanded message could be very similar in whole to another similar message since the message is itself included in the expanded version and consumes a considerable amount of space. This is somewhat circumvented by the use of the S-Box in the message expansion to choose a constant.
- The current order of the words contained in the expanded message maximizes differences but putting the second pseudo CRC at the end of the message might be more secure, leaving an attacker limited control of the initial and final parts of the expanded message.
- The round function and output function should be modified too. This is a work currently in progress.
- Tangle could benefit by a redesign with a 64 bit platform in mind. This type of platform is more common today than when Tangle was originally designed and is something under study.

5   Conclusions

We have proposed an alternative message expansion scheme for the Tangle hash function that addresses the flaws uncovered by the successful collision attacks discovered during the SHA-3 competition.

The proposed scheme is based on the fact that differences at the beginning of the expanded message contribute to a higher overall avalanche since they affect more rounds of the compression function. To achieve this goal two pseudo-CRC words are placed at the beginning of the message expansion and the expanded words follow, with the original message included at the end. The expansion scheme is, in itself, a complete redesign of the original.

The improved message expansion scheme presents much better security properties than the original version while maintaining the same high performance level. Nevertheless, modifications of the round and output functions are under study to further improve Tangle's security.

References

1. Daemen, J., Rijmen, V.: The Design of Rijndael: AES–the Advanced Encryption Standard. Springer, Heidelberg (2002)
2. Alvarez, R., McGuire, G., Zamora, A.: The Tangle Hash Function. NIST SHA-3 Competition submission (2008)
3. Coron, J.-S., Dodis, Y., Malinaud, C., Puniya, P.: Merkle-Damgård Revisited: How to Construct a Hash Function. In: Shoup, V. (ed.) CRYPTO 2005. LNCS, vol. 3621, pp. 430–448. Springer, Heidelberg (2005)
4. Esmaeili, Y.: Some observations on Tangle. Observations on Tangle, NIST SHA-3 Competition (2008)
5. McAuley, A.J.: Weighted Sum Codes for Error Detection and Their Comparison with Existing Codes. IEEE/IACM Transactions on Networking 2-1, 16–22 (1994)
6. Odoni, R.W.K., Varadharajan, V., Sanders, P.W.: Public Key Distribution in Matrix Rings. Electronic Letters 20, 386–387 (1984)
7. National Institute of Standards and Technology: Secure Hash Standard (with change notice). Federal Information Processing Standards Publication FIPS-180-2 (2002)
8. NIST SHA-3 Competition Resources, http://csrc.nist.gov/groups/ST/hash/sha-3/index.html
9. Thomsen, S.S.: Untangled. Observations on Tangle, NIST SHA-3 Competition (2008)

Cryptosystem with One Dimensional Chaotic Maps

J.A. Martínez-Ñonthe[1], A. Díaz-Méndez[2], M. Cruz-Irisson[1], L. Palacios-Luengas[1]
J.L. Del-Río-Correa[3] and R. Vázquez-Medina[1,*]

[1] Instituto Politécnico Nacional, ESIME-Culhuacan, Santa Ana 1000,
04430, D.F., México
[2] Instituto Nacional de Astrofísica, Óptica y Electrónica, Luis Enrique Erro 1,
Tonantzintla, Puebla, México
[3] Universidad Autónoma Metropolitana Iztapalapa, San Rafael Atlixco 186,
09340, D.F., México
{jmartinezn9800,ruvazquez}@ipn.mx, lpalacios@ieee.org,
ajdiaz@inaoep.mx, jlrc@xanum.uam.mx

Abstract. This paper presents a 64-bits chaotic block cryptosystem, which uses as noise generator one-dimensional chaotic maps with 8 bits sub-blocks data. These chaotic maps use a control parameter that allows them to operate in the chaotic region, which guarantees that each sub-block of data is mixed with un-predictable random noise. Statistical mechanic tools such as: bifurcation diagram, Lyapunov exponent, and invariant distribution have been used to analyze and evaluate the behavior of the noise generator. The cryptosystem has been evaluated using concepts of information theory, such as: entropy, as a diffusion measure in the encryption process, and mutual information as a measure of relationship between plaintext and its respective cryptogram. The noise generator has been used on the non-balanced and dynamic network proposed by L. Kocarev. The randomness of the cryptograms has been evaluated using the NIST random tests. The proposed cryptosystem can be a component in software applications that provides security to stored or communicated information. The proposed cryptosystem has a similar behavior to the one of currently used cryptosystems and it has been designed with chaotic sequence generators, which are aperiodic by definition.

Keywords: Chaotic cryptosystem, Block cryptosystem, Chaotic maps.

1 Introduction

The term chaos in scientific terms was popularized after 1961, it is related to mathematics and physics and it is connected to some kind of unpredictable behavior of Dynamic Systems (DS). A chaotic system (CS) is a non-linear, deterministic DS that has sensitive dependence on initial conditions, and presents an evolution through a phase space that seems to be random. Mathematicians agree that, for the special case of iterated functions, there are three common characteristics of the chaos [1]: Sensitive dependence on initial conditions, mixing, and dense periodic points. These properties are relevant for cryptographic applications, since it is very difficult to establish

---

* Correspondind author.

Á. Herrero and E. Corchado (Eds.): CISIS 2011, LNCS 6694, pp. 190–197, 2011.
© Springer-Verlag Berlin Heidelberg 2011

long-term predictions of chaotic systems [2]. Examples of discrete, deterministic and non-linear dynamic systems are the one-dimensional (1-D) chaotic maps. They offer identically distributed binary sequences and they can be used as deterministic generators of unpredictable sequences. Therefore, 1-D chaotic maps can be used in cryptographic, steganographic and digital marking systems. A 1-D chaotic map is specified by the following iterated expression:

$$x_{n+1} = \tau_\mu(x_n), \quad n = 0,1,2,\cdots \tag{1}$$

Where $\tau_\mu: I \rightarrow I$ is a non linear function, I denotes the interval in which the function is defined, n represents the actual iteration index of τ_μ (), x_0 is the initial condition and μ is the control parameter of the function.

1-D chaotic maps generate orbits, which are defined by,

$$\phi(x_0) = \{x_0, x_1, x_2, \cdots, x_n, \cdots\} = \{x_n\}_{n=0}^{\infty} \tag{2}$$

Note that each generated orbit depends on the initial condition and the control parameter μ of the used map. In this way, it is possible that these orbits tend to one or more fixed values, called map attractors. However, there are other values that are repellers and will produce unstable orbits in the map. Control parameter μ of the map τ_μ () defines that a point is an attractor or repeller.

Works related to the application of chaotic map on cryptographic systems can be found in [3], [4], [5], [6] and [7]. Therefore, chaos theory is currently used in the analysis and design of cryptosystems that provide technological solutions for information protection.

2 Chaotic Block Cryptosystem

2.1 Description

The block cryptosystem presented here, is based on G. Jakimoski and L. Kocarev proposal [3]. They suggest the use of logistic map in a balanced and dynamic ciphering structure that processes 64 bits blocks, considering 8 sub-blocks of 8 bits each one. The ciphering process consists of 8 rounds over the same data block B_j with $j = 0, 1, 2, ..., 7$. The block of the plaintext is B_0. The output block in a round is the input block of the following round, except in the last one, in which the output block corresponds to the ciphered block of the cryptogram. G. Jakimoski and L. Kocarev suggest to use a scaled and discretized logistic map in the noise function of the cryptosystem, according to the following equations:

$$x_{i,k+1} = x_{i-1,k} \oplus f_{k-1}(x_{i-1,1}, ..., x_{i-1,k-1}, z_{i-1,k-1}); k = 1, 2, ..., 8 \tag{3}$$

The values $x_{i,0}, x_{i,1}, ... x_{i,j}$ with $i = 1, 2, ..., r$, and $j = 0, 1, 2, ..., 7$ represent each 8-bits sub-block that conform the block B_i, which is the transformed version of B_{i-1}. In this way, B_r will be the ciphered block of every block B_0 from the plaintext. In the other hand, chaotic functions $f_j:[0, 255] \rightarrow [0, 255] \in \aleph$, receive and transform the sum of one or more sub-blocks with its corresponding sub key, except f_0. The function $\oplus$

represents the module 2 bit to bit sum considering words of 8 bits. Each round i is controlled by an 8 bytes sub-key $z_{i-1, k-1}$ and each function f_j has the form $f_j=(x_0, \ldots, x_j, z_j)$ and generate noise that will be applied in each round to each plaintext sub-block.

2.2 Use of Logistic Map

The logistic map is a chaotic system that generates sequences that exhibit a reproducible chaotic behavior. Moreover, using the bifurcation diagram and Lyapunov exponent (see Fig 1), the disadvantages of logistic map can be shown when it is used in cryptographic systems. These disadvantages are the presence of stability islands, in which the logistic map produces periodic signals into the chaotic region. This condition occurs when $\lambda \le 0$ (see Fig 1a), but when $\lambda \ge 0$ the logistic map will produce aperiodic signals. These stability islands appear according to Charkovsky sequence [8].

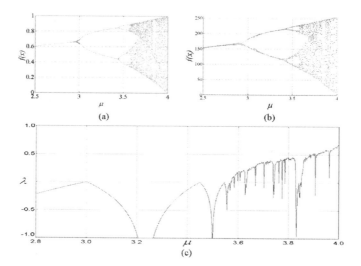

Fig. 1. Behavior of logistic map. a) Bifurcation diagram in $\Re$, b) Bifurcation diagram in $\aleph$ (scaled and discretized logistic map) and c) Lyapunov exponent in $\Re$.

2.3 Use of Piecewise Linear Maps

There are other 1-D chaotic maps that do not have stability islands and consequently they do not produce periodic signals into the chaotic region. These 1-D chaotic maps can be used as noise functions in cryptosystems, and they are known as piecewise linear maps. Examples of these maps are Bernoulli and Tent maps. When these maps are scaled and discretized, a non chaotic map is obtained, and the periodicity evidence can be obtained using its bifurcation diagram (see Fig. 2). Note that when an 8 bits precision is used in the tent map, the interval [0, 255] is not covered by the bifurcation diagram. There are few bands in which the energy is concentrated (see Fig 2a). In Fig 2c the statistical distribution of tent map is shown when $\mu = 0.8$, which is congruent with Fig. 2a. However, when the 16 bits precision is used in the tent map, the bifurcation diagram and statistical distribution is better respect to the 8 bits precision alternative (see Fig. 2b and 2d).

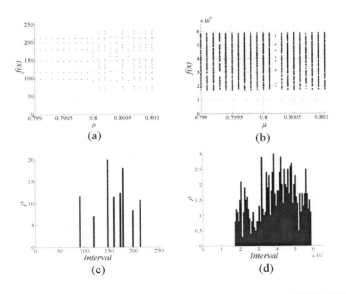

Fig. 2. Scaled and discretized tent map, a) 8 bits precision and $\mu \in$ [0.799, 0.801], b) 16 bits precision and $\mu \in$ [0.799, 0.801], c) Statistical distribution using an 8 bits precision and $\mu = 0.8$ and d) Statistical distribution using a 16 bits precision and $\mu = 0.8$.

2.4 Chaotic Noise Generator on Cryptosystem

Due to the problems encountered in the use of chaotic maps in noise generation for cryptographic systems, in this paper an alternative is proposed which does not require that the chaotic map is scaled and discretized. This alternative define for the chaotic map f; $[a,b] \rightarrow [a,b] \in \Re$ a regular partition of S intervals, in which each interval A_t with $t = 0, 1, 2, \ldots S$ has a length given by $L(A_t) = L = (b-a)/S$. The following membership function is defined:

$$I_{At}(x) = \begin{cases} 1, & si\ x \in A_t \\ 0, & si\ x \notin A_t \end{cases} \tag{4}$$

In this way, the new orbit $\wp_\aleph = \{y_0, y_1, y_2, \ldots\}$ in $[0,255] \in \aleph$ is constructed from the chaotic orbit $\wp_\Re = \{x_0, x_1, x_2, \ldots\}$ in $[a, b] \in \Re$, according to the following expression:

$$y_m = a_t \quad if\ (I_{At}(x_m)) = 1\ ;\ m = 1, 2, 3, \ldots \tag{5}$$

Where a_t represents the character t in the Extended ASCII alphabet. For the presented cryptosystem a tent map has been used, which is defined by the following equation:

$$f_\mu(x_n) = \begin{cases} 2\mu x_n + \dfrac{(1-\mu)}{2}; & 0 \le x_n \le \dfrac{1}{2} \\ -2\mu(x_n - 1) + \dfrac{(1-\mu)}{2}; & \dfrac{1}{2} \le x_n \le 1 \end{cases} \tag{6}$$

Parameter $\mu \in [0, 1]$ and the initial condition x_0 are known but arbitrary selected. Thus, μ and x_0 could be considered a key in the encryption process. Figure 3 shows the bifurcation diagram for a family of orbits $\{\wp_\aleph\}$ for a control parameter $\mu \in [0.799, 0.801]$.

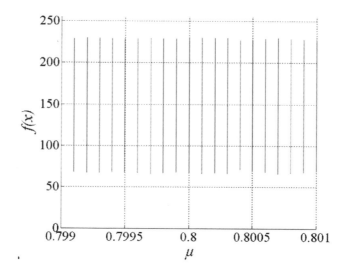

Fig. 3. Zoom on the bifurcation diagram for the family of orbits $\{\wp_\aleph\}$ with $m = 1, 2, 3, \ldots,$ when the tent map was not scaled and discretized and $\mu \in [0.799, 0.801]$

2.5 Chaos Annulling

When the 1-D chaotic maps are used in a computer, there are problems that must be considered. There is at least one initial condition for which chaos is not only sustained but also collapsed; this is an interesting result, and it can be noticed, that at the parameter value for which this occurs ($\mu = 4$, $x_0 = 0.5$ for logistic map), generates a condition called "*chaos annulling trap*" or CAT. CAT condition can be achieved as a result of the rounding off done by the computer; due to it, IEEE recommends calculations in double precision. In similar way, there are other x_0 values that produce a similar condition, which is called "chaos fixed trap" or CFT. There are two methods to determine the initial condition that cause either a CAT or a CFT condition for chaotic map: Analytic and brute force method [9]. Additionally, when a 1-D chaotic map is intended to be used as noise function in stream or block cryptosystems, a scaled and discretized version of the chaotic map must be considered, which is not necessarily a chaotic map, and therefore this condition must be analyzed.

3 Cryptosystem Behavior Analysis

The proposed algorithm evaluation was done using essentially three concepts: the entropy and randomness of the cryptograms and the mutual information of the encryption process. For this evaluation 5 files with different formats and sizes were used, and the proposed cryptosystem was compared with common cryptosystems as AES and IDEA.

The entropy is used as a measure of the message diffusion by the encryption process. So that, if the cryptogram entropy is maximum, it means that the cryptogram will be able to have a statistical distribution very near to the uniform distribution. This condition seeks to affect the statistical distribution of plaintext, and thus the cryptogram will achieve the state of greatest uncertainty. In the calculations a maximum entropy $H_{MAX} = 8$ has been considered for the cryptograms. Table 1 shows the results of the entropy for each cryptogram.

Mutual information measures the amount of information that contributes on a variable, the knowledge of another one. In this case, the mutual information is used as a measure of the relationship between plaintext and its respective cryptogram (see Table 2). A cryptosystem can be considered safe if the amount of information contributed by the knowledge of the cryptogram C in the entropy of the plaintext M is zero.

The randomness of the produced cryptograms has been evaluated using the NIST random tests [10]. Table 3 shows the results of applying the suite of NIST tests to a specific file, which was ciphered with each one of the different cryptosystems. In order to be able to apply the tests, the cryptosystems were binarized in a stream of 100 million bits. Note that proposed cryptosystem was successful in all the NIST SP800-22 test suite cases; this means that the cryptogram has the appearance of a random sequence.

Table 1. Entropy of the cryptograms using the proposed, AES and IDEA cryptosystems

File type	Entropy			
	Plaintext	Proposed cryptosystem	AES	IDEA
TXT	5.0802508	7.999173637	7.9989214	7.9992133
DOC	5.8174680	7.999426499	7.9994851	7.9995290
RTF	3.5727449	7.999939016	7.9999467	7.9999444
PPT	6.6895915	7.999671958	7.9995576	7.9996626
XML	5.4487835	7.999824941	7.9998163	7.9998091

Table 2. Mutual information of the proposed, AES, and IDEA cryptosystems

File type	Mutual Information		
	Proposed cryptosystem	AES	IDEA
TXT	0.069618783	0.0710524	0.0695141
DOC	0.144927532	0.1434934	0.1449023
RTF	0.004785542	0.0047777	0.0047549
PPT	0.100683255	0.1013163	0.1014454
XML	0.017484572	0.0177723	0.0177751

Table 3. Results of NIST SP800-22 Statistical tests

Results of NIST Pseudorandom tests				
Test	P-Value			Review
	Proposed Cryptosystem	AES	DES	
Frequency	0.5955	0.9463	0.0155	Approved
Block-Frequency	0.3669	0.4559	0.7399	Approved
Cumulative-sums Forward	0.9357	0.924	0.3504	Approved
Cumulative-sums Reverse	0.7197	0.7791	0.07571	Approved
Runs	0.9357	0.9558	0.2368	Approved
Longest-Runs of Ones	0.6579	0.7597	0.6371	Approved
Rank	0.3505	0.3504	0.319	Approved
Spectral FFT	0.0428	0.0757	0.2896	Approved
Overlapping-templates	0.7792	0.3838	0.419	Approved
Non-Overlapping-templates	0.4461	0.5749	0.3838	Approved
Universal	0.3345	0.6786	0.924	Approved
Approximate Entropy	0.4012	0.7597	0.3504	Approved
Random-Excursions	0.5047	0.02818	0.2492	Approved
Random-Excursions-Variant	0.3789	0.1005	0.1453	Approved
Serial	0.8669	0.6371	0.01559	Approved

4 Conclusions

In this paper, it is proposed a cryptosystem that includes pseudorandom sequences generators using 1-D chaotic maps. These generators have been built with piecewise linear maps because they do not have stability islands in the chaotic region. The partition made on the definition interval of the 1-D chaotic map and its association with the Extended ASCIII alphabet avoids the periodicity problems in the generated sequences. These problems are derived from the scaling and discretization of the chaotic map used in cryptosystems. In summary, the implementation of a block chaotic cryptosystem is shown, and its behavior is analyzed using the concepts of information theory and the suite of random test of NIST SP800-22. The proposed chaotic cryptosystem was made using a 1-D chaotic tent map, which has not stability islands into the chaotic region. The entropy and mutual information results show that the proposed cryptosystem is a good alternative to affect the syntactic, semantic and the statistical distribution of a plaintext. Cryptosystems as the one proposed in this paper can be useful components in software applications that provide security to stored or communicated information, because they have similar behavior to the one of the algorithms currently used, and they are designed with chaotic sequence generators, which are aperiodic by definition.

Acknowledgments. The authors are grateful to the financial support of the SIP-IPN 20110670 and ICYTDF 270/2010 projects.

References

1. Devanney, R.L.: An introduction to chaotic dynamical systems. Addison Wesley Publishing Company, Reading (1989)
2. Moon, F.C.: Chaotic and fractal in dynamics: an introduction for applied scientists and engineers. Wiley-IEEE (1992)
3. Jakimoski, G., Kocarev, L.: Chaos and Cryptography: Block Encryption Ciphers Based on Chaotic Maps. IEEE Transactions on Circuits and Systems I 48(2), 163–169 (2001)
4. Masuda, N., Aihara, K.: Cryptosystems with discretized chaotic maps. IEEE Transactions on Circuits and Systems-I: Fundamental Theory and Applications 49(1), 28–40 (2002)
5. He, J., Zheng, J., Li, Z.-b., Qian, H.-f.: Color Image Cryptography Using Multiple One-Dimensional Chaotic Maps and OCML. In: International Symposium on Information Engineering and Electronic Commerce, IEEC 2009, pp. 85–89 (2009)
6. Hussein, R.M., Ahmed, H.S., El-Wahed, W.: New encryption schema based on swarm intelligence chaotic map. In: 7th International Conference on Informatics and Systems (INFOS), pp. 1–7 (2010)
7. Rodríguez-Sahagún, M.T., Mercado-Sánchez, J.B., López-Mancilla, D., Jaimes-Reátegui, R., García-López, J.H.: Image Encryption Based on Logistic Chaotic Map for Secure Communications. In: IEEE Electronics, Robotics and Automotive Mechanics Conference, CERMA 2010, pp. 319–324 (2010)
8. Peitgen, H., Jürgens, H., Saupe, D.: Chaos and Fractals New Frontiers of Science, 2nd edn. Springer, Heidelberg (2010)
9. Kartalopoulos, S.V.: Annulling Traps & Fixed Traps in Chaos Cryptography. In: New Technologies, Mobility and Security, NTMS 2008, pp. 1–4, 5-7 (2008)
10. Rukhin A., Soto J., Nechvatal J., Smid M., Barker E., Leigh S., Levenson M., Vangel M., Banks D., Heckert A., Dray J., Vo S.: A Statistical Test Suite for Random and Pseudorandom Number Generators for Cryptographic Applications. NIST SP 800-22 Rev 1a (2010), http://csrc.nist.gov/groups/ST/toolkit/rng/documents/SP800-22rev1a.pdf

A Quantitative Analysis into the Economics of Correcting Software Bugs

Craig S. Wright and Tanveer A. Zia

School of Computing and Mathematics
Charles Sturt University, NSW 2678
cwrigh20@postoffice.csu.edu.au, tzia@csu.edu.au

Abstract. Using a quantitative study of in-house coding practices, we demonstrate the notion that programming needs to move from "Lines of Code per day" as a productivity measure to a measure that takes debugging and documentation into account. This could be something such as "Lines of clean, simple, correct, well-documented code per day", but with bugs propagating into the 6th iteration of patches, a new paradigm needs to be developed. Finding flaws in software, whether these have a security related cost or not, is an essential component of software development. When these bugs result in security vulnerabilities, the importance of testing becomes even more critical. Many studies have been conducted using the practices of large software vendors as a basis, but few studies have looked at in-house development practices. This paper uses an empirical study of in-house software coding practices in Australian companies to both demonstrate that there is an economic limit to how far testing should proceed as well as noting the deficiencies in the existing approaches.

Keywords: Software Development Life Cycle, Model Checking, Software Verification, Empirical studies.

1 Introduction

The deficiency of published quantitative data on software development and systems design has been a major ground for software engineering's failure to ascertain a proper scientific foundation. Past studies into coding practice have focused on software vendors. These developers have many distinctions from in-house projects that are not incorporated into the practices and do not align well with in-house corporate code development. In the past, building software was the only option but as the industry developed, the build vs. buy argument has swung back towards in-house development with the uptake of Internet connected systems. In general, this has been targeted towards specialized web databases and online systems with office systems and mainstream commercial applications becoming a 'buy' decision.

As companies move more and more to using the web and as 'cloud applications' become accepted, in-house development is becoming more common. This paper uses an empirical study of in-house software coding practices in Australian companies to both demonstrate that there is an economic limit to how far testing should proceed as well as noting the deficiencies in the existing approaches.

Á. Herrero and E. Corchado (Eds.): CISIS 2011, LNCS 6694, pp. 198–205, 2011.
© Springer-Verlag Berlin Heidelberg 2011

1.1 Related Work

Other studies of coding processes and reliability have been conducted over the last few decades. The majority of these have been based either on studies of large systems [3, 8] and mainframe based operations [8] or have analyzed software vendors [7]. In the few cases where coding practices within individual organization have been quantitatively analyzed, the organizations have been nearly always large telecommunications firms [1, 2, 5, 6, 8] or have focused on SCADA and other critical system providers [9] or are non-quantitative approaches [12, 13].

Whilst these results are extremely valuable, they fail to reflect the state of affairs within the vast majority of organizations. With far more small to medium businesses coupled with comparatively few large organizations with highly focused and dedicated large scale development teams (as can be found in any software vendor), an analysis of in-house practice is critical to both security and the economics of in-house coding.

As the Internet comes to become all persuasive, internal coding functions are only likely to become more prevalent and hence more crucial to the security of the organization.

1.2 Our Contribution

In section 2 we present an analysis of the empirical study completed to determine the cost of finding, testing and fixing software bugs. We model the discovery of bugs or vulnerabilities in Section 3 using Cobb-Douglas function and calculate the defect rate per SLOC (source line of codes) using Bayesian calculations. Finally paper is summarized and concluded in Section 4.

2 An Analysis of Coding Practice

A series of 277 coding projects in 15 companies with in-house developers was analyzed over multiple years. The costs, both in terms of time and as a function of financial expenditure were recorded. The analysis recorded: format string errors, integer overflows, buffer overruns, SQL injection, cross-site scripting, race conditions, and command injection. The code samples were analyzed by the authors using a combination of static tools and manual verification to the OWASP[1] and SANS[2] secure coding guidelines during both the development and maintenance phases. For the 277 coding projects, the following data fields have been collected:

- the total number of hours
    - o   Coding / Debugging (each recorded separately)
- tloc (thousand lines of source code)
- the number of bugs (both initially and over time as patches are released)

The coding projects where developed using a combination of the Java, C# (.Net), PhP and C++ languages. The authors collected data between June 2008 and December

---

[1] http://www.owasp.org/index.php/Secure_Coding_Principles
[2] http://www.sans-ssi.org/

2010 during a series of Audits of both code security and system security code associated with [14]. The code projects came from a combination of financial services companies, media companies and web development firms. The data will be released online by the authors.

It is clear from the results that there is an optimized ideal for software testing. Fig. 1 demonstrates the costs of testing and notes how each subsequent bug costs more to find than the previous one. The costs of finding bugs go up as the cost of software is tested to remove more bugs.

It has been noted that *"there is a clear intuitive basis for believing that complex programs have more faults in them than simple programs"* [9]. As the size and hence complexity of the code samples increased, the amount of time and costs required to write and debug the code increased (Fig. 2). What was unexpected was that the number of bugs/LOC did not significantly change as the size of the program increased (Fig. 3). Rather, there was a slight, but statistically insignificant decline in the number of bugs noted in more complex programs per line of code. So whilst the number of bugs did increase, this occurred in a linear fashion to the cost increase which occurred exponentially.

The calculated number of hours per line of code (Fig. 2) increased exponentially with an exponent of around 1.56. In this study, the largest program sampled was approximately 300,000 SLOC (source lines of code). This relates directly to complexity with longer programs costing more both in time and money.

A financial calculation of internal costs of mitigating the bugs was also conducted based on the bugs found within a year of the code being released. This period was selected as it comes to reason that if the bug has not been found in a 12 month period, it would be expensive to find.

The results of the analysis of the data demonstrated that the costs of testing can be analyzed. In Fig. 1, the cost (calculated as a function of analysis time) of finding each additional bug is exponentially more expensive than the last to find. As a consequence, this also increases the mean cost of the project. The more bugs are sought, the higher the cost. This is offset against the costs of fixing bugs in the field later in the paper.

Of particular interest is the distribution of bugs as a percentage of code. We can see that there is no strong correlation between the levels of bugs in code and the length of the code ($R^2 = -14.48$). There are more bugs in large code, but the number of bugs per line does not increase greatly.

The distribution of bugs was fairly even for all sizes of code in the study and was positively skewed. The numbers of bugs discovered was far too high. The reported numbers of bugs in large commercial software releases average around 4% [9]. The mean (Fig. 4) for the study was 5.529% (or 55 errors per 1,000 lines of source code). Many of these are functional and did not pose security threats, but the economics of repairing the remaining bugs remains.

We need to move from "*Lines of Code per day*" as a productivity measure to a measure that takes debugging and documentation into account. This could be something such as "*Lines of clean, simple, correct, well-documented code per day*" [3]. This also has problems, but it does go a long way towards creating a measure that incorporates the true costs of coding.

The primary issue comes from an argument to parsimony. The coder who can create a small, fast and effective code sample in 200 lines where another programmer would require 2,000 may have created a more productive function. The smaller number of lines requires less upkeep and can be verified far easier than the larger counterpart.

Software maintenance introduces more bugs. Through an analysis of the debugging progresses and the program fixes, it was clear that systems deteriorate over time. What we see is that the first iteration of bug fixes leads to a second and subsequent series of fixes. In each set of fixes, there is a 20-50% (mean of 34% $\pm$ 8%[1]) of the fix creating another round of bugs. This drops on the second round of fixes, but starts to rise on the 3rd and subsequent rounds. In a smaller set of code, the low overall volume of bugs limits the number of iterations, but the larger code samples led to up to 6 iterations. This would be expected to be even larger on extremely large programs (such as an Operating System).

The ratio of software bugs in the patching process was less than that of the initial release, but over the life of a program that has been maintained for several years, the total number of bugs introduced through patches can be larger than that of the initial release.

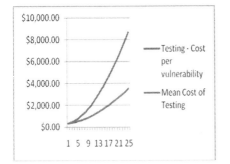

Fig. 1. Each vulnerability costs more than the last to mitigate

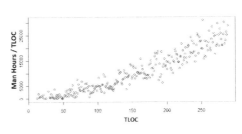

Fig. 2. Program size against Coding time

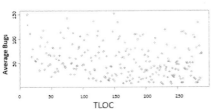

Fig. 3. Program size against Bugs

Fig. 4. Box plot of the distribution of Bugs/TLOC

---

[1] 95% Confidence Interval or $\alpha = 5\%$.

3 Vulnerability Modeling

Vulnerability rates can be modeled extremely accurately for major products. Those with an extremely small user base can also be modeled, but the results will fluctuate due to large confidence intervals. What most people miss is that the number of vulnerabilities or bugs in software is fixed at release. Once the software has been created, the number of bugs is a set value. What varies stochastically is the number of bugs discovered at any time.

This is also simple to model, the variance being based on the number of users (both benign and malicious) of the software. As this value tends to infinity (a large user-base), the addition of any further users makes only a marginal variation in the function. Small user-bases of course have large variations as more people pay attention (such as the release of software vulnerability).

This is a Cobb-Douglass function [10] with the number of users and the rate of decay as variables. For largely deployed software (such as Microsoft's Office suite or the Mozilla browser), the function of the number of vulnerabilities for a program given the size of the program can be approximated as a Poisson decay function.

3.1 Modeling the Discovery of Bugs/Vulnerabilities in Software

The discovery of software bugs can be mapped to the amount of time that has been used in both actively examining the product as well as the passive search for bugs (using the software).

The study found that a Cobb Douglass function with $\alpha=1.6$ and $F(x)= c \times TLOC +\varepsilon$ where c and C are constant values with the function $G(x)^{\beta}$ is constant for a given number of users or installations and expresses the rate at which users report bugs. This equation increases to a set limit as the number of users increase. In the case of widely deployed software installations (such as Microsoft Word or Adobe Acrobat) and highly frequented Internet sites, this value tends towards $G(x)=1$.

3.2 Equations for Bug Discovery

For a static software system under uniform usage the rate of change in, N, the number of defects discovered is directly proportional to the number of defects in the system,

$$\frac{d}{dt} N(t) = \alpha N(t) \tag{1}$$

A Static system is defined as one that experiences no new development, only defect repair. Likewise, uniform usage is based on same number of runs/unit time. As the user-base of the product tends to infinity, this becomes a better assumption.

If we set time T to be any reference epoch, then N satisfies

$$N(t) = N(t) e^{-\alpha(t-T)} \tag{2}$$

This means we can observe the accumulated number of defects at time t, A(t), where

$$A(t) = N(t)\left(1 - e^{-\alpha(t-T)}\right) \tag{3}$$

With continuous development, an added function to model the ongoing addition of code is also required. Each instantaneous additional code segment (patch fix or feature) can be modeled in a similar manner.

What we do not have is the decay rate and we need to be able to calculate this. For software with a large user-base that has been running for a sufficient epoch of time, this is simple.

This problem is the same as having a jar with an unknown but set number of red and white balls. If we have a selection of balls that have been drawn, we can estimate the ratio of red and white balls in the jar.

Likewise, if we have two jars with approximately the same number of balls in approximately the same ratio, and we add balls from the second jar to the first periodically, we have a most mathematically complex and difficult problem, but one that has a solution.

This reflects the updating of existing software. In addition, with knowledge if the defect rates as bugs are patched (that is the rate of errors for each patch), we can calculate the expected numbers of bugs over the software lifecycle. In each case, the number of bugs from each iteration of patching added *34% ± 8%* more bugs than the last iteration.

$$A(t) = \sum_{i=0}^{k} A_i(t) = A_0(t) + A_1(t) + \ldots + A_k(t)$$

$$\approx A_0(t) + \beta A_0(t) + \beta^2 A_0(t) + \ldots + \beta^k A_0(t) \qquad \beta \leq 1 \tag{5}$$

In the study, this would come to

$$A(t) = A_0(t) \sum_{i=0}^{6} (0.34)^i = 1.514 A_0(t) \tag{6}$$

So over the life of the software, there are 1.51 times the original number of bugs that are introduced through patching.

Where we have a new software product, we have prior information. We can calculate the defect rate per SLOC, the rate for other products from the team, the size of the software (in SLOC) etc. This information becomes the posterior distribution. This is where Bayesian calculations [11] are used.

t	=	time
λ_B	=	(Mean) Number of Bugs / TLOC (Thousand Lines of Code)
L	=	SLOC (Source Lines of Code)

So, more generally, if a software release has L lines of code and the expected number of lines of code per defect is λ_B, then the a priori distribution of defects in the release is a Poisson P_β distribution where β is the ratio of new lines of code to average number of lines/bug (L/ λ_B)

$$P_\beta(n_{defects}) = \frac{\beta^n e^{-\beta}}{n!} \tag{7}$$

The conditional distribution for the number of defects in a software release given a defect discovery T units of time since the last discovery is

$$P_\beta(n\_defects) = \frac{\beta^n}{n!} e^{-\beta} \tag{8}$$

Suppose the defect discovery (decay) constant is α and β is the a priori expected number of defects (code size/lines of code per defect). If we observe defects at time intervals of T_1, T_2, ..., T_k, then the conditional distribution of remaining defects is Poisson:

$$P_{(\beta e^{-\alpha(T_1+T_2+...+T_k)})}\left(n_{defects}\right) = \frac{(\beta e^{-\alpha(T_1+T_2+...+T_k)})^n}{n!} e^{-\beta e^{-\alpha(T_1+T_2+...+T_k)}} \tag{9}$$

This is the a priori expected number of defects scaled by the decay factor of the exponential discovery model.

As new releases to the software are made, the distribution of defects remains Poisson with the expected number of defects being the number remaining from the last release, γ plus those introduced, β, by the independent introduction of new functionality.

$$P_{(\beta+\gamma)}[n] = \frac{e^{-(\beta+\gamma)}(\beta+\gamma)^n}{n!} \tag{10}$$

It is thus possible to observe the time that elapses since the last discovery of a vulnerability. This value is dependent upon the number of vulnerabilities in the system and the number of users of the software. The more vulnerabilities, the faster the discovery rate of flaws. Likewise, the more users of the software, the faster the existing vulnerabilities are found (through both formal and adverse discovery).

4 Conclusion

To represent the effect of security expenditure in minimizing bugs against investment over time and the result as expected returns (or profit) we see that there are expenditure inflection points. What we see is that spending too much on security has a limiting function on profit. Also too little expenditure has a negative effect on profit as the cost of discovering bugs post release increases. This is where risk analysis comes into its own. The idea is to choose an optimal expenditure on security that limits the losses. Money should be spent on security until that last dollar returns at least a dollar in mitigated expected loss. Once the expenditure of a dollar returns less than a dollar, the incremental investment is wasted. Here, the software coder has to optimize the testing process.

Modeling and understanding program risks is essential if we are to minimize risk and create better code. It was clear from this study that organizational coding expresses a far higher rate of bugs per line of code than is expressed in specialized software companies. Insufficient testing is being conducted in many companies who have in-house coding teams. This is leading to higher costs and lower overall security.

The goal for any coding team should be how many lines of good code are produced, not how many lines of code are written and then sent to be fixed.

References

[1] Anderson., R.: Why information security is hard, an economic perspective. In: 17th Annual Computer Security Applications Conf., New Orleans, LA (December 2001)

[2] Carman, D.W., Dolinsky, A.A., Lyu, M.R., Yu, J.S.: Software Reliability Engineering Study of a Large-Scale Telecommunications System. In: Proc. Sixth Int'l Symp. Software Reliability Eng., pp. 350–359 (1995)

[3] Connell, C.: It's Not About Lines of Code, http://www.developer.com/java/other/article.php/988641 (viewed March 15, 2010)

[4] Daskalantonakis, M.K.: A Practical View of Software Measurement and Implementation Experiences within Motorola. IEEE Trans. Software Eng. 18(11), 998–1010 (1992)

[5] Kaaniche, K., Kanoun, K.: Reliability of a Telecommunications System. In: Proc. Seventh Int'l Symp. Software Reliability Eng., pp. 207–212 (1996)

[6] Khoshgoftaar, T.M., Allen, E.B., Kalaichelvan, K.S., Goel, N.: Early Quality Prediction: A Case Study in Telecommunications. IEEE Trans. Software Eng. 13(1), 65–71 (1996)

[7] Levendel, Y.: Reliability Analysis of Large Software Systems: Defects Data Modeling. IEEE Trans. Software Eng. 16(2), 141–152 (1990)

[8] Mills, H.D.: Top-down programming in large systems. In: Rustin, R. (ed.) Debugging Techniques in Large Systems. Prentice-Hall, Englewoods Cliffs (1971)

[9] Munson, J.C., Khoshgoftaar, T.M.: The Detection of Fault-Prone Programs. IEEE Transactions on Software Engineering 18(5), 423–433 (1992)

[10] Cobb, C.W., Douglas, P.H.: A theory of production. American Economic Review 18(1), 139–165 (1928); Supplement, Papers and Proceedings of the Fortieth Annual Meeting of the American Economic Association (1928)

[11] Bayes, T.: An essay towards solving a problem in the doctrine of chances. Philosophical Transactions of the Royal Society 53, 370–418 (1763)

[12] Bacon, D.F., Chen, Y., Parkes, D., Rao, M.: A market-based approach to software evolution. Paper Presented at the Proceeding of the 24th ACM SIGPLAN Conference Companion on Object Oriented Programming Systems languages and Applications (2009)

[13] Sestoft, P.: Systematic software testing IT University of Copenhagen, Denmark1 Version 2, 2008-02-25 (2008)

[14] Wright, C.S.: The not so Mythical IDS Man-Month: Or Brooks and the rule of information security. In: ISSRE (2010)

Rationally Opting for the Insecure Alternative: Negative Externalities and the Selection of Security Controls

Craig S. Wright and Tanveer A. Zia

School of Computing and Mathematics
Charles Sturt University, NSW 2678
cwrigh20@postoffice.csu.edu.au, tzia@csu.edu.au

Abstract. As with all aspects of business and the economy, information security is an economic function. Security can be modeled as a maintenance or insurance cost as a relative function but never in absolute terms. As such, security can be seen as a cost function that leads to the prevention of loss, but not one that can create gains (or profit). With the role of a capital investment to provide a return on investment, security is a defense against unforeseen losses that cost capital and reduce profitability. In this paper we assess the individual security cost and model our assessment in economic terms. This assessment is vital in determining the cost benefit in applying costly security controls in our systems in general and software in particular.

Keywords: Software Development Life Cycle, Model Checking, Software Verification, Empirical studies.

1 Introduction

Absolute security does not exist and nor can it be achieved. The statement that a computer is either secure or not is logically falsifiable [6], all systems exhibit a level of insecurity. An attacker with sufficient resources can always bypass controls. The goal is to ensure that the economic constraints placed upon the attacker exceed the perceived benefits to the attacker [15]. This generates a measure of relative system security in place of the unachievable absolute security paradigm that necessarily results in a misallocation of resources.

The result is that security is a relative risk measure that is related to organisational economics at the micro level and the economics of national security toward the macro level. This consequentially leads to a measure of security in terms of one's neighbour. The question is not, "*am I secure*", but rather, "am *I more secure than my neighbour?*"

This can be assessed in many ways as any other system is your neighbour on the Internet when viewed from the perspective of a Worm. Conversely, targeted attacks have a purpose. Neighbours may be other government systems, critical infrastructure, and a class of companies or an industry sector. In each instance, security is achieved in relative terms.

The rest of the paper is organised as follows: In section 2 we assess individual security costs. We then provide analysis and discussion on security assessment in terms of its economic value in Section 3. Finally, the paper is concluded in Section 4.

Á. Herrero and E. Corchado (Eds.): CISIS 2011, LNCS 6694, pp. 206–213, 2011.
© Springer-Verlag Berlin Heidelberg 2011

2 Assessing Individual Security Costs

The most effective security solution is that which provides the best level (that which is optimised) for "the least cost". Costs to the consumer are minimised at the point where security costs exactly equal the expected loss that is associated with the risk function.

More security costs = higher costs to the consumer.
Higher expected loss from risk = higher costs to the consumer.

As expenditure on security is expected to decrease the expected loss, the costs to the consumer are minimised were the additional expenditure of $1 on security reduces the expected risk based loss by exactly $1.

Security is a cost function that is passed to the consumer if profitability is to be retained or which reduces profit directly where alternatives exist (this is the product is elastic or consumers are willing to reduce their use if costs increase). The expected cost formula for the supply of these types of services against a loss function can be expressed by:

$$C_s = D(x, y) + x + y \tag{1}$$

Where the loss function $D(x,y)$ and the damage to x (the producer) and y (the consumer) are modelled arithmetically. As in all areas of economics, the marginal gains in D_x offset those of D_y.

In these calculations, calculations, $D_{xy} D_{xy} > D_{xx} D_{xy}$ which creates the inference that the inputs are substitutes. As the producer spends more on security, the consumer spends less and vice versa. The exact composition of these values varies based on the nature of the product with elastic supply being affected more than an inelastic supply.

The real issue and goal in security becomes the creation of a Cournot-Nash equilibria [11]. This is an outcome where X_e and Y_e are together form a Cournot-Nash equilibria for a given value of Y_e the x which maximises X's utility is X_e and given X_e that y which maximises Y's utility is Y_e. This does not require that the equilibria be Pareto optimal [12].

At present, the cost functions directed towards many industries (such as banks in regulated countries including Australia) are sufficient in that there is but a trivial increase in marginal demand for the consumer for an incremental increase in security expenditure. The producing company is likely to do little and that which they do conduct has a minimal effect. For instance, Microsoft is unlikely to greatly improve the security of its operating system through minimising patches due to the increasing cost of finding additional bugs in its software. If it did so, the cost point is such that Microsoft's profit would be diminished as consumers are generally unwilling to bear the cost increment that this would entail. The incremental cost of finding additional bugs exceeds the total cost to all consumers of taking an alternative course of action such as installing HIDS (Host Intrusion Detection Software) and Host firewalls.

The loss for the consumer is lessened to a lower extent than the loss of the producer. With fraud loss limits of $50 in countries such as Australia for online transactions, banks in these locations have an incentive to minimise the loss to the consumer. Perversely, this can incentivise the consumer against adequately securing their system. If the consumer expects to lose a maximum of L_{iy} (which is set at \$50 for credit card transaction fraud in Australia) for any given incident i where the total expected damage is defined as:

$$D_y = \sum_{i=1}^{n} L_{iy} \qquad D_x = \sum_{i=1}^{n} L_{ix} \qquad (2)$$

The expected annual number of incidents per consumer n can be calculated as the total number of incidents that have occurred divided by the total number of consumers of a class (i.e. the total pool of credit card users).

$$E(n) = \frac{\#incidents}{\#consumers} \qquad (3)$$

Setting C_{Ty} as the total cost to the consumer of implementing controls, if the expected total loss to the consumer $D_y < C_{Ty}$, it is doubtful that the consumer will pay for additional protection. For instance, if a high-end HIDS and anti-malware product costs $C_{Ty}= \$225$, and the consumer experiences $n=4$ incidents in a usual year, the expected damage $D_y = \sum_{i=1}^{n} L_{iy} = \$200.$ As $D_y < C_{Ty}$, it is not in the interest of the consumer to adequately protect their system. The user of a system that requires more security then the mean level of control provided by a vendor can implement increased security controls on their system, but this would either require that the consumer experience other measurable losses or that $D_y > C_{Ty}$ for this consumer.

Here we see that the anti-fraud efforts by banks and credit card companies create a negative incentive to consumers. The loss to the vendor L_{ix} currently averages \$237 [1] for each lost set of credentials. The result is that it is in the interest of the financial company to provide the consumer with a compensating control. Holding the consumer liable if they had failed to use the enhanced controls over security would result in $D_y > C_{Ty}$ and hence an incentive for the consumer to protect their system.

Capital invested by the consumer in securing their system has a greater marginal effect than that of the producer in the case of an organisation such as Microsoft. A consumer can purchase HIDS and host firewall software for less than the cost that it would cost Microsoft to perfect their software through formal verification and hence remove more bugs.

The expected damage, $E(Damage)_i = P(x_{ai}).D_{Tot}$ or the expected damage is equal to the probability of a breach times the amount of damage suffered in a breach. This can be expressed as a function for each user or as a total cost function for all users, $E(Damage) = \sum_i (P(x_{ai}).D_{Tot})$. Here we can clearly see that the total amount of damage is a function of not only the producer, but also the consumer. The optimal solution is to find a point that minimises the total costs. This is the expected damage as a loss function plus the costs of damage prevention of a compromise of other loss. The damage can also be expressed as a function of both the producer and consumer (user) costs,

$$C_T = Cost_{Tot} = \sum_i [P(x_{ai})D(x_{ai})] + C_v + \sum_i [C_u(i)] \qquad (4)$$

The first order conditions are:

$$P'(x_{ai})D(x_{ai}) + 1 = 0 \qquad (5)$$

$$D'(x_{ai})P(x_{ai}) + 1 = 0 \qquad (6)$$

That is, the user should increase the expenditure on precaution (preventing a breach) until the last dollar spent on precaution by the user reduces the expected damage by \$1. And the producer should increase the expenditure on reducing the possible damage in case of a breach until the last dollar spent on precaution by the producer reduces the expected damages by \$1.

Clearly, the greater the likelihood of the user experiencing a breach, or the larger $P(x_{ai})$ is for the user, the greater the precaution that they should undertake. In the case of a producer who is a software vendor, they will (generally) sell their products to a wide range of users with varying levels of likelihood that each will experience a breach. That is, the software vendor is acting with imperfect information.

The optimal amount of precaution is the solutions to Equations (2) and (3) and is denoted by the expressions C_v^{Ω}, $C_u^{\Omega}(i)$ and where the total costs for all users is optimised at $\sum_i [C_u^{\Omega}(i)]$.

The marginal utility expenditure of security means that the value of security decreases the more we add. There is reason for this. If we spend more than the value of the organisations capital, it is simple to see that the producer will not survive long. It is more than this, we only need to reduce profitability for a producer to fail, not the capital.

The level of damages suffered by a user depends on both the pre-breach behaviour of the user and the vendor. The vendor is in a position where reputation impacts sales (demand) and hence the willingness to add layers of testing and additional controls (all of which increase the cost of the software). As the market for software varies in its elasticity [9] from the highly inelastic in small markets with few competitors (e.g. Electricity markets) to highly elastic (e.g. Operating Systems), the user has the ability to best determine their needs. The user may select customised software with warranties designed to reduce the levels of breach that can occur. This comes with an increased cost.

Software vendors normally do not face strict liability for the damage associated with a breach due to a software vulnerability [4, 7]. Although negligence rules for software vendors have been called for [7], this creates a sub-optimal outcome. The user can: (1) select different products with an expectation of increased security [2], (2) add external controls (through the introduction of external devices, create additional controls or use other software that enhances the ability of the primary product), and (3) increase monitoring for attacks that may be associated with the potentially vulnerable services such as by the use of IDS (Intrusion Detection System).

By limiting the scope of the user's responsibility, the user's incentive to protect their systems is also limited [4]. That is the user does not have the requisite incentive to take the optimal level of precautions. Most breaches are not related to zero day attacks [3]. Where patches have been created for known vulnerabilities that could lead to a breach, users will act in a manner (rational behaviour) that they expect to minimise their costs [10]. Whether risk seeking or risk adverse, the user aims to minimise the costs that they will experience. This leads to a wide range of behaviour with risk adverse users taking additional precautions and risk neutral users can accept their risk by minimising their upfront costs, which may lead to an increase in loss later.

In any event, the software vendor as the cause of a breach is not liable for any consequential damages. This places the appropriate incentives on the user to mitigate the risk. At the same time, the vendor has a reputational incentive to minimise the risk to their reputation. This was seen a number of years ago where the costs of bugs to the consumer from Microsoft was deemed as being exceedingly high. The vendor response was to change their coding practices and to significantly reduce the number of vulnerabilities in their released code.

A better game model for the software industry is the "Stag Hunt". This was based on Jean Jacques Rousseau's postulations of a co-operation strategy between two hunters [8]. These individuals can either jointly hunt a stag or individually hunt a rabbit. The largest payoff is assigned against the capture of a stag which provides a larger return than the hare. The hunting of a stag is more demanding and requires mutual cooperation. If either player hunts a stag alone, the chance of success is negligible and sub-optimal. Hunting stags is most beneficial for society in that this activity creates the optimal returns. The problem with this game is that it requires a lot of trust among the players.

| | | Software User | |
		Create Secure Software	Add Features
Software Vendor	Create Secure Software	10, 10 A, W	1, 7 B, X
	Add Features	7, 1 C, Y	5, 5 D, Z

Fig. 1. Software Markets as a "Stag Hunt"

This game has two pure strategy equilibria in which both of the players prefer the lower risk equilibrium to the higher payoff equilibrium. The game is both Pareto optimal and Hicks optimal, but the sub-optimal and hence inefficient equilibrium poses a lower risk to either player. As the payoff variance over the other player's strategies is less than that of the optimal solution, it is more likely that this option will be selected. Another way of stating this is that the equilibrium is payoff-dominant while the other strategy is risk-dominant.

The strategy between the Software Vendor and the Software User is displayed in Fig 1. In this, the numerical representations represent the payoff figures for the specific case (the software market) and the generalized relations take the form:

$$A > C \geq D > B$$
$$W > X \geq Z > Y$$
(7)

The outcomes are not definitive statements of what will be produced. In this game, the "Stag" is a desire to "Create Secure Software" and the "Hare" the fallback to adding more features. A desire is not a case of creating fewer bugs by itself, but rather a combination of adding controls and testing to software. Such an example would be the addition of the XP to Windows XP SP2 by Microsoft. Additional testing is effective to a point and more can be done than is occurring at present.

The payoffs for creating more secure software are great for both the vendor and the user, but the risk of a misaligned strategy leads to the sub-optimal equilibria. What is needed is a signaling process. A signal will allow the players to align to the more optimal strategy. It is not only in the user's interest to have more secure software, but also is in the interest of the vendor. Patching is expensive and the vendor can reasonably charge more for secure software.

As the ratio between the payoff for stag hunting and the payoff for hare hunting is reduced, the incentives to move towards stag hunting decreases. As a result, it becomes less likely that software security will be made into a primary goal of either party. As such, where the introduction of features and the "*new killer app*" occur more frequently, software security lags and it becomes more likely that a change from a stag hunting equilibrium to a hare hunting equilibrium will occur. It is hence less probable that an alteration of the players strategy from hare to stag.

Since neither player has an incentive to deviate, this probability distribution over the strategies is known as a correlated equilibrium of the game. Notably, the expected payoff for this equilibrium is $7(1/3) + 2(1/3) + 6(1/3) = 5$ which is higher than the expected payoff of the mixed strategy Nash equilibrium.

3   Assessing Economic Value of Security

Being a relative function, not only does the profitability of an individual class (be that organization, group or nation) factor into the calculation of security risk, but the relation to a classes neighbors also needs to be measured.

The cost function is in the criminals favor without additional input from the consumer. There is no impetuous for the bank to move to a more secure (and also more costly) means of protecting consumers when the criminal can still gain to the consumers system. One part of the problem is the regulations that plague banking. The requirement to authenticate customers when calling for their privacy makes it simple for a criminal to pose as the bank and obtain the information. So even if a more secure means is selected, it is trivial to bypass many controls using social engineering and other less technical methods.

Whilst there are greater losses from consumer inaction then supplier inaction, the consumer's failure to secure their system and refrain from the use of systems at insecure locations all compound to make it more likely to have a loss through this means.

At all points of an assessment, we have to also take the time value of money into account. The value of capital is not set and fluctuates with time. To evaluate costs, we need to take both cost and the point at which the cost is expressed into account.

In order to compare any set of two or more alternatives, the financial characteristics of the alternatives must be compared on an equivalent basis. Two options are said to be equivalent when they have the same effect. Monetary values are termed as equivalent when they have the same exchange value. This can be defined as:

1. The comparative amount of each monetary sum,
2. The times of the occurrence of the sums can be aligned.
3. An interest rate can be used to compare differences in the time of payment.

The general equivalence function is defined as:

$$\text{PE, AE or FE} = f(F_i, i, n) \tag{8}$$

This equation holds for values of t between 0 and n. The equivalence equation uses:

$F_t =$ the rate of monetary flow at the end of time period t.
$i =$ the rate of interest for the time period.
$n =$ the number of discrete time periods.

The security and risk product lifecycle defines the function of the acquisition and utilisation phases. A system with a longer MTBF (Mean Time Between Failure) has a greater return on the initial investment. Similarly, larger upfront investments in security reduce the amount of capital available for investment. The financial present equivalent function [PE(i)] is defined as a value calculation that is related to the difference between the present equivalent capital value and the present equivalent costs for a given alternative at a given interest rate.

The present equivalent value at interest rate i over a total of n years is stated as:

$$PE(i) = F_0\left(^{P/F,i,0}\right) + F_1\left(^{P/F,i,1}\right) + \ldots + F_n\left(^{P/F,i,n}\right)$$
$$= \sum_{t=0}^{n} F_t\left(^{P/F,i,t}\right) \tag{9}$$

The addition on measures that take externalities into account act as a signaling instrument that reduce information asymmetry and improve the overall risk position of both the consumer and the vendor. The development of a software risk derivative mechanism would be beneficial to security [5] through the provision of a signaling process to security and risk.

4 Conclusion

As we move security expenditure from a lower to higher value, the returns on that expenditure increases to a maxima and then decreases. The optimal point is where security expenditure and expected returns result in positive growth. In this paper we have rigorously assessed the security expenditure and their expected returns and conclude that the rational choice for selection of security controls is important. Before we invest our valuable resources into protecting the information assets it is vital to address concerns such as the importance of information or the resource being protected, the potential impact if the security is breached, the skills and resources of the attacker and the controls available to implement the security. The value on stack is not the capital, but rather expected return on capital. In any event, security expenditure fails where it costs more than it is expected to save [14]. This paper validates reasons why the cost of vendors in share price [13] and reputational losses exceed the perceived gains from technical reasons where the fix might break existing applications.

References

[1] Ben-Itzhak, Y.: Organised cybercrime and payment cards. Card Technology Today 21(2), 10–11 (2009)

[2] Devanbu, P.T., Stubblebine, S.: Software engineering for security: a roadmap. In: Proceedings of the Conference on The Future of Software Engineering. ACM, Limerick (2002)

[3] DShield (2006-2010), http://www.dshield.org

[4] Hahn, R.W., Layne-Farrar, A.: The Law and Economics of Software Security, p. 283. Harv. J.L. & Pub., Pol'y (2007)

[5] Jaziar, R.: Understanding Hidden Information Security Threats: The Vulnerability Black Market. Paper presented at the 40th Annual Hawaii International Conference on System Sciences HICSS (2007)

[6] Peisert, S., Bishop, M.: How to Design Computer Security Experiments. In: WG 11.8 International Federation of Information Processing. Springer, Boston (2007)

[7] Scott, M.D.: Tort Liability for Vendors of Insecure Software: Has the Time Finally Come. Md. L. Rev. 67(425) (2007-2008)

[8] Skyrms, B.: The Stag Hunt and the Evolution of Social Structure. Cambridge University Press, Cambridge (2004)

[9] Stolpe, M.: Protection Against Software Piracy: A Study Of Technology Adoption For The Enforcement Of Intellectual Property Rights. Economics of Innovation and New Technology 9(1), 25–52 (2000)

[10] White, D.S.D.: Limiting Vulnerability Exposure through effective Patch Management: threat mitigation through vulnerability remediation. Master of Science Thesis, Department of Computer Science, Rhodes University (2006)

[11] Kolstad, C.D., Mathiesen, L.: Computing Cournot-Nash Equilibria. Operations Research 39, 739–748 (1991)

[12] Kurz, M., Hart, S.: Pareto-Optimal Nash Equilibria Are Competitive in a Repeated Economy. Journal of Economic Theory 28, 320–346 (1982)

[13] Arora, A., Telang, R.: Economics of Software Vulnerability Disclosure. IEEE Security and Privacy 3(1), 20–22 (2005)

[14] Bacon, D.F., Chen, Y., Parkes, D., Rao, M.: A market-based approach to software evolution. Paper presented at the Proceeding of the 24th ACM SIGPLAN Conference Companion on Object Oriented Programming Systems Languages and Applications (2009)

[15] Cavusoglu, H., Cavusoglu, H., Zhang, J.: Economics of Security Patch Management. In: The Fifth Workshop on the Economics of Information Security, WEIS 2006 (2006)

An Approach for Adapting Moodle into a Secure Infrastructure⋆

Jesus Diaz, David Arroyo, and Francisco B. Rodriguez

Grupo de Neurocomputacion Biologica, Departamento de Ingenieria Informatica,
Escuela Politecnica Superior, Universidad Autonoma de Madrid
{j.diaz,david.arroyo,f.rodriguez}@uam.es

Abstract. Moodle is one of the most popular open source e-learning
platforms. It makes available a very easy-to-deploy environment, which
once installed, is ready to be used. These two characteristics, make it a
very attractive choice. But regarding information security and privacy,
it presents several and important drawbacks. This is mainly due to the
fact that it leaves the most serious tasks, like server configuration or
access control in the hands of the system administrator or third-party
module developers. This approach is understandable, as is that very fact
what makes Moodle easy and therefore attractive. The aim of this paper
is not to discredit this option, but to enhance it by means of standard
cryptographic and information security infrastructures. We focus in the
registration process, which ends with the distribution of a user certificate.
To link the users' real identity with their virtual one, we have taken an
approach that merges EBIAS (Email Based Identification and Authentication System) with a kind of challenge-response method involving secure
pseudo random number generation based in a fast chaos-based Pseudo
Random Number Generator.

1 Introduction

Moodle is one of the most popular e-learning platforms, due to its easy installation and deployment. Nevertheless, a standard Moodle installation encloses some
security and privacy drawbacks (see [21,12]). To avoid them, we present a registration protocol that allows the incorporation of a PKI into a Moodle platform.
In this scenario, any user can use the cryptographic funcionalities of his/her personal certificate. Additionally, an important challenge for interactive systems is
to make the underlying security infrastructure as invisible as possible. Indeed,
security cannot be achieved at the cost of ease of use [22, Principle 6]. One could
make a perfectly secure tool, but if the human interface is not easy to use, nobody
will employ it. Even worst, someone could use it incorrectly leading to a false

---

⋆ This work was supported by the UAM projects of Teaching Innovation and the
Spanish Government projects TIN2010-19607. The work of David Arroyo was supported by a Juan de la Cierva fellowship from the Ministerio de Ciencia e Innovación
of Spain, and by the Ministerio de Ciencia e Innovación of Spain project CUCO
(MTM2008-02194).

Á. Herrero and E. Corchado (Eds.): CISIS 2011, LNCS 6694, pp. 214–221, 2011.

feeling of security. Beyond the problem of usability, the need for security and privacy improvements in e-learning systems has been studied in the last years and considered as a very necessary and desirable property. In [19] the benefits of a secured e-learning system are shown in an empirical test. This work compares a secure environment against a non-secure one, concluding that a major users' trust in the secured environment produced a higher participation. Nevertheless, we want to emphasize that our proposal does not make a so extended Moodle distribution an impenetrable fortress. However, it will enormously ease the task of incorporating any cryptographic functionality into the platform. Actually, it endorses an increase of the overall security of the system information, providing the basic protocols to implement desired security requirements like demanding from every user to sign every document he/she uploads to the system.

The rest of the paper is organized as follows: in Sec. 2 we introduce the context in which our work has been developed, and the requirements to provide cryptographic functionality in a proper way; in Sec. 3 we explain the main protocol used for remote digital certificate distribution; finally, Sec. 4 will introduce some basic functionality we have provided to a default Moodle distribution thanks to the integration with a PKI, concluding with some potentially uses one could give to it.

2   Description of Moodle's Default Framework and Proposed Improvements

Moodle is an open source e-learning environment. Although the default distribution comes ready to be used, its modular architecture is what makes it a powerful and successful tool. This, together with being open source, makes possible to any third party developer to add new modules and extend Moodle's functionality without the need of touching its "core". Just by adding some basic files and folders, one can add his own contribution to Moodle by copying them into the corresponding directory. For the registration protocol proposed here, an authentication module has been created. Also, for testing some basic functionality (digital signatures), new upload and quiz modules have been created. For more information about Moodle's architecture, one can see the official Moodle's webpage[1] or [14].

Regarding the main functionality we are dealing with, which is the registration process, Moodle has several registration modules available. Maybe, the most used is the one called *email based authentication*, which allows users to be registered in the system using their email address as identifier. With a default Moodle installation, it is possible to enhance security by limiting the valid email accounts to those pertaining to the organizational domain. A pure Email Based Identification and Authentication System (EBIAS, see [10]) bases users registration solely in the assumption that if someone can access an email account, then he is the legitimate owner of the email account. Its major advantage against other authentication methods is the ease of use and the familiarity of users with

---

[1] http://moodle.org

emails. Even assuming that a user who has access to an organizational email account demonstrates he is its legitimate owner, one cannot be certain that the email communications have not been intercepted and a man in the middle attack is being performed. An approach suggested at the end of [10], consists of using a hybrid system which makes use of EBIAS and PKI. This method provides the ease of use of EBIAS, and the cryptographic security provided by PKI. Since our goal is to achieve security without eroding users' activity, we have designed an authentication procedure combining the main properties of both techniques. Other approaches for adapting emails with public key cryptography are those based on Shamir's Identity-Based Cryptosystems (see [20,1]).

Once we have pointed out the basics required from Moodle, it is time to go into the details of PKI and email configuration. First of all, we have adopted the general recommendation for PKI architectures and, consequently, we have distinguished between Registration Authority (RA) and a Certification Authority (CA)[2] [18, p. 437]. The RA plays the role of intermediary between users and the CA, whereas the CA is on charge of generating new certificates according to the different requests from the RA. This being the case, the user will interact with the Moodle Server and with the RA, but never with the CA directly. Furthermore, users' applications must be recorded. This task is performed by the RA, which implies a communication channel between the RA and the Moodle Server. On the other hand, with respect to the email service, a highly recommended measure is to use SSL/TLS enabled email clients and servers. Almost every email provider offers this possibility. Although enabling SSL/TLS in this step does not guarantee the security of transmitted emails, it makes the access to the email server secure, preventing, e.g., impersonation attacks [9, p. 406]. But, as this will depend on users configuring correctly their email clients, we have introduced another control measure based on the generation of a *ticket ID*. If this ticket is *unique*, it prevents, e.g., man in the middle attacks, possible when the registration depends only on responding to the received email.

Finally, all the communications, except the email sending, are protected with the SSL protocol.

3   Registration Protocol

In short, the registration protocol is a two step verification based in the generation of a nonce (see [5, Chapter 3]) that will be presented to the user at the first step. This nonce will serve as response for a challenge sent by the RA server at the second step (see [13, Chapter 10] for an explanation of challenge-response methods involving nonces). We explain it in more detail below.

The very first step in the registration phase is to request for registration. The user does this through the usual registration Moodle web page, by filling up some personal information data. Once the user submits the form, the Moodle Server sends to the RA the data introduced by the user. This information will

---

[2] An example of secure architecture can be seen in http://www.ejbca.org/architecture.html

be used later by the CA to generate the user's digital certificate. The RA replies with a ticket ID, which is a SHA-2 hash generated from the concatenation of a random number and the username. The RA will also store the generated pseudo random number in order to finalize the user's registration in a subsequent step. To end this first step, the user has to download his ticket ID, which he will have to provide later in order to confirm his identity. This prevents an attacker from asking for certificates directly, as one must first pass the Moodle registration form and obtain a valid ticket ID. We have to underline that all communications between the user and the Moodle Server (MS), and between the MS and the RA are protected with SSL.

Once this first step is completed, the user receives an email with a link (just as in a default Moodle distribution), requesting him to access the site provided by the link, to confirm he is the owner of the email account. The user is challenged by the RA to provide a valid ticket ID, along with his username. The RA will check the result of the ticket ID by repeating its calculation from the pseudo random number stored in the previous step and the username provided in the current step. If the result matches the ticket ID provided by the user, then the challenge will be successfully passed, and the RA will proceed to request the CA to issue a new certificate for the new user.[3]

Finally, the user will be shown a dialog to download his new certificate, in PKCS#12 format, and the password used to armor it. The complete process is depicted in figure 1. It is very important to emphasize the use of SSL to secure every communication between the user and the MS and between the user and the RA, making all the information exchanges secure during the registration process. The only step not protected with SSL is the activation email sending and receiving, but this weak link is strengthen by the introduction of the ticket ID, provided securely through SSL.

3.1   Chaos-Based Generation of Nonces

A critical element in our authentication scheme is the procedure to create nonces associated to the different users. As it has been underlined above, nonces are derived from the SHA-2 hash of the concatenation of a pseudo random number and the username. Since the username is accessible to a possible attacker, the touchstone in delivering nonces is the method used in the generation of (pseudo) random numbers. There are many deterministic procedures to implement PRNGs, but we must choose a secure (by means of randomness tests) and efficient one. In this sense, we should adhere to the commitments of eSTREAM project[4]. In this regard, chaos-based PRNGs can be considered as an option. Certainly, chaotic systems can be employed as skeleton of new, secure and efficient PRNGs ([4]). Furthermore, cryptanalysis work in the field of chaos-based cryptography shows that security and efficiency can be achieved when there exists a proper combination of chaotic dynamics and the standards of conventional cryptography [3,7,6].

---

[3] Here, additional functionality can be added, e.g., to use different certificate profiles depending on the email subdomain.

[4] http://www.ecrypt.eu.org/stream/

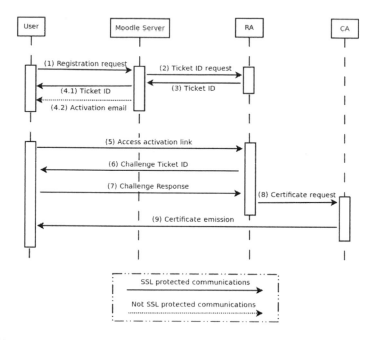

Fig. 1. Users registration protocol. (1): User requests registration (2): Moodle Server sends to the RA the user info (3): RA generates a new Ticket ID (nonce) and sends it to the Moodle Server (4.1): The Moodle Server sends the Ticket ID to the user (4.2) The Moodle Server sends an email with an activation link to the user (5): The user accesses the activation link (6): The RA asks the user for his Ticket ID and user name (7): The user sends his user name and the Ticket ID he received in step 4 (8): If the challenge result is successful, the RA asks the CA to send the user his new certificate (9) The CA sends the user his new certificate

This is the case of the PRNG proposed in [16], which is the PRNG used in our implementation.

3.2   Preliminary Analyisis of Usability

We have emphasized that usability is of major importance for interactive systems, and maybe even more when securing environments, because a misuse of the functionality could lead to huge losses. This is why we expose here some thoughts on this matter. Also, some reflections about the ease of use of the functionality are presented. Nevertheless, we are planning to test our contribution in a real scenario, which will provide us real users' feedback to improve our functionality.

The analysis we have carried out for the introduced overload is not intended to be exhaustive. For a detailed study of the extra cost introduced by the SSL protocol one can consult existing works like [11,15], where it is proved that a well designed server architecture can provide good results in terms of throughput and response time. We have performed some tests simulating a basic scenario, consisting in sending a file of 400 KB every 30 seconds, during 10 minutes.

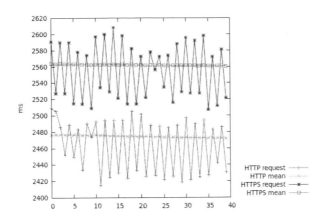

Fig. 2. Overload introduced by the SSL secured communications, in terms of the time response seen by the user compared to not SSL secured communications

In one case, the files were sent just like a normal Moodle distribution will do it; in the other, they are signed by the client, sent using SSL, and verified (the signature) by the server. The tests have been carried out in an Intel Core Duo with 2.80 GHz, 1MB L2 cache size and 2GB RAM, acting as MS, RA and CA. Therefore, and following the results in [11], a much better performance could be achieved with a better designed architecture (e.g. using different machines for the MS, RA and CA). Nevertheless, our tests show that, for this basic scenario, the differences in terms of time responses are not too high. We show the results obtained of one of the runs of the test in image 2. For the sake of clarity we only depict the time response for the last 40 samples (which behave like the 80 previous samples) and the evolution of the mean values obtained from them. We can observe that the time responses are quite similar, although the mean values are a little bigger for SSL protected communications than for not protected communications. The mean value of the response time obtained for unprotected communications and SSL protected communications, is of roughly 2471 ms and 2560 ms, respectively, although in some tests the difference was slightly bigger, but no more than a few hundreds of ms.

With respect to the changes a user will experience in the way he/she must interact with the system, they are just minor ones. During the registration protocol, there are only two extra steps to the eyes of the user: the ticket ID and the certificate that he will have to download. Once this is done, the added functionalities affect users' day to day experience only when signing files and quizzes (through the private keys stored in users' certificate to sign files and quizzes). In order to do this, the user just have to tell the browser where his/her certificate is located and introduce the corresponding password. As we have explained above, these are just minor changes. Nevertheless, we are planning to make some tests involving real users to obtain true feedback in this matter.

4   Conclusions and Future Work

In the current work, a registration protocol that allows the incorporation of a PKI infrastructure into an interactive environment like Moodle has been designed, making possible the introduction of all the functionalities that public key cryptography provides. This incorporation means a big step towards a more robust, privacy enhancing and secure system, a matter that does not usually get the deserved attention in this kind of systems, probably due to the fact that they are oriented to make third-party contributions easier and system configuration faster. Also, we have made a preliminary analysis showing that the added functionality does not worsen usability and the introduced overload is bearable.

We have developed Moodle modules to sign files and quizzes by students, which can be afterwards verified by the teachers in the corresponding course. This will allow to further expand system functionalities. For example, it has been studied the benefits that an adequate anonymity model can provide in order to improve the students experience (see [2,8]). E.g., an exam being submitted anonymously will ensure the maximum level of neutrality during correction, or an option for making anonymous posts in a forum could make introverted students to lose fear and have a more active participation in a course. Or even an anonymous model with direct non-repudiation (similar to the one in [17]) can be used to avoid "hooligans" to take advantage of anonymity. Also, public key watermarking methods can be used to protect digital contents uploaded to the system ([23]).

Currently, we are also working on the verification of the proposed protocol, using tools for secure protocols verification and preparing a test involving real users to measure their acceptance to the system.

References

1. Adida, B., Chau, D., Hohenberger, S., Rivest, R.L.: Lightweight email signatures (2006)
2. Aïmeur, E., Hage, H., Onana, F.S.M.: Anonymous credentials for privacy-preserving e-learning. In: Proceedings of the 2008 International MCETECH Conference on e-Technologies, pp. 70–80. IEEE Computer Society, Washington, DC, USA (2008), http://portal.acm.org/citation.cfm?id=1397754.1397777
3. Alvarez, G., Li, S.: Some basic cryptographic requirements for chaos-based cryptosystems. Int. J. Bifurc. Chaos 16(8), 2129–2151 (2006)
4. Amigó, J.M.: Chaos-based cryptography. In: Kocarev, L., Galias, Z., Lian, S. (eds.) Chaos-based cryptography, pp. 291–314. Springer, Heidelberg (2009)
5. Anderson, R.J.: Security Engineering: A Guide to Building Dependable Distributed Systems, 2nd edn. Wiley Publishing, Chichester (2008)
6. Arroyo, D., Alvarez, G., Amigó, J.M., Li, S.: Cryptanalysis of a family of self-synchronizing chaotic stream ciphers. Communications in Nonlinear Science and Numerical Simulation 16(2), 805–813 (2011), http://arxiv.org/abs/0903.2928
7. Arroyo, D., Rhouma, R., Alvarez, G., Li, S., Fernandez, V.: On the security of a new image encryption scheme based on chaotic map lattices. Chaos: An Interdisciplinary Journal of Nonlinear Science 18, 033112, 7 pages (2008)

8. Borcea, K., Donker, H., Franz, E., Pfitzmann, A., Wahrig, H.: Towards privacy-aware eLearning. In: Danezis, G., Martin, D. (eds.) PET 2005. LNCS, vol. 3856, pp. 167–178. Springer, Heidelberg (2006), http://dx.doi.org/10.1007/11767831_11

9. Cross, M.: Web Application Security. Syngress Publishing Inc. (2007)

10. Garfinkel, S.L.: Email-based identification and authentication: An alternative to PKI? IEEE Security and Privacy 1, 20–26 (2003), http://portal.acm.org/citation.cfm?id=1435589.1435788

11. Guitart, J., Carrera, D., Beltran, V., Torres, J., Ayguadé, E.: Designing an overload control strategy for secure e-commerce applications. Comput. Netw. 51, 4492–4510 (2007), http://portal.acm.org/citation.cfm?id=1284912.1285118

12. Kumar, S., Dutta, K.: Investigation on security in LMS moodle. International Journal of Information Technology and Knowledge Management 4, 223–238 (2011)

13. Menezes, A., van Oorschot, P., Vanstone, S.: Handbook of Applied Cryptography. CRC Press, Boca Raton (1997)

14. Moore, J., Churchward, M.: Moodle 1.9 Extension Development. Packt Publishing (2010)

15. Oppliger, R.: SSL and TSL: Theory and practice. Arthec House, Boston (2009)

16. Orue, A.B., Álvarez, G., Guerra, A., Pastor, G., Romera, M., Montoya, F.: Trident, a new pseudo random number generator based on coupled chaotic maps. In: Herrero, Á., Corchado, E., Redondo, C., Alonso, Á., et al. (eds.) Computational Intelligence in Security for Information Systems 2010. Advances in Intelligent and Soft Computing, vol. 85, pp. 183–190. Springer, Heidelberg (2010)

17. Pfitzmann, B., Sadeghi, A.-R.: Anonymous fingerprinting with direct non-repudiation. In: Okamoto, T. (ed.) ASIACRYPT 2000. LNCS, vol. 1976, pp. 401–414. Springer, Heidelberg (2000), http://portal.acm.org/citation.cfm?id=647096.716985

18. Pfleeger, C.P., Pfleeger, S.L.: Security in computing, 3rd edn. Pearson Educatin Inc., London (2003)

19. Raitman, R., Ngo, L., Augar, N.: Security in the online e-learning environment. In: Proceedings of the Fifth IEEE International Conference on Advanced Learning Technologies, ICALT 2005, pp. 702–706. IEEE Computer Society, Washington, DC, USA (2005), http://dx.doi.org/10.1109/ICALT.2005.236

20. Shamir, A.: Identity-based cryptosystems and signature schemes. In: Blakely, G.R., Chaum, D. (eds.) CRYPTO 1984. LNCS, vol. 196, pp. 47–53. Springer, Heidelberg (1985), http://portal.acm.org/citation.cfm?id=19478.19483

21. Stapic, Z., Orehovacki, T., Danic, M.: Determination of optimal security settings for LMS moodle. In: 31st International Convention on Information and Communication Technology, Electronics and Microelectronics, MIPRO (2008)

22. Stoneburner, G., Hayden, C., Feringa, A.: Nist special publication 800-27: Engineering principles for information technology security (a baseline for achieving security). Tech. rep., National Institute Standards and Technology (2001)

23. Weippl, E.: Security in E-Learning. Springer, Heidelberg (2005)

On Secure JAVA Application in SOA-Based PKI Mobile Government Systems

Milan Marković[1] and Goran Đorđević[2]

[1] Banca Intesa ad Beograd
Bulevar Milutina Milankovića 1c, 11070 Novi Beograd, Serbia
milan.markovic@bancaintesabeograd.com
[2] Institute for Manufacturing banknotes and coins NBS,
Pionirska 2, 11000 Beograd, Serbia
djg_goran@mail.com

Abstract. In this paper, we describe a possible model of secure m-government system based on secure JAVA mobile application and SOA-Based m-government platform. The proposed model consists of additional external entities/servers, such as: PKI, XKMS, STS, UDDI and TSA. The main parts of the proposed model are secure JAVA mobile application and secure Web Service implemented on the SOA-based platform. One example of the possible mobile government online services is particularly emphasized: sending m-residence certificate request and obtaining the m-residence electronic document (m-residence certificate) as a government's response. This scenario could serve as a model of any m-government online services consisting of sending some requests to the m-government platforms and obtaining responses as corresponding governmental electronic messages or documents.

Keywords: Java based mobile phone application, m-government platform, Web Service, SOAP protocol, XML-Security, WS-Security, XKMS protocol, SAML, Timestamp.

1 Introduction

This work is related to the consideration of some possible SOA-based m-government online systems, i.e. about secure communication between citizens and companies with the small and medium governmental organizations, such as municipalities, or other governmental organizations and/or agencies. We have considered a general model of such systems consisting of three main parts:

- Secure JAVA mobile client application,
- SOA-Based m-government platform, and
- External entities: PKI (Public Key Infrastructure), STS (Security Token Service), XKMS (XML Key Management Service), TSA (Time Stamping Authority), and UDDI (Universal Description Discovery and Integration).

Although the generic m-government model is proposed and considered, and although the model supports the usage of desktop JAVA web service application too, a main

Á. Herrero and E. Corchado (Eds.): CISIS 2011, LNCS 6694, pp. 222–229, 2011.
© Springer-Verlag Berlin Heidelberg 2011

emphasis and contribution of the paper is the Secure JAVA Mobile Web Service application communicating with the Web Service of the proposed m-government platform. In a process of development the secure JAVA Mobile Application we have used the J2ME development environment [1].

The work presented and examples described are included in the general framework of the EU IST FP6 SWEB project (Secure, interoperable cross border m-services contributing towards a trustful European cooperation with the non-EU member Western Balkan countries, SWEB) [2].

The paper is organized as follows. A consideration of security in mobile communication is given in Chapter 2 whike description of the possible m-Governmental architecture is given in Chapter 3. Chapter 4 is dedicated to the consideration about secure JAVA mobile Web Service application. Conclusions are given in Chapter 5.

2 Security in Mobile Communication

This paper mainly identifies the need for security in mobile communications, such as mentioned in [3], and presents a secure mobile framework that is based on widely used XML-based standards and technologies such as XML-Security (XML-Signature, and XML-Encryption) and Web Services Security (WS-Security).

Besides security aspects of the XML communication, a possible Federation ID system based on security token service is considered too. In this work, SAML (Security Assertion Markup Language) tokens/assertions have a role of security tokens. Communication between JAVA mobile application, or the SOA-Based platform itself, and STS server is realized by using WS-Secured SOAP communication.

We have also used XKMS protocol [3] in the proposed m-government system. It enables the integration of keys and certificates into mobile applications as well as the implementation of PKI X.509v3 digital certificate registration, revocation, validation and update mechanisms.

Besides STS and XKMS, the client applications and the platform used also the time stamping functionalities in order to create timely valid electronic documents with digital signatures of long-term validities. In this sense, a suitable TSA also represents an important part of the proposed model.

Regarding security needs in m government online systems, the proposed model addresses main security functionalities (business security needs) in a following way:

- **User authentication** – the Secure JAVA Mobile application needs the user password based authentication to launch the application itself. This prevents accessing the application from non-authorized persons. In fact, there is a two-step user authentication procedure since the user needs to present another password (passphrase) to enable application access to its asymmetric private key stored in the JAVA key store inside the application for the functions that needs the user's electronic signature.
- **User identity** – as reliable electronic identities of different users and entities in the proposed system, PKI X.509v3 electronic certificates are used issued by corresponding Certification Authorities (CA).

- **Federation Identity** – in the proposed model, we used SAML token as the federation ID. SAML token is issued to users, government civil servants or platforms itselves after proper entity's authentication to the STS server. The STS server issues the SAML token to the users after successful entity's authentication based on the entity's electronic certificate.
- **User authorization to the proposed platform** – a process of the user authorization to the platform is based on the obtained SAML token carrying the user's role which is presented to the m-government platform together with the signed m-governmental service request. The SAML token could also serve as the Federation ID to access any other Web service-based governmental platform without a need for the user to be authenticated again.
- **Authenticity, Integrity and Non-repudiation of transactions** – the user applies digital signature (XML Signature) on each request sending to different entities (STS server, m-government platform) based on RSA algorithm.
- **Confidentiality** – in the proposed model, the WS-Security mechanism (WS-Encryption) is used to encrypt all communication between the Secure JAVA Mobile application and STS server and/or m-government platform. This request-response application protocol is much more suitable for the mobile communication system compared to session-based SSL/TLS protocols, proposed in [4], since it does not need much more expensive session establishment between the user and the server side.
- **Electronic signature verification on the user's side** – Secure JAVA mobile application has functions of electronic signature verification of transactions (Web service responses from different entities) including electronic certificate validation function. The latter function is implemented by applying communication with XKMS server which is more natural solution to SOAP based request-response Web service systems than using CRL (Certificate Revocation List) validation or other techniques described in [4].
- **Long-term validity of transactions** – in order to justify reliable time of creating m-government requests and documents, we used time stamping in order to include reliable and signed time stamps both to the user's requests and governmental responses (m-government documents). This enables a more reliable proof of time when requests/documents are created as well as a fact if that signer's electronic certificates were valid in the moment of signing. Besides, implemented time stamping functionality enables possibility to realize functions of long-term validity of stored requests/documents.

3 Possible m-Government Architecture

The proposed m-government model is presented on Fig. 1 [2], [3] and consists of:

- Mobile users (citizen, companies) who send some Web Services requests to m-government platform for a purpose of receiving some governmental documents (e.g. residence certificate, birth or marriage certificates, etc.). These users use secure JAVA mobile Web Service application for such a purpose.
- Fixed/Desktop users connecting to the proposed Web Service governmental platform through some desktop secure Web Service application (could be JAVA-based too).

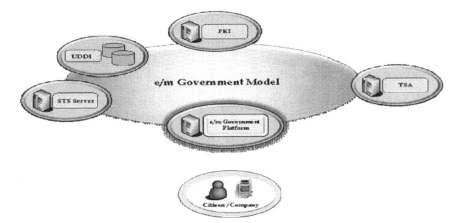

Fig. 1. Proposed m-government model

- Web Service endpoint implementation on the platform's side that implements a complete set of security features. Well processed requests with all security features positively verified, the Web Service platform's application proceeds to other application parts of the proposed SOA-Based platform, including the governmental Legacy system for issuing actual governmental certificates requested. In fact, the proposed platform could change completely the application platform of some governmental organization or could serve as the Web Service „add-on" to the existing Legacy system implementation. In the latter case, the Legacy system will not be touched and only a corresponding Web Service interface should be developped in order to interconnect the proposed SOA-Based platform and the Legacy governmental system.
- External entities, such as: PKI server with XKMS server as a front end, STS, UDDI and TSA.

Functions of the proposed external entities are following:

- **STS server** – is responsible for strong user authentication and authorization based on PKI X.509v3 electronic certificate issued to users and other entities in the proposed model. Communication between STS server and the user's JAVA mobile application is SOAP-based and secured by using WS-Security features. After the succesful user authentication and authorization, the STS server issues a SAML token to the user which will be subsequently used for the user authentication and authorization to the Web Service of the proposed m-government platform. The SAML token is signed by the STS server and could consist of the user role for platform's user authentication and authorization.
- **UDDI server** – is a platform-independent, XML based registry for businesses worldwide to list themselves on the Internet. In this paper, UDDI server is used to store information about SWEB-enabled municipal organizations including WSDLs and URLs defining a way to access these SWEB platforms.
- **PKI server** - is responsible for issuing PKI X.509v3 electronic certificates for all users/entities in the proposed m-governmental model (users, civil servants, administrators, servers, platforms, etc.). Since some certificate processing

functions could be too heavy for mobile users, the PKI services are exposed by the XKMS server which could register users, as well as locate or validate certificates on behalf of the mobile user. This is of particular interests in all processes that request signature verification on mobile user side.

- **TSA server** - is responsible for issuing time stamps for user's requests as well as for platform's responses (signed m-documents).

4 Secure JAVA Mobile Web Service Application

In this Chapter, we give a functional description of the secure JAVA mobile Web Service application for a purpose of secure communication with the described m-government SOA-based platform [2].

The assumption is that the user already has the JAVA application on his mobile phone/terminal and thus a procedure of downloading and activating the application is beyond a scope of this document. Possible usages are described in [5].

This client application comprises of following functionalities objects:

- Graphical User Interface (GUI) for presenting business functionalities to the end user. The GUI object of the proposed JAVA mobile web service application is responsible to show user interface that enable calling of function for authentication of the end user and presenting the core functionalities to the end user.
- Business functionalities object is responsible for implementation of the core SWEB client-base functionalities:
  - o Secure requesting and receiving the m-residence certificate from the corresponding municipality SOA-based platform, receiving a notification and delivering the obtained certificate to some interested party.
  - o Secure sending of other kind of predefined message (for example m-invoice) to the corresponding municipality platform and receiving the notification from the platform.
- The Security object of the considered JAVA mobile application is responsible for overall application-level security functionalities.
- Communication object.

The Java mobile client used for communication with the platform is developed by using J2ME CDC1.1 platform. There are forms (screens) on mobile phone application used to perform communication with the platform.

The first form is 'Logon form'. The user should enter its username and password after which verification will be passed to the next form. Also, the language that will be used in the whole application can be chosen on this form. After successful verification of username and password, 'Functions form' will be passed to the user where a task that needs to be done can be chosen. The available tasks are:

1. Change Password - used for changing login password in order to access the mobile application.
2. mResidence Certificate Request - used for sending request for mResidence certificate to the municipality (to the Web service of the m-government platform).

3. Download mResidence Certificate - used for downloading prepared mResidence certificate from the municipality.
4. Send m-Invoice - used for preparing and sending m-invoices to the municipality.

The change of logon password can be done via 'New Password' simple form. By pressing button for sending of mResidence Certificate Request, user will jump to 'Residence Cert' form where the receiving municipality should be chosen from the list that appears on the form.

The next step is entering PIN used for reading user private key that is stored in KeyStore on the file system on the user mobile device. This should be done on the 'PIN' form. The result of request processing (error or success) is displayed on the 'Final' form. All communications between client and servers are here synchronous. It means that each request produces response.

After successful processing of user's mResidence Certificate Request, the platform prepares the required mResidence Certificate and sends the SMS message to the user mobile device as an approval that the m-government document is ready for this user. This part of communication between user and the platform is asynchronous.

Received SMS message is a signal for the user to perform download of mResidence Certificate via option of Download certificate. On the 'Doc ID' form, the Task ID should be chosen from the list. The Task ID uniquely identifies the mRCertificate that should be downloaded. The result of download will also be displayed on the 'Final' form (see Fig 2).

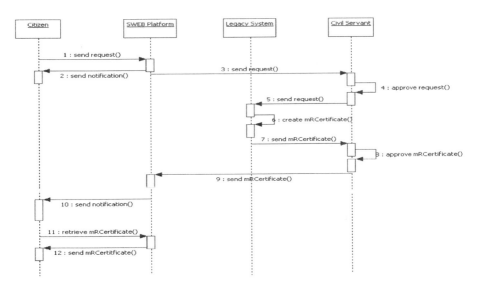

Fig. 2. mResidence Scenario details

In order to realize the abovementioned functionalities, the mobile JAVA application communicates with following external entities:

- STS server,
- XKMS server,
- TSA server,
- M-government platform – Web service exposed for the SOAP based m-government platform.

The communication between JAVA mobile application and STS server is realized by using WS-Secured SOAP communication. According to the scenarios, the JAVA mobile application sends the RST (Request for Security Token) to the STS server and, if everything is ok, receives back the RSTR (RST Response) which consist of URL of the municipality and the SAML token with the user's role on the SWEB platform.

The communication between the JAVA mobile application and the Web service of the platform is realized as WS-Encrypted SOAP communication. According to the scenarios, the JAVA mobile application sends the signed mRCertificate request or m-invoice (signing is done by using XML signature mechanisms) to the Web service platform of the municipality. Before sending it to the municipality, signed mResidence Certificate request or m-invoice must be timestamped. In order to accomplish this, the JAVA mobile application communicates with TSA server via HTTP communication. In this sense, the JAVA mobile application sends a hash of the signature of the mResidence Certificate or m-invoice to the TSA server and receives back a timestamp (signed hash with added time information) which is signed by the private key of the TSA server.

Only in the mResidence Certificate scenario, when the mResidence Certificate is ready for delivery at the platform, the platform sends a SMS to the mobile user informing him that the mResidence Certificate with the given TaskID is ready for download. After that, the JAVA mobile application will send a request for mResidence Certificate download also as a signed and timestamped request in a body of the WS-Encrypted SOAP message to the platfom's Web service.

During the abovementioned communication, in order to verify signatures and validate different X.509v3 certificates, the JAVA mobile application needs to communicate with XKMS server which outsources a part of the time and resource consuming PKI functionalities from the JAVA mobile application. Namely, the JAVA mobile application could obtain a suitable certificate from the XKMS server (by using LocateRequest XKMS function) and, more importantly, could validate certificate of some party (by using ValidateRequest XKMS function). This way, the most time consuming PKI operations, like certificate validation, will be excluded from the mobile phone. The communication with the XKMS server is SOAP communication without applying security features. Only, the XKMS server's response is always digitally signed by using the XML signature mechanism.

5   Conclusions

In this paper, we present a possible model of secure SOA-Based m-government system based on JAVA mobile Web service application. In fact, this work is related to the consideration about secure mobile communication between citizens and companies with the small and medium governmental organizations, such as municipalities.

We elaborated some m-government framework which is based on secure JAVA mobile application, PKI certificates, SOA-based platform, XML-security, WS-Security, SAML, Time Stamping and XKMS. The work presented and examples described are included in the general framework of the EU IST FP6 SWEB project. Future work could include implementation of SIM-based security solution into the proposed global (SWEB-like) m-governmental model and create a secure environment for additional m-governmental services, such as: sending electronic document with qualified signature through JAVA mobile application, etc.

Having in mind the above mentioned text, main contributions of the paper are:

- Proposal of a possible secure m-government model based on JAVA mobile/desktop application and SOA-based m-government platform.
- Usage of secure JAVA mobile application in which all modern security techniques are implemented (XML-security, WS-Security, SAML, Time Stamping, PKI, XKMS) which are used in optimum way in order to cope with majority of security issues of the mobile Web Service communication.
- Usage of SOA-based request-response m-government platform (Web Services) which is far more suitable in the mobile communication systems instead of session-based Web application platform.
- Usage of XKMS service which is more suitable for mobile PKI system since it outsources complex operations such as PKI validation services to the external entity – the XKMS server, compared to usages of other techniques [4].

References

1. Kolsi, O., Virtanen, T.: MIDP 2.0 Security Enhancements. In: Proceedings of the 37th Hawaii International Conference on System Sciences, Honolulu, Hawaii, USA (January 2004)
2. Marković, M., Đorđević, G.: On Possible Model of Secure e/m-Government System. Information Systems Management 27, 320–333 (2010)
3. Papastergiou, S., Karantjias, A., Polemi, D., Marković, M.: A Secure Mobile Framework for m-Services. In: Proceedings of the Third International Conference on Internet and Web Applications and Services, ICIW 2008, Athens, Greece (June 2008)
4. Lee, Y., Lee, J., Song, J.: Design and implementation of wireless PKI technology suitable for mobile phone in mobile-commerce. Computer Communication 30(4), 893–903 (2007)
5. Cuno, S., Glickman, Y., Hoepner, P., Karantjias, T., Marković, M., Schmidt, M.: The Architecture of an Interoperable and Secure eGovernment Platform Which Provides Mobile Services. In: Cunningham, P., Cunningham, M. (eds.) Collaboration and the Knowledge Economy: Issues, Applications, Case Studies, pp. 278–256. IOS Press, Amsterdam (2008); ISBN 978-1-58603-924-0
6. Đorđević, G., Marković, M.: Simulation and JAVA Programming of Secure Mobile Web Services. In: Proceedings of Balkan Conference on Operational Research, Balcore, Zlatibor, Serbia (October 2007)
7. Marković, M., Đorđević, G.: On Secure SOA Based e/m Government Online Services. Accepted for publication in Handbook Service Delivery Platforms: Developing and Deploying Converged Multimedia Services, ch. 11, pp. 251–278. Taylor & Francis, Abington (2010)
8. Kanneganti, R., Chodavarapu, P.: SOA Security, Sound View Court 3B. Manning Publications Co., Greenwich (2008)

Structural Feature Based Anomaly Detection for Packed Executable Identification

Xabier Ugarte-Pedrero, Igor Santos, and Pablo G. Bringas

S³Lab, DeustoTech - Computing, Deusto Institute of Technology
University of Deusto,
Avenida de las Universidades 24, 48007
Bilbao, Spain
{xabier.ugarte,isantos,pablo.garcia.bringas}@deusto.es

Abstract. Malware is any software with malicious intentions. Commercial anti-malware software relies on signature databases. This approach has proven to be effective when the threats are already known. However, malware writers employ software encryption tools and code obfuscation techniques to hide the actual behaviour of their malicious programs. One of these techniques is executable packing, which consists of encrypting the real code of the executable so that it is decrypted in its execution. Commercial solutions to this problem try to identify the packer and then apply the corresponding unpacking routine for each packing algorithm. Nevertheless, this approach fails to detect new and custom packers. Therefore, generic unpacking methods have been proposed which execute the binary in a contained environment and gather its actual code. However, these approaches are very time-consuming and, therefore, a filter step is required that identifies whether an executable is packed or not. In this paper, we present the first packed executable detector based on anomaly detection. This approach represents not packed executables as feature vectors of structural information and heuristic values. Thereby, an executable is classified as packed or not packed by measuring its deviation to the representation of normality (not packed executables). We show that this method achieves high accuracy rates detecting packed executables while maintaining a low false positive rate.

Keywords: malware, anomaly detection, computer security, packer.

1 Introduction

Malware (or malicious software) is defined as computer software that has been explicitly designed to harm computers or networks. The amount, power and variety of malware programs increases every year, as does its ability to overcome all kinds of security barriers [1]. Currently, malware writers use executable packing techniques (cyphering or compressing the actual malicious code) to hide the actual behaviour of their creations. Packed programs have a decryption routine that extracts the real payload from memory and then executes it. Currently, up to the 80 % of the detected malware is packed [2].

Á. Herrero and E. Corchado (Eds.): CISIS 2011, LNCS 6694, pp. 230–237, 2011.

Signatures have been applied for the detection of packed executables (e.g., PEID [3] and Faster Universal Unpacker (FUU) [4]). However, this approach has the same shortcoming as signatures for malware detection: it is not effective with unknown obfuscation techniques or custom packers. Indeed, according to Morgenstern and Pilz [5], the 35 % of malware is packed by a custom packer.

Dynamic unpacking approaches monitor the execution of a binary in order to extract its actual code. These methods execute the samples inside an isolated environment that can be deployed as a virtual machine or an emulator [6]. Several dynamic unpackers use heuristics to determine the exact point where the execution jumps from the unpacking routine to the original code and once reached, bulk the memory content to obtain an unpacked version of the malicious code (e.g., Universal PE Unpacker [7] and OllyBonE [8]). Notwithstanding, concrete heuristics cannot be applied to all the packers in the wild, as all of them work in very different manners. In contrast, not so highly heuristic-dependant approaches have been proposed for generic dynamic unpacking (e.g., PolyUnpack [9], Renovo [10], OmniUnpack [11] and Eureka [12]). Nonetheless, these methods are very tedious and time-consuming, and cannot counter conditional execution of unpacking routines, a technique used for anti-debugging and anti-monitoring defense [13,14,15]. Another common approach is using the structural information of the PE executables to determine if the sample under analysis is packed or if it is suspicious of containing malicious code (e.g., PE-Miner [16], PE-Probe [17] and Perdisci et al. [18]).

In light of this background, we propose here the first method that applies anomaly detection to packed executable filtering as a previous phase to dynamic and generic unpacking. This approach is able to determine whether an executable is packed or not by comparing some structural features with a dataset composed only of not packed executables. If the executable under inspection presents a considerable deviation to what it is considered as usual (not packed executables), it is considered suspicious and is isolated for a further analysis. This method does not need updated data about packed executables, and thus, it reduces the efforts of labelling executables manually.

Summarising, our main contributions are: (i) we select a set of structural characteristics extracted from PE executables to determine whether a sample is packed or not and provide a relevance measure for each characteristic based on information gain, (ii) we propose an anomaly-detection-based architecture for packed executable filtering, by means of weighted comparison against a dataset composed of only not packed executables and (iii) we evaluate the method using three different deviation measures.

2   Structural Features of the Portable Executable Files

Given the conclusions obtained in previous work [16,17,18], we selected a set of 211 structural features from the PE executables. Some of the features were obtained directly from the PE file header while the rest are calculated values based on certain heuristics commonly used by the research community. Shafiq et al. [17] used PE executable structural features were used to determine if an executable is benign or malicious but it was not considered if the executable was packed or not. Perdisci et al. [18] and later Farooq et al. [16] used some heuristics like entropy, or certain section characteristics to determine whether an executable is packed or not, as a previous step to a deeper analysis. In this paper, we combine both points of view, structural characteristics and heuristics, providing a statistical analysis to determine their true relevance for determining the packed state of an executable.

We consider that one of the main requisites of our anomaly detection system is speed, as it constitutes a filtering step for a heavier unpacking process. Therefore, we selected a set of features whose extraction does not require a significant processing time, and avoided techniques such as code disassembly, string extraction or n-gram analysis [18], which slow down the sample comparison.

Features can be divided into four main groups: 125 raw header characteristics [17], 33 section characteristics (i.e., number of sections that meet certain properties), 29 characteristics of the section containing the entry point (the section which will be executed first once the executable is loaded into memory) and, finally, 24 entropy values. We apply relevance weights to each feature based on Information Gain (IG) [19]. IG provides a ratio for each feature that measures its importance to consider if a sample is packed or not. These weights were calculated from a dataset composed of 1,000 packed and 1,000 not packed executables, and are useful not only to obtain a better distance rating among samples, but also to reduce the amount of selected features, given that only 151 of them have a non-zero IG value.

- **DOS header characteristics (31).** The first bytes of the PE file header correspond to the DOS executable header fields. IG results showed that these characteristics are not specially relevant, having a maximum IG value of 0.23, corresponding to a reserved field, which intuitively may not be a relevant field. 15 values range from 0.10 to 0.16, and the rest present a relevance bellow 0.10.
- **File header block (23).** This header block is present in both image files (.EXE) and object files. From a total of 23 characteristics, 14 have an IG value greater than 0, and only 2 of them have an IG value greater than 0.01: the number of sections (0.3112) and the time stamp (0.1618).
- **Optional Header Block (71).** This optional block is only present in image files and contains data about how the executable must be loaded into memory. 37 features have an IG value over 0, but the most relevant ones are: the address of entry point (0.5111), the Import Address Table (IAT) size (0.3832) and address (0.3733) (relative to the number of imported DLLs), the size of the code (0.3011), the base of the data (0.2817), the base of the code (0.2213),the major linker version (0.1996), checksum (0.1736), the size of initialized data (0.1661), the size of headers (0.1600), the size of relocation table (0.1283) and the size of image (0.1243).
- **Section characteristics (33).** From the 33 characteristics that conform this group, 22 have an IG value greater than 0. The most significant ones are: the number of non-standard sections (0.7606), the number of executable

sections (0.7127); the maximum raw data per virtual size ratio (0.5755) ($rawSize/virtualSize$, where $rawSize$ is defined as the section raw data size and $virtualSize$ is the section virtual size, both expressed in bytes), the number of readable and executable sections (0.5725) and the number of sections with a raw data per virtual size ratio lower than 1 (0.4842).

- **Section of entry point characteristics (29).** This group contains characteristics relative to the section which will be executed once the executable is loaded into memory. 26 characteristics have an IG value greater than 0, from which 11 have a significant relevance: the characteristics field in its raw state (0.9757), its availability to be written (0.9715), the raw data per virtual size ratio (0.9244), the virtual address (0.7386), whether is a pointer to raw data or not (0.6064), whether is a standard section or not (0.5203), the virtual size (0.4056), whether it contains initialized data (0.3721), the size of raw data (0.2958) and its availability to be executed (0.1575).

- **Entropy values (24).** We have selected 24 entropy values, commonly used in previous works [18], from which 22 have an IG value greater than 0, and 9 have a relevant IG value: max section entropy (0.8375), mean code section entropy (0.7656), mean section entropy (0.7359), file entropy (0.6955), entropy of the section of entry point (0.6756), mean data section entropy (0.5637), header entropy (0.1680), number of sections with an entropy value greater than 7.5 (0.7445), and number of sections with an entropy value between 7 and 7.5 (0.1059).

In this way, every feature is represented as a decimal value and then normalized, dividing each value by the maximum value for that feature in the whole dataset. This way, we can represent each executable as a vector of decimal values that range from 0 to 1. The final step is to apply the relevance obtained from IG, and it consists of multiplying each value in the normalized vector by its relevance.

3   Anomaly Detection

Through the features described in the previous section, our method represents unpacked executables as points in the feature space. When an executable is being inspected our method starts by computing the values of the point in the feature space. This point is then compared with the previously calculated points of the unpacked executables.

To this end, distance measures are required. In this study, we have used the following distance measures:

- **Manhattan Distance.** This distance between two points v and u is the sum of the lengths of the projections of the line segment between the points onto the coordinate axes: $d(x, i) = \sum_{i=0}^{n} |x_i - y_i|$ where x is the first point; y is the second point; and x_i and y_i are the ith component of first and second point, respectively.
- **Euclidean Distance.** This distance is the length of the line segment connecting two points. It is calculated as: $d(x, y) = \sum_{i=0}^{n} \sqrt{v_i^2 - u_i^2}$ where x is

the first point; y is the second point; and x_i and y_i are the ith component of first and second point, respectively.

- **Cosine Similarity.** It is a measure of similarity between two vectors by finding the cosine of the angle between them [20]. Since we are measuring distance and not similarity we have used $1 - Cosine\ Similarity$ as a distance measure: $d(x, y) = 1 - \cos(\theta) = 1 - \frac{v \cdot u}{||v|| \cdot ||u||}$ where v is the vector from the origin of the feature space to the first point x, u is the vector from the origin of the feature space to the second point y, $v \cdot u$ is the inner product of v and u. $||v|| \cdot ||u||$ is the cross product of v and u. This distance ranges from 0 to 1, where 1 means that the two executables are completely different and 0 means that the executables are the same (i.e., the vectors are orthogonal between them).

By means of these measures, we are able to compute the deviation of an executable respect to a set of not packed executables. Since we have to compute this measure with the points representing not packed executables, a combination rule is required in order to obtain a final value of distance which considers every measure performed. To this end, our system employs 3 simple rules: (i) select the mean value, (ii) select the lowest distance value and (iii) select the highest value of the computed distances. In this way, when our method inspects an executable a final distance value is acquired, which will depend on both the distance measure and the combination rule.

4   Empirical Validation

To evaluate our anomaly-based packed executable detector, we collected a dataset comprising 500 not packed executables and 1,000 packed executables. The first one is composed of 250 benign executables and 250 malicious executables gathered from the VxHeavens [21] website. The packed dataset is composed of 500 benign executables and 500 malicious executables from VxHeavens [21]. To generate the packed dataset, we employed not packed executables and we packed them using 10 different packing tools with different configurations: Armadillo, ASProtect, FSG, MEW, PackMan, RLPack, SLV, Telock, Themida and UPX.

Then, using this dataset we performed a 5-fold cross-validation to divide the not packed dataset into 5 different divisions of 400 executables for representing normality and 100 for measuring deviations. In this way, each fold is composed of 400 not packed executables that will be used as representation of normality and 1,100 testing executables, from which 100 are not packed and 1,000 are packed.

Hereafter, we extracted their structural characteristics and employed the 3 different measures and the 3 different combination rules described in Section 3 to obtain a final deviation measure for each tested executable. For each measure and combination rule, we established 10 different thresholds to determine whether an executable is packed or not.

We evaluated accuracy by measuring False Negative Ratio (FNR) and False Positive Ratio (FPR). FNR is defined as: $FNR(\beta) = \frac{FN}{FN+TP}$ where TP is the number of packed executable cases correctly classified (true positives) and FN is

Table 1. Results for different combination rules and distance measures. The results in bold are the best for each combination rule and distance measure. Our method is able to detect more than 99 % of the packed executable while maintaining FPR lower than 1 %.

Combination	$1 - Cosine\ Similarity$			$Euclidean Distance$			$Manhattan Distance$		
	Threshold	FNR	FPR	Threshold	FNR	FPR	Threshold	FNR	FPR
Mean	0.05000	0.000	0.332	0.70000	0.000	0.816	1.70000	0.000	0.544
	0.08400	0.001	0.166	0.84000	0.001	0.288	2.17000	0.001	0.260
	0.11800	0.001	0.126	0.98000	0.001	0.172	2.64000	0.001	0.150
	0.15200	0.001	0.018	1.12000	0.001	0.130	3.11000	0.001	0.048
	0.18600	**0.001**	**0.012**	1.26000	0.001	0.014	3.58000	0.001	0.012
	0.22000	0.042	0.010	1.40000	0.001	0.010	**4.0500**	**0.002**	**0.010**
	0.25400	0.532	0.010	**1.54000**	**0.002**	**0.008**	4.52000	0.017	0.008
	0.28800	0.625	0.006	1.68000	0.096	0.006	4.9900	0.086	0.006
	0.32200	0.728	0.004	1.82000	0.298	0.006	5.4600	0.247	0.002
	0.35600	0.888	0.000	1.96000	0.568	0.000	5.93000	0.379	0.000
Maximum	0.36300	0.000	0.262	1.90000	0.000	0.768	5.90000	0.000	0.570
	0.38200	0.003	0.138	1.96000	0.000	0.594	6.20000	0.000	0.340
	0.40100	0.004	0.118	2.02000	0.000	0.232	6.50000	0.000	0.194
	0.42100	**0.020**	**0.108**	2.08000	0.00	0.050	6.80000	0.001	0.048
	0.43900	0.085	0.100	2.14000	0.001	0.024	7.10000	0.002	0.028
	0.45800	0.102	0.098	**2.20000**	**0.002**	**0.014**	**7.40000**	**0.008**	**0.018**
	0.47700	0.122	0.086	2.26000	0.004	0.012	7.70000	0.033	0.008
	0.49600	0.195	0.012	2.32000	0.020	0.008	8.00000	0.077	0.004
	0.51500	0.329	0.010	2.38000	0.061	0.008	8.30000	0.239	0.004
	0.53400	0.509	0.000	2.44000	0.146	0.000	8.60000	0.378	0.000
Minimum	0.00032	0.000	0.682	0.06000	0.000	0.736	0.06000	0.000	0.736
	0.01962	**0.003**	**0.012**	0.20000	0.001	0.396	0.20000	0.001	0.396
	0.03892	0.107	0.008	0.34000	0.001	0.106	0.34000	0.001	0.106
	0.05822	0.189	0.004	0.48000	0.001	0.030	0.48000	0.001	0.03
	0.07752	0.213	0.004	**0.62000**	**0.002**	**0.014**	**0.62000**	**0.002**	**0.014**
	0.09682	0.374	0.004	0.76000	0.032	0.006	0.76000	0.032	0.006
	0.11612	0.477	0.002	0.90000	0.054	0.004	0.90000	0.054	0.004
	0.13542	0.692	0.002	1.04000	0.163	0.004	1.04000	0.163	0.004
	0.15472	0.792	0.002	1.18000	0.262	0.002	1.18000	0.262	0.002
	0.17402	0.860	0.000	1.32000	0.386	0.000	1.32000	0.386	0.000

the number of packed executable cases misclassified as not packed software (false negatives). FPR is defined as: $FPR(\alpha) = \frac{FP}{FP+TN}$ where FP is the number of not packed executables incorrectly detected as packed while TN is the number of not packed executables correctly classified.

Table 1 shows the obtained results. Euclidean and Manhattan distances, despite of consuming less processing time, have achieved better results than cosine-similarity-based distance for the tested thresholds. In particular, our anomaly-based packed executable detector is able to correctly detect more than 99 % of unknown packers while maintaining the rate of misclassified not packed executable lower than 1 %. As it can be observed, mean combination rule presents slightly better results both for FNR and FPR. These results show that this method is a valid pre-process step for a generic unpacking schema. Since the main limitation of these unpackers is their performance overhead, a packed executable detector like our anomaly-based method can improve their workload, acting as a filter for these systems.

236 X. Ugarte-Pedrero, I. Santos, and P.G. Bringas

5 Discussion and Conclusions

Like the previous work, our method is focused on executable pre-filtering, as an initial phase to decide whether to analyse samples on a generic unpacker or not. Our main contribution is the anomaly-detection-based approach employed for packed executable identification. In contrast to previous approaches, this method does not need previously labelled packed and not packed executables, as it measures the deviation of executables respect to normality (not packed executables). Moreover, as it does not use packed samples for comparison, it is independent of the packer used to protect the executables. Although anomaly detection systems tend to produce high false positive rates, our experimental results show very low values in all cases. This fact proofs the validity of our initial hypothesis.

Anyway, it presents some limitations that should be studied in further work. First, it cannot identify the packer nor the family of the packer used to protect the executable. Such information would help the malware analyst in the task of unpacking the executable. Sometimes, generic unpacking techniques are very time consuming or fail and it is easier to use specific unpacking routines, created for most commonly used packers.

Secondly, the features extracted can be modified by malware writers in order to bypass the filter. In the case of structural features, packers could build executables using the same flags and patterns as common compilers, for instance importing common DLL files or creating the same number of sections. Heuristic analysis, in turn, can be evaded by using standard sections instead of not standard ones, or filling sections with padding data to unbalance byte frequency and obtain lower entropy values. What is more, our system is very dependant on heuristics due to the relevance values obtained from IG, making it vulnerable to such attacks.

Finally, it is important to consider efficiency and processing time. Our system compares each executable against a big dataset (400 vectors). Despite Euclidean and Manhattan distances are easy to compute, cosine distance and more complex distance measures such as Mahalanobis distance may take too much time to process every executable under analysis. For this reason, in further work we will emphasize on improving the system efficiency by clustering not packed vectors and reducing the whole dataset to a limited amount of samples.

Acknowledgements

This research was partially supported by the Basque Government under a pre-doctoral grant given to Xabier Ugarte-Pedrero. We would also like to acknowledge Iker Pastor López for his help in the experimental configuration.

References

1. Kaspersky: Kaspersky security bulletin: Statistics (2008), http://www.viruslist.com/en/analysis?pubid=204792052

2. McAfee Labs: Mcafee whitepaper: The good, the bad, and the unknown (2011), `http://www.mcafee.com/us/resources/white-papers/wp-good-bad-unknown.pdf`
3. PEiD: PEiD webpage (2010), `http://www.peid.info/`
4. Faster Universal Unpacker (1999), `http://code.google.com/p/fuu/`
5. Morgenstern, M., Pilz, H.: Useful and useless statistics about viruses and anti-virus programs. In: Proceedings of the CARO Workshop (2010), `www.f-secure.com/weblog/archives/Maik_Morgenstern_Statistics.pdf`
6. Babar, K., Khalid, F.: Generic unpacking techniques. In: Proceedings of the 2nd International Conference on Computer, Control and Communication (IC4), pp. 1–6. IEEE, Los Alamitos (2009)
7. Data Rescue: Universal PE Unpacker plug-in, `http://www.datarescue.com/idabase/unpack_pe`
8. Stewart, J.: Ollybone: Semi-automatic unpacking on ia-32. In: Proceedings of the 14th DEF CON Hacking Conference (2006)
9. Royal, P., Halpin, M., Dagon, D., Edmonds, R., Lee, W.: Polyunpack: Automating the hidden-code extraction of unpack-executing malware. In: Proceedings of the 2006 Annual Computer Security Applications Conference (ACSAC), pp. 289–300 (2006)
10. Kang, M., Poosankam, P., Yin, H.: Renovo: A hidden code extractor for packed executables. In: Proceedings of the 2007 ACM Workshop on Recurring Malcode, pp. 46–53. ACM, New York (2007)
11. Martignoni, L., Christodorescu, M., Jha, S.: Omniunpack: Fast, generic, and safe unpacking of malware. In: Proceedings of the 2007 Annual Computer Security Applications Conference (ACSAC), pp. 431–441 (2007)
12. Yegneswaran, V., Saidi, H., Porras, P., Sharif, M., Mark, W.: Eureka: A framework for enabling static analysis on malware. Technical report, Technical Report SRI-CSL-08-01 (2008)
13. Danielescu, A.: Anti-debugging and anti-emulation techniques. CodeBreakers Journal 5(1) (2008), `http://www.codebreakers-journal.com/`
14. Cesare, S.: Linux anti-debugging techniques, fooling the debugger (1999), `http://vx.netlux.org/lib/vsc04.html`
15. Julus, L.: Anti-debugging in WIN32 (1999), `http://vx.netlux.org/lib/vlj05.html`
16. Farooq, M.: PE-Miner: Mining Structural Information to Detect Malicious Executables in Realtime. In: Proceedings of the 12th International Symposium on Recent Advances in Intrusion Detection (RAID), pp. 121–141. Springer, Heidelberg (2009)
17. Shafiq, M., Tabish, S., Farooq, M.: PE-Probe: Leveraging Packer Detection and Structural Information to Detect Malicious Portable Executables. In: Proceedings of the Virus Bulletin Conference (VB), pp. 29–33 (2009)
18. Perdisci, R., Lanzi, A., Lee, W.: McBoost: Boosting scalability in malware collection and analysis using statistical classification of executables. In: Proceedings of the 2008 Annual Computer Security Applications Conference (ACSAC), pp. 301–310 (2008)
19. Kent, J.: Information gain and a general measure of correlation. Biometrika 70(1), 163–173 (1983)
20. Tata, S., Patel, J.: Estimating the Selectivity of tf-idf based Cosine Similarity Predicates. SIGMOD Record 36(2), 75–80 (2007)
21. VX Heavens, `http://vx.netlux.org/`

Produre: A Novel Proximity Discovery Mechanism in Location Tagging System*

Jianbin Hu, Yonggang Wang, Tao Yang, Zhi Guan, Nike Gui, and Zhong Chen

Key Laboratory of High Confidence Software Technologies, Ministry of Education, China
School of Electronics Engineering and Computer Science, Peking University, China
{hjbin,wangyg,yangtao,guanzhi,guink,chen}@infosec.pku.edu.cn

Abstract. Proximity discovery is a very interesting and useful technique which helps a user to find out his proximities who have the same or similar location with him during a certain period of time. However, current methods of discovering proximities are difficult to adopt and vulnerable when wrong location tags are provided. This paper proposes Produre, a novel proximity discovery mechanism in location tagging system based on users' credibility degrees and online social network. The introduction of online social network helps to maintain the relationship and location exposure policies between friends. The users' credibilities help to diminish the bad influence of malicious users who always annotate wrong location tags because the credibility scores change based on users' performance. The experimental results by our prototype illustrate Produre can effectively discover proximities of a user in an efficient and accurate way with high quality and fewer mistakes.

Keywords: Proximity discovery, location tagging system, credibility degree, online social network.

1 Introduction

With the development of online social networks(OSN), such as Facebook [1] in U.S. and Renren [2] in China, more and more applications have emerged to provide personalized and useful services. Among all these services, proximity discovery has attracted so many people and is being discussed almost everywhere. Here we define the term "proximity discovery" as "finding out the persons who have the same or similar geographical location with a certain user". In other words, according to proximity discovery, we can find out the geographical neighbors with respect to a certain user. In practice, we usually refer to the proximity of a user u as a user p the distance between whom and u is no more than a threshold D_t. In this paper, we would like to use "online social network" as an information pool which can provide useful information (e.g., friend relationship, location tags, maps...) to support proximity discovery. We define "user" as a real person behind an individual account in an online social network.

---

* This work was supported in part by the NSFC under grant No. 60773163, No. 60873238, No. 60970135 and No. 61003230, the National Significant Science and Technology Projects under grant No. 2009ZX01039-001-001, as well as the PKU PY Project under grant No. PKU-PY2010-005.

Á. Herrero and E. Corchado (Eds.): CISIS 2011, LNCS 6694, pp. 238–245, 2011.

An example of proximity discovery. *Alice* and *Bob* are friends. Now *Alice* is shopping in a shopping mall. Her mobile is turned on and so is the bluetooth in the mobile. *Bob* has just stepped into that mall, then *Alice* is being noticed by her mobile that *Bob* is in the same hall too. Therefore, they will meet and have a pleasant time together.

Typical proximity discovery. In typical proximity discovery systems, users repeatedly annotate location tags according to the information given by their handheld devices (e.g., mobile phone and PDA), send the location tags to the server, and then the server will find out proximities of each user based on doing comparisons between those tags. For example, if the server discovers that the location in a location tag M_1 sent by user U_1 is the same as or similar with the location in another location tag M_2 sent by user U_2. Then the server may notice U_1 and U_2 that they are proximities of each other. However, there may be tag spam in the location tags. Here we define "tag spam" as a location tag whose content doesn't match the location where the user resides. Obviously, if there are tag spam, then the server will do wrong comparisons and therefore return wrong results (i.e., wrong proximities) to the users. For example, *Bob* sends a location tag, which indicates that he is shopping however he is at home actually, to the server. One friend of *Bob* (say *Alice*) also sends a location tag, which indicates that she is shopping which is true, to the server. The server will tell *Alice* that *Bob* is nearby based on comparison between location tags, however, *Alice* will find herself be cheated.

Our goal. This paper aims to answer the following questions: *Is it possible to design an approach that helps the users to discover their proximities with fewer mistakes which are caused by wrong location tags?* To answer the question, we aim for effective mechanism that helps users to discover their proximities with high efficiency and fewer wrong results.

Our approach and contributions. In this paper we present Produre, a novel proximity discovery mechanism based on users' credibilities in location tagging system and online social network. The introduction of online social network helps to maintain the relationship and location exposure policies between friends. The users' credibilities help to diminish the bad influence of malicious users who always annotate wrong location tags because the credibility scores change based on users' performance. The experimental results by our prototype illustrate Produre can effectively discover proximities of a user in an efficient and accurate way with high quality and fewer mistakes.

To the best of our knowledge, there is not any study, using the method similar with Produre. The contributions of this paper are as follows:

- We propose Produre, a novel proximity discovery mechanism in location tagging system based on users' credibilities.
- We introduce online social network to maintain the relationship and location exposure policies between users in Produre.
- We are the first to introduce approach to overcome the proximity discovery problem in current social-network services.

Outline. The rest of this paper is organized as follows. Section 2 describes the design rationale of Produe. Then, the evaluation results are discussed in Section 3. We present the related work in Section 4. Finally, we present conclusion and future work in Section 5.

2   Produre

In this section, first, we introduce our model of location tagging system in Section 2.1 which also includes model of location tags and location exposure policy. In Section 2.2, we mainly describe the working process of Produre. In Section 2.3 and Section 2.4, we describe algorithm for users' credibilities and issues about key management to supplement Section 2.2.

2.1   Location Tagging System

Location Tag Model. In traditional tagging system, users annotate tags to resources in the system to show their subjective feelings about the resources. In this paper, we define a *location tag* [3] as an ephemeral, unpredictable nonce associated with a location and can be derived from various electromagnetic signals available in the environment, such as WiFi and Bluetooth. It can be thought of as a shared pool of entropy between all users at a given location at a given time. A location tag lt can be represented as follows:

$$lt = \langle u, l, t \rangle \tag{1}$$

where

- u: the user who sends the location tag lt, i.e., the annotator of the location tag.
- l: the location of user u when he is sending the location tag lt, which is the main content of the location tag. Apparently, there may be more information in a location tag due to different kinds of location services and in this paper we just extract several main items to design Produre.
- t: the time when the location tag lt is sent, which means at the time of t, user u is in the location of l.

System Model. We define a *location tagging system* (say S_{lt}) as a system which provides location services according to location tags. We also define the user who raises a proximity discovery request as a "client". The system model which meets the design requirement of Produre is given as follows:

$$S_{lt} = \langle U, LT, C, K \rangle \tag{2}$$

where

- U: the set of users in the tagging system, among whom there are friendship relations because of introducing online social network.
- C: the processing center of the whole system, which is in charge of communication, computation, and storage of friendship relations between users and their location exposure policies.
- LT: the set of location tags in the system. Users in the system repeatedly send location tags to the processing center.
- K: the key management center. It is responsible for generating public and private key pairs for the processing center and each user in the location tagging system, maintaining and destroying the public and private key pairs when necessary.

Location Exposure Policy. Produre combines traditional location tagging system and online social network. Therefore, the friend relationship in ONS can be used to make location exposure policy in location tagging system. In other words, a user u in the system can decide which users are allowed to know his location so that these users will be notified when u is one of their proximities (i.e., is near them). A location exposure policy of u's can be represented as $P_{ui} = \langle F, A, ST, ET \rangle$, where F is the set of target users of this policy, i.e., the users who are covered in this policy item. A is the set of action of this policy. An action can be allowing or not allowing users in F to know the location information of u.

2.2   Steps of Produre

The working process of Produre which is shown in Fig. 1 is described as follows.

- **Step 1 - Request Generation:** A client c raises a request of proximity discovery, and the processing center receives the request.
- **Step 2 - Policy Checking:** The processing center C checks c's location exposure policy to determine the set of users who are allowed to exist in the returning results to c.
- **Step 3 - Proximity Calculation:** For each user u_i obtained in Step 2, the processing center C makes comparison of the set of u_i's location tags with the set of c's location tags, and calculates the size (say N_{ci}) of the intersection of those two sets. If $N_{ci} > N_m$, then the processing center C will regard user u_i as a proximity of the client c and put u_i into a proximity set S_p of c.
- **Step 4 - Proximity Ranking:** The processing center C ranks each element u_{pi} (i.e., a user) in S_p according to c's credibility degree with respect to u_{pi}. At last, the processing center C returns the first θ elements in S_p to c and the value of θ can be adjusted according to the system requirement.
- **Step 5 - Credibility Adjustment:** The client c views some of the results (users) who possibly are his proximities, and contacts some proximities to do something (e.g., going shopping together, or sharing the fee of a taxi...). After that, the client will adjust his credibility degrees with respect to those users according to his own evaluation on them.

After Step 5, the working process of a single proximity request is done. The changed credibility degrees are stored in the system for later use, i.e., dealing with the following proximity requests.

2.3   Algorithm for Users' Credibilities

In Produre, when a client issues a proximity discovery request, the system will present the result page. Then he may view some of the results (users) who possibly are his proximities, and contact some proximities to do something (e.g., going shopping together, or sharing the fee of a taxi...). After that, the client will have his own evaluation with respect to the proximities who the client has contacted with. According to the evaluation, if the client regards a proximity as a true proximity, the credibility of the client with respect to that proximity will increase. In contrast, if the client regards that proximity

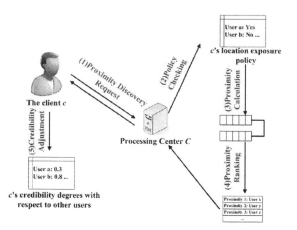

Fig. 1. Steps of Produre

as a false one, the credibility will decrease faster than it increase. Considering the client c and a proximity p in the results, the credibility of c with respect to p, $R_{c(p)}$, is as follows (the initial value to an unknown proximity is always 0):

$$R_{c(p)} = \begin{cases} \min(1, R_{c(p)} + \alpha_i) & \text{if } c \text{ regards } p \text{ as a true proximity,} \\ \max(-1, R_{c(p)} - \alpha_d n^2) & \text{otherwise.} \end{cases} \tag{3}$$

where

- $\alpha_i(\alpha_d)$: the reward (penalty) given to p for each good (bad) proximity feedback. The relation $\alpha_d > \alpha_i$ assures that $R_{c(u)}$ decreases faster than it increases. The selections of α_i and α_d are based on the specific requirement of application.
- n: the number of consecutive wrong proximity results which means $R_{c(p)}$ decreases exponentially when n increases.

In Equation 3, the credibility of c with respect to p decreases faster than it increases. The advantage is obvious: malicious users who always try to pretend to be proximities of others will be severely penalized because of the weight which is α_d by the square of the number of consecutive wrong proximity results.

2.4 Key Management

The key management center K mentioned in Equation 2 is in charge of generating public and private key pairs for the processing center and each user in the location tagging system, maintaining and destroying the public and private key pairs when necessary.

In Produre, all the users and the processing center have their own public and private key pair. During the transmission of location tags, the content is encrypted by the receiver's public key and the sender's private key for confidentiality and authentication. The sending content when considering encryption from the client's perspective is

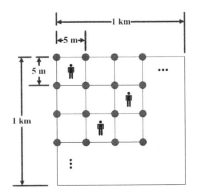

Fig. 2. Experimental area of evaluation on Produre

$\langle u_{id}, K_{R_{pub}}(K_{S_{prv}}(Cont)), t_{stamp_i} \rangle$, where u_{id} is the identity of the sender (i.e., user). $K_{R_{pub}}$ and $K_{S_{prv}}$ are respectively the receiver's public key and the sender's private key. t_{stamp_i} is the sending timestamp while $Cont$ is the sending content.

3 Evaluation

In this section, we describe the evaluation of performance of Produre. First, we introduce the experimental environment and the evaluation metric. Then, we describe the result of evaluation.

3.1 Experiment Setup

To evaluate our approach, we develop a prototype location tagging system where the whole mechanism of Produre is implemented. We recruit several volunteers who behave as users in the tagging system. They are required to generate the location tags based on their handheld wireless devices (e.g., mobile phones, GPS, or RFID tags). In other words, users first check the position information given by handheld devices and then give their subjective location tags. The experimental area is shown in Fig. 2. It is a square whose length and width are both 1 kilometer. It is divided into many little $5m \times 5m$ squares. Ideally, there should be location tag receivers at each red point in Fig. 2 to assure high accuracy of transmission. However, lacking of so many receivers, we only put some receivers at several red pints (one at one) in the area. We assume that the accuracy of transmission has been affected quite a little. The users randomly walk in the experimental area and repeatedly send location tags to the receivers and then to the processing center. However, some devices are malicious by providing wrong information about locations.

To discover the proximity set of a user, it is necessary to define a distance threshold of D_t two users who can be viewed as each other's proximities. In the experiment, we set D_t to 5, 10, 50 meters to see how the performance of the whole location tagging system is. We use the ratio of successful detection (SDR) as the evaluation metric which is defined as the ratio of the number of successful detection of wrong tags to the number of all the wrong tags.

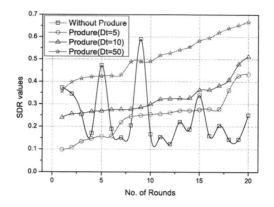

Fig. 3. Evaluation result

3.2 Evaluation Result

From Fig. 3 we can see that without Produre, the SDR values fluctuate heavily as the number of experimental rounds increase. However, the adopting of Produre makes the SDR values increase as the number of rounds increase. Different D_t values get different results. Generally speaking, SDR values with D_t of a higher value are easily high. However, the accuracy is very low because D_t of a higher value cannot reveal more detail of users' proximities' locations. Therefore, in practice, there is always a trade-off between the SDR value and the accuracy of Produre.

4 Related Work

Tagging systems (e.g., Flickr [4], Del.icio.us [5] and YouTube [6]) have grown in significance on the global Internet. In tagging systems, users search their wanted resources with related tags and annotate their resources (e.g., photos in Flickr and URLs in Del.icio.us) with their interested tags. Location tagging system is one kind of tagging system which provide location services, among which proximity discovery is the most useful and practical to most of the users.

As to proximity discovery, it has been provided by many websites, such as Google [7] and Netease Bang [8]. Users of these sites now and then obtain their locations according to GPS and post location tags on sites. They can change the policy which defines whether their locations can be exposed to their friends or other strangers.

There have been several studies which focus on location privacy protection by now. Obviously, it is based on the assumption that the processing center may be compromised by malicious users or hackers, which is different from the assumption in this paper. A privacy-aware friend locator was studied in [9]. Unfortunately the technique used therein has many flaws including the fact that the server always learns the result of proximity testing. Many papers have taken the anonymization approach to location privacy. The work of Gruteser and Grunwald [10] kicked off a long line of papers in this area. This approach has several limitations including the highly identifying nature of location information [11] and the limited location resolution resulting from the obfuscation or quantization needed for anonymization. At any rate, this approach is not suitable for proximity detection because identity is important in a social network context. There is a body of work on location-based encryption. Some of it assumes the existence of tamper-proof ("anti-spoof") hardware [12]. Other work such as [13] is more rigorous and involves securely verifying the location of the receiver based on timing or strength of electromagnetic signals.

5 Conclusion and Future Work

Proximity discovery is very practical and interesting in location tagging systems. We have proposed Produre, a novel proximity discovery mechanism based on users' credibilities. Our experiments based on real environment show that Produre can effectively discover proximities of a user in an efficient and accurate way with high quality and fewer mistakes.

In the future, we plan to apply Produre mechanism with more secure cryptographic features. Some improvements may be added, such as the use of attribute-based encryption (ABE) and identity-based encryption (IBE).

References

1. Facebook, http://www.facebook.com/
2. Renren, http://www.renren.com/
3. Narayanan, A., Thiagarajan, N., Lakhani, M., Hamburg, M., Boneh, D.: Location Privacy via Private Proximity Testing. In: NDSS (2011)
4. Flickr, http://www.flickr.com/
5. Del.icio.us, http://del.icio.us/
6. YouTube, http://www.youtube.com/
7. Google, http://www.google.com/
8. Netease Bafang, http://bafang.163.com/
9. Šikšnys, L., Thomsen, J.R., Šaltenis, S., Yiu, M.L., Andersen, O.: A location privacy aware friend locator. In: Mamoulis, N., Seidl, T., Pedersen, T.B., Torp, K., Assent, I. (eds.) SSTD 2009. LNCS, vol. 5644, pp. 405–410. Springer, Heidelberg (2009)
10. Gruteser, M., Grunwald, D.: Anonymous usage of location-based services through spatial and temporal cloaking. In: MobiSys 2003, pp. 31–42 (2003)
11. Golle, P., Partridge, K.: On the anonymity of home/Work location pairs. In: Tokuda, H., Beigl, M., Friday, A., Brush, A.J.B., Tobe, Y. (eds.) Pervasive 2009. LNCS, vol. 5538, pp. 390–397. Springer, Heidelberg (2009)
12. Scott, L., Denning, D.E.: A location based encryption technique and some of its applications. Institute of Navigation National Technical Meeting, pp. 734–740 (2003)
13. Sastry, N., Shankar, U., Wagner, D.: Secure verification of location claims. In: Proceedings of the 2nd ACM workshop on Wireless security (WiSe 2003), pp. 1–10 (2003)

Scientific Gateway and Visualization Tool

Eva Pajorová and Ladislav Hluchý

Institute of Informatics, Slovak Academy of Sciences, Slovakia
utrrepaj@savba.sk

Abstract. The science gateway is important component of many large-scale Earth, astronomical, environmental and natural disasters science projects. Developing the sciences portals and the science gateways is coverage of requirements of large scale sciences such as Earth science, astronomy and all sciences which are using last one platform of HPC (high-performance computing infrastructure) as are grid, cloud or cluster computing. The paper shows the main position of *visualization* in Science Gateway and describes architecture of the Visualization Tool (VT), for Earth and astrophysics simulations and shows some examples. VT is integrated in the web portal, as is e-science gateway for astronomy and astrophysics.

Keywords: Scientific gateway, Earth science, Grid.

1 Introduction

Since 2004 numerous scientific gateways have been developed lot of scientific gateways funded by the Tera-Grid Science Gateways program [1]. The gateway paradigm requires gateway developers to compile and install scientific applications on a variety of HPC clusters available from the resource providers in TeraGrid, to build service middleware for the management of the applications, and to develop web interfaces for delivering the applications to a user's web browser. Consequently, lot of web-service frameworks [2], [3], [4] have been designed and applied in building domain-specific science gateways. Some of them enable workflow based on the web services [4], but they commonly don't provide solutions to support web interface generation. Developers were usually hindered. Usually they need to spend a lot of time learning web programming, especially JavaScript and AJAX Technologies to implement a user-friendly and interactive web interface to these services.

Scientific gateways are able to provide a community-centric view, workflow/ dataflow services and a strong support in accessing the last one platform of HPC infrastructure including grid and cloud based resources. In each of science contexts, scientific gateways play a key role since they allow scientists to transparently access distributed data repositories (across several domains and institutions) and metadata sources to carry out search & discovery activities, as well as *visualization* and analysis ones, etc. Finally, scientific gateways can play an important role in training students (at academic level) in different scientific disciplines, attract new users and represent a relevant centralized knowledge repository in the sciences context. It is also a collaborative cyber-environment on which researchers working the same or similar

Á. Herrero and E. Corchado (Eds.): CISIS 2011, LNCS 6694, pp. 246–250, 2011.
© Springer-Verlag Berlin Heidelberg 2011

domains can easily team up to perform computational thinking on challenging scientific problems by sharing their computational software tools and elevating experimental datasets to scientific knowledge and innovative theories. Our paper deals with the position of *visualization* as one of the main components of scientific gateway. The scientific web portal - gateway cumulate all types of *visualization*. This paper describes VT for Earth science and for astrophysics, in which is cumulate all types of *visualization*.

Visualization tool is a part of gateway and proposes a new web based application framework for Earth science and astrophysics environment. The framework including the can import the astronomy specific workflow scripts easily can generate web appliance for running astronomical application workflows and *visualization* the outputs results directly from workflow execution, online visualization through their web browsers.

2   Visual Representation of Datasets

Simulation and execution with a huge data usually spend long execution time. Good solution for execution is represented by grown in platforms as is grid, HPC, cloud or cluster infrastructures. In each of infrastructures *visualization* has the main position as a way to control the execution process. Visual control has in all infrastructures very useful position. The modal parametric studies applications include, for example, astronomical simulations. The simulation was realized as a sequence of parameter studies, where each sub-simulation was submitted to the grid as a separate parameter study. The job management was rather time consuming due to the analysis of failed jobs and to their re-submission.

Visualization is included as a visual control process. Client asks for visualization is a "visualization client". Output data on the storage element are the inputs data for visualization jobs. Visualization workers are to modify data to the formats, which can be visualized, but also to prepare the typical visualization scenes. Client can render such scenes on the browser, can make the visual control and modify executions. For example, to immediately understand the evolution of the investigated proto-planetary disc we have developed a Visualization Tool (VT). The VT is composed of several modules, which are responsible for creating scenes and converting data to the "visualize" format. The VT is designed as a plug-in module. The components generating rendering scenes are easy to exchange, according to the requirements of the given application. In case of our gridified application the output data of the simulation located on the SE can be used directly as the input for the VT. The final product of the VT includes a set of files containing data in the VRML (Virtual Reality Modeling Language) format. These output files can be rendered by many available VRML web-browsers. The whole visualization process is maintained through visualization scripts, whose basic function is invoking the individual VT components in successive steps, transferring data, and handling error events. The script is written using the Bourne shell scripts and all VT modules are implemented in the C++ language. The VT can be embedded into the framework described above, or can be used separately as a stand-alone program. By using the on-line VT the client can stop the execution process, change the input parameters and restart the execution process again. In grid environment, such architecture can be used for all applications from different science spheres which have the character of a parametric study.

Actually, the research community needs not only "traditional" batch computations of huge bunches of data but also the ability to perform complex data processing; this requires capabilities like on-line access to databases, interactivity, fine real-time job control, sophisticated *visualization* and data management tools (also in real time), remote control and monitoring. The user can completely control the job during execution and change the input parameters, while the execution is still running. Both tools, the tool for submission designed before and continued sequential visualization tool, provide complete solution of the specific main problem in HPC environment. The position of the visualization tool as a visual control process is shown in figure 1. Astrophysics scientists are able to run scientific simulations, data analysis, and visualization through web browsers.

Through Earth and astronomical science gateway scientists are able to import they sophisticated scripts by which the VT can be activated as well, as the output from workflow executions without writing any web related code [5].

2.1 VT as a New Discovery for Presenting Academic Research Results

Advance in sciences and engineering results in high demand of tools for high-performance large-scale visual data exploration and analysis. For example, astronomical scientists can now study evolution of all Solar systems on numerous astronomical simulations. These simulations can generate large amount of data, possibly with high resolution (in three-dimensional space), and long time series. Single-system visualization software running on commodity machines cannot scale up to the large amount of data generated by these simulations. To address this problem, a lot of different grid-based visualization frameworks have been developed for time-critical, interactively controlled file-set transfer for visual browsing of spatially and temporally large datasets in a grid environment. To address the problem, many frameworks for grid and cloud based visualization are used. We can go through evolution of sophisticated grid-based visualization frameworks with actualized functionality, for example, Reality Grid, UniGrid and TerraGrid.

All of the frameworks have been included in the *visualization*. Frameworks were created during grid-based projects and create new features for presentations of the academic research results in visualization. Visualization resources enabled by the astronomical science gateway the top of research experiences.

Multiple visualizations generated from a common model will improve the process of creation, reviewing and understanding of requirements. Visual representations, when effective, provide cognitive support by highlighting the most relevant interactions and aspects of a specification for a particular use. The goal of scientific visualization is to help scientists view and better understand their data. This data can come from experiments or from numerical simulations. Often the size and complexity of the data makes them difficult to understand by direct inspection. Also, the data may be generated at several times during an experiment or simulation and understanding how the data varies with time may be difficult. Scientific visualization can help with these difficulties by representing the data so that it may be viewed in its entirety. In the case of time data varying in time, animations can be created that show this variation in a natural way. Using virtual reality techniques, the data can be viewed and handled naturally in a true three-dimensional environment (e.g. depth is explicitly perceived and not just implied). All these techniques can allow scientists to better understand their data. Viewing the data in this way can quickly draw the scientist's attention to interesting and/or anomalous portions of the data. Because of this, we encourage scientists to use scientific visualization from the beginning of their experiments and simulations and not just when they think they have everything operating correctly. This also allows scientists to develop a set of visualization tools and techniques that will help them understand their data as their research matures. For example, depending on of our astronomical example, in order to understand immediately the evolution of the investigated proto-planetary disc help us the final products of Visualization Tool (VT) for astronomers as are lot of video files and pictures.

VT tool for Earth Science provides pictures from simulations of the big Fire in Crompla region and from flood in river Vah, see Figure 1. Pictures shows simulations results of the evolution of proto-planetary disc from 1Myr to 1000 Myr. Specifically, Figure 2 shows the evolution of proto-planetary disc in the time of 1 Myr. We can see that during the 1000 Myr time that the particles were replaced from inside to outside of the spheres. Figure 2 shows the result of dynamical evolution of Oort-cloud as a part of proto-planetary disk after its evolutionary stage which was the first Gyr (giga year) [6].

Fig. 1. Visualization outputs from research results in Earth science natural disasters simulations

Fig. 2. Visualization outputs from research results in Astrophysics science simulations

2.2 Directly Visual Education Form

Educational visualization uses a simulation normally created on a computer to develop an image of something so it can be taught about. This is very useful when teaching a topic which is difficult to see otherwise, for example, proto-planetary disk, its evolution or evolution in Solar system. It can also be used to view past events, such as looking at the Solar system during its evolution stage, or look at things that are difficult. For astronomers, the VT has in education roles well.

3 Conclusion

The goal of the paper was to describe the VT architecture as the essential component in new portals - gateways technologies and to show some examples. For the future we want to extend the use of the VT for other scientific disciplines in addition to astronomy, but also for Earth Sciences with all *visualization* aspects. Now we are preparing the proposal for a new project of a new astronomical sciences gateway. For the future we plan to participate in a project in which the main activity will be to create and operate a pan-European e-Science

Acknowledgement

This work was supported by Slovak Research and Development Agency under the RPEU-0024-06 project, and by VEGA project No. 2/0211/09, as well as by EGEE III EU FP7 RI project: Enabling Grids for E-science III (2008-2010) FP7-222667 and also projects RECLER ITMS: 26240220029 and SMART II ITMS: 26240120029.

References

1. Wilkins-Diehr, N., Gannon, D., Klimeck, G., Oster, S., Pamidighantam, S.: TeraGrid Science Gateways and Their Impact on Science. IEEE Computer 41(11), 32–41 (2008)
2. Kandaswamy, G., Fang, L., Huang, Y., Shirasuna, S., Marru, S., Gannon, D.: Building Web Services for Scientific Grid Applications. IBM Journal of Research and Development 50(2-3) (2006)
3. Krishnan, L., Stearn, B., et al.: Opal: Simple Web Services Wrappers for Scientific Applications. In: IEEE International Conference on Web Services (ICWS 2006), Chicago, September 18-22 (2006)
4. Oinn, T., Addis, M., et al.: Taverna: A tool for the composition and enactment of bioinformatics workflows. Bioinformatics Journal 20(17), 3045–3054 (2004)
5. Paulech, T., Jakubík, M., Neslušan, L., Dobczynski, P.A., Leto, G.: Extended modeling of the Oort cloud formation from the initial protoplanetary disc. In: On 4th International Workshop on Grid Computing for Complex Problems, October 27-29, pp. 142–150 (2008)
6. Astaloš, J.: Experiences from porting the astrophysical simulation The unified theory of Kuiper-belt and Oort-cloud formationi to EGEE grid. In: The 3rd EGEE UF

An Innovative Framework for Securing Unstructured Documents

Flora Amato, Valentina Casola, Antonino Mazzeo, and Sara Romano

Dipartimento di Informatica e Sistemistica
University of Naples Federico II, Napoli, Italy
{flora.amato,casolav,mazzeo,sara.romano}@unina.it

Abstract. The coexistence of both structured and unstructured data represents a huge limitation for documents management in public and private contexts. In order to identify and protect specific resources within monolithic documents we have exploited the adoption of different techniques aiming to analyze texts and automatically extract relevant information. In this paper we propose an innovative framework for data transformation that is based on a semantic approach and can be adapted in many different contexts; in particular, we will illustrate the applicability of such a framework for the formalization and protection of e-health medical records.

Keywords: Knowledge extraction, document transformation, fine-grain document protection.

1 Introduction

The adoption of innovative systems for electronic document management is today very common in many domains as, for example, e-government, e-health and many other professional and social fields. Indeed, in such domains there is the need to manage the coexistence of traditional not-structured documents, mainly stored on paper or digital supports, with new, structured documents built with modern open standards and technologies (opendoc, XML, etc.). In the practice, the innovative management and elaboration techniques are unuseful for not-structured documents and, even if desirable, it is impossible to think of operations like semantic search, knowledge extraction, text elaboration and so on, unless a proper of unstructured data is performed.

Furthermore, people working in "traditional contexts" (medical, juridical, humanistic etc.,) are not interested in structuring their data/documents (like textual documents, e-mails, web pages, multimedia files) treating the document production as a monolith block without understanding the possible improvements of data management and protection when information are well structured. For example, a lawyer writes juridical records containing both sensitive and non sensitive information that can be physically accessible (read and/or modified) by different actors of the law domain; he has no competence to understand that information systems can enforce the data management and fine-grained access

Á. Herrero and E. Corchado (Eds.): CISIS 2011, LNCS 6694, pp. 251–258, 2011.

control rules but it is important for him that data are in the right place, protected by unauthorized accesses and can be easily retrieved when it is needed. So the data confidentiality is strongly related to the structure of data itself and to the physical support. Although producing data without following structural rules can be faster, as time goes by, it can result very difficult to maintain consistency of not structured data as well as to query and process not structured data. At this aim we are exploiting the adoption of semantic techniques to analyze texts and automatically extract relevant information, concepts and complex relations; the final goal is to be able to format not structured information in a structured way and with automatic or human-assisted tools. Once structured data and resources, it is possible to associate to each of them different protection mechanisms. In previous works we proposed a methodology for the classification and the protection of sensitive data, able to retrieve and associate the security rules to the resource to protect. It is based on semantic approaches for relevant concepts identification in textual data by means of lexical-statistical techniques [6,7]. The main idea of our work is to design a reconfigurable framework for documents processing that accepts in inputs a collection of heterogeneous data, including textual and multimedia, belonging to specialist domains and provides semiautomatic procedures for structuring data and extracting information of interest. Each domain has in common the activity of knowledge extraction from texts that includes different kinds of text analysis methodologies. The state of the art in this field is related to techniques of NLP and to cross-disciplinary perspectives including Statistical Linguistics whose objective is the study and the analysis of natural language through computational tools and models. The framework that we propose is based on transformation rules that are strongly related to the application domain, we were able to locate a set of tools, techniques and methodologies that can be adopted in different contexts and can be easily personalized and tuned. Once structured, the "monolithic" documents can be seen as a set of resources that can be separately accessible; we will represent them as XML files and we can easily enforce fine-grained access control policies with available security enforcer modules as XACML [12]. We will illustrate the applicability of the framework with a real case study to structure and protect e-health documents.

The reminder of the paper is structured as follows: in Section 2 we will illustrate the document processing framework for data transformation; in Section 3 we propose a detailed example of the framework implementation for the security domain, in Section 4 a simple case study will be presented to put in evidence how the framework can be used for medical record structuring and protection. Finally, in Section 5 some conclusion and future work are drawn.

2   A Model for Document Processing Framework

In several contexts as medical, juridical, humanistic, knowledge management dealing with acquiring, maintaining, and accessing knowledge within data can improve public and private services providers. Difficulties arise when the informations are

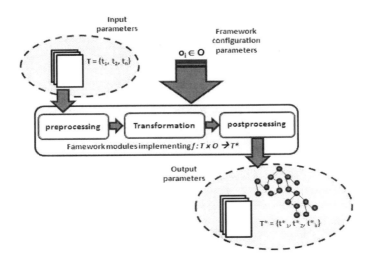

Fig. 1. Document processing framework

not structured and contained in textual format (for example electronic or paper document) without any support so that the contents could be machine-readable and processable. At this aim we have defined a framework for document processing for analyze texts and automatically extract relevant information, concepts and complex relations organizing the originally not structured information in a structured fashion.

In Figure 1 a framework schema is depicted. It is composed of three main blocks: *(i)* preprocessing module for extracting textual elements from documents in input; *(ii)* transformation module for applying on textual elements a set of transformation rules, identified by the set of parameters configuration as input; *(iii)* postprocessing module for providing a proper encoding for the transformed textual elements in order to make use of them in different application areas. We have formailzed the document processing framework as follow: let $T = \{t_1, t_2, ..., t_n\}$ be the set of textual documents; let $T^* = \{t_1^*, t_2^*, ..., t_k^*\}$ be the set of data structure (textual documents, XML, RDF, etc.) and finally let $O = \{o_1, o_2, ..., o_s\}$ be the set of *targets* defined by parameters configurations. Each target o_i represent, in turn, a set of parameters configuration aimed at selecting the appropriate set of algorithms and techniques for documents transformation according to the context in which the framework has to be instantiated. Such parameters configuration could act on the three modules that make up the framework. In particular, each module takes as input a subset of configuration parameters that select specific algorithms and eventually data inputs for a selected algorithm. So let $A = \{\alpha_1, \alpha_2, ..., \alpha_h\}$, $B = \{\beta_1, \beta_2, ..., \beta_l\}$ and $C = \{\gamma_1, \gamma_2, ..., \gamma_r\}$ be the input parameters of the preprocessing, transformation and postprocessing modules respectively, the set O can be defined as $O \subseteq A \times B \times C$. The framework is defined as a function $f : T \times O \to T^*$ that giving a target o_i and a document t_j implements a set of transformation rules (identified by o_i) and provides as output an elements t_j^*.

3 Adopting the Framework in the Security Domain

Organizing not structured text in order to obtain the same information content in a semantically structured fashion is a challenging research field that can be applied in different contexts. For example, a possible scenario is represented by structuring information using a semantic approach (with techniques for knowledge extraction and representation) in order to develop a semantic search engine that enables the access to information contents (semantic) of a not structured document set. Another interesting scenario is represented by the development of a semantic interpretation module that enables software or hardware agents to identify situations of interest and enhancing the cognition ability (for example by the recognition and learning of vocal and/or gestural commands). Moreover a semantic approach can be used on unstructured information in order to detect sensible information and for enforcing fine grained access control on these.

These scenarios have motivated the proposal of the framework: it can be instantiated in different contexts. Each context has in common the need to organize and transform heterogeneous documents in a structured form. In order to contextualize the framework in a particular domain, it is necessary to perform a tuning phase by means of techniques, algorithms and input parameters selection.

In order to properly locate and characterize text sections, the application of semantic text processing techniques is needed. The comprehension of a particular concept within a specialized domain, as the medical one, requires information about the properties characterizing it, as well as the ability to identify the set of entities that the concepts refer to. At this aim the preprocesing, transformation and postprocessing modules should respectively: *(i)* breaking a stream of text up into a list of words, phrases, or other meaningful elements called tokens and marking up the tokens as corresponding to a particular part of speech; *(ii)* filtering the token list obtaining the relevant ones in order to build concepts; *(iii)* identifying the text macro-structures (sections).

In order to process the input text and produce a list of words, the **preprocessing module** implements in sequence text tokenization, text normalization, part-of-speech tagging and lemmatization procedures. *Text Tokenization* consist in sentences segmentation into minimal units of analysis, which constitute simple or complex lexical items, including compounds, abbreviations, acronyms and alphanumeric expressions; *Text Normalization* takes variations of the same lexical expression back in a unique way; *Part-Of-Speech (POS) Tagging* consists in the assignment of a grammatical category (noun, verb, adjective, adverb, etc.) to each lexical unit identified within the text collection; *Text Lemmatization* is performed in order to reduce all the inflected forms to the respective lemma, or citation form, coinciding with the singular male/female form for nouns, the singular male form for adjectives and the infinitive form for verbs. These procedures are language dependent, consisting of several sub-steps, and are implemented by using the state of the art NLP modules [5]. At this point, a list of tokens is obtained from the raw data. In order to identify concepts, not all words are equally useful: some of them are semantically more relevant than others, and among these words there are lexical items weighting more than other. The **transformation**

module aims at filtering the token list in order to obtain a reduced list, containing only the relevant tokens. To do that, there are several techniques in literature that "weight" the importance of a term in a document, based on the statistics of occurrence of the term. TF-IDF index (*Term Frequency - Inverse Document Frequency*) [4] is actually the most popular measure used to evaluate terms semantic relevance. Having the list of relevant terms, concepts are detected by relevant token sets that are semantically equivalent (synonyms). In order to determine the synonym relation among terms, it is possible to use statistic-based techniques of unsupervised learning, as clustering, or external resources like thesaurus (an example is wordnet). At this point it is possible to codify concepts by means of ontology data models (RDF, OWL, etc..). Once the set of textual concepts is identified, the **postprocessing module** performs resource recognition that implies textual macro-structures identification. The macro-structures identification process consists of a classification task, exploiting as features the presence of the absence of concepts identified in the previous section. In literature the classification is a statistic-based technique of supervised learning and there are several different implementation of classifiers as, for example, Naive Bayes [1], Decision Tree [2], K-Nearest Neighbor [3]. Once the sensible resources are identified, we are able to represent the "monolithic" documents as a set of resources that can be separately controlled and accessed. This modules enables to codify the information in a structured fashion by means of common data models (as for example XML, HL7,...) and we can easily enforce fine-grained access control policies with available security enforcer modules. In particular, it is possible to write and enforce fine grained access control policies based on the well-known Role Based Access control Model. We will implement this module according to the XACML standard [12] where each security rule is applicable to each sensible resource (e.g. patient personal information, diagnosis, therapy,....) and it is based on user roles (e.g. Doctor, Nurse,....) and, eventually, on other resource information (e.g. time, place, environmental constraints,...).

4   Case Study: Structuring E-Health Documents

In order to process documents belonging to the E-Heath domain, the general framework is instantiated by means of input parameters o_i selection. In this way specific tools are selected in order to implement each module. The system accepts in input the corpus (made of unstructured medical records) and performs the formalization activities in order to structure it. In this way the resources to protect, representing the objects of the security roles, are identified.

In order to detect sensible resource we adopted a semantic based methodology, exploiting the presence/absence identification of relevant concepts [6]. As showed in Fig. 2, the system is composed by different modules.

In particular, in the *Preprocessing* module, all procedures are implemented by using a state of the art tool suitable for text analysis: TaLTaC^2[11] (in Italian language). In the *Trasformation* module the procedure responsible for *TF-IDF* calculation is computed again by TaLTaC^2. The *Concepts Builder* component is implemented by means of an innovative software designed by our research group. It takes as input a list of relevant words (those having higher TF-IDF value) and, exploiting a domain thesaurus [8] for semantic relations identification, clusterize them in concepts.

The resources identification of the *Postprocessing* module uses the classification procedure offered by KNIME [9] workflow tool.

In order to illustrate the processing phases, let's consider a fragment of an Italian medical record:

"La Signora si presenta con un anamnesi di precedenti ricoveri presso differenti reparti di questo ospedale. Inquieta ed a tratti aggressiva, manifesta un forte stato d'ansia e dolori allo stomaco. Vista la storia clinica di patologie ansiogene del paziente, le sono stati somministrati 10mg di Maalox."

Although the example is formulated in Italian the concepts to whom the relevant terms refer to, are indicated in English.

The fragment states that "the patient presents a history of previous admissions in different departments of a hospital. Restless and aggressive, shows a strong state of anxiety and stomach pain. Given the patient's anxiety-inducing conditions, she was given 10mg of Maalox".

Once the terms of this fragment were extracted by means of *Preprocessing* module (for brevity sake this step is not described, nevertheless, the interested reader can find details in [6]), the *Transformation* module extracts the relevant terms using, as described above, statistical measure; all the terms having a TF-IDF value over an established threshold are selected: "paziente"(4.1), "ansia"(4.2), "dolori allo stomaco"(3.8), "aggressiva" (3.1), "storia clinica"(4.8), and "Maalox" (4.7). These terms are then linked to the synsets to which they belong. Each synset refers to a concept, and each concept is then associated to a document section as summarized in Figure 3.

In our example we obtain the concepts associated to the extracted terms: "Patient" ,"anxiety" and "stomach pain", "aggressive", "Patient History" and "Maalox". The relevant concepts are structured in RDF format and the list of

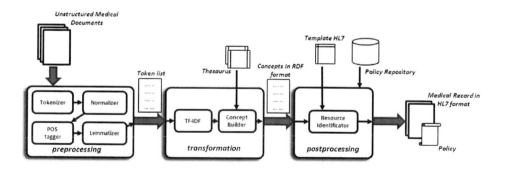

Fig. 2. Instanced architecture for E-Health documents processing

Extracted Terms	Associated Synset	Concept	Associated Section
paziente	ammalato, degente, malato, paziente	Patient	Invest. and Diagnosis
ansia	ansioso, ansiogeno, anxiety	Anxiety	Invest. and Diagnosis
dolori allo stomaco	dolori_allo_stomaco, mal_di_somaco,	Stomach Pain	Invest.and Diagnosis
aggressiva	aggressivo, aggressiva, aggressive	Aggressive	Patient Status
storia clinica	storia clinica, patient history	Patient History	Patient Status
Maalox	Maalox	Maalox	Therapy

Fig. 3. Association between extracted terms and corresponding concepts

identified resource are coded in XML files according to the HL7 standard [10] for medical records by the *Postprocessing* module.

The presence of concepts "Patient", "Anxiety" and "Stomach_Pain" in the underlined part of the example, and the absence of concepts belonging to the other sections, constitutes the features by which the subsection of the fragment under analysis will be classified as "Investigation and Diagnosis" section.

This kind of resource can be accessible only by those people having proper rights. In a role-based access control mechanism, these rights are associated to a role and they are usually assigned by security administrators according to governmental laws (on privacy in e-health, for example) and enterprise regulations. In previous works we designed security policies for this domain [7] and located roles were: *Doctors, Administrative Managers, Nurses* and *Patient*. For each role the possible actions considered are: "read" and "write". In our example, being the selected text fragment identified as "Investigation and Diagnosis" section, the following access control rules are enforced on it:

R1: $\{Doctor, Investigation\,and\,Diagnosis, (Read, Write,)\}$
R2: $\{Nurse, Investigation\,and\,Diagnosis, (Read, \neg Write)\}$
R3: $\{Administrative\,Manager, Investigation\,and\,Diagnosis, (\neg Read, \neg Write)\}$
For example, R1 states that the Doctor can Read and Write on resources of type "Investigation and Diagnosis" while a Nurse can just Read it (R2) and an Administrative Manager cannot access it (R3). The set of rules defines the security policy that can be associated to this document; according to the XACML architecture, these policies are stored in proper repositories and can be easily enforced by a Policy Evaluation Point [12] to secure any structured resources.

5   Conclusion and Future Works

Up to date, many systems are based on document management applications and cannot benefit of new design techniques to structure data because of the presence of old unstructured documents written by doctors, lawyers, administrative people and so on. Indeed, documents, especially the old ones, are just digitalized and made available to users. Among the other limitations, this prevents access control mechanisms from enforcing fine-grain security policies. In this paper we proposed an innovative framework that is based on a semantic methodology to transform unstructured data in a structured way by extracting relevant information and to identify critical resources to protect. We also illustrated its adoption on a simple case study to put in evidence the potentiality of the proposed approach from a security perspective by formalizing e-health records and defining fine grained access control rules. We think that the formalization of this general framework is very promising and we intend to investigate other methodologies to integrate different analysis approaches with a close look at the huge number of new applications that can derive.

References

1. Yang, Y., Webb, G.I.: Discretization for naive-Bayes learning: managing discretization bias and variance. In: Machine Learning, vol. 74(1), pp. 39–74. Springer, Heidelberg (2009)
2. Safavian, S.R., Landgrebe, D.: A survey of decision tree classifier methodology. IEEE Transactions on Systems, Man and Cybernetics 21(3), 660–674 (2002)
3. Kim, B.S., Park, S.B.: A Fast k Nearest Neighbor Finding Algorithm Based on the Ordered Partition. IEEE Transactions on Pattern Analysis and Machine Intelligence, 761–766 (2009)
4. Dagan, I., Termight, C.K.: Identifying and translating technical terminology. In: Proceedings of the fourth conference on applied natural language processing, pp. 34–40. Morgan Kaufmann Publishers Inc., San Francisco (1994)
5. Manning, C., Schtze, H.: Foundations of Statistical Natural Language Processing. MIT Press, Cambridge (1999)
6. Amato, F., Casola, V., Mazzeo, A., Romano, S.: A semantic based methodology to classify and protect sensitive data in medical records. In: IEEE Proc. of IAS 2010, Atlanta, USA, pp. 240–246 (2010)
7. Amato, F., Casola, V., Mazzocca, N., Romano, S.: A semantic-based document processing framework: a security perspective. Accepted in: Complex, Intelligent, and Software Intensive Systems 2011, Seoul, Korea (June 2011)
8. The Medical Subject Headings comprise the National Library of Medicine's www.nlm.nih.gov/mesh/
9. Berthold, M.R., Cebron, N., Dill, F., Di Fatta, G., Gabriel, T.R., Georg, F., Meinl, T., Ohl, P.: KNIME: The Konstanz Information Miner. In: Proceedings of the 4th Annual Industrial Simulation Conference, Workshop on Multi-agent Systems and Simulations, Palermo (2006)
10. HL7 CDA Release 2.0 2005. The HL7 Version 3 Standard: Clinical Data Architecture, Release 2.0, ANSI Standard
11. Bolasco, S.: Statistica testuale e text mining: alcuni paradigmi applicativi, Quaderni di Statistica, Liguori Ed., 7, p. 17-53 (2005)
12. The OASIS technical commitee: Xacml: extensible access control markup language (2005), http://www.oasisopen.org/committees/xacml/repository/

Use of Schema Associative Mapping for Synchronization of the Virtual Machine Audit Logs

Sean Thorpe[1], Indrajit Ray[2], and Tyrone Grandison[3]

[1] Faculty of Engineering and Computing, University of Technology
Kingston, Jamaica
thorpe.sean@gmail.com
[2] Colorado State University
Fort Collins, USA
indrajit@cs.colostate.edu
[3] IBM Almaden Research
Silicon Valley, USA
tyroneg@us.ibm.com

Abstract. Compute cloud interoperability across different domains represents a major challenge for the System administrator community. This work takes a look at the issues for enabling heterogeneous synchronization of virtual disk log attributes by use of an associative mapping technique. We explore this concern as a function of providing secure log auditing for the virtual machine (VM) cloud. Our contribution provides novel theoretical foundations that can be used to establish these synchronized log audit requirements supported by practical case study results.

Keywords: Log audit, Attribute, Synchronized, Virtual Machine, Associative.

1 Introduction

Enabling security within the compute cloud presents serious challenges which the VM system administrator has to face. These challenges range from third party trust, malicious insiders, and distributed storage just to name a few. Arguably the benefits of economies of scale for cloud deployment is matched by the security risk.

This paper articulates using a formal approach, the specific components required in designing an audit compute cloud. We achieve this by synchronizing the log file data between the actual physical disk and the virtual disk using associative mapping techniques of the adopted cloud components [7]. The rest of the paper is divided into four (4) sections. Section 2 looks at related work, Section 3 looks at an Attribute Log Graph context model, Section 4 looks at Experimental Results and Section 5 provides the conclusion and future work.

2 Related Work

Cloud computing arguably is seen by many as virtualization on steroids. The first deployment of virtual machines started as early as 2003, and by 2006 it's acceptance as

Á. Herrero and E. Corchado (Eds.): CISIS 2011, LNCS 6694, pp. 259–264, 2011.
© Springer-Verlag Berlin Heidelberg 2011

a mainstream service oriented computing model became evident. It is well understood that virtual compute clouds provide tremendous economies of scale for users.

We look at the work defined by Arenas et.al. [6] and others [2] [4] [8] [9] to develop our own algorithms. We posit the use of schema mapping techniques to correlate log file designs for the synchronized Virtual log auditing functions. Schema mapping composition is a fundamental operation in data management and data exchange. The mapping composition problem has been extensively studied for a number of mapping languages most notably source to target tuple generating dependencies (s-t tgds). We adopt these constraints as apart of our own specification semantics for a Global Virtual Machine Attribute Policy Auditor (GVMAPA) which is currently ongoing work within our research group. An important class of s-t tgds are local as view (LAV) tgds. This class of mapping is prevalent in practical data integration and exchange systems. We use these ideas to develop heterogeneous source-target Virtual Machine log maps, given the rich and desirable structural properties that these mappings possess and we think it can offer to such abstract domains.

3   Audit Log Graph Context Model

The authors posit a synchronized log file based audit mechanism for the cloud environment. The following formalisms below represent the attribute parameters required for defining these types of digital log footprints:

Definition 1: Virtual log (VL) footprint contains the attributes: We adopt the formal definition from [7].

$$c_a = \{e_1^t, \ldots, e_n^t)$$

$$c_a \in C, e_x^i \in E, 1 \le i \le l, 1 \le x \le m$$

l represents the maximum number of active log context and m represents the maximum number of VM environments defined for any given active context. Each context environment must be sensitive to the identified data, machine, and time allocated to a specified context

$$e_x^i = \{t_x^i, \{m_1^{i^x}, \ldots, m_a^{i^x}\}, \{d_1^{i^x}, \ldots, d_b^{i^x}\}, \{cn_1^{i^x}, \ldots, cn_e^{i^x}\}\}$$

Where

$$m_a^{i^x} \in M, d_b^{i^x} \in D, cn_e^{i^x} \in CN, 1 \le a \le \infty, 1 \le b \le \infty, 1 \le e \le \infty.$$

M is the set of all machines, D is the set of all related data and CN is the set of all connected nodes. M is assumed to be a collection of physical machines only a is the maximum number of machines, b is the maximum number of data transactions and e is the maximum number of nodes within a data center. As the number of machines comprises virtual machines and connections may exist between machines of different data centers, the value of e may be significantly larger than n-1, i.e. the number of other data centers in this cloud instance The values for a and b are assumed to have no upper limit as the number of machines and storage units for a particular cloud will grow or shrink as needed The location of the xth data center of the ith cloud, l x is a latitude-longitude pair. A machine consists of at least one central processing unit indexed by a unique CPU_ID and bandwidth.

The storage component is either a physical storage unit or a virtual storage unit. Note that S = PS ∪VS where PS is the set of all physical storage and VS is the set of all virtual storage. The next connected data center contains the source node bandwidth and the next or target node. Both source and target nodes are either a data center, a physical machine address (i.e. MAC address and associated I.P. address) or a virtual machine (i.e. a logical address mapped to a binding I.P address).

Due to the fact that a few of the base constructs in our model are composite data types, we define a base function called in (Composite Object O, Sub-Element Type T) that returns a set of the elements of type T in object O. The implicit assumption is that all types in a composite object are unique. In our articulation of a cloud log instance, we declare that the data centers are connected as a reminder.

Definition 2: Each VM node is stored as apart of a cloud log graph G .

Algorithm 1. CloudLogGraph (Cloud ci)
1: Create an empty graph G
2: For each data center dx in ci
3: Create a group graph node (ggn) in G for dx
4: For each machine m contained in dx
5: Build a node m in ggn dx for machine m
6: For each dx in ci
7: For each next element e contained in dx
8: Find the associated node or ggn associated to e's source
9: Find the associated node or ggn associated to e's target
10: Create a link between source and target
11: Assign bandwidth to the weight of the edge
12: return G

Definition 3: The Virtual Log Data Set Graph GD is a set of labelled graphs, GD={G1,G2, . . . ,Gn}, and |M| denotes the number of log graphs in a log graph dataset, that is the size of the graph dataset. |E| denotes the number of edges of the log graph dataset.

Definition 4: The size of a Virtual Log Graph(G) is the number of edges in E(G).

Definition 5: A log sub-graph of a Virtual log graph $G1 = \{V, E\}$ is a log graph $G2 = \{W, F\}$, where $W \subseteq V$ and $F \subseteq E$. A sub-graph G2 of G1 is a proper log sub-graph of G1 if $G2 \notin G1$.

Given two labelled graphs $G1 = \{V,E,\Sigma_v,\Sigma_e, l\}$ and $G2 = \{V,E,\Sigma_v,\Sigma_e, l\}^1$, G2 is a log sub graph of G1 iff
    1. $V^1 \subseteq V$.
    2. $\forall u \in V^1 \; ((l(u)) = (l^1(u)))$
    3. $\forall u, v \in V, (u, v) \in E, (l(u,v) = l^1 f(u),f(v) \in E^1)$

Definition 6: A labeled log graph G2 is sub-graph isomorphic to labeled sub graph G1, denoted by G2 ⊆ G1.

Definition 7: Virtual Log graph assumes the use of the Frequency Graph mining algorithm. G is frequent iff supG >∞. The frequent subgraph threshold is set to∞. where $0 ≤ ∞ ≥ 1$ and a graph database GD, is used to find all frequent sub-graphs in GD. To obtain the frequency of a sub-graph G2, we should count the number of graphs which contains this sub graph. During the frequent subgraph search step, the expansion of sub-graphs may cause similar sub-graphs to grow in different ways. The use of canonical order techniques is adopted to evaluate log graph consistency among similar graphs.

In the next section we demonstrate how we have developed a software prototype called a virtual machine log auditor that synchronizes these log formalisms within the actual working environment.

4   Experimental Results

In order to evaluate the effectiveness of our approach we have implemented a prototype tool called the "Global Virtual Machine Log Auditor (GVLMA)." We have applied GVLMA within the context of a University wide deployment for monitoring it's private VCentre cloud. GVLMA as a software application maps the VMware essx3i host ran on a Windows 7 operating system. The coordinated mapping task involves making a read and copy of the source log on the VM kernel host. GVLMA polls the VCentre disk through a secure ftp session (SENDER shell script) to the VCentre production storage area network (SAN). At this point it should be noted that our SENDER script actually does a semantic mapping of the log source schema on the kernel. We also deploy a LOADER script which initiates an Oracle 11g stored procedure, and this allows for transformation mapping between the source and target schema. In this case the target schema is the log auditor's database.

We use JASPER reporting (i.e. Java's web-based GUI reports) to show the outcome of the semantic translation. In the test environment, we maintain GVLMA also running on Windows 7, using our own VCentre essx 3i test host. The production source SAN runs a 1 Terabyte disk storage whereas our test SAN runs a 100GB disk storage. The production VCentre cloud runs fifteen (15) virtual machine server instances connected to the local VM host.

The mapped log events are polled over different time points, to determine a suitable VM log footprint of consistent transactions ran by this host. In Figure 1 below we show a snapshot of these time points for the System Log Events as of 9/11/10. The table frequency shows that between the time interval 9:51 a.m. to 16:36 p.m. a consistent signature of failed disk starts. These results corroborate a chain of basic evidence to suggest that the security administrator should have swapped out these disks on the production SAN as well as to perform further forensic analysis on the same at that instant of noted failure.

The summary evaluation of these failed disk events also lead to obvious application instances errors on the SAN. For example failed buffer writes of the application logs, antivirus shutdown on the host etc.

LOG_ DATE	EVENT	LOG-SOURCE	DESCRIPTION	OCCURRENCE
			Most Frequent Errors	
VM Log Type: Error		Log type: Error	Date loaded 20110128 /first vm-log dump	
11/102010 9:51	15	Symmpi	The \Device\Scsi\symmpi1 is not ready for access yet.	36
11/10/201 0 9:51	11	Disk	The driver detected a controller error on \Device\Harddisk0.	36
11/10/201 0 9:50	15	Symmpi	The\ Device\Scsi\symmpi1 is not ready for access yet.	34
11/10/201 0 9:50	11	Disk	The driver detected a controller error on \Device\Harddisk0.	34
11/9/2010 16:36	11	Disk	The driver detected a controller error on \Device\Harddisk0.	26

Fig. 1. Shows the synchronized VM Host disk over the time period 9/11/10 between 9:00 a.m. to 16:36 p.m. for a sequence of time events and their Frequency of occurrence

What we cannot say from these results is why the VM system administrator took so long to detect the failures, but a reasonable assumption is that before we had done this automated prototype to perform the audit, the administrator appeared to have been doing manual entries to perform security validations on the VM kernel. And hence may have somehow missed these entries at that point in time. Notable to the production environment however at that time point, is the fact that there was no archival security analysis done on these system event logs. The commissioning of our automated log auditor since the 28/11/2011 is what the University currently uses to demonstrate these mapped log errors on the synchronized VM kernel. And hence we could argue that the administrator task could have been made easier, if this automation was done earlier.

It is also useful for the reader to understand that the automated synchronized logs audits are read from the VMware essx3i kernel \var\log directory. Hence for this reason we can generate a schema for both the device and application instances running within this virtualization stack.

The results captured in this study have been limited to the VMware cloud; however ongoing work explores further testing on the Citrix Xen-Kernel host, as well as VCentre newer infrastructure 4, to demonstrate further schematic mapping constraints by our log auditor. Also, we use static snapshot analysis of the log events to perform this system study.

5 Conclusion and Future Work

In this paper the authors have presented formal structural properties for auditing a synchronized VM cloud environment. We used schematic associative mapping formalisms to link these properties. We substantiated our formalisms by a preliminary experimental study. Further work explores associative mining rules that not only correlate log frequency on a synchronized event but also classifies the behavior of these events as forensic concern for this virtual machine log auditor.

References

1. Agrawal, R., Srikant, R.: Fast algorithms for mining association rules in large databases. In: VLDB Conference, pp. 487–499 (1994)
2. Dehaspe, L., Toivonen, H.: Discovery of frequent, datalog patterns. Data Mining. Knowledge. Discovery 3(1), 7–36
3. Ordonez, C.: Models for association rules based on clustering and correlation. Intelligent Data Analysis 13(2), 337–358 (2009)
4. Yan, X., Cheng, H., Han, J., Yu, P.S.: Mining significant graph patterns by leap search. In: SIGMOD, Conference, pp. 433–444 (2008)
5. http://www.usenix.org/events/osdi99/full_papers/wang/wang_html/node8.html
6. Arenas, et.al.: Inverting Schema Mappings: Bridging the Gap between Theory and Practice. PVLDB 2(1), 1018–1029 (2009)
7. Grandison, T., Maximillen, E.M., Thorpe, S., Alba, A.: Towards a formal definition of Cloud Computing. In: Proceedings of IEEE Services (2010)
8. Mahavan, J., Harvey, A.: Composing Mappings among Data Sources. In: VLDB, pp. 251–262 (1996)
9. ten Cate, B., Kolaitis, P.: Structural Characterizations of Schema Mapping Languages. In: ICDT, pp. 63–72 (2009)

Enforcing Data Quality Rules for a Synchronized VM Log Audit Environment Using Transformation Mapping Techniques

Sean Thorpe[1], Indrajit Ray[2], and Tyrone Grandison[3]

[1] Faculty of Engineering and Computing, University of Technology,
Kingston, Jamaica
`thorpe.sean@gmail.com`
[2] Colorado State University,
Fort Collins, USA
`indrajit@cs.colostate.edu`
[3] IBM Almaden Research
Silicon Valley, USA
`tyroneg@us.ibm.com`

Abstract. In this paper we examine the transformation mapping mechanisms required in synchronizing virtual machine (VM) log audit data for the system administrator environment. We explain the formal constraints that are required by the transformation mapping process between the source and target log schemas for these VMs. We discuss the practical considerations of using these formalisms in establishing the suitable data quality rules that provides for security within these abstract domains.

Keywords: Transformation, Mapping, Log, Quality, Audit.

1 Motivation

Often when one thinks about the virtual machine cloud environment one sees economies of scales for the business. To this end enabling security across these domains are critical. The integrity of the disparate data sources however has proven a major interoperability challenge within these hybrid compute clouds. Hence efforts to provide data quality as apart of the VM data centre needs to be meticulous. Customarily data integration systems are automated systems that permit the transformation, integration, and exchange of structured data that has been designed and developed independently. The often subtle and complex interdependencies within data can make the creation, maintenance, and use of such systems quite challenging for database security. When one thinks about these traditional challenges as a new and urgent concern within the cloud computing arena the issues become even more problematic.

There are five (5) sections in this paper. Section 2 looks at the related work. Section 3 looks at the formal transformation mapping constraint definitions. Section 4 provides a case study analysis of the security challenges in the transformation mapping processes for our log auditor deployment. Section 5 summarizes the conclusion and future work in our research.

Á. Herrero and E. Corchado (Eds.): CISIS 2011, LNCS 6694, pp. 265–271, 2011.
© Springer-Verlag Berlin Heidelberg 2011

2   Related Work

Mapping composition and schema changes are fundamental operations in modeling consistent data quality for the traditional database systems. In this work we reference the semantics for mapping composition that was introduced by Fagin et. al [3]. Schema Mappings, and declarative constraints that model relationships between schemas, are the main enabler of data integration and data exchange. They are used to translate queries over target schema into queries over source schema or to generate executable transformations that produce a target instance from a source instance. These transformations are generated from the logical specification of the mappings. Such schema mappings are normally generated semi-automatically from using well established mapping tools like Clio, BEA Aqualogic [4][5]. The complexity of large schemas, lack schema documentation, and the iterative, semi-automatic process of mapping and transformation generation are common sources of errors. These issues are compounded by the nuisances of mapping tools (which can produce supposedly a wide variety of transformations is far from trivial and often time consuming and expensive). In addition, schema mapping is often done over several data sources that are themselves dirty or inconsistent. We contend that errors caused by faulty data cannot be easily separated from errors caused by an incorrect or inconsistent mapping and/or transformation. In the context of a synchronized VM environment, such inconsistencies are multiplied ten fold.

3   Transformation Mapping Constraints

If this section we identify the types of mapping constraints and how we apply enforcements to over come these constraints for enabling data quality within the synchronized virtual machine environment. We articulate these constraints as a set of formal mathematical definitions.

Definition 1: Rules $R_i, R_j \in \Re$ are mutually inconsistent if

1) $\forall A_k \in A \quad v(R_i, A_k) = v(R_j, A_k)$
2) $v(R_i, C) \neq v(R_j, C)$

Informally condition 1 in the above definition states that all decision making VM attribute values of R_i are the same as the corresponding attribute values of rule R_j and condition 2 states the category attribute value of rule R_j. Note that one assumes that decision making attributes will be in the same order for all rules, a condition that can easily be satisfied.

One has indirect inconsistency if the two rules are present in different policy sets lead to contradictory conclusions.Such inconsistencies are difficult to see because they may not be visible at the time of defining policies and can only be triggered only when some specific event occur. For example on the VM server a Professor T is allowed to create a student exam account and Mary a student is allowed to delete accounts. A policy may state that create and delete operation cannot be performed by the same entity or identity. Inconsistency could occur if Professor T delegates his rights to Mary. However from the perspective of having a synchronized VM log audit policy that can perform data mining on the attribute identities , one could formally define inconsistency in the following manner.

Definition 2: Algorithm 1.0. VM Node Inconsistency Detection Algorithm
Input: Decision tree
Output: Context of VM node inconsistency
1:         Let $A(bi)$ be the set of all attributes present in one branch.
2:         Bool *consistent = true*;
3:         **for** each branch *bi* in Decision tree **do**
4:         **if** more than 1 category attribute is assigned to terminal
            node *bi.tnode* **then**
5:         $A(bi)$ = fetch all attributes of brah(bi);
6:         **for** each actual rule *Ra* in the policy set **do**
7:         **if** $v(A(Ra)) = v(A(bi))$ **then**
8:         Highlight: $Ra : A1 \ldots An \rightarrow C$;
9:         **end if**
10:       **end for**
11:       *consistent = false*;
12:       **end if**
13:       **end for**
14:       **if** *consistent = true* **then**
15:       No inconsistency found;
16:       end if

In such a decision tree, each branch *bi* (from the root to a VM terminal node) represents one rule. In order to detect inconsistency, one will apply the above algorithm. First one checks the terminal node of each branch (Lines: 3-4). If any terminal node *tnode* contains more than one category (C) attribute value (Line: 4), this means that some rules in the policy set are mutually inconsistent. In order to determine which particular rules in the VM policy are mutually inconsistent, first one fetch all the attributes of the particular branch (Line: 5). After that the algorithm will start searching the attribute-values in the actual VM policy set (Lines: 6-10). All the rules in the policy set that contain those attribute-values will be highlighted as inconsistent (Lines: 7-9). If in a decision tree, no terminal node has more than one category attribute-value then this means that no inconsistency has been found in the policy set (Lines: 14-16).

To eliminate the inconsistency constraint in definitions (1) and (2) above, we define the notion of association to describe a set of associated atomic type schema elements in our transformation mapping mechanism. Intuitively, an association is a query that returns all the atomic type elements in a Log query.

Definition 3: A VM Log mapping system is a triple $< V_{LS}, VT_{LS}, M >$ where V_{LS} and VT_{LS} are the source and target schemas and M is a set of mappings between V_{LS} and VT_{LS}.

Definition 4: A schema element in schema V_{LS} is a path query, that is query of the form:

$$\underline{select} \; e_{n+1} \; \underline{from} \; x_0 \; \underline{in} \; L_0 \;, x_1 \; \underline{in} \; L_1 \ldots\ldots x_n \; \underline{in} \; L_n$$

where each L_k with $k \geq 1$ uses variable x_{k-1}, L_0 is an expression starting at a Log schema root in V_{LS} and expression e_{n+1} uses variable x_n. If the details of the <u>from</u> clause are unimportant, we refer to a Log schema element using the notation <u>select</u> e <u>from</u> L.

Constraints. For Log schema constraints we consider a very general form of referential constraints called nested referential integrity constraints (NRIs) [21] extended to support choice types. NRIs capture naturally relational foreign key constraints.

Definition 5: An association is a query on a VM log schema V_{LS}

$$\underline{select}\ e_{n+1}\ \underline{from}\ x_0\ \underline{in}\ L_0\ ,x_1\ \underline{in}\ L_1 \ldots\ldots x_n\ \underline{in}\ L_n$$
$$\underline{where}\ e_1 = e^1{}_1\ \underline{and}\ e_2 = e^1{}_2\ \underline{and} \ldots\ldots\ e_n = e^1{}_n$$

Definition 6: A mapping is a constraint for each A^{VLs} exist A^{VTs} with C, where A^{VLs} is an association on a virtual machine log source schema V_{LS} and A^{VTs} is an association on a virtual machine log target schema VT_{LS} and C is a conjunction of equality conditions relating atomic type expressions over V_{LS} with atomic expressions over VT_{LS}.

Definition 7: A correspondence is a specification that describes how the value of an atomic target VM log schema element is generated from the VM Log source schema. A correspondence can be represented as simple inter-schema referential constraints. A correspondence from a source element select e^{VLS} from from L^{VLS} to a target element select e^{VTLS} from from L^{VTLS} is an inter-schema NRI for each L^{VLS} exist L^{VTLS} with $e^{VLS} = e^{VTLS}$. Correspondences are implicit within the mappings (and view definitions) can be easily extracted from them.

Definition 8: A VM Log association A is dominated by association **B** (noted as $A \preceq B$) if there is a renaming function h from the variables of A to the variables of B such that the from and where clauses of h(A) are subsets, respectively of the from and where clauses of B.

   Domination can naturally extend to mappings as follows. VM log Mapping m_1: for each $A^{VLs}{}_1$ exist $A^{VTs}{}_1$ with C_1 is dominated by mapping m_2 for each $A^{VLs}{}_2$ exist $A^{VTs}{}_2$ with C_2 (denoted as $m_1 \preceq m_2$) if $A^{VLs}{}_1 \preceq A^{VTs}{}_2$ and for every equality condition $e = e^1$ in C_1, $h_1(e) = h_2(e^1)$ is in C_2 (or implied by C_2) where $h_1(e) = h_2(e^1)$ are renaming functions from $A^{VLs}{}_1$ to $A^{VTs}{}_1$ and from $A^{VLs}{}_2$ to $A^{VTs}{}_2$ respectively.

   There are three (3) ways in which semantic relationships between schema elements can be encoded. The first is through the structure of the schema. Elements may be related by their placement in the same record type or more generally through parent child relationship in nested schemas. An association containing elements that are related only through the schema structure is referred to as a structural association. Structural associations correspond to the primary paths used in where it is shown that they can be computed by one time traversal over this log schema.

Definition 9: A structural VM Log association is an association *select* e_{n+1} *from* x_0 *in* L_0 , x_1 *in* L_1 ....x_n *in* L_n with no where clause and where the expression L_1 must start at a schema root and every expression I_{-k} , $k > 0$ starts with variable x_{k-1} .

The schema structure encodes a set of VM Log semantic relationships that the VM administrator chose to model explicitly. A second way of encoding semantic associations is in a mapping. A mapping is an encoding of a pair of source and target associations (which may or may not be explicitly present in the VM Log schema structure. A VM Log mapping may expose hidden semantic relations between schema elements. In our case study on same our software prototype of the VM Log auditor acts as such a mapping tool.

Definition 10: Let M be a set of given VM Log schema mappings. A user association is an association that has been provided to the system via a mapping $m \in$ M.

Definition 11: A Logical association R is the result of chasing a structural or a user association L with the set S of all the NRIs of the VM Log schema (denoted as $chase_x (L))^1$.

Definition 12: Chasing is a classical relational method that can be used to assemble elements that are semantically related to each other through constraints. In other words this should be observed as schema constraint against the set of all the VM Log related elements. A chase is a series of chase steps. A chase step of association say R with an NRI Z : for each W exist Y with C, can be applied if, by definition, the association R contains (a renaming of) W but doesn't satisfy the constraint, in which case the Y clause and the C conditions (under respective naming) are added to the association. The chase can be used to enumerate logical join paths, based on the set of dependencies in the VM Log schema. We use a variation of a nested chase that can handle choice types NRIs. We define more formally an extended version of the chase in our next paper.

Definition 13: Let V_{LS} and VT_{LS} be the pair of VM Log source and target schemas and M a set of VM Log mappings between them. Consider C to be the set of correspondences specified by mappings in M. A semantically valid VM Log mapping is an expression of the form for each A^{VLs} exist A^{VTs} with D , where A^{VLs} and A^{VTs} are logical associations in the source and target schema correspondingly, and D is the conjunction of the conditions of the correspondences in C that are covered by the pair $\prec A^{VLs}$, $A^{VTs} \succ$ (provided that at least one such correspondence exist.) A correspondence v : for each L^{VLS} exist L^{VTLS} with D is covered by the associations $< A^{VLs}$, $A^{VTs} >$ if $L^{VLS} \prec A^{VLs}$ and $L^{VTLS} \prec A^{VTs}$.

Definition 14: Given a source and target VM Log schema V_{LS} and VT_{LS} along with the set of mappings M from V_{LS} to VT_{LS} , a VM Log mapping universe $U^M_{VLS, VTLS}$ is the set of all semantically valid mappings.

4 Case Study Evaluation

At the University of Technology (UTECH) we demonstrate the design of a synchronized virtual machine log auditor using VMWare essx3i data centre. Our goal in this research was to guarantee data consistency between the source and target schemas as a data quality concern. We achieve this by applying transformation mapping to our log auditor. The auditor runs a LOADER script, which happens to be an Oracle stored procedure that reads the source schema after we had successfully mapped it to our staging database. At the staging area, the LOADER script scans the column values of the source and matches its attribute parameters before copying it to the auditor's target database. However there are cases when an associatively mapped VM instance, shows different transformation attributes from what is registered in the auditor's logical target schema. This observation reflects changes in the source schema composition due to adaptation at the source VM host. For example we noted this as a concern, when data sets were mapped from a new test VMware host in the production centre. The CPU World ID strings appeared to have had a concatenated string length as compared to it's original attribute values on the current production host VM. This resulted in null column value update on the target. We treat this as a referential integrity constraint error at the target, and record such transformation events as a new and unknown within the VM. Realistically, this may be considered an inconclusive observation, as the attribute type is legitimate, it just had an unknown format to our auditor's target schema. In this context these results will subject the auditor to its own lack of integrity, due to human misunderstanding of these database constraints or some other anomaly. Hence we have started to look at the various intelligent adaptation and inference mechanisms to handle this log schema concern. One approach is the use of chasing methods in our transformation, by running a parser that periodically checks column formats and updates the auditor of any semantic changes. Ongoing work explores this chasing technique not only as a function of our static log monitoring auditor but also as dynamic monitoring parameter for the synchronized virtual machine environment. We still don't have any conclusive empirical study on these transformations, as our work is still in its preliminary stages. We however are testing application log profiles to determine the different real issues of these transformation formatting arguments.

5   Conclusion and Future Work

We have presented a formal theoretical approach on how we can establish virtual machine log synchronization using transformation mapping mechanisms. We relate from our case study deployment of our log auditor prototype how these transformation mapping mechanisms prove critical to data quality assurance and invariably the security within such logical domains. Our ongoing work assesses the transformation mapping issues for both the homogenous and heterogeneous VM cloud environments.

References

1. Grandison, T., Maximillen, E.M., Thorpe, S., Alba, A.: Towards a Formal Cloud Computing definition. In: Proceedings of IEEE Services (July)
2. Thorpe, S., Ray, I.: Global Virtual Machine Policy Auditor. CSU PhD Discussion Forum (September 2010)

3. Fagin, R., Kolatis, P., Miller, R.J., Popa, L.: Data Exchange Semantics and Query Answering. Theory of Computer Science 336(1), 89–124
4. Miller, R.J., Haas, L.M., Hernandez, M.: Schema Mapping as a Query Discovery. In: VLDB, pp. 77–88 (2000)
5. Chiticariu, L., Tan, W.: Debugging Schema Mappings with routes. In: VLDB, pp. 79–90 (2006)
6. Van den Bussche, J., Vansummeren, S., Vossen, G.: Towards Practical Meta Querying. Information Systems 30(4), 317–332 (2005)

Evaluating User-Centered Privacy Model (UPM) in Pervasive Computing Systems

Ali Dehghantanha[1], Nur Izura Udzir[2], and Ramlan Mahmod[2]

[1] Faculty of Computing and Technology- Asia-Pacific University College of
Technology and Innovation, Kuala Lumpur, Malaysia
`Ali_Dehqan@ucti.edu.my`
[2] Faculty of Computer Science and Information Technology, University of Putra
Malaysia, Kuala Lumpur, Malaysia
{`izura,ramlan`}`@fsktm.upm.edu.my`

Abstract. The fact that pervasive systems are typically embedded and
invisible makes it difficult for users to know when, where, and how these
devices are collecting data. So privacy is a major issue for pervasive
computing applications and several privacy models have been proposed
for pervasive environments. In this paper we present the evaluation of
a XML based User-centered Privacy Model (UPM) and measure this
model unobtrusiveness and discuss privacy policies' expressiveness, and
user control over private information. We show that the model provides
content, identity, location, and time privacy with low unobtrusiveness
while privacy policies are highly expressive and support mandatory and
discretionary rules, context sensitivity, uncertainty handling, and conflict
resolution.

Keywords: Privacy, Pervasive Computing, Privacy Evaluation.

1 Introduction

Providing users with enough privacy level is a basic requirement in pervasive
systems which provide services seamlessly everywhere, at any time for all the
users.

Different evaluation methods have been proposed for security and privacy in
pervasive computing systems. Ranganathan et al [1] proposed a benchmark for
pervasive computing systems which considered three characteristics for privacy
models as follow:

1. User control over private information which is the model ability to provide
   content, identity, and location privacy.
2. Unobtrusiveness of privacy mechanisms which is the percentage of time user
   consumes on interacting with privacy sub-system.
3. Expressiveness of privacy policies which is the policys ability to support
   mandatory and discretionary rules, context sensitivity, uncertainty handling,
   and conflict resolution.

Á. Herrero and E. Corchado (Eds.): CISIS 2011, LNCS 6694, pp. 272–284, 2011.
© Springer-Verlag Berlin Heidelberg 2011

The main unobtrusiveness challenge is to provide a balance between usability and privacy [2].

Several projects and models have already addressed some concerns of privacy protection. Privacy Sensitive Information Diluting Mechanism (PSIDM) [3] provides location privacy without any concern about model unobtrusiveness. Mix networks and mix nodes model [4] provides location privacy without looking into model unobtrusiveness. Pseudonyms and mix-zones model [5] provides both location and identity privacy but it does not have any concern for model unobtrusiveness. LocServ [6] model just supports location privacy with attention to its unobtrusiveness. Mist model [7] provides location and identity privacy for the user regarding the model for unobtrusiveness. Paws (Privacy Awareness System) [8] supports user identity and location privacy with concern about model unobtrusiveness. Geopriv model [9] provides user location privacy but it was not concerned about model unobtrusiveness. Spirit [10] provides location privacy with concern about model unobtrusiveness. QoP (Quality of Privacy) model [11] provides location, content, and identity privacy and provides a balance between user privacy and services that can be provided for him.

Today enhanced pervasive devices providing real time user information necessitates researchers to provide user with control over his time privacy.

In this paper we first present a brief description of UPM [12] at section 2, to provide needed background for describing the model proposed evaluation. Then in section 3, we evaluate the model in detail and show the models ability to provide users with control over content, identity, location, and time privacy with less than 10% unobtrusiveness. Conclusion and future works are presented in section 4.

2   The User-centered Privacy Model

Five parties are communicating in UPM as follows:

1. User: User requests for services.
2. Service provider: Provides services for the user using the data that is provided by the owner.
3. Owner: Owner is the content provider.
4. User light houses: Each user has one or more light houses. Light houses are user trusted parties that contain user identity information but they never have any information regarding user location, content, and time. Light houses provide other parties with user identity information based on user identity privacy policy.
5. Portals: portals are wireless nodes managing user context. Each context consists of one portal which plays two roles:
   (a) All devices of the context - including users device - sending and receiving data through the portal.
   (b) Portal manages all devices that gather user private information in the context. By default a portal has access just to user location information but it does not have any access to user identity, content, and time information.

These parties are communicating within three layers as follow:

1. User context layer: This layer surrounds user. Context includes one portal and several devices which are capable of gathering user private data. These devices are managed and controlled by the portal. In a specific time, user can be just within one portal covered environment but user might move between several portals experiencing different context.
2. Service layer: User light houses and service providers are in this layer.
3. Owner layer: Information owners are in this layer to provide required contents for service providers.

In this model, user sends data to the portal without sending any information of his identity. Portal hides user location and forwards data to the light house. So the user portal just knows user location and the user light house just knows user identity. User light house will be responsible to communicate with the service provider. Service provider receives its needed contents through owners.

2.1   The Model Privacy Files

The model privacy management method is based on XML files for describing privacy policies and preferences. Each user, portal, and service provider has two XML privacy files, namely privacy policy file and privacy preferences file. These two files format and tags are similar for each party. The privacy preferences file describes preferred level of privacy to communicate with other parties. Privacy policy file describes each party current and agreed privacy level during communication with other parties.

These XML files define each party identity, location, and time privacy. The identity privacy tag value can be *No ID*, *Confirm ID*, or *Real ID*.

Real ID value means the party will provide or ask the real identity in communication with other parties.

Confirm ID means the party will use a pseudonym ID that its trust ability and access level has been confirmed by a common trusted third party.

No ID means the party will use or ask an anonymous ID in communicating with other parties. Location privacy tag value can be *No Loc*, *Confirm Loc*, or *Real Loc*.

Real Loc value means the party will provide or ask the exact location information of the other communicating parties.

Confirm Loc value means the party will confirm its existence in a certain area through a common trusted third party or ask the other parties to confirm their existence in a certain area.

No Loc value means the party will not reveal or ask any location information in communicating with other parties. The time privacy tag value can be *No time*, *Confirm time*, and *Real time*.

No time value means there is no time limitation to communicate with other parties.

Confirm time value means the parties are confined to communicate just within a pre-specified time period.

Real time value means the communication between parties is confined to the real time communication.

Owner will just have privacy preferences file that describes the content privacy and all parties should follow these content privacy policies during communication. So the owner does not need to have privacy policy file.

Portal privacy policy file defines just ID and location privacy. Since there is no long term data transmission in portal and user communication and portal services are real times, so there is no need for a time privacy policy control mechanism.

Owner privacy preferences file defines just time and location privacy for each service. Since service provider presents contents for the end users, so it only checks user identity privacy. Owner just specifies required privacy for the content saving locations and the content availability time.

All remaining privacy files have time, location, and identity tags.

2.2   The Model Phases

The UPM contains five phases. Figure 1 shows UPM phases and relations with different parties.

In authentication phase, users are able to authenticate to the system through various authentication methods. System assigns a number called Authentication Precision Level (APL) in [0,100] to each authentication method. More precise authentication methods get higher APLs (These levels should be set previously by device manufacturer or system administrator).

System works on different automation level based on APL.

With APL in [0, 25), functionality is more important than privacy for the user. In this case, in any conflicts or uncertain privacy situation between user and other parties (when the other party cannot provide user required privacy level), user automatically accepts and applies the other party highest provided privacy level and start communication.

With APL in [25, 75], user receives alarms on communication with the parties with lower privacy levels than user requested. In this case, user has the ability to accept or deny communication offer. So the model provides user notice and choice in this level.

With APL in (75,100], user does not accept any privacy level less than his required privacy. So if the other party could not provide user required privacy level, the system will not let user to use the other party services.

APL would be saved in APL tag of user privacy policy file for later comparisons and decision making during the other phases.

Each context device that gathers user private information has a device privacy policy file. Context privacy policy file will reflect lowest level of each privacy type in the context.

In context joining phase user sends his required privacy level to the context portal. If context is able to provide that privacy level then user will join to the context. The agreed privacy level between user and context will be written in Context Privacy Policy tag of user privacy policy file.

To start using a service, user sends requested service privacy level to the service provider. Service provider has preferred identity, location, and time privacy for each service that it provides in service provider privacy policy file.

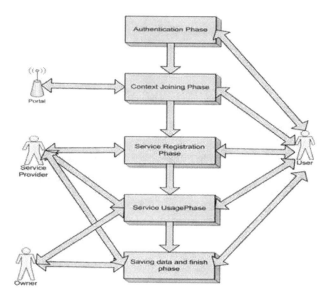

Fig. 1. Model phases

In service registration phase, if service provider would be able to provide user requested privacy level, then it sends service usage key to the user otherwise user will not be able to use that service. The agreed privacy policy would be written in user privacy policy and service provider privacy policy files that consist of the agreed ID, location, and time privacy.

There is an information space tag for each content part of a service on the service provider, each of which defines time and location privacy of related content part. In service usage phase, service provider should get assurance that user provides requested content privacy level before sending content to the user.

When user finishes using a part of the content or tries to save the content, system first applies content privacy policy on the saved content part, so that in future access to the content, user needs to provide required privacy level.

3   Results and Discussion

In this part we measure the UPM unobtrusiveness of privacy policies level and show that the model unobtrusiveness is less than 10%. Then we discuss the UPM expressiveness of privacy policies and show the models privacy policies' ability to support mandatory and discretionary rules, reflecting context sensitive information, handling uncertain situations, and resolving conflict situations. We continue by inspecting the user control over private information through describing the model's ability to provide identity, content, location, and time privacy. Finally, we discuss the UPM scalability through its support for XML as a common communication platform and distributed decision making processes.

3.1   Measuring the Models Unobtrusiveness of Privacy Mechanisms

The unobtrusiveness of privacy policies is the percentage of time the user consumes on dealing with the privacy subsystem to make decision. The designed experiment to measure the model unobtrusiveness includes the following steps:

1. Categorizing all system situations based on the number of privacy alarms into groups of scenarios. The model consists of the three groups of scenarios with zero, one or two privacy alarms.
2. Design cases in a way that each has one scenario with zero, one scenario with one, and one scenario with two privacy alarms. Each case should have at least one scenario that none of the other cases had before and all the model scenarios should be covered.
3. Each experiment participant does one case to measure the whole time of work and the amount of time that a user consumes on dealing with the privacy alarms in each scenario. The unobtrusiveness of each case computes as follow:
   Each case unobtrusiveness = (Sum of all times that user consumes on dealing with privacy alarms during that case / Total time of experimenting the case)* 100. (1)
4. The model average unobtrusiveness computes as follow:
   Average Model Unobtrusiveness= (Sum of all cases unobtrusiveness / number of cases). (2)

To measure the total time of experiment, the implemented software writes an entry into the windows event viewer at two specific times, starting work and finishing work. Whenever the user receives a privacy alarm, an entry would be written into the event viewer and when the user makes a decision for that alarm, another entry would be registered in the event viewer. The sum of all times that user spends to make decision is used in formula (2).

We use C#.Net 2005 (.Net2.00) mobile web applications to implement the model. We implemented three different tasks namely Buying Ticket, Reserving Appointment Time with University Lecturers, and Using University Smart Board and then based on the case design we measure the model unobtrusiveness.

Table 1 show results of the experiment (all times are measured in seconds). The Total Time of Work (TTW) column shows the amount of time from the user authentication phase until the user finishes using the service and saves data, Joining Context Interruption Time (JCIT), Service Registration Interruption Time (SRIT), and Login Page Interruption Time (LPIT) columns show the amount of time the user consumes on dealing with each privacy alarm in that phase. The other columns are calculated as follow:

Table 1. Experiment results of unobtrusiveness of privacy mechanisms (B standsfor Best, M for Medium, W for Worst scenarios)

Experiment ID.	Scenario ID	JCIT	SRIT	LPIT	TIT	TTW	U	AU
Case 1	B1	N/A	N/A	N/A	N/A	16.67	0%	8.41%
	M1	N/A	1.68	N/A	1.68	20.92	8.03%	
	W1	1.86	1.87	N/A	3.73	21.66	17.22%	
Case 2	B2	N/A	N/A	N/A	N/A	16.71	0%	6.88%
	M2	1.65	N/A	N/A	1.65	22.30	7.39%	
	W1	1.65	1.80	N/A	3.45	25.99	13.27%	
Case 3	B3	N/A	N/A	N/A	N/A	19.54	0%	7.83%
	M3	1.61	N/A	N/A	1.61	26.64	6.04%	
	W1	2.79	2.73	N/A	5.52	31.62	17.45%	
Case 4	B4	N/A	N/A	N/A	N/A	22.99	0%	7.55%
	M4	N/A	1.41	N/A	1.41	20.71	6.80%	
	W1	2.12	2.45	N/A	4.57	28.80	15.86%	
Case 5	B5	N/A	N/A	N/A	N/A	18.09	0%	7.44%
	M5	N/A	0.97	N/A	0.97	19.60	4.94%	
	W1	2.04	2.10	N/A	4.14	23.82	17.38%	
Case 6	B6	N/A	N/A	N/A	N/A	21.48	0%	7.10%
	M6	N/A	N/A	0.69	0.69	15.75	4.38%	
	W1	3.16	3.18	N/A	6.34	37.47	16.92%	
Case 7	B7	N/A	N/A	N/A	N/A	20.71	0%	7.13%
	M7	N/A	N/A	0.54	0.54	14.57	3.70%	
	W1	3.19	3.02	N/A	6.21	35.08	17.70%	
Case 8	B8	N/A	N/A	N/A	N/A	17.70	0%	8.19%
	M8	N/A	N/A	0.75	0.75	14.58	5.02%	
	W1	1.74	2.16	N/A	3.90	19.92	19.57%	
Case 9	B9	N/A	N/A	N/A	N/A	23.68	0%	7.36%
	M9	N/A	N/A	0.87	0.87	16.11	5.40%	
	W1	2.57	2.17	N/A	4.74	28.37	16.70%	
Case 10	B10	N/A	N/A	N/A	N/A	19.54	0%	8.06%
	M1	N/A	2.21	N/A	2.21	25.10	8.80%	
	W1	2.02	2.18	N/A	4.20	27.29	15.39%	
Case 11	B11	N/A	N/A	N/A	N/A	17.48	0%	6.88%
	M2	2.08	N/A	N/A	2.08	34.78	5.98%	
	W1	2.39	2.44	N/A	4.83	32.92	14.67%	
Case 12	B12	N/A	N/A	N/A	N/A	18.35	0%	8.37%
	M3	5.28	N/A	N/A	5.28	59.67	8.84%	
	W1	4.07	3.90	N/A	7.97	48.95	16.28%	
Case 13	B13	N/A	N/A	N/A	N/A	16.43	0%	7.61%
	M4	N/A	2.80	N/A	2.80	43.90	6.37%	
	W1	3.90	3.74	N/A	7.64	46.35	16.48%	
Case 14	B14	N/A	N/A	N/A	N/A	17.88	0%	7.43%
	M5	N/A	1.90	N/A	1.90	32.92	5.77%	
	W1	2.86	2.87	N/A	5.73	34.65	16.53%	
Case 15	B15	N/A	N/A	N/A	N/A	20.20	0%	6.97%
	M6	N/A	N/A	0.70	0.70	14.01	4.99%	
	W1	1.63	1.68	N/A	3.31	20.79	15.92%	
Case 16	B16	N/A	N/A	N/A	N/A	16.83	0%	6.68%
	M7	N/A	N/A	1.27	1.27	35.11	3.61%	
	W1	4.09	3.74	N/A	7.83	47.65	16.43%	
Case 17	B17	N/A	N/A	N/A	N/A	18.51	0%	7.44%
	M8	N/A	N/A	1.80	1.80	34.89	5.15%	
	W1	4.33	4.27	N/A	8.6	50.03	17.18%	
Average Unobtrusiveness of the model								7.49%

Total Interruption Time (TIT) = JCIT + SRIT + LPIT. (3)

Unobtrusiveness(U)=(TIT / TTW) * 100. (4)

Average Unobtrusiveness (AU)=(U Best +U Medium+U Worst)/3(for each experiment). (5)

The last line of the table 3 shows Average Unobtrusiveness of the Model (AUM), that is, the result of adding all experiments unobtrusiveness divided by the number of all cases. The experiment result shows that the AUM is 7.49%.

The factors that decrease the model unobtrusiveness are as follow:

1. The integrated privacy design of the model which considers the user privacy from user authentication phase until saving data phase.
2. As it was described earlier, the privacy alarms only rise for APL in the range of 25-75 which reduces the probability of rising privacy alarm.

3.2   Measuring the Model Expressiveness of Privacy Policies

The Expressiveness of Privacy Policies is determined by the support that privacy policies and privacy mechanisms of the model provide for mandatory and discretionary rules, context sensitivity, uncertainty handling, and conflict resolution.

To evaluate the model privacy policys ability to support mandatory and discretionary rules, the privacy policies should be expressed in a way that communicating parties can reliably distinguish between mandatory and discretionary rules and the model should have some trusted mechanisms to guarantee the use of mandatory rules on all parties. The model should provide some mechanisms to let communicating parties to choose among discretionary rules as well.

The model privacy policies are context sensitive if these privacy policies show context captured information, and have the ability to reflect context preferred and current privacy levels.

The model handles uncertain situations and resolve conflicts if its privacy policies have the ability to define these uncertain situations and the model has suitable mechanisms to manage each one.

We implemented three different tasks with different privacy levels and to show that the privacy files support mandatory and discretionary rules, reflect context sensitivity, handle uncertain situations, and resolve conflicts.

The following describes how the UPM fulfills each of the above mentioned factors:

1. Support for mandatory rules: The UPM has the ability to support mandatory rules through the mechanism that is used for applying owner-provided content privacy preferences on all parties. As it was said earlier, the content privacy preferences are mandatory rules defined by the owner and they have to be applied on all parties, the owner provides the service contents just after receiving the confirmation of applying content privacy policies on all parties. The same mechanism can be applied for all other mandatory rules as well. The mandatory rules position on each party defined in the model are designed to be distinguishable from discretionary rules.

The developed model support for this factor can be shown by comparing user and service provider privacy policy files before and during service usage phase.

2. Support for discretionary rules: Discretionary rules are the rules that each party defines on its own side and tries to adhere in communicating with other parties. Privacy preferences files reflect their related party discretionary rules. Each party tries to achieve these preferred privacy levels in communicating with other parties but it might communicate with lower or higher privacy levels based on the privacy agreements too. The mechanism for applying discretionary rules is based on the user APL. If the user APL is less than 25 or more than 75, the system decides automatically on applying the proper privacy policy, however in APL between 25 and 75 the user receives an alarm and has to make a decision. The implemented model shows the support for discretionary rules by comparing the privacy preferences and privacy policy files of each party before and after each phase. The similarities between these two show the situation that the partys discretionary rules have been applied while the differences show the situations that other partys discretionary rules have been applied.

3. Context sensitivity: Our model portals gather context information in the device level. The current status of the context devices is reflected in Device Privacy Policy File but the device's preferred privacy levels are reflected in the Device Privacy Preferences File. Context Privacy Preferences File shows the preferred context privacy but the Context Privacy Policy File reflects the current context privacy. The above files provide context sensitivity for the model.

4. Managing uncertain situations: The uncertain situations happen when the user requested privacy level is less than the privacy level that can be provided by the other party. Our models privacy policies are expressive in a way that uncertain situations can be detected with simple comparison and they get managed in a way to provide the highest possible privacy level for the user. For example if the user connects to the bank portal which provides higher privacy level than the requested level by the user, the system works with a higher privacy level of the bank portal. The same mechanism is used in all other uncertain situations.

5. Conflict resolution: A conflict occurs when the other party could not provide the requested privacy level. The mechanisms for resolving the conflicts are based on the APL. If the APL is less than 25 the system resolves conflict situation through accepting other party provided privacy level. If APL is more than 75 the user gives up using the service in any conflict situation. For the APL between 25 and 75 the system provides choice and consent for the user.

The above discussion shows that the UPM supports all four characteristics of Expressiveness of privacy policies.

3.3   Discussion of User Control over Private Information

The model user control over private information is measured by the number of content, identity, location, and time privacy types that model supports.

The model is able to provide the content privacy if it supports some mechanisms to assure user that during content production, transferring, using, and saving, only the parties which previously authorized by the user get access to the contents.

The model is able to provide user control over identity privacy if it lets users choose to be anonymous, use pseudonym identities, or use their real identity in communicating with other parties, inform other parties about the current user identity privacy policy, and reliably apply it in user communications.

The model is able to provide user control over location privacy if it lets users choose the level of location information that other parties have access to and applies the user selected level in communications. The user should be able to select among not providing any location information, or confirming his existence in a certain area, or providing his exact location information to the other parties.

The model provides user control over time privacy if it lets users define time periods for all of their privacy policies and controls other parties' access to user time policy and guarantees the application of time policy on all parties that have related data to a specific time policy. The following discusses the UPM ability to support each privacy type.

1. Content privacy: The UPM provides two levels of content privacy, privacy of the content in communication, and content privacy for the services contents. The UPM provides content privacy in communication by using two kinds of keys as follow:
   (a) The location dependent keys that encrypts and decrypts information based on the geographical location information of the user. These keys are used in location dependent privacy policies.
   (b) The public/private keys with ECC algorithms that provide content confidentiality for transferring information between mobile devices.
   The UPM provides content privacy through defining ¡Information Space¿ tags that specify the location and time privacy for each parts of the content on each party in the service using and saving data phases, so the UPM provides content privacy without increasing the size of the transformed or saved content.
   The above two mechanisms guarantee the content privacy for the entire data life time and provide user control over his content privacy.
2. Identity privacy: All parties specify their ID privacy preferences in their privacy preferences files that can be one of transparent ID, protected ID, or private ID in communication with other parties. The user light house plays the main role in preserving user identity, in private ID policy the light house does not divulge any information of the user, in protected ID the light house confirms user access level through a third trusted party, and in transparent ID status the light house divulges real user identity to the other parties. The UPM provides identity privacy in three levels for all communicating parties.

3. Location privacy: The UPM provides three levels of location privacy namely transparent location, protected location, or private location. The user portal plays the main role to preserve location privacy. In private location privacy, the portal completely hides the user location from other parties. In protected location, the portal confirms the user existence in its controlled area without divulging the users exact location. In transparent location policy, the portal provides the exact geographical location of the user to the other parties.

4. Time privacy: The UPM provides three levels of time privacy namely transparent time, protected time, and private time for each party which specifies in its privacy preferences file. Control of time privacy is on the party that receives services or data. In transparent time the parties do not put any time restriction, protected time confines all parties communication, services, or data saving only to a specific time period, and real time policy limits the communication and data saving period to only the communication time between these parties.

As described, the UPM could provide all communicating parties with control over content, identity, location, and time.

3.4   Discussion of Model Scalability

A model is scalable if it provides the following supports:

1. A common communication platform for communicating between devices. This platform should be supported by different device vendors and it has to have the ability to transfer privacy policies properly.

2. Distribution of decision making processes. There should not be any centralized point for decision in the model that confines the model scalability.

As it was described the models scalability measures two factors namely the model platform independence and its ability to make all decisions distributed. The following discusses the proposed UPM supports for both of the above factors:

1. Platform independence: The UPM provides platform independence by using XML as a common communication platform. XML format lets any devices with any embedded platform which just has the ability to send and receive data through XML tags, to join and use the model. With fast spreading of XML acceptance on different platforms, selecting XML provides higher level of platform independence.

2. No centralized decision making point: There is no centralized decision making point in the UPM. All decisions and responsibilities are distributed among three parties in three layers of the model. Portals are responsible for location privacy in context layer, light houses are responsible for identity privacy in services layer, and time privacy decisions are making on the receiver party itself. So there is no centralized decision making point in our model which confines the model scalability.

So the UPM could provide both scalability factors.

4   Conclusion

In this paper we showed that the UPM could provide users full control over private information by providing user control over content, identity, location, and time privacy. The model is highly scalable because of its distributed decision making processes and its platform independence and its unobtrusiveness is less than 10%. Finally we showed that the UPM policies are able to support mandatory and discretionary rules, context sensitivity, uncertainty handling, and conflict resolution to provide high expressiveness. This research can be extended to the following areas:

1. Adding mechanisms to support concurrent, multiple authentication methods to increase the accuracy of the user APL that increases the model privacy.
2. Applying secret sharing techniques to overcome the probability of collusion attack that can result from the collusion of light houses and portals that will divulge parties private information, this technique can be used for eliminating the software trust-ability assumption too.
3. Adding ontology to the model that allows devices to communicate without any information of their XML schema format or any prior agreement about it.

References

1. Ranganathan, A., Al-Muhtadi, J., Biehl, J., Ziebart, B., Campbell, R.H., Bailey, B.: Towards a pervasive computing benchmark. In: 3rd International Conf. on Pervasive Computing and Communications Workshop, pp. 194–198 (2005)
2. Bhaskar, P., Sheikh, S.I.: Privacyin Pervasive Computing and Open Issues. In: International Conference on Availability, Reliability, and Security, pp. 110–118 (2007)
3. Cheng, H.S., Zhang, D., Tan, J.G.: Protection of Privacy in Pervasive Computing Environments. In: International Conference on Information Technology: Coding and Computing, pp. 242–247 (2005)
4. Beresford, A.R., Stajano, F.: Location Privacy in Pervasive Computing. IEEE Pervasive Computing 2(2), 40–46 (2003)
5. Beresford, A.R., Stajano, F.: Mix Zones- User Privacy in Location-aware Services. In: International Workshop on Pervasive Computing and Communication Security. IEEE, Los Alamitos (2004)
6. Myles, G., Friday, A., Davies, N.: Preserving privacy in environments with location-based applications. IEEE Pervasive Computing 2(1), 56–64 (2003)
7. Campbell, R., Al-Muhtadi, J., Naldurg, P., Sampemane, G., Mikunas, M.D.: Towards Security and Privacy for Pervasive Computing. In: Proceeding of International Symposium on Software Security (2002)
8. Langheinrich, M.: A Privacy Awareness System for Ubiquitous Computing Environments. In: Ubicomp, pp.72-74 (2006)
9. Myles, G., Firday, A., Davies, N.: Preserving privacy in environments with location-based applications. IEEE Pervasive Computing 2(1), 56–64 (2003)

10. Beresford, A.R., Stajano, F.: Location Privacy in Pervasive Computing. IEEE Pervasive Computing 2(1), 46–55 (2003)
11. Tentori, M., Favela, M.J., Rodriguez, D., Gonzalez, V.M.: Supporting Quality of Privacy (QoP) in Pervasive Computing. In: Mexican International Conference on Computer Science, pp. 58–67 (2005)
12. Dehghantanha, A., Mahmod, R., Udzir, N.: A XML based, User-centered Privacy Model in Pervasive Computing Systems. International Journal of Computer Science and Networking Security 9(10), 167–173 (2009)

An Innovative Linkage Learning Based on Differences in Local Optimums

Hamid Parvin, Behrouz Minaei-Bidgoli, and B. Hoda Helmi

School of Computer Engineering, Iran University of Science and Technology (IUST),
Tehran, Iran
{parvin,b_minaei,helmi}@iust.ac.ir

Abstract. Genetic Algorithms (GAs) are categorized as search heuristics and have been broadly applied to optimization problems. These algorithms have been used for solving problems in many applications, but it has been shown that simple GA is not able to effectively solve complex real world problems. For proper solving of such problems, knowing the relationships between decision variables which is referred to as linkage learning is necessary. In this paper a linkage learning approach is proposed that utilizes the special features of the decomposable problems to solve them. The proposed approach is called Local Optimums based Linkage Learner (LOLL). The LOLL algorithm is capable of identifying the groups of variables which are related to each other (known as linkage groups), no matter if these groups are overlapped or different in size. The proposed algorithm, unlike other linkage learning techniques, is not done along with optimization algorithm; but it is done in a whole separated phase from optimization search. After finding linkage group information by LOLL, an optimization search can use this information to solve the problem. LOLL is tested on some benchmarked decomposable functions. The results show that the algorithm is an efficient alternative to other linkage learning techniques.

Keywords: Linkage Learning; Optimization Problems, Decomposable Functions.

1 Introduction

GAs are the most popular algorithms in the category of Evolutionary Algorithms (EAs). These algorithms are widely used to solve real-world problems. However when it comes to solve difficult problems, GA has deficiencies. One of the main problems of simple GAs is their blindness and oblivion about the linkage between the problem variables. It is long time that the importance of the linkage learning is recognized in success of the optimization search. There are a lot of linkage learning techniques. Some are based on perturbation methodology, some are categorized in the class of probabilistic model building approaches and some are the techniques that adapt the linkages along with the evolutionary process by employing special operators or representations.

In this paper a new linkage learning approach, which is called LOLL is proposed. The proposed algorithm as its title implies, does not fall in the above mentioned categories, but it is a linkage group identification approach which tries to identify

Á. Herrero and E. Corchado (Eds.): CISIS 2011, LNCS 6694, pp. 285–292, 2011.

multivariate dependencies of complex problems in acceptable amount of time and with admissible computational complexity.

2   Background

In this section, Deterministic Hill Climbers (DHC) which will be used later in our algorithm and challenging problems which are used to explain and test the proposed algorithm are described. Firstly, some terms should be defined. A partial solution denotes specific bits on a subset of string positions. For example, if we consider 100-bit binary strings, a 1 in the second position and a 0 in the seventh position is a partial solution. A building block is a partial solution which is contained in an optimum and is superior to its competitors. Each additively separable problem is composed of number of partitions each of which is called a "linkage group".

In this study, DHC [10] are used to search for local optimums. In each step, the DHC flips the bit in the string that will produce the maximum improvement in fitness value. This process can be allowed to iterate until no single bit flip produces additional movement. DHC starts with a random string.

2.1   Challenging Problems

Deficiencies of GAs were first demonstrated with simple fitness functions called deceptive functions of order k. Deception functions of order k are defined as a sum of more elementary deceptive functions of k variables. In a deceptive function the global optimum $(1, ,1)$ is isolated, whereas the neighbors of the second best fitness solution $(0, ,0)$ have large fitness values. Because of this special shape of the landscape, GAs are deceived by the fitness distribution and most GAs converge to $(0, ,0)$. This class of functions has a great theoretical and practical importance. An n-bit Trap5 function has one global optimum in the string where the value of all the bits is 1, and it has $(2^{n/5}) - 1$ local optimums. The local optimums are those individuals that the values of the variables in a linkage group are either 1 or 0 (they are all 1, or they are all 0) [8].

Also another additively separable function called deceptive3 [8]. An n-bit Deceptive3 function like an n-bit Trap3 function has one global optimum in the string where the value of all the bits is 1, and it has $(2^{n/3}) - 1$ local optimums.

For yet another more challenging problem we use an additively separable function, one bit Overlapping-Trap5. An n-bit Overlapping-Trap5 function has one global optimum in the string where the value of all the bits is 1 just similar to Trap5 function, and it has $(2^{(n-1)/4}) - 1$ local optimums. The local optimums are those individuals that the values of the variables in a linkage group are either 1 or 0 (they are all 1, or they are all 0) again similar to Trap5 function [8].

2.2   Linkage Learning

There are lots of approaches in the class of linkage adaptation techniques. Linkage learning GA [2] uses a special probabilistic expression mechanism and a unique combination of the (gene number, allele) coding scheme and an exchange crossover operator to create an evolvable genotypic structure. In [4] punctuation marks are added to the chromosome representation. These bits indicate if any position on the chromosome is a crossover point or in another words, a linkage group boundary. Linkage evolving genetic operator (LEGO) [5] is another linkage adaptation strategy that in order to achieve the linkages, each gene has associated with it two Boolean flags. These two flags determine whether the gene will link to the genes to its left and right. The two adjacent genes are assumed to be linked if the appropriate flags are both set to true. Therefore building blocks are consecutive linked genes on the chromosome.

Linkage learning is necessary when there are epistatic linkages between variables. Estimation of distribution algorithms (EDAs) are among the most powerful GAs which try to find these epistatic linkages through building probabilistic models that summarize the information of promising solutions in the current population. In another words, by using probabilistic models these algorithms seek to find linkage between variables of the problem. In each generation they find as much information as possible about the variable dependencies from the promising solutions of the population. Knowing this information, the population of the next generation is created. There are numbers of estimation of distribution algorithms which their differences are often in the model building part. Bayesian Networks and marginal product models are examples of the probabilistic models that have been used by Bayesian Optimization Algorithm (BOA) [1] and Extended Compact Genetic Algorithm (ECGA) [3]. Although EDAs scale polynomial in terms of number of fitness evaluations, the probabilistic model building phase is usually computationally expensive. Perturbation-based method, detect linkage group by injecting perturbations in the population of individuals and inspecting the fitness change caused by the perturbation. Gene expression messy genetic algorithm (gemGA) which uses transcription operator for identifying linkage group is classified in this category.

Dependency Structure Matrix Genetic Algorithm (DSMGA) [8] is another approach which models the relationship among variables using Dependency Structure Matrix (DSM). In DSMGA a clustering method is used for identifying the linkage groups. In spite of these efforts, none of the algorithms have been claimed to be stronger that than Hierarchical Bayesian Optimization Algorithms (HBOA) [6] and [7] which itself in spite of its polynomial scalability in terms of the number of fitness evaluations, is computationally expensive.

3 Local Optimum Based Linkage Learner: LOLL

The main idea in the proposed approach for identifying the multivariate dependencies is using local optimums. But how the local optimums can lead us to identification of the linkage groups?

Local optimums of "Additively Separable problems" have some unique features. As it is obvious, the global optimum of an additively separable problem is the one that all of its building blocks are identified. In another words, in the global optimum, all of the linkage groups of the problem have the highest possible contribution to the overall fitness. But in local optimum solutions, not all of the building blocks are found and those partitions or sub-problems of the problem which their optimum values are not found are occupied by the best competitors of the superior partial solution.

In additively separable problems there are lots of these local optimum solutions. Actually number of such solutions is directly dependant on length of the problem and number of partitions (or sub-problems or linkage groups) of the problem. It can be said that each local solution contains at least one building block (except the one with all 0s) and therefore comparison of the optimum solutions can lead us to identification of the linkage groups.

The following example can reveal this concept more clearly. Consider a 12 bit Trap3 function. This function has one global optimum 111111111111 and $(2^{12/3}) - 1 =$ (15) local optimums. The strings are local optimum if the bits corresponding to each trap partition are equal, but the value of all the bits in at least one trap partition is 0. Some of local optimums are shown in table 1: A simple comparison between first local solution and fifth local solution helps us find the second linkage group and comparison between third local solution and fourth local solution helps us find the first linkage group.

Now, the algorithm can be explained and the example is continued later. In an overall view, there are two phases of search and analysis. In search phase some local optimums are found and in analysis phase the comparisons between these local solutions are done. If number of local solutions is not enough to discover all the linkage groups of the problem, the local solutions for the remained bits of the problem that are not assigned to a linkage group yet are to be found by the comparison of the newly found local optimums. This process repeats until remained undiscovered linkage groups of the problem are identified. The process will end if all the variables of the problem are assigned to a linkage group. In the search phase, K DHCs are initialized randomly and set to search the landscape (with length (Xs) number of variables). When each DHC finds a peak in the landscape and no movements are possible, that solution which is a local optimum will be saved in a set named *HighModals*.

After the search phase, analysis phase starts. In the analysis phase, linkage groups should be identified by comparing different local optimum solutions.

Table 1. Some of the local optimums for Trap3 size 12

1	1	1	0	0	0	0	0	0	1	1	1
0	0	0	1	1	1	1	1	1	0	0	0
0	0	0	1	1	1	0	0	0	1	1	1
1	1	1	1	1	1	0	0	0	0	0	0
1	1	1	1	1	1	0	0	0	1	1	1

A comparison method is needed for the analysis phase. The comparison method should be able to segregate the BBs of the local solutions and yet be simple and uncomplicated. XOR operation is a good candidate for this purpose. This is due to the fact that the local and global solutions of a decomposable function are the two strings with the most differences in their appearance and binary strings are used to code the individuals.

Therefore in the analysis phase, each two local optimum solutions in the *HighModals* set are *XORed* with each other and the results are stored in *XORed* set. Therefore *XORed* is an array of arrays. The strings with least number of ones are found. Number of 1s (r) in these strings is considered the length of linkage group. And these strings (string with length r) are put in the set *DiscoveredBBs* which is an array of arrays and contains the ultimate results (all the identified linkage groups). All of the other members of *XORed* set with more than r 1s are put in the set *XsArray* which is again array of arrays. After identifying some of the linkage groups, the algorithm is recursively called for finding linkage groups in other parts of the string which are not identified yet. The undiscovered parts are the *XORed* strings which their length is more than r or those variables of the problem which are not in the *XORed* set. Therefore those bits in the *Xs* which are not in the*XORed* set are added as a separate member to the *XsArray* (step A.4 in the algorithm).

As it is mentioned before we need a mechanism to balance the time spent in the search phase. For this reason a parameter, *sp* is contrived which determines when to leave the search phase. Leaving the search phase takes place with the probability *sp*. If *sp* is small, the set *HighModals* will become bigger because the search phase takes longer and as a consequence more local solutions are found. Analysis of huge number of solutions is difficult and unnecessary. On the other hand by comparison of too few local solutions there is a little chance of identifying all the linkage groups of the problem. So *sp* parameter should be determined wisely considering the length of the problem. If the length of the problem is more, the number of local solutions needed to identify the linkage groups is more. If each variable of the problem is assigned to at least one linkage group, the LOLL algorithm terminates. The pseudo code of LOLL algorithm is shown in Algorithm 1.

Xs is an array with length *n* containing the indexes of the problem variables. *DiscoveredBBs* is an array of arrays, containing the discovered linkage groups. Each linkage group is shown with an array containing the indexes of the variables in the linkage group. *HighModals* is an array containing the local optimums of the problem. *XORed* is an array of arrays containing the result of XOR operation on local solutions. Each XOR result is shown with an array containing the indexes of bits which their value is 1 after doing XOR operation. *DeterminedBits* is an array which contains the indexes of the variables which their corresponding linkage group is identified. *XsArray* is an array of arrays containing those parts which should be searched again for identification of the remaining linkage groups.

As it is obvious, the only parameter which should be set wisely is *sp*. In the future work, we address solutions to adjust this parameter automatically. Complexity of the algorithm will be discussed later. Now, we go back to our simple example: *Xs* is here the array *Xs* = { 1, 2, …, 12} *HighModals* set is in Table 1.

XORed set of our simple example: [1,2,3,4,5,6] , [1,2,3,7,8,9] , [7,8,9,10,11,12] , [4,5,6] , [1,2,3,7,8,9,10,11,12] , [1,2,3]
DiscoveredBBs set so far: [4,5,6] , [1,2,3]
DeterminedBits set: [1,2,3,4,5,6]
XsArray: [1,2,3,7,8,9] , [7,8,9,10,11,12] , [1,2,3,7,8,9,10,11,12]

LOLL algorithm is again called for three sub-problems in *XsArray*. The algorithm could be simplified but it is developed in a general form so that it can also identify the overlapping linkage groups. The experimental results regarding overlapping linkage groups and complexity analysis of them are kept to be reported in our future work.

```
X_s=(1...n);
r=0;
DiscoveredBBs=LOL(X_s)
    Search Phase:
        S.1. Run DHC_s;
        S.2. Save local solutions to HighModals set.
        S.3. If p--exit--search < (sp) goto Analysis phase.
             Else goto S.1.
    Analysis Phase:
        A.1. Perform XOR between each two members of HighModals set.
             Put the XORed into XORed set.
        A.2. Find the strings with least number of 1s in XORed set.
             Set its number of 1s = r as length of BB, and put those XORed members
             to set DiscoveredBBs.
        A.3. Delete those XORed members which their length is equal to length X_s.
        A.4. Put all the indexes of bits of each member of XORed set which its length
             is equal to r into a set DeterminedBits.
        A.5. For each member of XORed set i,
             If((length(i)>r)^all of the bits of i which are not in DeterminedBits)
                  Put that in the set XsArray;
        A.6. Put the (X_s-(indexes of all the bits which value 1 in the XORed set)) into
             XsArray;
        A.7. If all of the variables of the problem ∈ DeterminedBits
                  \*all of the variables are assigned to linkage group (at least) *\
                  Terminates the algorithm.
             Else
                  for i=1 to length XsArray Do
                      DiscoveredBBs=LOL(XsArray[i]);
```

Fig. 1. Local Optimum based Linkage Learning Algorithm

If we have two or more optimums in each building block, the method has some drawbacks in finding the final *DiscoveredBBs*. For handling this drawback we use each of these *DiscoveredBBs* as one cluster. Then cluster ensemble problem can be solved by cutting a minimal number of clusters (hyperedges) using approach the HyperGraph-Partitioning Algorithm (HGPA) [9].

4   Empirical Results

For all tested problems, 30 independent runs are performed and our approach is required to find all the linkage groups accurately in all the 30 runs. The performance of LOLL is measured by the average number of fitness evaluations until it terminates. The results are summarized in the Fig 2-3. All this results are obtained without applying the clustering algorithm. As it is obvious, the finding of building blocks is sub-quadratic either in non-overlapping challenging problems, or in overlapping ones. It is worthy to note that the time order of the algorithm in the challenging problems increases as the size of building blocks increases no matter it is overlapping functions. This is very important result, because as the size of building blocks in the BOA and in the HBOA, the times orders of these algorithms increase exponentially [8].

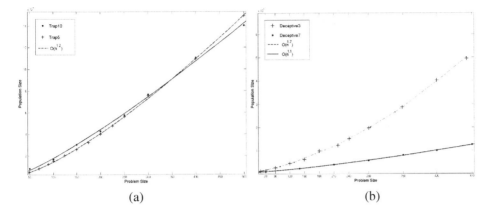

(a)   (b)

Fig. 2. (a) Number of fitness evaluations vs. problem size for trap5 and trap10. (b) Number of fitness evaluations vs. problem size for deceptive3 and deceptive7.

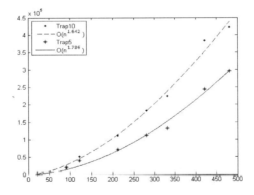

Fig. 3. Number of fitness evaluations vs. problem size one-bit overlap trap5 and trap10

5 Conclusions

With the purpose of learning the linkages in the complex problem a novel approach is proposed. There are other approaches that are claimed to be able to solve those challenging problems in tractable polynomial time. But the proposed approach does not classified into the existence categories. This work has looked at the problem from whole different points of view. Our method is based on some properties of additively decomposable problems in order to identify the linkage groups. The amazing property of additively decomposable problems that our method is based on is the special form of their local optimums which a bunch of them would give us lots of information about the linkage groups. The proposed algorithm is called LOLL. The algorithm is capable of solving the challenging problems effectively.

LOLL is capable of identifying the linkage groups in a simple and straightforward manner. As it is shown in terms of numbers of fitness evaluation the complexity of LOLL has been $O(n^{1.2})$ in the two test cases over a trap problem and $O(n^{1.7})$ and $O(n^{1.1})$ in deceptive3 and deceptive7 problems. Moreover we believe that the proposed algorithm (without any major changes) is capable of finding the overlapping building blocks. The result testing the proposed approach on overlapping problems and more detailed analysis of the algorithm will be represented in our future work. Analyzing the proposed algorithm in the context of optimization problem and along with an optimization search is one of the tasks that can be done as future works. Comparing the results with the other approaches is also left as future work.

References

1. Audebert, P., Hapiot, P.: Effect of powder deposition. J. Electroanal. Chem. 361, 177 (1993)
2. Newman, J.: Electrochemical Systems, 2nd edn. Prentice-Hall, Englewood Cliffs (1991)
3. Hillman, A.R.: Electrochemical Science and Technology of Polymers, vol. 1, ch. 5. Elsevier, Amsterdam (1987)
4. Miller, B.: Geelong, Vic. J. Electroanal. Chem. 168, 19–24 (1984)
5. Jones: Personal Communication (1992)
6. Pelikan, M., Goldberg, D.E.: Escaping hierarchical traps with competent genetic algorithms. In: Genetic and Evolutionary Computation Conference, GECCO, pp. 511–518 (2001)
7. Pelikan, M., Goldberg, D.E.: A hierarchy machine: Learning to optimize from nature and humans. Complexity 8(5) (2003)
8. Pelikan, M.: Hierarchical Bayesian optimization algorithm: Toward a new generation of evolutionary algorithms. Springer, Heidelberg (2005)
9. Strehl, A., Ghosh, J.: Cluster Ensembles — A Knowledge Reuse Framework for Combining Multiple Partitions. Journal of Machine Learning Research 3, 583–617 (2002)
10. Stuart, R., Peter, N.: Artificial Intelligence: A Modern Approach, 2nd edn., pp. 111–114. Prentice-Hall, Englewood Cliffs (2003)

A New Particle Swarm Optimization for Dynamic Environments

Hamid Parvin[1], Behrouz Minaei[1], and Sajjad Ghatei[2]

[1] School of Computer Engineering, Iran University of Science and Technology (IUST),
Tehran, Iran
{parvin,minaei}@iust.ac.ir
[2] Department of Computer Engineering, Islamic Azad University Ahar Branch,
Young Researchers Club, Ahar, Iran
s.ghatei@qiau.ac.ir

Abstract. Dynamic optimization in which global optima and local optima change over time is always a hot research topic. It has been shown that particle swarm optimization works well facing into dynamic environments. From another hands, learning automata is considered as an intelligent tool (agent) which can learn what action is the best one interacting with its environment. The great deluge algorithm is also a search algorithm applied to optimization problems. All these algorithms have their special drawbacks and advantages. In this paper it is examined can the combination of these algorithms results in the better performance dealing with dynamic problems. Indeed a learning automaton is employed per each particle of the swarm to decide whether the corresponding particle updates its velocity (and consequently its position) considering the best global particle, the best local particle or the combination global and local particles. Water level in the deluge algorithm is used in the progress of the algorithm. Experimental results on different dynamic environments modeled by moving peaks benchmark show that the combination of these algorithms outperforms Particle Swarm Optimization (PSO) algorithm, Fast Multi-Swarm Optimization (FMSO) method, a similar particle swarm algorithm for dynamic environments, for all tested environments.

Keywords: Particle Swarm Optimization, Great Deluge, Learning Automaton, Moving Peaks, Dynamic Environments.

1 Introduction

The standard particle swarm optimization algorithms have been performed well for static environment. Also it is shown that original PSO can't handle dynamic environments. So researchers turn to new variations of PSO to overcome its inefficiency [1].

Hu and Eberhart proposed re-randomization PSO (RPSO) for optimization in dynamic environments [13] in which some particles randomly are relocated after a change is detected or when the diversity is lost, to prevent losing the diversity. Li and Dam [14] showed that a grid-like neighborhood structure used in FGPSO [11] can

Á. Herrero and E. Corchado (Eds.): CISIS 2011, LNCS 6694, pp. 293–300, 2011.

perform better than RPSO in high dimensional dynamic environments by restricting the information sharing and preventing the convergence of particles to the global best position, thereby enhancing population diversity. Janson and Middendorf [7] proposed hierarchical PSO (HPSO), a tree-like structure hierarchical PSO, and reported improvements over standard PSO for dynamic environments. They also suggested Partitioned Hierarchical PSO in which a hierarchy of particles is partitioned into several sub-swarms for a limited number of generations after a change in the environment is detected [8]. Lung and Dumitrcsc [19] used two collaborating populations with same size which one swarm is responsible for preserving the diversity of the particles by using a crowding differential evolutionary algorithm [20] while the other keeps track of global optimum with a PSO algorithm.

Li and Yang proposed a FMSO method which maintains the diversity through the run [16]. To meet this goal two types of swarm are used: a parent swarm which maintains the diversity and detects the promising search area in the whole search space using a fast evolutionary programming algorithm, and a group of child swarms which explore the local area for the local optima found by the parent using a fast PSO algorithm. This mechanism makes the child swarms spread out over the highest multiple peaks, as many as possible, and guarantees to converge to a local optimum in a short time. Moreover, in [15], the authors introduced a clustering particle swarm optimizer in which a clustering algorithm partitions the swarm into several sub-swarms each searching for a local optimum.

Liu et al. [17] introduced compound particle swarm optimization (CPSO) utilizing a new type of particles which helps explore the search space more comprehensively after a change occurred in the environment. In another work, they used composite particles which help quickly find the promising optima in the search space while maintaining the diversity by a scattering operator [18].

Hashemi and Meybodi introduced cellular PSO, a hybrid model of cellular automata and PSO [6]. In cellular PSO, a cellular automaton partitions the search space into cells. At any time, in some cells of the cellular automaton a group of particles search for a local optimum using their best personal experiences and the best solution found in their neighborhood cells. To prevent losing the diversity, a limit on the number of particles in each cell is imposed. Furthermore, to track the changes in the environment, in [6] particles in cellular PSO change their role to quantum particles and perform a random search around the previously found optima for a few iterations after a change is detected in the environment.

Kamosi et al. propose some variations of PSO that can perform well for dynamic environments [9]. In their work, they proposed a multi-swarm algorithm for dynamic environments which address the diversity loss problem by introducing two types of swarm: a parent swarm, which explores the search space to find promising area containing local optima and several non-overlapping child swarms, each of which is responsible for exploiting a promising area found by the parent swarm.

2 Related Work

A learning automaton (LA) is an adaptive decision-making unit that is situated in a random environment and learns the optimal state-action set through many repeated interactions with its environment. The actions are chosen according to a specific probability distribution which is updated based on the environment responses to the action taken by the automaton. Given a finite number of actions that can be performed in a random environment, when a specific action is taken place the environment provides a random response which is either favorable or unfavorable. The objective in the design of the automaton is to determine how the choice of the action at any stage should be guided by past actions and responses [21].

The PSO is first introduced by Kennedy and Eberhart [10]. In PSO, a potential solution for a problem is considered as a bird, which is called a particle, flies through a D-dimensional space and adjusts its position according to its own experience and other particles'. In PSO, a particle is represented by its position vector x and its velocity vector v.

The great deluge algorithm (GD) is first introduced by Dueck [5], but unfortunately was not widely useful in succeeding years. This local search meta-heuristic is different from its predecessors (e.g. Hill-Climbing or Simulated Annealing) in the acceptance of a candidate solution from a neighborhood. The GD algorithm accepts all solutions, for which absolute values of the cost function are less than or equal to the current boundary value, called "level". The local search starts with the initial value of "level" equal to an initial cost function and during the search its value is monotonically reduced. A decrement of the reduction (defined by the user) appears as a single algorithmic parameter.

3   Proposed Combination Framework of PSO, LA and GD Algorithms

To get rid of the premature convergence of PSO algorithm, it is needed to use a mechanism that produces perturbation in population. A very promising method is to turn to multi-swarm mechanisms. In the multi-swarm mechanism, there must be a parent swarm which is responsible for finding promising area in the search space and also some child swarms which are created to exploit the new found promising area [1-3] and [10].

This paper differently deals with the premature problem. It uses a PSO in which each particle uses a learning automaton based on which the particle decides how to update its velocity. Indeed each automaton learns how to behave in predefined situations. These situations contain variance of the best fitness of local optima and the distance of the particle to its local and global optima. The learning of the automaton is based on feedbacks received from the environment. A feedback per each particle is set according to its current position's fitness and the previous position's fitness. It means that if the previous position's fitness is higher than the current position's, the action taken on the previous position to reach the current position is punishes else it is rewarded.

In the proposed method, the states of learning automaton A_j is a triple denoted by (var, dis^j_1, dis^j_2), where var, dis^j_1 and dis^j_2 are three quantitative variables belong to $\{0,1,2\}$. To calculate var first maximum distance between two arbitrary selected X^i_l ($i \in 1..N$) is defined as max_disqp.

$$\max\_disqp = \max(\|X_l^q - X_l^p\|) \quad q, p \in 1..N \tag{1}$$

Then the normalized variance of X_l^i ($i \in 1..N$) denoted by $nvar$ is defined as follow.

$$n\,var = Var(X_l^q)/\max\_disqp \quad q \in 1..N \tag{2}$$

where $Var(X_l^q)$ is the variance of X^q_1. Now var is calculated according the following equations.

$$var = \begin{cases} 0 & n\,var < v_1 \\ 1 & v_1 \le n\,var < v_2 \\ 2 & v_2 \le n\,var \end{cases} \tag{3}$$

where v_1 and v_2 are two user-specified thresholds. For calculating $dis^j{}_1$, max_disp is first defined as following equation.

$$\max\_disp = \max(\|X_g - X_l^p\|) \quad p \in 1..N \tag{4}$$

Then the normalized distance between $X^j{}_l$ and X_g denoted by $ndis^j{}_l$ is defined as follow.

$$ndis_1^j = (X_g - X_l^j)/\max\_disp \tag{5}$$

Now $dis^j{}_l$ is calculated according the following equations.

$$dis_1^j = \begin{cases} 0 & ndis_1^j < d_{11} \\ 1 & d_{11} \le ndis_1^j < d_{12} \\ 2 & d_{12} \le ndis_1^j \end{cases} \tag{6}$$

where d_{11} and d_{12} are two user-specified thresholds. And finally for calculating $dis^j{}_2$, max_disq is first defined as following equation.

$$\max\_disq = \max(\|X_p - X_l^p\|) \quad p \in 1..N \tag{7}$$

Then the normalized distance between $X^j{}_l$ and x_j denoted by $ndis^j{}_2$ is defined as following.

$$ndis_2^j = (X_p - X_l^p)/\max\_disq \tag{8}$$

Now $dis^j{}_2$ is calculated according the following equation.

$$dis_2^j = \begin{cases} 0 & ndis_2^j < d_{21} \\ 1 & d_{21} \le ndis_2^j < d_{22} \\ 2 & d_{22} \le ndis_2^j \end{cases} \tag{9}$$

where d_{21} and d_{22} are two user-specified thresholds. Pseudo code of the proposed algorithm is presented in the Fig. 1. In this code r_1 and r_2 are both 0.5. Also all w_1, w_2 and w_3 are 0.33.

```
counter=0
max_fitness=maximum of possible fitness in an arbitrary problem setting
level= max_fitness
Repeat
    counter=counter+1
    step = exp( -1*counter)*max_fitness
    each particle i
    Update particle position x_i According to one of the three below equations
            For each particle i
                compute situation according to equation 3, 6 and 9
                a=make_decide(Automata_i, situation)
                if(a=0)
```

$$v_i(t+1) = w_1 v_i(t) + w_2(x_i^l(t) - x_i(t)) + w_3(x^g(t) - x_i(t))$$

```
                elseif(a=1)
```

$$v_i(t+1) = r_1 v_i(t) + r_2(x_i^l(t) - x_i(t))$$

```
                elseif(a=2)
```

$$v_i(t+1) = random$$

```
            Endif
            End for
    x_i'=x_i+v_i
    if(f(x_i')>f(x_i))
        punish(Automata_i,situation,a)
    else
        reward(Automata_i,situation,a))
    End if
    if(f(x_i')<level)
        x_i=x_i'
    End if
    if(f(xi')<f(xg))
        x_g=x_i'
    End if
    if(f(x_i')<f(x_i^l))
        x_i^l=x_i
    End if
    level=level+step
Until termination criterion reached
```

Fig. 1. Pseudo code of the proposed algorithm

4 Experimental Study

Branke [4] introduced a dynamic benchmark problem, called moving peaks benchmark (MPB) problem. In this problem, there are some peaks in a multi-dimensional space, where the height, width and position of each peak change during the environment change. This function is widely used as a benchmark for dynamic environments in literature [12] and [17].

Table 1. Parameters of Moving Peaks Benchmark

Parameter	Value
number of peaks	10
f	every 5000 evaluations
height severity	7.0
width severity	1.0
peak shape	cone
shift length s	{0.0}
number of dimensions D	5
A	[0, 100]
H	[30.0, 70,0]
W	[1, 12]
I	50.0

The default parameter setting of MPB used in the experiments is presented in Table 1. In MPB, shift length, s, is the radius of peak movement after an environment change. m is the number of peaks. f is the frequency of environment change as number of fitness evaluations. H and W denote range of height and width of peaks which will change after a change in environment by height severity and width severity respectively. I is the initial heights for all peaks. Parameter A denotes minimum and maximum value on all dimensions. For evaluating the efficiency of the algorithms, we use the offline error measure, the average deviation of the best individual from the optimum in all iterations.

Table 2. Offline error ±Standard Error for f =500 and f =1000

	Proposed algorithm f=500	MultiSw armPSO f=500	CellularP SO f=500	FMSO f=500	mQSO10 f=500	Proposed algorith m f=1000	MultiSw armPSO f=1000	CellularP SO f=1000	FMSO f=1000	mQSO10 f=1000
1	12.49±0.21	5.46±0.30	13.4±0.74	27.58±0.9	33.67±3.4	6.12±0.22	2.90±0.18	6.77±0.38	14.42±0.4	18.6±1.6
5	11.87±0.24	5.48±0.19	9.63±0.49	19.45±0.4	11.91±0.7	5.66±0.20	3.35±0.18	5.30±0.32	10.59±0.2	6.56±0.38
10	9.26±0.12	5.95±0.09	9.42±0.21	18.26±0.3	9.62±0.34	5.88±0.16	3.94±0.08	5.15±0.13	10.40±0.1	5.71±0.22
20	7.39±0.17	6.45±0.16	8.84±0.28	17.34±0.3	9.07±0.25	5.36±0.16	4.33±0.12	5.23±0.18	10.33±0.1	5.85±0.15
30	7.74±0.11	6.60±0.14	8.81±0.24	16.39±0.4	8.80±0.21	5.37±0.16	4.41±0.11	5.33±0.16	10.06±0.1	5.81±0.15
40	6.32±0.14	6.85±0.13	8.94±0.24	15.34±0.4	8.55±0.21	4.45±0.11	4.52±0.09	5.61±0.16	9.85±0.11	5.70±0.14
50	5.97±0.16	7.04±0.10	8.62±0.23	15.54±0.2	8.72±0.20	4.49±0.15	4.57±0.08	5.55±0.14	9.54±0.11	5.87±0.13
100	5.65±0.12	7.39±0.13	8.54±0.21	12.87±0.6	8.54±0.16	3.79±0.09	4.77±0.08	5.57±0.12	8.77±0.09	5.83±0.13
200	5.55±0.11	7.52±0.12	8.28±0.18	11.52±0,6	8.19±0.17	3.93±0.10	4.76±0.07	5.50±0.12	8.06±0.07	5.54±0.11

In the proposed method the acceleration coefficients c_1 and c_2 are set to 2.8 and 1.3 and the inertial weight w is set to mean of c_1 and c_2 (2.05). The number of particles in the swarm is set to 20 particles. Parameters d_{11}, d_{21}, d_{12}, d_{22}, v_1 and v_2 are user-specified which are experimentally set to 0.4, 0.4, 0.6, 0.6, 0.4 and 0.6 respectively. The proposed algorithm is compared with Multi-Swarm PSO [9], mQSO [1], FMSO [16], and cellular PSO [6]. In Multi-Swarm PSO the acceleration coefficients c_1 and c_2 are set to 1.496180 and the inertial weight w is set to 0.729844. The number of particles in the parent swarm and the child swarms (π) are set to 5 and 10 particles, respectively in Multi-Swarm PSO. The radius of the child swarms (r), the minimum allowed distance between two child swarm (*rexcl*) and the radius of quantum particles (*rs*) are set to 30.0, 30.0, and 0.5, respectively. For mQSO we adapted a configuration 10(5+5q) which creates 10 swarms with 5 neutral (standard) particles and 5 quantum particles with $rcloud=0.5$ and $rexcl=rconv=31.5$, as suggested in [1]. For FMSO, there are at most 10 child swarms each has a radius of 25.0. The size of the parent and the child swarms are set to 100 and 10 particles, respectively [16]. For cellular PSO, a 5-Dimensional cellular automaton with 105 cells and Moore neighborhood with radius of two cells is embedded into the search space. The maximum velocity of particles is set to the neighborhood radius of the cellular automaton and the radius for the random local search (r) is set to 0.5 for all experiments. The cell capacity θ is set to 10 particles for every cell [6].

As depicted in the Table 2 and Table 3, the proposed algorithm outperforms other tested PSO algorithms when the number of peaks increases.

Table 3. Offline error ±Standard Error for f =5000 and f =10000

	Proposed algorithm f=5000	MultiSwarmPSO f=5000	CellularPSO f=5000	FMSO f=5000	mQSO10 f=5000	Proposed algorithm f=10000	MultiSwarmPSO f=10000	CellularPSO f=10000	FMSO f=10000	mQSO10 f=10000
1	2.54±0.19	**0.56±0.04**	2.55±0.12	3.44±0.11	3.82±0.35	1.52±0.17	**0.27±0.02**	1.53±0.12	1.90±0.06	1.90±0.18
5	1.49±0.11	**1.06±0.06**	1.68±0.11	2.94±0.07	1.90±0.08	0.88±0.11	**0.70±0.10**	0.92±0.10	1.75±0.06	1.03±0.06
10	**1.44±0.10**	1.51±0.04	1.78±0.05	3.11±0.06	1.91±0.08	**0.91±0.06**	0.97±0.04	1.19±0.07	1.91±0.04	1.10±0.07
20	**1.85±0.11**	1.89±0.04	2.61±0.07	3.36±0.06	2.56±0.10	**1.32±0.07**	1.34±0.08	2.20±0.10	2.16±0.04	1.84±0.08
30	**2.00±0.09**	2.03±0.06	2.93±0.08	3.28±0.05	2.68±0.10	**1.35±0.05**	1.43±0.05	2.60±0.13	2.18±0.04	2.00±0.09
40	**2.02±0.08**	2.04±0.06	3.14±0.08	3.26±0.04	2.65±0.08	**1.27±0.04**	1.47±0.06	2.73±0.11	2.21±0.03	1.99±0.07
50	**2.03±0.08**	2.08±0.02	3.26±0.08	3.22±0.05	2.63±0.08	**1.30±0.03**	1.47±0.04	2.84±0.12	2.60±0.08	1.99±0.07
100	2.23±0.04	**2.14±0.02**	3.41±0.07	3.06±0.04	2.52±0.06	**1.32±0.03**	1.50±0.03	2.93±0.09	2.20±0.03	1.85±0.05
200	2.54±0.19	**0.56±0.04**	2.55±0.12	3.44±0.11	3.82±0.35	**1.51±0.02**	**1.48±0.02**	2.88±0.07	2.00±0.02	1.71±0.04

For all algorithms we reported the average offline error and 95% confidence interval for 100 runs. Offline error of the proposed algorithm, mQSO10(5+5q) [1], FMSO [16], cellular PSO [6], and Multi-Swarm PSO [9] for different dynamic environment is presented in Table 2 and Table 3. For each environment, result of the best performing algorithm(s) with 95% confidence is printed in bold.

5 Conclusions

In this paper, a new PSO algorithm is proposed to deal with the dynamic environments. In the proposed PSO there is one Learning Automaton per each particle which it is to learn for its corresponding particle how to act during the evolution. To prevent redundant search in the same area, the LA belonging to particle P_i, which is denoted by L_i, learns the relationship between the variance of the solutions, normalized distance between the position x_i and position of its local optima and normalized distance between the position of its local optima and global optima, and the behavior of the particles i. Indeed the proposed PSO is a kind of indirect niching method. In addition, the deluge water level is employed during the evolution.

Results of the experiments show that for many tested dynamic environments the proposed algorithm outperforms all competent tested PSO algorithms.

References

1. Blackwell, T., Branke, J.: Multi-Swarms, Exclusion, and Anti-Convergence in Dynamic Environments. IEEE Transactions on Evolutionary Computation 10, 459–472 (2006)
2. Blackwell, T., Branke, J.: Multi-Swarm Optimization in Dynamic Environments. Applications of Evolutionary Computing, 489–500 (2004)

3. Blackwell, T., Branke, J., Li, X.: Particle Swarms for Dynamic Optimization Problems. Swarm Intelligence, 193–217 (2008)
4. Branke, J.: Memory Enhanced Evolutionary Algorithms for Changing Optimization Problems. In: 1999 Congress on Evolutionary Computation, Washington D.C., USA, vol. 3, pp. 1875–1882 (1999)
5. Dueck, G.: New Optimization Heuristics. The Great Deluge Algorithm and the Record-to-Record Travel. Journal of Computational Physics 104, 86–92 (1993)
6. Hashemi, A.B., Meybodi, M.R.: Cellular PSO: A PSO for Dynamic Environments. Advances in Computation and Intelligence, 422–433 (2009)
7. Janson, S., Middendorf, M.: A Hierarchical Particle Swarm Optimizer for Dynamic Optimization Problems. Applications of Evolutionary Computing, 513–524 (2004)
8. Janson, S., Middendorf, M.: A hierarchical particle swarm optimizer for noisy and dynamic environments. Genetic Programming and Evolvable Machines 7, 329–354 (2006)
9. Kamosi, M., Hashemi, A.B., Meybodi, M.R.: A New Particle Swarm Optimization Algorithm for Dynamic Environments. In: Panigrahi, B.K., Das, S., Suganthan, P.N., Dash, S.S. (eds.) SEMCCO 2010. LNCS, vol. 6466, pp. 129–138. Springer, Heidelberg (2010)
10. Kennedy, J., Eberhart, R.C.: Particle Swarm Optimization. In: IEEE International Conference on Neural Networks, Piscataway, NJ, vol. IV, pp. 1942–1948 (1995)
11. Kennedy, J., Mendes, R.: Population structure and particle swarm performance. In: Evolutionary Computation Congress, Honolulu, Hawaii, USA, pp. 1671–1676 (2002)
12. Moser, I.: All Currently Known Publications on Approaches Which Solve the Moving Peaks Problem. Swinburne University of Technology, Melbourne (2007)
13. Hu, X., Eberhart, R.C.: Adaptive particle swarm optimization: detection and response to dynamic systems. In: IEEE Congress on Evolutionary Computation, Honolulu, HI, USA, vol. 2, pp. 1666–1670 (2002)
14. Li, X., Dam, K.H.: Comparing particle swarms for tracking extrema in dynamic environments. In: IEEE Congress on Evolutionary Computation, Canberra, Australia, pp. 1772–1779 (2003)
15. Li, C., Yang, S.: A clustering particle swarm optimizer for dynamic optimization. In: IEEE Congress on Evolutionary Computation, pp. 439–446 (2009)
16. Li, C., Yang, S.: Fast Multi-Swarm Optimization for Dynamic Optimization Problems. In: Fourth International Conference on Natural Computation, Jinan, Shandong, China, vol. 7, pp. 624–628 (2008)
17. Liu, L., Wang, D., Yang, S.: Compound Particle Swarm Optimization in Dynamic Environments. Applications of Evolutionary Computing, 616–625 (2008)
18. Liu, L., Yang, S., Wang, D.: Particle Swarm Optimization with Composite Particles in Dynamic Environments. IEEE Transactions on Systems, Man, and Cybernetics, Part B: Cybernetics, 1–15 (2010)
19. Lung, R.I., Dumitrescu, D.: A collaborative model for tracking optima in dynamic environments. In: IEEE Congress on Evolutionary Computation, Singapore, pp. 564–567 (2007)
20. Thomsen, R.: Multimodal optimization using crowding-based differential evolution. In: IEEE Congress on Evolutionary Computation, Portland, Oregon, USA, pp. 1382–1389 (2004)
21. Viswanathan, R.: Learning automaton: Models and applications. Ph.D. dissertation, Yale Univ., New Haven, CT (1972)

A Classifier Ensemble for Face Recognition Using Gabor Wavelet Features

Hamid Parvin, Nasser Mozayani, and Akram Beigi

School of Computer Engineering, Iran University of Science and Technology
(IUST), Tehran, Iran
{parvin,mozayani,beigi}@iust.ac.ir

Abstract. Gabor wavelet-based methods have been proven that are useful in many problems including face detection. It has been shown that these features tackle well facing into image recognition. In image identification, while there is a number of human faces in a repository of employees, it is aimed to identify the face of an arrived employee is which one? So the application of gabor wavelet-based features is reasonable. We propose a weighted majority average voting classifier ensemble to handle the problem. We show that the proposed mechanism works well in an employees' repository of our laboratory.

Keywords: Classifier Ensemble, Gabor Wavelet Features, Face Recognition, Image Processing.

1 Introduction

Gabor wavelet-based methods have been successfully employed in many computer-vision problems, such as fingerprint enhancement and texture segmentation [10, 11]. Also similar to the human visual system, Gabor wavelets represent the characteristics of the spatial localities and the orientation selectivity, and are locally optimal in the space and frequency domains [12]. Therefore, Gabor Wavelets are proper the choice for image decomposition and representation when the goal is to derive local and discriminating features [13].

Combinational Classifiers are so versatile in the fields of artificial intelligence. It has been proved that a single classifier is not able to learn all the problems because of three reasons:

1. Problem may inherently be multifunctional.
2. From other side, it is possible that a problem is well-defined for a base classifier which its recognition is very hard problem.
3. And finally, because of the instability of some base classifiers like Artificial Neural Networks, Decision Trees, and Bayesian Classifier and so on, the usage of Combinational Classifiers can be inevitable.

There are several methods to combine a number of classifiers in the field of image processing. Some of the most important are sum/mean and product methods, ordering (like max or min) methods and voting methods. There is a good coverage over their comparisons and evaluations in the [1], [2], [3] and [4]. In [5] and [6] it is shown that

Á. Herrero and E. Corchado (Eds.): CISIS 2011, LNCS 6694, pp. 301–307, 2011.

the product method can be considered as the best approach when the classifiers have correlation in their outputs. Also it is proved that in the case of outliers, the rank methods are the best choice [4]. For a more detailed study of combining classifiers, the reader is referred to [7].

Applications of combinational classifiers to improve the performance of classification have had significant interest in image processing recently. Sameer Singh and Maneesha Singh [8] have proposed a new knowledge-based predictive approach based on estimating the Mahalanobis distance between the test sample and the corresponding probability distribution function from training data that selectively triggers classifiers. They also have shown the superior performance of their method over the traditional challenging methods empirically.

This paper aims at producing an ensemble-based classification of face recognition by use of gabor features with different frequencies. The face images are first gave to the gabor feature extractor with different frequencies, then the features of all trainset union with the test data are compared with each other in each frequency. This results in a similarity vector per each frequency. The similarity vectors are finally combined to vote to which image the test data is belonged.

2 Voting Classifier Ensemble

Classifier ensemble works well in classification because different classifiers with the different characteristics and methodologies can complement each other and cover their internal weaknesses. If a number of different classifiers votes as an ensemble, the overall error rate will decrease significantly rather using each of them individually.

One of the oldest and the most common policy in classifier ensembles is majority voting. In this approach as it is obvious, each classifier of the ensemble is tested for an input instance and the output of each classifier is considered as its vote. The class is the winner which the most of the classifiers vote for it. The correct class is the one most which is often chosen by different classifiers. If all the classifiers indicate different classes, then the one with the highest overall outputs is selected to be the correct class.

Let us assume that E is the ensemble of n classifiers $\{e_1, e_2, e_3 \ldots e_n\}$. Also assume that there are m classes in the case. Next, assume applying the ensemble over data sample d results in a binary D matrix like equation 1.

$$D = \begin{bmatrix} d_{1\ 1} & d_{1\ 2} & . & d_{1\ n} \\ . & . & . & . \\ d_{m-1\ 1} & d_{m-1\ 2} & . & d_{m-1\ n} \\ d_{m\ 1} & d_{m\ 2} & . & d_{m\ n} \end{bmatrix} \tag{1}$$

where $d_{i,j}$ is equal to one if the classifier j votes that data sample belongs to class i. Otherwise it is equal to zero. Now the ensemble decides the data sample to belong class b according to equation 2.

$$b = \arg\max_i \left| \sum_{j=1}^{n} d_i \;_j \right| \qquad (2)$$

Another method to combine a number of classifiers which employs d_{ij} as confidence of classifier j for belonging the test data sample to class i is called majority average voting. The majority average voting uses equation 2 as majority voting.

Weighted majority vote is another approach of voting; in this method members' votes have different worths. Unlike the previous versions of voting this is not like democracy. For example if a classifier has 99% recognition ratio, it is more worthy to use its vote with a more effect than the vote of another classifier with 80% accuracy rate. Therefore in weighted majority vote approach, every vote is multiplied by its worth. Kuncheva [7] has shown that this worth can optimally be a function of accuracy.

To sum up assume that the classifiers existing in the ensemble E have accuracies $\{p_1, p_2, p_3 \ldots p_n\}$ respectively. According to Kuncheva [7] the worth of them are $\{w_1, w_2, w_3 \ldots w_n\}$ respectively where

$$w_i = \log \frac{p_i}{1 - p_i} \qquad (3)$$

Weighted majority vote mechanism decides the data sample to belong class b according to equation 2.

$$b = \arg\max_i \left| \sum_{j=1}^{n} w_j * d_i \;_j \right| \qquad (4)$$

Similarly another method of combining which again employs d_{ij} as confidence of classifier j for belonging the test data sample to class i is called weighted majority average voting. Weighted majority average voting uses equation 4 as weighted majority voting.

3   Feature Extraction

Gabor filter can capture salient visual properties such as the spatial localization, the orientation selectivity, and the spatial frequency characteristics. The Gabor responses describe a small patch of gray values in an image $I(x)$ around a given pixel $x=(x,y)^T$. It is based on a wavelet transformation, given by the equation 5.

$$R_i(x) = \int I(x')\psi_i(x - x')dx' \qquad (5)$$

which $\psi_i(x)$ is a convolution of image with a family of Gabor kernels like equation 6.

$$\psi_i(x) = \frac{\|k_i\|^2}{\sigma^2} e^{\frac{\|k_i\|^2 \|x^2\|}{2\sigma^2}} \left[e^{jk_i x} - e^{\frac{\sigma^2}{2}} \right] \qquad (6)$$

where

$$k_i = \begin{pmatrix} k_{ix} \\ k_{iy} \end{pmatrix} = \begin{pmatrix} k_v \cos \theta_\mu \\ k_v \sin \theta_\mu \end{pmatrix} \tag{7}$$

Each $\Psi_i(x)$ is a plane wave characterized by the vector k_i enveloped by a Gaussian function, where σ is the standard deviation of this Gaussian. The center frequency of ith filter is given by the characteristic wave vector k_i having a scale and orientation given by (k_v, θ_μ). Convolving the input image with a number of complex Gabor filters with 5 spatial frequencies ($v = 0,...4$) and 8 orientations ($\mu = 0,...7$) will capture the whole frequency spectrums, both amplitude and phase as illustrated in [9].

According to equation 5, each image I^q of face train dataset is mapped to 40 images $I^q{}_{v,\mu}$, where $v \in \{0,...4\}$ and $\mu \in \{0,...7\}$. Test Image H is also mapped to $H'_{v,\mu}$. Now orientation matching between each train image and the test image is gained using equation 8.

$$r_{q,H,f} = n_{q,H,f} - m_{q,H,f} \tag{8}$$

where m_{qf} and n_{qf} are extracted from equation 9.

$$[m_{q,H,f}, n_{q,H,f}] = \arg \max_{m,n} (mean_{x \in Center}(|I''^q_{f,m}(x) - H'_{f,n}(x)|)) \tag{9}$$

where $Center$ is a 9×9 square in the middle of the image, e.g. for image with size 80×40, it is $\{36,...44\} \times \{16,...24\}$. Now the orientation matched image denoted by $OMI^q{}_{v',\mu'}$ is defined as equation 10.

$$OMI^q_{v,H,\mu'} = I'^q_{v,\mu} \tag{10}$$

where

$$\mu' = (\mu + r_{q,H,f}) \bmod 8 \tag{11}$$

Now we define the similarity vector $\textbf{\textit{sim}}^f$ whose ith element indicates the similarity between ith train image and the test image, according to equation 12.

$$sim^f_i(H) = \frac{1}{8} \sum_{m=0}^{7} mean_{x \in C}(|OMI^q_{f,H,m}(x) - H'_{f,m}(x)|) \tag{12}$$

4   Employed Classification

Let assume that there exist n training images and one test image. Also assume that the training images are indexed as number one to n respectively and the test image indexed as number $n+1$. The goal is to understand to which training image the test image is similar. The Gabor Wavelet features of r_1 frequency and eight directions are first extracted from images number one to $n+1$. Then the similarities between each of train images and test image are evaluated according to equation 12, as discussed in the previous section. It is obvious that in order to become these similarities comparable they must be normalized in such a way that the sum of similarities vector of test image becomes unit. So they are normalized in range [0,1]. After calculating each of these similarities between each two training and test images, a similarity vector named sim^{r1} which is a vector with n elements, is obtained. It is important to note that the $sim^{r1}{}_i$ means the similarity between images number i and test image.

As the reader can guess, the problem mentioned here, is an n class problem. sim^{r1} can be also served as a simple classifier C_{r1} which uses image number 1 to n as its train dataset. So as to the index of the maximum value in the vector can be considered as class label of test image.

Considering sim^{r1}, $r1 \in \{0,...4\}$ there are five classifiers to classify the test image. Now the majority-votes ensemble is employed to classify the test image. Assume that the accuracy of classifier C_{r1} is denoted by p_{r1}, the weight vector w can straightforwardly be calculated in the weighted-majority-votes ensemble.

5   Parameters of Classification

In the experiments, there exist 2×300 training images. Here there are 300 real classes, 2 images per each class denoted by TI_i and VI_i where $i \in \{1,...300\}$. Indeed one image of class i is denoted by TI_i and the other by VI_i. 300 fixed images i.e. TI_i, are selected as training dataset. Running the algorithm 299 times, each time one of VI_i is considered as test image and the other 299 images as validation dataset. In zth running of algorithm image VI_z is selected as test image and images VI_j where $j \in \{1,...300\}$-$\{VI_z\}$ are considered as validation dataset. Now we obtain 5 classifiers C_{r1}, $r1 \in \{0,...4\}$ based on sim^{r1}. To calculate the accuracies of C_{r1} the mentioned validation dataset is used as following. The similarities between each pairs of images denoted by TI_i and VI_i, where $i \in \{1,...300\}$ and $j \in \{1,...300\}$-$\{VI_z\}$ are evaluated employing equation 13.

$$SIMILARITY_{i,j}^{r1} = sim_i^{r1}(I^j) \qquad (13)$$

It is obvious that these similarities must also again be normalized in order to become them comparable. So they are again normalized in range [0,1] as mentioned before. After calculating each of these similarities between each two of training datasets, a similarity matrix named $SIMILARITY^{r1}$ which is an $n \times n$ matrix, is obtained. It is important to note that the $SIMILARITY^{r1}{}_{i,j}$ means the similarity between image number i of training dataset and image number j of validation dataset and the VI_z^{th} column of that matrix is invalid.

Now the accuracy of classifier C_{r1}, on the training data, is the number of training data that correctly assigned to its correct class, divided to n. In other words, the number of the columns which its maximum value is over matrix diagonal, divided to n can be considered as the accuracy of this classifier as stated in equation 14. Although it is obvious that diagonal elements of this matrix must be the largest in their columns, it is not true in many cases.

$$p_{r1} = \frac{1}{299} \sum_{j \in \{1,...,300\}-\{VI_z\}} isequal(\arg \max_i (SIMILARITY_{i,j}^{r1}), j)$$ (14)

where $isequal(x,y)$ is defined as equation 15.

$$isequal(x, y) = \begin{cases} 1 & x == y \\ 0 & otherwise \end{cases}$$ (15)

6 Experimental Study

Experimental results are reported over 300 pairs of images. Each pair of images belongs to an employee (personnel) of our laboratory. All the images have the same resolution. All of them are first equalized using equalizing their histograms.

Live-one-out technique is used to test ensemble classifier over these images. Also features of 5 different frequencies and 8 orientations are extracted. So, there are forty similarity matrices. 599 images, except in weighted majority voting, are used as training set because there is no longer need to validation set. It is worthy to mention that the best classifier using only one of the similarity matrix, has just 76.63% recognition ratio. While recognition ratio of classifier mentioned above has 90.17% recognition ratio with majority voting, by use of the average voting as final results the 89.32% recognition ratio is achieved. But the combinational proposed approach has 92.67% recognition ratio. The Table 1 summarizes the results.

Table 1. Face recognition ratios of different methods

Best C^f	MV(C^f)	MAV(C^f)	WMAV
76.63	89.32	90.17	92.67

7 Conclusions

In this paper, new face identification algorithm is proposed. In the proposed algorithm first gabor wavelet features with different frequencies are extracted maximizing over different orientations. Defining one classifier per each frequency an ensemble is obtained. The ensemble uses weighted majority average voting as the consensus function. It is shown that the proposed mechanism works well in an employees' repository of laboratory.

References

1. Ross, A., Jain, A.K.: Information fusion in biometrics. Pattern Recognition Letters 24(13), 2115–2125 (2003)
2. Pekalska, E., Duin, R., Skurichina, M.: A discussion on the classifier projection space for classifier combining. In: Roli, F., Kittler, J. (eds.) MCS 2002. LNCS, vol. 2364, pp. 137–148. Springer, Heidelberg (2002)

3. Kittler. J., Li. Y.P., Matas. J., Sánchez, M.U.R.: Combining evidence in multimodal personal identity recognition systems. Audio- and Video-Based Biometric Authentication (1997)
4. Kittler, J., Matas, G., Jonsson, K., Sánchez, M.: Combining evidence in personal identity verification systems. Pattern Recognition Letters 18(9), 845–852 (1997)
5. Bilmes, J., Kirchhoff, K.: Directed graphical models of classifier combination: Application to phone recognition. Spoken Language Processing (2000)
6. Tax, D.M.J., Breukelen, M.V., Duin, R.P.W., Kittler, J.: Combining multiple classifiers by averaging or by multiplying. Pattern Recognition 33, 1475–1485 (2000)
7. Kuncheva, L.I.: Combining Pattern Classifiers, Methods and Algorithms. Wiley, New York (2005)
8. Singh, S., Singh, M.: A dynamic classifier selection and combination approach to image region labeling. Signal Processing: Image Communication 20, 219–231 (2005)
9. Štruc, V., Pavešić, N.: Gabor-Based Kernel Partial-Least-Squares Discrimination Features for Face Recognition. INFORMATICA 20(1), 115–138 (2009)
10. Hong, L., Jain, A., Pankanti, S., Bolle, R.: Fingerprint enhancement. In: IEEE WACV, Sarasota, pp. 202–207 (1996)
11. Bashar, M.K., Matsumoto, T., Ohnishi, N.: Wavelet transform-based locally orderless images for texture segmentation. Pattern Recognition Letters 24(15), 2633–2650 (2003)
12. Žibert, J., Mihelič, F.: Zhao–Atlas–Marks representation of speech signals. Electrotechnical Review 69(3-4), 159–164 (2002)
13. Liu, C.: Gabor-based kernel PCA with fractional power polynomial models for face recognition. IEEE Transactions on Pattern Analysis and Machine Intelligence 26(5), 572–581 (2004)

Author Index